STRATEGIC MARKETING PLANNING
PLANNING
in the
HOSPITALITY INDUSTRY

Educational Institute Books

STRATEGIC MARKETING PLANNING
in the
HOSPITALITY INDUSTRY

Edited by
Robert L. Blomstrom, Ph.D.

the EDUCATIONAL INSTITUTE
OF THE AMERICAN HOTEL & MOTEL ASSOCIATION

Disclaimer

Nothing contained in this publication shall constitute an endorsement by the Educational Institute of the American Hotel & Motel Association (the Institute) or the American Hotel & Motel Association (AH&MA) of any information, opinion, procedure, or product mentioned, and the Institute and AH&MA disclaim any liability with respect to the use of any such information, procedure, or product, or reliance thereon.

The information contained herein is in no way to be construed as a recommendation by the Institute or AH&MA of any industry standard, or as a recommendation of any kind to be adopted by or binding upon any member of the hospitality industry.

Accredited by the Accrediting
Commission of the National
Home Study Council.

Library of Congress Cataloging in Publication Data

Strategic marketing planning for the hospitality industry.

   1. Marketing. 2. Hotels, taverns, etc.—Addresses,
   essays, lectures, 3. Motels—Addresses, essays, lec-
   tures. 4. Food service—Addresses, essays, lectures.
   I. Blomstrom, Robert L.
TX911.3.M3S847 1982   647′.94′0688   82-18312
ISBN 0-86612-013-0

Copy editor: Cindy J. Sillman

Contents

Preface

The term "strategic marketing planning" is relatively new and a strategic marketing approach to operations is less frequent in the hospitality industry than in the manufacturing and product distribution industries. Nevertheless, a metamorphosis is taking place in the way hospitality firms plan, and a variety of terms are appearing that suggest a strategic approach to the way hospitality firms are run. Terms such as "strategic planning," "business planning," "market planning," "marketing planning," and "strategic marketing planning" are fairly common in manufacturing and product distribution. But the concept of strategic planning, by whatever name, as a central way of managing the business has been slower to emerge in the hospitality and other service industries.

This book of readings will help managers in the hospitality field to apply marketing concepts and tools that have been, for the most part, developed for use in other industries. Important to strategic marketing planning is the concept that both long-range and short-range planning require the coordinated efforts of managers at all levels, and that a property's health and viability depend increasingly on knowledge about markets.

The teaching of marketing to undergraduate students of hotel and restaurant management motivated the assembly of these readings. There are a number of excellent texts available on general marketing, and also an abundance of articles on strategic marketing planning in periodic literature. However, there is a shortage of good literature about the specialized marketing problems of the hospitality industry. Good articles do exist, but they are widely scattered in a variety of publications. This book pulls together many excellent articles, for the first time, to provide an integrated insight into the strategic marketing process as it applies to the hospitality industry.

Intended for two groups of people, this book was produced primarily as a teaching tool for hospitality marketing courses. It was not meant to be a principal text; but rather, to supplement other texts, providing instructors with a single source of useful material. Managers in the hospitality industry who have responsibility for business performance should also find the book valuable; particularly managers of independent properties who do not benefit from planning support at the corporate level.

Part I discusses strategic marketing planning philosophy that focuses on consumers' needs and wants. The second part explains the "how to" process of strategic marketing planning. Specialized activities or parts of the process are detailed in the next four parts. The last two parts illustrate cases that provide observations about specialized markets, and also some success stories.

Part I

Strategic Marketing Planning — The Concept

All hospitality firms, regardless of size, do some planning. The on-going nature of business requires that management make estimates about what is likely to happen in the future. Based on these estimates, management must decide how the business may adjust to future events.

Like all other businesses, firms in the hospitality industry operate in a competitive environment. They compete with properties across the street, down the block, or across town. They compete with properties in other cities, and sometimes in other countries. In whatever competitive arena they function, all hospitality firms have at least three things in common. They try to develop new sources of business; they try to create a core market of repeat business; they must make a profit if they are to survive.

To accomplish these objectives managers use strategies. Strategies are statements about what should be done to achieve desired results. Strategies are courses of action designed to reach goals. For example, it is one thing to have a goal of increasing weekend occupancy by ten percent. But it is quite another thing to determine what has to be done to achieve that ten percent increase. One manager might cut prices to increase occupancy. Another manager might increase services. Yet another manager might rely more on travel agents to create this increase.

Choosing courses of action for the future implies planning. Planning, at the same time, requires knowledge or judgments about the future and a set of decisions concerning what is to be done in the future. Planning can be formal or informal, organized or unorganized, structured or unstructured, intuitive or research based. The increasing complexity of today's business climate suggests that managers who plan strategies for the changing markets will fare better than those who don't.

The Need for Strategic Marketing Planning

Historically, hospitality firms have lagged behind manufacturing firms in the use of strategic marketing planning. There are several reasons for the lag. First, the hospitality industry, until relatively recently, has been composed largely of small firms, many of whom considered marketing to be either too expensive or irrelevant. Second, for a substantial period of time, the demand for hospitality services was so high that managers saw little need for strategic marketing activities. Finally, many managers simply mistook promotion and merchandising for marketing.

Today there are compelling reasons for hospitality firms to become more marketing oriented. Competition is stronger than at any time in the recent past. Consumer buying preferences are changing. Chains continue to grow and to dominate the industry. Costs continue to escalate. Productivity in the hospitality industry, which has never been high, seems to be stagnating and even declining. Lastly, consumers' views about the relationship of price and value appear to be changing. These reasons suggest a new approach to marketing planning in the hospitality industry. That is what this book is about.

A New Approach

The concept of strategic marketing planning for the hospitality industry revolves around customers and the business environment in which hospitality firms operate. It demands extensive knowledge about customers and potential customers—their needs and wants, how they buy, and what they consider to be value. Strategic marketing planning focuses on finding opportunities or "strategic windows" that have not been discovered by competitors. It means finding different and/or better ways of satisfying the wants of consumers. Thus, the concept goes beyond the functional approach of marketing and sales and incorporates marketing into a general management approach to survival and growth of the business. The emphasis is not only on how to sell what we have to offer, but also on how to develop services and products that are more attractive than those of competitors. Strategic marketing planning includes *all* of the organization's strategies in the market place.

The Nature of Strategic Marketing Planning

Strategic marketing planning "is the process of developing and maintaining a strategic fit between the organization and its changing marketing opportunities." [1] It is essentially a process of figuring out where to go and how to get there.

Strategic marketing planning is a dynamic, on-going process based on the ever changing marketing environment in which hospitality firms function. Needs and wants of customers change with time, as do our economic environment and competition. Transitions in these and other forces create new opportunities for alert hospitality managers. They might also create threats which, if not heeded, could endanger the profitability and perhaps even the survival of hospitality properties. Thus, strategic marketing planning cannot be viewed as a one-time exercise. Good planning is a continuous cycle, with one plan becoming the base for the following updated plan.

Strategic marketing planning, then, is both a philosophy and a process used by managers to ensure that current strategies match existing competitive conditions and that newly developed strategies will take advantage of emerging marketing opportunities. Stated another way, strategic marketing planning is knowing everything possible about the business and the environment in which it operates, identifying marketing opportunities, and choosing strategies that will put the property in a stronger market position than that of competitors. Strategic marketing planning is both a process and a managerial state of mind.

This book is about strategic marketing planning and how it can be applied successfully and profitably in the hospitality industry. The articles bring together the expert views of many hospitality marketers and produce a blend of theory and practice, forming a practical foundation for strategic marketing planning. The principles and practices contained herein are as relevant to small independent hotels, motels, and restaurants as they are to large chain-operated properties.

---

1. Kotler, Philip, *Principles of Marketing,* Englewood Cliffs, N.J., Prentice Hall, Inc. 1980, p. 74.

Part I sets the stage. It begins with a classic marketing article which is general in nature, yet has immense applications for the hospitality industry. Focusing on how managers ought to think about running a business, this lead article is as applicable to managers in the hospitality business as it is to those in manufacturing or distribution. The remaining articles in this section deal with the concepts and tools of strategic marketing planning in the hospitality industry.

Marketing Myopia

by Theodore Levitt

Shortsighted managements often fail to recognize that in fact there is no such thing as a growth industry

How can a company ensure its continued growth? In 1960 "Marketing Myopia" answered that question in a new and challenging way by urging organizations to define their industries broadly to take advantage of growth opportunities. Using the archetype of the railroads, Mr. Levitt showed how they declined inevitably as technology advanced because they defined themselves too narrowly. To continue growing, companies must ascertain and act on their customers' needs and desires, not bank on the presumptive longevity of their products. The success of the article testifies to the validity of its message. It has been widely quoted and anthologized, and HBR has sold more than 265,000 reprints of it. The author of 14 subsequent articles in HBR, Mr. Levitt is one of the magazine's most prolific contributors. In a retrospective commentary, he considers the use and misuse that have been made of "Marketing Myopia," describing its many interpretations and hypothesizing about its success.

At the time of the article's publication, Theodore Levitt was lecturer in business administration at the Harvard Business School. Now a full professor there, he is the author of six books, including The Third Sector: New Tactics for a Responsive Society *(1973) and* Marketing for Business Growth *(1974).*

Every major industry was once a growth industry. But some that are now riding a wave of growth enthusiasm are very much in the shadow of decline. Others which are thought of as seasoned growth industries have actually stopped growing. In every case the reason growth is threatened, slowed, or stopped is *not* because the market is saturated. It is because there has been a failure of management.

Fateful purposes: The failure is at the top. The executives responsible for it, in the last analysis, are those who deal with broad aims and policies. Thus:

The railroads did not stop growing because the need for passenger and freight transportation declined. That grew. The railroads are in trouble today not because the need was filled by others (cars, trucks, airplanes, even telephones), but because it was *not* filled by the railroads themselves. They let others take customers away from them because they assumed themselves to be in the railroad business rather than in the transportation business. The reason they defined their industry wrong was because they were railroad-oriented instead of transportation-oriented; they were product-oriented instead of customer-oriented.

Hollywood barely escaped being totally ravished by television. Actually, all the established film companies went through drastic reorganizations. Some simply disappeared. All of them got into trouble not because of TV's in-roads but because of their own myopia. As with the railroads, Hollywood defined its business incorrectly. It thought it was in the movie business when it was actually in the entertainment business. "Movies" implied a specific, limited product. This produced a fatuous contentment which from the beginning led producers to view TV as a threat. Hollywood scorned and rejected TV when it should have welcomed it as an opportunity—an opportunity to expand the entertainment business.

Today, TV is a bigger business than the old narrowly defined movie business ever was. Had Hollywood been customer-oriented (providing entertainment), rather than product-oriented (making movies), would it have gone through the fiscal purgatory that it did? I doubt it. What ultimately saved Hollywood and accounted for its recent resurgence was the wave of new young writers, producers, and directors whose previous successes in television had decimated the old movie companies and toppled the big movie moguls.

There are other less obvious examples of industries that have been and are now endangering their futures by improperly defining their purposes. I shall discuss some in detail later and analyze the kind of policies that lead to trouble. Right now it may help to show what a thoroughly customer-oriented management *can* do to keep a growth industry growing, even after the obvious opportunities have been exhausted; and here there are two examples that have been around for a long time. They are nylon and glass—specifically, E.I. duPont de Nemours & Company and Corning Glass Works.

Both companies have great technical competence. Their product orientation is unquestioned. But this alone does not explain their success. After all, who was more pridefully product-oriented and product-conscious than the erstwhile New England textile companies that have been so thoroughly massacred? The DuPonts and the Cornings have succeeded not primarily because of their product or research orientation but because they have been thoroughly customer-oriented also. It is constant watchfulness for opportunities to apply their technical know-how to the creation of customer-satisfying uses which accounts for their prodigious output of successful new products. Without a very sophisticated eye on the customer, most of their new products might have been wrong, their sales methods useless.

Aluminum has also continued to be a growth industry, thanks to the efforts of two wartime-created companies which deliberately set about creating new customer-satisfying uses. Without Kaiser Aluminum & Chemical Corporation and Reynolds Metals Company, the total demand for aluminum today would be vastly less.

Error of analysis: Some may argue that it is foolish to set the railroads off against aluminum or the movies off against glass. Are not aluminum and glass naturally so versatile that the industries are bound to have more growth opportunities than the railroads and movies? This view commits precisely the error I have been talking about. It defines an industry, or a product, or a cluster of know-how so narrowly as to guarantee its premature senescence. When we mention "railroads," we should make sure we mean "transportation." As transporters, the railroads still have a good chance for very considerable growth. They are not limited to the railroad business as such (though in my opinion rail transportation is potentially a much stronger transportation medium than is generally believed).

What the railroads lack is not opportunity, but some of the same managerial imaginativeness and

audacity that made them great. Even an amateur like Jacques Barzun can see what is lacking when he says:

"I grieve to see the most advanced physical and social organization of the last century go down in shabby disgrace for lack of the same comprehensive imagination that built it up. [What is lacking is] the will of the companies to survive and to satisfy the public by inventiveness and skill." [1]

Shadow of Obsolescence

It is impossible to mention a single major industry that did not at one time qualify for the magic appellation of "growth industry." In each case its assumed strength lay in the apparently unchallenged superiority of its product. There appeared to be no effective substitute for it. It was itself a runaway substitute for the product it so triumphantly replaced. Yet one after another of these celebrated industries has come under a shadow. Let us look briefly at a few more of them, this time taking examples that have so far received a little less attention:

Dry cleaning—This was once a growth industry with lavish prospects. In an age of wool garments, imagine being finally able to get them safely and easily clean. The boom was on.

Yet here we are 30 years after the boom started and the industry is in trouble. Where has the competition come from? From a better way of cleaning? No. It has come from synthetic fibers and chemical additives that have cut the need for dry cleaning. But this is only the beginning. Lurking in the wings and ready to make chemical dry cleaning totally obsolescent is that powerful magician, ultrasonics.

Electric utilities—This is another one of those supposedly "no-substitute" products that has been enthroned on a pedestal of invincible growth. When the incandescent lamp came along, kerosene lights were finished. Later the water wheel and the steam engine were cut to ribbons by the flexibility, reliability, simplicity, and just plain easy availability of electric motors. The prosperity of electric utilities continues to wax extravagant as the home is converted into a museum of electric gadgetry. How can anybody miss by investing in utilities, with no competition, nothing but growth ahead?

But a second look is not quite so comforting. A score of nonutility companies are well advanced

1. Jacques Barzun, "Trains and the Mind of Man," *Holiday*, February 1960, p. 21.

toward developing a powerful chemical fuel cell which could sit in some hidden closet of every home silently ticking off electric power. The electric lines that vulgarize so many neighborhods will be eliminated. So will the endless demolition of streets and service interruptions during storms. Also on the horizon is solar energy, again pioneered by nonutility companies.

Who says the utilities have no competition? They may be natural monopolies now, but tomorrow they may be natural deaths. To avoid this prospect, they too will have to develop fuel cells, solar energy, and other power sources. To survive, they themselves will have to plot the obsolescence of what now produces their livelihood.

Grocery stores – Many people find it hard to realize that there ever was a thriving establishment known as the "corner grocery store." The supermarket has taken over with a powerful effectiveness. Yet the big food chains of the 1930s narrowly escaped being completely wiped out by the aggressive expansion of independent supermarkets. The first genuine supermarket was opened in 1930, in Jamaica, Long Island. By 1933 supermarkets were thriving in California, Ohio, Pennsylvania, and elsewhere. Yet the established chains pompously ignored them. When they chose to notice them, it was with such derisive descriptions as "cheapy," "horse-and-buggy," "cracker-barrel storekeeping," and "unethical opportunists."

The executive of one big chain announced at the time that he found it "hard to believe that people will drive for miles to shop for foods and sacrifice the personal service chains have perfected and to which Mrs. Consumer is accustomed."[2] As late as 1936, the National Wholesale Grocers convention and the New Jersey Retail Grocers Association said there was nothing to fear. They said that the supers' narrow appeal to the price buyer limited the size of their market. They had to draw from miles around. When imitators came, there would be wholesale liquidations as volume fell. The current high sales of the supers was said to be partly due to their novelty. Basically people wanted convenient neighborhood grocers. If the neighborhood stores "cooperate with their suppliers, pay attention to their costs, and improve their service," they would be able to weather the competition until it blew over.[3]

It never blew over. The chains discovered that survival required going into the supermarket business. This meant the wholesale destruction of their huge investments in corner store sites and in established distribution and merchandising methods. The companies with "the courage of their convictions" resolutely stuck to the corner store philosophy. They kept their pride but lost their shirts.

Self-deceiving cycle: But memories are short. For example, it is hard for people who today confidently hail the twin messiahs of electronics and chemicals to see how things could possibly go wrong with their galloping industries. They probably also cannot see how a reasonably sensible businessman could have been as myopic as the famous Boston millionaire who 50 years ago unintentionally sentenced his heirs to poverty by stipulating that his entire estate be forever invested exclusively in electric streetcar securities. His posthumous declaration, "There will always be a big demand for efficient urban transportation," is no consolation to his heirs who sustain life by pumping gasoline at automobile filling stations.

Yet, in a casual survey I recently took among a group of intelligent business executives, nearly half agreed that it would be hard to hurt their heirs by tying their estates forever to the electronics industry. When I then confronted them with the Boston streetcar example, they chorused unanimously, "That's different!" But is it? Is not the basic situation identical?

In truth, *there is no such thing* as a growth industry, I believe. There are only companies organized and operated to create and capitalize on growth opportunities. Industries that assume themselves to be riding some automatic growth escalator invariably descend into stagnation. The history of every dead and dying "growth" industry shows a self-deceiving cycle of bountiful expansion and undetected decay. There are four conditions which usually guarantee this cycle:

1. The belief that growth is assured by an expanding and more affluent population.

2. The belief that there is no competitive substitute for the industry's major product.

3. Too much faith in mass production and in the advantages of rapidly declining unit costs as output rises.

4. Preoccupation with a product that lends itself to carefully controlled scientific experimentation, improvement, and manufacturing cost reduction.

I should like now to begin examining each of these conditions in some detail. To build my case as boldly as possible, I shall illustrate the points

---

2. For more details see M.M. Zimmerman, *The Super Market: A Revolution in Distribution* (New York, McGraw-Hill Book Company, Inc., 1955), p. 48

3. Ibid, pp. 45-47.

with reference to three industries— petroleum, automobiles, and electronics—particularly petroleum, because it spans more years and more vicissitudes. Not only do these three have excellent reputations with the general public and also enjoy the confidence of sophisticated investors, but their managements have become known for progressive thinking in areas like financial control, product research, and management training. If obsolescence can cripple even these industries, it can happen anywhere.

Population Myth

The belief that profits are assured by an expanding and more affluent population is dear to the heart of every industry. It takes the edge off the apprehensions everybody understandably feels about the future. If consumers are multiplying and also buying more of your product or service, you can face the future with considerably more comfort than if the market is shrinking. An expanding market keeps the manufacturer from having to think very hard or imaginatively. If thinking is an intellectual response to a problem, then the absence of a problem leads to the absence of thinking. If your product has an automatically expanding market, then you will not give much thought to how to expand it.

One of the most interesting examples of this is provided by the petroleum industry. Probably our oldest growth industry, it has an enviable record. While there are some current apprehensions about its growth rate, the industry itself tends to be optimistic.

But I believe it can be demonstrated that it is undergoing a fundamental yet typical change. It is not only ceasing to be a growth industry, but may actually be a declining one, relative to other business. Although there is widespread unawareness of it, I believe that within 25 years the oil industry may find itself in much the same position of retrospective glory that the railroads are now in. Despite its pioneering work in developing and applying the present-value method of investment evaluation, in employee relations, and in working with backward countries, the petroleum business is a distressing example of how complacency and wrongheadedness can stubbornly convert opportunity into near disaster.

One of the characteristics of this and other industries that have believed very strongly in the beneficial consequences of an expanding population, while at the same time being industries with a

generic product for which there has appeared to be no competitive substitute, is that the individual companies have sought to outdo their competitors by improving on what they are already doing. This makes sense, of course, if one assumes that sales are tied to the country's population strings, because the customer can compare products only on a feature-by-feature basis. I believe it is significant, for example, that not since John D. Rockefeller sent free kerosene lamps to China has the oil industry done anything really outstanding to create a demand for its product. Not even in product improvement has it showered itself with eminence. The greatest single improvement — namely, the development of tetraethyl lead — came from outside the industry, specifically from General Motors and DuPont. The big contributions made by the industry itself are confined to the technology of oil exploration, production, and refining.

Asking for trouble: In other words, the industry's efforts have focused on improving the *efficiency* of getting and making its product, not really on improving the generic product or its marketing. Moreover, its chief product has continuously been defined in the narrowest possible terms, namely, gasoline, not energy, fuel, or transportation. This attitude has helped assure that:

Major improvements in gasoline quality tend not to originate in the oil industry. Also, the development of superior alternative fuels comes from outside the oil industry, as will be shown later.

Major innovations in automobile fuel marketing are originated by small new oil companies that are not primarily preoccupied with production or refining. These are the companies that have been responsible for the rapidly expanding multipump gasoline stations, with their successful emphasis on large and clean layouts, rapid and efficient driveway service, and quality gasoline at low prices.

Thus, the oil industry is asking for trouble from outsiders. Sooner or later, in this land of hungry inventors and entrepreneurs, a threat is sure to come. The possibilities of this will become more apparent when we turn to the next dangerous belief of many managements. For the sake of continuity, because this second belief is tied closely to the first, I shall continue with the same example.

Idea of indispensability: The petroleum industry is pretty much persuaded that there is no competitive substitute for its major product, gasoline — or, if there is, that it will continue to be a derivative of crude oil, such as diesel fuel or kerosene jet fuel.

There is a lot of automatic wishful thinking in this assumption. The trouble is that most refining companies own huge amounts of crude oil reserves. These have value only if there is a market for products into which oil can be converted — hence the tenacious belief in the continuing competitive superiority of automobile fuels made from crude oil.

This idea persists despite all historic evidence against it. The evidence not only shows that oil has never been a superior product for any purpose for very long, but it also shows that the oil industry has never really been a growth industry. It has been a succession of different businesses that have gone through the usual historic cycles of growth, maturity, and decay. Its overall survival is owed to a series of miraculous escapes from total obsolescence, of last-minute and unexpected reprieves from total disaster reminiscent of the Perils of Pauline.

Perils of petroleum: I shall sketch in only the main episodes.

First, crude oil was largely a patent medicine. But even before that fad ran out, demand was greatly expanded by the use of oil in kerosene lamps. The prospect of lighting the world's lamps gave rise to an extravagant promise of growth. The prospects were similar to those the industry now holds for gasoline in other parts of the world. It can hardly wait for the underdeveloped nations to get a car in every garage.

In the days of the kerosene lamp, the oil companies competed with each other and against gaslight by trying to improve the illuminating characteristics of kerosene. Then suddenly the impossible happened. Edison invented a light which was totally nondependent on crude oil. Had it not been for the growing use of kerosene in space heaters, the incandescent lamp would have completely finished oil as a growth industry at that time. Oil would have been good for little else than axle grease.

Then disaster and reprieve struck again. Two great innovations occurred, neither originating in the oil industry. The successful development of coal-burning domestic central-heating systems made the space heater obsolescent. While the industry reeled, along came its most magnificent boost yet — the internal combustion engine, also invented by outsiders. Then when the prodigious expansion for gasoline finally began to level off in the 1920s, along came the miraculous escape of a central oil heater. Once again, the escape was provided by an outsider's invention and development. And when that market weakened, wartime demand for aviation fuel came to the rescue. After the war the expansion of civilian aviation, the

dieselization of railroads, and the explosive demand for cars and trucks kept the industry's growth in high gear.

Meanwhile, centralized oil heating — whose boom potential had only recently been proclaimed — ran into severe competition from natural gas. While the oil companies themselves owned the gas that now competed with their oil, the industry did not originate the natural gas revolution, nor has it to this day greatly profited from its gas ownership. The gas revolution was made by newly formed transmission companies that marketed the product with an aggressive ardor. They started a magnificent new industry, first against the advice and then against the resistance of the oil companies.

By all the logic of the situation, the oil companies themselves should have made the gas revolution. They not only owned the gas, they also were the only people experienced in handling, scrubbing, and using it, the only people experienced in pipeline technology and transmission, and they understood heating problems. But, partly because they knew that natural gas would compete with their own sale of heating oil, the oil companies pooh-poohed the potentials of gas.

The revolution was finally started by oil pipeline executives who, unable to persuade their own companies to go into gas, quit and organized the spectacularly successful gas transmission companies. Even after their success became painfully evident to the oil companies, the latter did not go into gas transmission. The multibillion dollar business which should have been theirs went to others. As in the past, the industry was blinded by its narrow preoccupation with a specific product and the value of its reserves. It paid little or no attention to its customers' basic needs and preferences.

The postwar years have not witnessed any change. Immediately after World War II the oil industry was greatly encouraged about its future by the rapid expansion of demand for its traditional line of products. In 1950 most companies projected annual rates of domestic expansion of around 6% through at least 1975. Though the ratio of crude oil reserves to demand in the Free World was about 20 to 1, with 10 to 1 being usually considered a reasonable working ratio in the United States, booming demand sent oil men searching for more without sufficient regard to what the future really promised. In 1952, they "hit" in the Middle East; the ratio skyrocketed ro 42 to 1. If gross additions to reserves continue at the average rate of the past five years (37 billion barrels annually), then by 1970 the reserve ratio will be up to 45 to 1. This abundance of oil has weakened crude and product prices all over the world.

Uncertain future: Management cannot find much consolation today in the rapidly expanding petrochemical industry, another oil-using idea that did not originate in the leading firms. The total United States production of petrochemicals is equivalent to about 2% (by volume) of the demand for all petroleum products. Although the petrochemical industry is now expected to grow by about 10% per year, this will not offset other drains on the growth of crude oil consumption. Furthermore, while petrochemical products are many and growing, it is well to remember that there are nonpetroleum sources of the basic raw material, such as coal. Besides, a lot of plastics can be produced with relatively little oil. A 50,000-barrel-per-day oil refinery is now considered the absolute minimum size for efficiency. But a 5,000-barrel-per-day chemical plant is a giant operation.

Oil has never been a continuously strong growth industry. It has grown by fits and starts, always miraculously saved by innovations and developments not of its own making. The reason it has not grown in a smooth progression is that each time it thought it had a superior product safe from the possibility of competitive substitutes, the product turned out to be inferior and notoriously subject to obsolescence. Until now, gasoline (for motor fuel, anyhow) has escaped this fate. But, as we shall see later, it too may be on its last legs.

The point of all this is that there is no guarantee against product obsolescence. If a company's own research does not make it obsolete, another's will. Unless an industry is especially lucky, as oil has been until now, it can easily go down in a sea of red figures — just as the railroads have, as the buggy whip manufacturers have, as the corner grocery chains have, as most of the big movie companies have, and indeed as many other industries have.

The best way for a firm to be lucky is to make its own luck. That requires knowing what makes a business successful. One of the greatest enemies of this knowledge is mass production.

Production Pressures

Mass-production industries are impelled by a great drive to produce all they can. The prospect of steeply declining unit costs as output rises is more than most companies can usually resist. The profit possibilities look spectacular. All effort focuses on production. The result is that marketing gets neglected.

John Kenneth Galbraith contends that just the opposite occurs.[4] Output is so prodigious that all effort concentrates on trying to get rid of it. He says this accounts for singing commercials, desecration of the countryside with advertising signs, and other wasteful and vulgar practices. Galbraith has a finger on something real, but he misses the strategic point. Mass production does indeed generate great pressure to "move" the product. But what usually gets emphasized is selling, not marketing. Marketing, being a more sophisticated and complex process, gets ignored.

The difference between marketing and selling is more than semantic. Selling focuses on the needs of the seller, marketing on the needs of the buyer. Selling is preoccupied with the seller's need to convert his product into cash, marketing with the idea of satisfying the needs of the customer by means of the product and the whole cluster of things associated with creating, delivering, and finally consuming it.

In some industries the enticements of full mass production have been so powerful that for many years top management in effect has told the sales departments, "You get rid of it; we'll worry about profits." By contrast, a truly marketing-minded firm tries to create value-satisfying goods and services that consumers will want to buy. What it offers for sale includes not only the generic product or service, but also how it is made available to the customer, in what form, when, under what conditions, and at what terms of trade. Most important, what it offers for sale is determined not by the seller but by the buyer. The seller takes his cues from the buyer in such a way that the product becomes a consequence of the marketing effort, not vice versa.

Lag in Detroit: This may sound like an elementary rule of business, but that does not keep it from being violated wholesale. It is certainly more violated than honored. Take the automobile industry.

Here mass production is most famous, most honored, and has the greatest impact on the entire society. The industry has hitched its fortune to the relentless requirements of the annual model change, a policy that makes customer orientation an especially urgent necessity. Consequently the auto companies annually spend millions of dollars on consumer research. But the fact that the new compact cars are selling so well in their first year indicates that Detroit's vast researches have for a

---

4. *The Affluent Society* (Boston, Houghton-Mifflin Company, 1958) pp. 152-160.

long time failed to reveal what the customer really wanted. Detroit was not persuaded that he wanted anything different from what he had been getting until it lost millions of customers to other small car manufacturers.

How could this unbelievable lag behind consumer wants have been perpetuated so long? Why did not research reveal consumer preferences before consumers' buying decisions themselves revealed the facts? Is that not what consumer research is for — to find out before the fact what is going to happen? The answer is that Detroit never really researched the customer's wants. It only researched his preferences between the kinds of things which it had already decided to offer him. For Detroit is mainly product-oriented, not customer-oriented. To the extent that the customer is recognized as having needs that the manufacturer should try to satisfy, Detroit usually acts as if the job can be done entirely by product changes. Occasionally attention gets paid to financing, too, but that is done more in order to sell than to enable the consumer to buy.

As for taking care of other customer needs, there is not enough being done to write about. The areas of the greatest unsatisfied needs are ignored, or at best get stepchild attention. These are at the point of sale and on the matter of automotive repair and maintenance. Detroit views these problem areas as being of secondary importance. That is underscored by the fact that the retailing and servicing ends of this industry are neither owned and operated nor controlled by the manufacturers. Once the car is produced, things are pretty much in the dealer's inadequate hands. Illustrative of Detroit's arm's-length attitude is the fact that, while servicing holds enormous sales-stimulating, profit-building opportunities, only 57 of Chevrolet's 7,000 dealers provide night maintenance service.

Motorists repeatedly express their dissatisfaction with servicing and their apprehensions about buying cars under the present selling setup. The anxieties and problems they encounter during the auto buying and maintenance processes are probably more intense and widespread today than 30 years ago. Yet the automobile companies do not *seem* to listen to or take their cues from the anguished consumer. If they do listen, it must be through the filter of their own preoccupation with production. The marketing effort is still viewed as a necessary consequence of the product, not vice versa, as it should be. That is the legacy of mass production, with its parochial view that profit resides essentially in low-cost full production.

What Ford put first: The profit lure of mass production obviously has a place in the plans and strategy of business management, but it must always *follow* hard thinking about the customer. This is one of the most important lessons that we can learn from the contradictory behavior of Henry Ford. In a sense Ford was both the most brilliant and the most senseless marketer in American history. He was senseless because he refused to give the customer anything but a black car. He was brilliant because he fashioned a production system designed to fit market needs. We habitually celebrate him for the wrong reason, his production genius. His real genius was marketing. We think he was able to cut his selling price and therefore sell millions of $500 cars because his invention of the assembly line had reduced the costs. Actually he invented the assembly line because he had concluded that at $500 he could sell millions of cars. Mass production was the *result* not the cause of his low prices.

Ford repeatedly emphasized this point, but a nation of production-oriented business managers refuses to hear the great lesson he taught. Here is his operating philosophy as he expressed it succinctly:

"Our policy is to reduce the price, extend the operations, and improve the article. You will notice that the reduction of price comes first. We have never considered any costs as fixed. Therefore we first reduce the price to the point where we believe more sales will result. Then we go ahead and try to make the prices. We do not bother about the costs. The new price forces the costs down. The more usual way is to take the costs and then determine the price; and although that method may be scientific in the narrow sense, it is not scientific in the broad sense, because what earthly use is it to know the cost if it tells you that you cannot manufacture at a price at which the article can be sold? But more to the point is the fact that, although one may calculate what a cost is, and of course all of our costs are carefully calculated, no one knows what a cost ought to be. One of the ways of discovering . . . is to name a price so low as to force everybody in the place to the highest point of efficiency. The low price makes everybody dig for profits. We make more discoveries concerning manufacturing and selling under this forced method than by any method of leisurely investigation."[5]

Product provincialism: The tantalizing profit possibilities of low unit production costs may be the

5. Henry Ford. *My Life and Work* (New York, Doubleday, Page & Company, 1923), pp. 146-147.

most seriously self-deceiving attitude that can afflict a company, particularly a "growth" company where an apparently assured expansion of demand already tends to undermine a proper concern for the importance of marketing and the customer.

The usual result of this narrow preoccupation with so-called concrete matters is that instead of growing, the industry declines. It usually means that the product fails to adapt to the constantly changing patterns of consumer needs and tastes, to new and modified marketing institutions and practices, or to product developments in competing and complementary industries. The industry has its eyes so firmly on its own specific product that it does not see how it is being made obsolete.

The classical example of this is the buggy whip industry. No amount of product improvement could stave off its death sentence. But had the industry defined itself as being in the transportation business rather than the buggy whip business, it might have survived. It would have done what survival always entails, that is, changing. Even if it had only defined its business as providing a stimulant or catalyst to an energy source, it might have survived by becoming a manufacturer of, say, fanbelts or air cleaners.

What may some day be a still more classical example is, again, the oil industry. Having let others steal marvelous opportunities from it (e.g., natural gas, as already mentioned, missile fuels, and jet engine lubricants), one would expect it to have taken steps never to let that happen again. But this is not the case. We are not getting extraordinary new developments in fuel systems specifically designed to power automobiles. Not only are these developments concentrated in firms outside the petroleum industry, but petroleum is almost systematically ignoring them, securely content in its wedded bliss to oil. It is the story of the kerosene lamp versus the incandescent lamp all over again. Oil is trying to improve hydrocarbon fuels rather than develop *any* fuels best suited to the needs of their users, whether or not made in different ways and with different raw materials from oil.

Here are some things which nonpetroleum companies are working on:

Over a dozen such firms now have advanced working models of energy systems which, when perfected, will replace the internal combustion engine and eliminate the demand for gasoline. The superior merit of each of these systems is their elimination of frequent, time-consuming, and irritating refueling stops. Most of these systems are fuel cells designed to create electrical energy directly from chemicals without combustion. Most of them use chemicals that are not derived from oil, generally hydrogen and oxygen.

Several other companies have advanced models of electric storage batteries designed to power automobiles. One of these is an aircraft producer that is working jointly with several electric utility companies. The latter hope to use off-peak generating capacity to supply overnight plug-in battery regeneration. Another company, also using the battery approach, is a medium-size electronics firm with extensive small-battery experience that it developed in connection with its work on hearing aids. It is collaborating with an automobile manufacturer. Recent improvements arising from the need for high-powered miniature power storage plants in rockets have put us within reach of a relatively small battery capable of withstanding great overloads or surges of power. Germanium diode applications and batteries using sintered-plate and nickel-cadmium techniques promise to make a revolution in our energy sources.

Solar energy conversion systems are also getting increasing attention. One usually cautious Detroit auto executive recently ventured that solar-powered cars might be common by 1980.

As for the oil companies, they are more or less "watching developments," as one research director put it to me. A few are doing a bit of research on fuel cells, but almost always confined to developing cells powered by hydrocarbon chemicals. None of them are enthusiastically researching fuel cells, batteries, or solar power plants. None of them are spending a fraction as much on research in these profoundly important areas as they are on the usual run-of-the-mill things like reducing combustion chamber deposit in gasoline engines. One major integrated petroleum company recently took a tentative look at the fuel cell and concluded that although "the companies actively working on it indicate a belief in ultimate success . . . the timing and magnitude of its impact are too remote to warrant recognition in our forecasts."

One might, of course, ask: Why should the oil companies do anything different? Would not chemical fuel cells, batteries, or solar energy kill the present product lines? The answer is that they would indeed, and that is precisely the reason for the oil firms having to develop these power units before their competitors, so they will not be companies without an industry.

Management might be more likely to do what is needed for its own preservation if it thought of itself as being in the energy business. But even that would not be enough if it persists in imprisoning itself in the narrow grip of its tight product orientation. It has to think of itself as taking care of customer needs, not finding, refining, or even selling oil. Once it genuinely thinks of its business as taking care of people's transportation needs, nothing can stop it from creating its own extravagantly profitable growth.

'Creative destruction': Since words are cheap and deeds are dear, it may be appropriate to indicate what this kind of thinking involves and leads to. Let us start at the beginning — the customer. It can be shown that motorists strongly dislike the bother, delay, and experience of buying gasoline. People actually do not buy gasoline. They cannot see it, taste it, feel it, appreciate it, or really test it. What they buy is the right to continue driving their cars. The gas station is like a tax collector to whom people are compelled to pay a periodic toll as the price of using their cars. This makes the gas station a basically unpopular institution. It can never be made popular or pleasant, only less unpopular, less unpleasant.

To reduce its unpopularity completely means eliminating it. Nobody likes a tax collector, not even a pleasantly cheerful one. Nobody likes to interrupt a trip to buy a phantom product, not even from a handsome Adonis or a seductive Venus. Hence, companies that are working on exotic fuel substitutes which will eliminate the need for frequent refueling are heading directly into the outstretched arms of the irritated motorist. They are riding a wave of inevitability, not because they are creating something which is technologically superior or more sophisticated, but because they are satisfying a powerful customer need. They are also eliminating noxious odors and air pollution.

Once the petroleum companies recognize the customer-satisfying logic of what another power system can do, they will see that they have no more choice about working on an efficient, long-lasting fuel (or some way of delivering present fuels without bothering the motorist) than the big food chains had a choice about going into the supermarket business, or the vacuum tube companies had a choice about making semiconductors. For their own good the oil firms will have to destroy their own highly profitable assets. No amount of wishful thinking can save them from the necessity of engaging in this form of "creative destruction."

I phrase the need as strongly as this because I think management must make quite an effort to break itself loose from conventional ways. It is all too easy in this day and age for a company or in-

dustry to let its sense of purpose become dominated by the economies of full production and to develop a dangerously lopsided product orientation. In short, if management lets itself drift, it invariably drifts in the direction of thinking of itself as producing goods and services, not customer satisfactions. While it probably will not descend to the depths of telling its salesmen, "You get rid of it; we'll worry about profits," it can, without knowing it, be practicing precisely that formula for withering decay. The historic fate of one growth industry after another has been its suicidal product provincialism.

Dangers of R&D

Another big danger to a firm's continued growth arises when top management is wholly transfixed by the profit possibilities of technical research and development. To illustrate I shall turn first to a new industry — electronics — and then return once more to the oil companies. By comparing a fresh example with a familiar one, I hope to emphasize the prevalence and insidiousness of a hazardous way of thinking.

Marketing shortchanged: In the case of electronics, the greatest danger which faces the glamorous new companies in this field is not that they do not pay enough attention to research and development, but that they pay *too much* attention to it. And the fact that the fastest growing electronics firms owe their eminence to their heavy emphasis on technical research is completely beside the point. They have vaulted to affluence on a sudden crest of unusually strong general receptiveness to new technical ideas. Also, their success has been shaped in the virtually guaranteed market of military subsidies and by military orders that in many cases actually preceded the existence of facilities to make the products. Their expansion has, in other words, been almost totally devoid of marketing effort.

Thus, they are growing up under conditions that come dangerously close to creating the illusion that a superior product will sell itself. Having created a successful company by making a superior product, it is not surprising that management continues to be oriented toward the product rather than the people who consume it. It develops the philosophy that continued growth is a matter of continued product innovation and improvement.

A number of other factors tend to strengthen and sustain this belief:

1. Because electronic products are highly com-

plex and sophisticated, managements become top-heavy with engineers and scientists. This creates a selective bias in favor of research and production at the expense of marketing. The organization tends to view itself as making things rather than satisfying customer needs. Marketing gets treated as a residual activity, "something else" that must be done once the vital job of product creation and production is completed.

2. To this bias in favor of product research, development, and production is added the bias in favor of dealing with controllable variables. Engineers and scientists are at home in the world of concrete things like machines, test tubes, production lines, and even balance sheets. The abstractions to which they feel kindly are those which are testable or manipulatable in the laboratory, or, if not testable, then functional, such as Euclid's axioms. In short, the managements of the new glamour-growth companies tend to favor those business activities which lend themselves to careful study, experimentation, and control—the hard, practical, realities of the lab, the shop, the books.

What gets shortchanged are the realities of the *market*. Consumers are unpredictable, varied, fickle, stupid, shortsighted, stubborn, and generally bothersome. This is not what the engineer-managers say, but deep down in their consciousness it is what they believe. And this accounts for their concentrating on what they know and what they can control, namely, product research, engineering, and production. The emphasis on production becomes particularly attractive when the product can be made at declining unit costs. There is no more inviting way of making money than by running the plant full blast.

Today the top-heavy science-engineering-production orientation of so many electronics companies works reasonably well because they are pushing into new frontiers in which the armed services have pioneered virtually assured markets. The companies are in the felicitous position of having to fill, not find markets; of not having to discover what the customer needs and wants, but of having the customer voluntarily come forward with specific new product demands. If a team of consultants had been assigned specifically to design a business situation calculated to prevent the emergence and development of a customer-oriented marketing viewpoint, it could not have produced anything better than the conditions just described.

Stepchild treatment: The oil industry is a stunning example of how science, technology, and mass production can divert an entire group of companies from their main task. To the extent the consumer is studied at all (which is not much), the focus is forever on getting information which is designed to help the oil companies improve what they are now doing. They try to discover more convincing advertising themes, more effective sales promotional drives, what the market shares of the various companies are, what people like or dislike about service station dealers and oil companies, and so forth. Nobody seems as interested in probing deeply into the basic human needs that the industry might be trying to satisfy as in probing into the basic properties of the raw material that the companies work within trying to deliver customer satisfactions.

Basic questions about customers and markets seldom get asked. The latter occupy a stepchild status. They are recognized as existing, as having to be taken care of, but not worth very much real thought or dedicated attention. Nobody gets as excited about the customers in his own backyard as about the oil in the Sahara Desert. Nothing illustrates better the neglect of marketing than its treatment in the industry press.

The centennial issue of the *American Petroleum Institute Quarterly,* published in 1959 to celebrate the discovery of oil in Titusville, Pennsylvania, contained 21 feature articles proclaiming the industry's greatness. Only one of these talked about its achievements in marketing and that was only a pictorial record of how service stations' architecture has changed. The issue also contained a special section on "New Horizons," which was devoted to showing the magnificent role oil would play in America's future. Every reference was ebulliently optimistic, never implying once that oil might have some hard competition. Even the reference to atomic energy was a cheerful catalogue of how oil would help make atomic energy a success. There was not a single apprehension that the oil industry's affluence might be threatened or a suggestion that one "new horizon" might include new and better ways of serving oil's present customers.

But the most revealing example of the stepchild treatment that marketing gets was still another special series of short articles on "The Revolutionary Potential of Electronics." Under that heading this list of articles appeared in the table of contents:
"In the Search for Oil"
"In Production Operations"
"In Refinery Processes"
"In Pipeline Operations"
Significantly, *every* one of the industry's major

functional areas is listed, *except* marketing. Why? Either it is believed that electronics holds no revolutionary potential for petroleum marketing (which is palpably wrong), or the editors forgot to discuss marketing (which is more likely, and illustrates its stepchild status).

The order in which the four functional areas are listed also betrays the alienation of the oil industry from the consumer. The industry is implicitly defined as beginning with the search for oil and ending with its distribution from the refinery. But the truth is, it seems to me, that the industry begins with the needs of the customer for its products. From the primal position its definition moves steadily backstream to areas of progressively lesser importance, until it finally comes to rest at the "search for oil."

Beginning & end: The view that an industry is a customer-satisfying process, not a goods-producing process, is vital for all businessmen to understand. An industry begins with the customer and his needs, not with a patent, a raw material, or a selling skill. Given the customer's needs, the industry develops backwards, first concerning itself with the physical *delivery* of customer satisfactions. Then it moves back further to *creating* the things by which these satisfactions are in part achieved. How these materials are created is a matter of indifference to the customer, hence the particular form of manufacturing, processing, or what-have-you cannot be considered as a vital aspect of the industry. Finally, the industry moves back still further to *finding* the raw materials necessary for makings its products.

The irony of some industries oriented toward technical research and development is that the scientists who occupy the high executive positions are totally unscientific when it comes to defining their companies' overall needs and purposes. They violate the first two rules of the scientific method — being aware of and defining their companies' problems, and then developing testable hypotheses about solving them. They are scientific only about the convenient things, such as laboratory and product experiments.

The reason that the customer (and the satisfaction of his deepest needs) is not considered as being "the problem" is not because there is any certain belief that no such problem exists, but because an organizational lifetime has conditioned management to look in the opposite direction. Marketing is a stepchild.

I do not mean that selling is ignored. Far from it. But selling, again, is not marketing. As already pointed out, selling concerns itself with the tricks and techniques of getting people to exchange their cash for your product. It is not concerned with the values that the exchange is all about. And it does not, as marketing invariably does, view the entire business process as consisting of a tightly integrated effort to discover, create, arouse, and satisfy customer needs. The customer is somebody "out there" who, with proper cunning, can be separated from his loose change.

Actually, not even selling gets much attention in some technologically-minded firms. Because there is a virtually guaranteed market for the abundant flow of their new products, they do not actually know what a real market is. It is as if they lived in a planned economy, moving their products routinely from factory to retail outlet. Their successful concentration on products tends to convince them of the soundness of what they have been doing, and they fail to see the gathering clouds over the market.

Conclusion

Less than 75 years ago American railroads enjoyed a fierce loyalty among astute Wall Streeters. European monarchs invested in them heavily. Eternal wealth was thought to be the benediction for anybody who could scrape a few thousand dollars together to put into rail stocks. No other form of transportation could compete with the railroads in speed, flexibility, durability, economy, and growth potentials.

As Jacques Barzun put it, "By the turn of the century it was an institution, an image of man, a tradition, a code of honor, a source of poetry, a nursery of boyhood desires, a sublimist of toys, and the most solemn machine — next to the funeral hearse — that marks the epochs in man's life."[6]

Even after the advent of automobiles, trucks, and airplanes, the railroad tycoons remained imperturbably self-confident. If you had told them 60 years ago that in 30 years they would be flat on their backs, broke, and pleading for government subsidies, they would have thought you totally demented. Such a future was simply not considered possible. It was not even a discussable subject, or an askable question, or a matter which any sane person would consider worth speculating about. The very thought was insane. Yet a lot of insane notions now have matter-of-fact accept-

6. Jacques Barzun, "Trains and the Mind of Man," *Holiday*, February 1960, p. 20.

ance—for example, the idea of 100-ton tubes of metal· moving smoothly through the air 20,000 feet above the earth, loaded with 100 sane and solid citizens casually drinking martinis—and they have dealt cruel blows to the railroads.

What specifically must other companies do to avoid this fate? What does customer orientation involve? These questions have in part been answered by the preceding examples and analysis. It would take another article to show in detail what is required for specific industries. In any case, it should be obvious that building an effective customer-oriented company involves far more than good intentions or promotional tricks; it involves profound matters of human organization and leadership. For the present, let me merely suggest what appear to be some general requirements.

Visceral feel of greatness: Obviously the company has to do what survival demands. It has to adapt to the requirements of the market, and it has to do it sooner rather than later. But mere survival is a so-so aspiration. Anybody can survive in some way or other, even the skid-row bum. The trick is to survive gallantly, to feel the surging impulse of commercial mastery; not just to experience the sweet smell of success, but to have the visceral feel of entrepreneurial greatness.

No organization can achieve greatness without a vigorous leader who is driven onward by his own pulsating *will to succeed.* He has to have a vision of grandeur, a vision that can produce eager followers in vast numbers. In business, the followers are the customers.

In order to produce these customers, the entire corporation must be viewed as a customer-oriented and customer-satisfying organism. Management must think of itself not as producing products but as providing customer-creating value satisfactions. It must push this idea (and everything it means and requires) into every nook and cranny of the organization. It has to do this continuously and with the kind of flair that excites and stimulates the people in it. Otherwise, the company will be merely a series of pigeonholed parts, with no consolidating sense of purpose or direction.

In short, the organization must learn to think of itself not as producing goods or services but as *buying customers,* as doing the things that will make people *want* to do business with it. And the chief executive himself has the inescapable responsibility for creating this environment, this viewpoint, this attitude, this aspiration. He himself must set the company's style, its direction, and its goals. This means he has to know precisely where he himself wants to go, and to make sure the whole organization is enthusiastically aware of where that is. This is a first requisite of leadership, for *unless he knows where he is going, any road will take him there.*

If any road is okay, the chief executive might as well pack his attache case and go fishing. If an organization does not know or care where it is going, it does not need to advertise that fact with a ceremonial figurehead. Everybody will notice it soon enough.

Retrospective Commentary

Amazed, finally, by his literary success, Isaac Bashevis Singer reconciled an attendant problem: "I think the moment you have published a book, it's not any more your private property. . . . If it has value, everybody can find in it what he finds, and I cannot tell the man I did not intend it to be so." Over the past 15 years, "Marketing Myopia" has become a case in point. Remarkably, the article spawned a legion of loyal partisans—not to mention a host of unlikely bedfellows.

Its most common and, I believe, most influential consequence is the way certain companies for the first time gave serious thought to the question of what business they are really in.

The strategic consequences of this have in many cases been dramatic. The best-known case, of course, is the shift in thinking of oneself as being in the "oil business" to being in the "energy business." In some instances the payoff has been spectacular (getting into coal, for example) and in others dreadful (in terms of the time and money spent so far on fuel cell research). Another successful example is a company with a large chain of retail shoe shores that redefined itself as a retailer of moderately priced, frequently purchased, widely assorted consumer specialty products. The result was a dramatic growth in volume, earnings, and return on assets.

Some companies, again for the first time, asked themselves whether they wished to be masters of certain technologies for which they would seek markets, or be masters of markets for which they would seek customer-satisfying products and services.

Choosing the former, one company has declared, in effect, "We are experts in glass technology. We intend to improve and expand that expertise with the object of creating products that will attract customers." This decision has forced the company into a much more systematic and customer-sensitive look at possible markets and users, even though its stated strategic object has been to capitalize on glass technology.

Deciding to concentrate on markets, another company has determined that "we want to help people (primarily women) enhance their beauty and sense of youthfulness." This company has expanded its line of cosmetic products, but has also entered the fields of proprietary drugs and vitamin supplements.

All these examples illustrate the "policy" results of "Marketing Myopia." On the operating level, there has been, I think, an extraordinary heightening of sensitivity to customers and consumers. R&D departments have cultivated a greater "external" orientation toward uses, users, and markets — balancing thereby the previously one-sided "internal" focus on materials and methods; upper management has realized that marketing and sales departments should be somewhat more willingly accommodated than before; finance departments have become more receptive to the legitimacy of budgets for market research and experimentation in marketing; and salesmen have been better trained to listen to and understand customer needs and problems, rather than merely to "push" the product.

A Mirror, Not a Window

My impression is that the article has had more impact in industrial-products companies than in consumer-products companies — perhaps because the former had lagged most in customer orientation. There are at least two reasons for this lag: (1) industrial-products companies tend to be more capital intensive, and (2) in the past, at least, they have had to rely heavily on communicating face-to-face the technical character of what they made and sold. These points are worth explaining.

Capital-intensive businesses are understandably preoccupied with magnitudes, especially where the capital, once invested, cannot be easily moved, manipulated, or modified for the production of a variety of products — e.g., chemical plants, steel mills, airlines, and railroads. Understandably, they seek big volumes and operating efficiencies to pay off the equipment and meet the carrying costs.

At least one problem results: corporate power becomes disproportionately lodged with operating or financial executives. If you read the charter of one of the nation's largest companies, you will see that the chairman of the finance committee, not the chief executive officer, is the "chief." Executives with such backgrounds have an almost trained in-

capacity to see that getting "volume" may require understanding and serving many discrete and sometimes small market segments, rather than going after a perhaps mythical batch of big or homogeneous customers.

These executives also often fail to appreciate the competitive changes going on around them. They observe the changes, all right, but devalue their significance or underestimate their ability to nibble away at the company's markets.

Once dramatically alerted to the concept of segments, sectors, and customers, though, managers of capital-intensive businesses have become more responsive to the necessity of balancing their inescapable preoccupation with "paying the bills" or breaking even with the fact that the best way to accomplish this may be to pay more attention to segments, sectors, and customers.

The second reason industrial products companies have probably been more influenced by the article is that, in the case of the more technical industrial products or services, the necessity of clearly communicating product and service characteristics to prospects results in a lot of face-to-face "selling" effort. But precisely because the product is so complex, the situation produces salesmen who know the product more than they know the customer, who are more adept at explaining what they have and what it can do than learning what the customer's needs and problems are. The result has been a narrow product orientation rather than a liberating customer orientation, and "service" often suffered. To be sure, sellers said, "We have to provide service," but they tended to define service by looking into the mirror rather than out the window. They *thought* they were looking out the window at the customer, but it was actually a mirror — a reflection of their own product-oriented biases rather than a reflection of their customers' situations.

A Manifesto, Not a Prescription

Not everything has been rosy. A lot of bizarre things have happened as a result of the article:

Some companies have developed what I call "marketing mania" — they've become obsessively responsive to every fleeting whim of the customer. Mass production operations have been converted to approximations of job shops, with cost and price consequences far exceeding the willingness of customers to buy the product.

Management has expanded product lines and added new lines of business without first establishing adequate control systems to run more complex operations.

Marketing staffs have suddenly and rapidly expanded themselves and their research budgets without either getting sufficient prior organizational support or, thereafter, producing sufficient results.

Companies that are functionally organized have converted to product, brand, or market-based organizations with the expectation of instant and miraculous results. The outcome has been ambiguity, frustration, confusion, corporate infighting, losses, and finally a reversion to functional arrangements that only worsened the situation.

Companies have attempted to "serve" customers by creating complex and beautifully efficient products or services that buyers are either too risk-averse to adopt or incapable of learning how to employ — in effect, there are now steam shovels for people who haven't yet learned to use spades. This problem has happened repeatedly in the so-called service industries (financial services, insurance, computer-based services) and with American companies selling in less-developed economies.

"Marketing Myopia" was not intended as analysis or even prescription; it was intended as manifesto. It did not pretend to take a balanced position. Nor was it a new idea — Peter F. Drucker, J.B. McKitterick, Wroe Alderson, John Howard, and Neil Borden had each done more original and balanced work on "the marketing concept." My scheme, however, tied marketing more closely to the inner orbit of business policy. Drucker — especially in *The Concept of the Corporation* and *The Practice of Management* — originally provided

me with a great deal of insight.

My contribution, therefore, appears merely to have been a simple, brief, and useful way of communicating an existing way of thinking. I tried to do it in a very direct, but responsible, fashion, knowing that few readers (customers), especially managers and leaders, could stand much equivocation or hesitation. I also knew that the colorful and lightly documented affirmation works better than the tortuously reasoned explanation.

But why the enormous popularity of what was actually such a simple preexisting idea? Why its appeal throughout the world to resolutely restrained scholars, implacably temperate managers, and high government officials, all accustomed to balanced and thoughtful calculation? Is it that concrete examples, joined to illustrate a simple idea and presented with some attention to literacy, communicate better than massive analytical reasoning that reads as though it were translated from the German? Is it that provocative assertions are more memorable and persuasive than restrained and balanced explanations, no matter who the audience? Is it that the character of the message is as much the message as its content? Or was mine not simply a different tune, but a new symphony? I don't know.

Of course, I'd do it again and in the same way, given my purposes, even with what more I now know — the good and the bad, the power of facts and the limits of rhetoric. If your mission is the moon, you don't use a car. Don Marquis's cockroach, Archy, provides some final consolation: "an idea is not responsible for who believes in it."

Strategy is Different in Service Businesses

by Dan R.E. Thomas

Understanding the basic nature of the service company is the key to effectiveness

Most managers of service businesses continue to think of strategy in product-oriented terms, despite the fact that much of this approach is actually irrelevant to their companies. Important consequences flow from whether a service business is equipment-based or people-based, according to this author, who shows how managers can analyze their companies and take advantage of the strategies that are uniquely available to them.

Dan Thomas is assistant professor of business administration at the Harvard Business School.

Many managers of service businesses are aware that the strategic management (by which I mean the total process of selecting and implementing a corporate strategy) of service businesses is different from that of manufacturing businesses. This article discusses how pure service businesses are different from product-oriented businesses and why they require different strategic thinking. A pure service business is one in which the service is the primary entity that is sold.

That distinction is important because everyone in every type of business sells some element of service. In pure service businesses any transfer of a physical or concrete product is incidental to the service — for example, the written report of a management consultant. Examples of pure service businesses include airlines, banks, computer service bureaus, law firms, plumbing repair companies, motion picture theaters, and management consulting firms.

Top managers should ask themselves six questions about strategic management. The questions are fairly common, but the answers for service businesses are often unique. Each question will be raised here and discussed in depth later.

1. *Do we fully understand the specific type of service business we are in?* Although service-oriented businesses are different from product-oriented businesses, the nature of the difference depends a great deal on the specific type of service business. I will present a classification scheme to help distinguish between service businesses along some important strategic dimensions.

2. *How can we defend our business from competitors?* Every business must consider how it can build and protect a strong competitive position. To do this, the economics of the business must be carefully analyzed. Service businesses often require different competitive strategies from those of product-oriented companies. If an enduring institution is to be created, some attention must be given to the management of economies of scale, proprietary technology, and reputation of the company.

3. *How can we obtain more cost-efficient operations?* Manufacturing companies can improve operating leverage by, for example, purchasing faster and more reliable machinery. But most service businesses are not able to follow this approach. Other methods must be explored.

4. *What is the rationale for our pricing strategy?* The pricing of services is a nebulous area. Cost-based pricing is often difficult to determine, and there are few formulas for effective value-based pricing. It is important to look at pricing strategy and think about the economic and psychological effects of a change in that strategy.

5. *What process are we using to develop and test new services?* Every company depends on an ability to renew its franchise in the marketplace. The service-oriented company must pay particular attention to this area because of the difficulty of developing protectable competitive positions. The process of new-service development and testing must recognize the abstract, perishable nature of services.

6. *What acquisitions, if any, would make sense for our company?* Once the nature of the current business is understood, the acquisition question can be faced. The acquisition game in the service

sector can be dangerous. More than one company has acquired a service business using only criteria that would be used in the acquisition of a product-oriented company. As several of these companies have learned, this type of analysis, although necessary, is insufficient.

Describing Services

In product-oriented businesses, the physical reality of the product provides a simple but powerful base on which to build a business description. The question is far more difficult for service-oriented businesses to answer because services are more abstract than products. For example, it may be difficult to describe management consulting as a business to someone who has never experienced the consulting relationship. What does a consultant do?

One way to deal with the difficulty of describing services has been to talk about them as if they were products. G. Lynn Shostack, a vice president in charge of business planning and analysis at Citibank, has noted:

"Banks often devote significant resources to an activity they call 'new product development.' The phrase is so alluring that groups are regularly set up to create these 'new products.' The realization seldom seems to occur to such banks that they are not in the *product* development business at all. In fact, many banks do not seem to have arrived at the insight that *things* are not the basis for their industry. Even marketers in such banks apparently do not understand that they are engaged in perhaps the most difficult and dimly understood realm of business endeavor — the development and marketing of financial services." [1]

The predominant mental image about "the way things work" in business is a product-based image. This image leads to a product-oriented language, and the language in turn constrains communication in such a way that one cannot develop really innovative approaches to managing the service business.

Because they are often lumped together, service businesses can be misunderstood. As we shall see later, they differ greatly, and an understanding of their differences can help the thoughtful manager to understand the nature of the strategic opportunities in each.

The traditional image of the service business is

that the service is "invariably and undeviatingly personal, as something performed by individuals for other individuals." [2] This perspective is erroneous. Automatic car washes, automated banking services, and computer time-sharing are just three of the many examples of service businesses in which the service is provided by automated equipment. The strategic requirements for these businesses are obviously quite different from those in which individuals perform services for other individuals.

The *Exhibit* shows one way to separate service businesses into general types, with different strategic management requirements. At the pinnacle of the pyramid is the service that is provided by the business. To place a specific business on the spectrum in the exhibit, it is necessary to answer two questions: (1) How is the service rendered? (2) What type of equipment or people render the service?

Placement of a specific service business along the spectrum may be difficult, but two general observations may ease the difficulty: (1) as service businesses evolve, they often move along the spectrum from people-based to equipment-based or vice versa, and (2) many companies are in more than one type of service business. Virtually all banks, for example, operate multiple-service businesses. Some of these are equipment-based, as in the transfer and storage of funds. Others are people-based, as in the financing of a home, car, or business, because they require judgment about the financial management of funds.

Building Barriers

In product-oriented companies, capital is the most commonly used barrier to the entry of competition. As a product-oriented company grows, it can take advantage of economies of scale in producing the product, invest in technology that will become proprietary, and offer a differentiated product through product development and marketing. These efforts pay off largely because they are centered on a uniform product that has concrete dimensions and is sold as a package. They are made possible by the fact that the production, distribution, and sale of the product can be uncoupled, often being accomplished by different companies.

Service businesses rarely have this luxury. The service, because it is an abstract, perishable quantity, must be produced and delivered by a single company, often by a single unit of equipment or

1. G. Lynn Shostack, "Banks Sell Services—Not Things," *The Banker's Magazine,* Winter, 1977, p. 40.
2. Theodore Levitt, "Production-Line Approach to Service," HBR September-October, 1972, p. 43.

Exhibit
A spectrum of types of service businesses

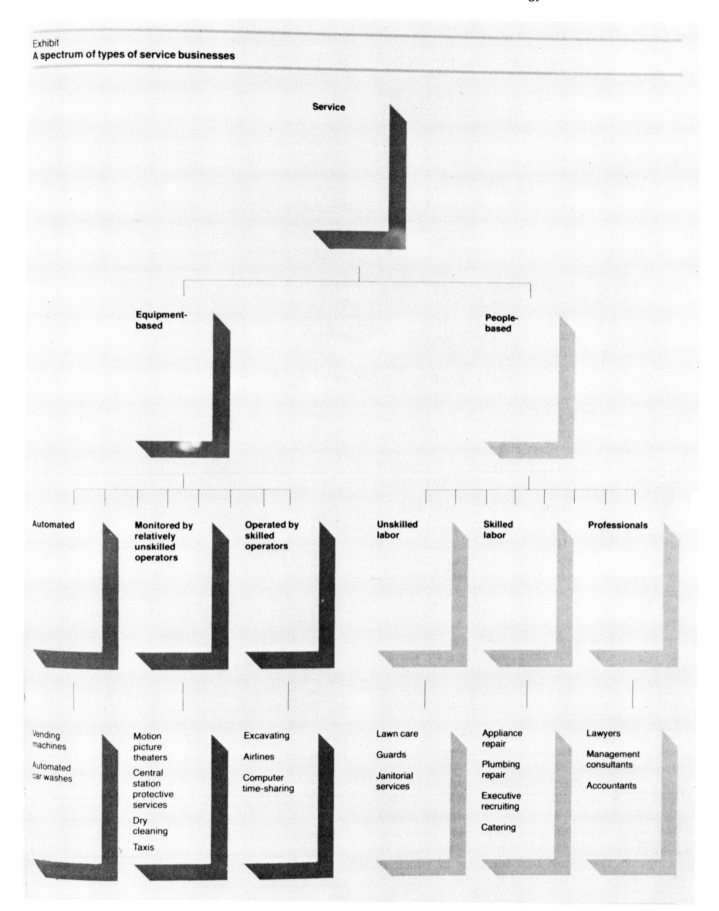

Service

Equipment-based

People-based

Automated

Monitored by relatively unskilled operators

Operated by skilled operators

Unskilled labor

Skilled labor

Professionals

Vending machines

Automated car washes

Motion picture theaters

Central station protective services

Dry cleaning

Taxis

Excavating

Airlines

Computer time-sharing

Lawn care

Guards

Janitorial services

Appliance repair

Plumbing repair

Executive recruiting

Catering

Lawyers

Management consultants

Accountants

people. The result is a decentralization of the service production process to the local level and a reduction in the opportunity for developing economies of scale. As a result, location decisions are often very important and multiple locations can serve as a barrier to entry. One example is the car rental business, where a large number of airport locations is very important.

Economies of Scale

Managers of service businesses should not conclude that they have no opportunities for scale economies and the resulting capital barriers to entry. On the contrary, there are many examples of scale economies, especially in equipment-based service businesses. The introduction of wide-bodied jets by the airlines enabled them to fly twice as many passengers with the same number of high-salaried pilots and flight engineers. Although not on the same scale, other reductions in maintenance and ground handling personnel were possible.[3]

A second example of economies of scale is the multiple-unit motion picture theater that can be found in most suburban locations in the United States. These facilities may have four or five theaters, some of which may be fairly small. The refreshment stand and the ticket selling booths are centralized, thus requiring both less floor space and fewer people to operate them. In some cases, there is a single projection room for more than one theater, and the equipment is almost completely automated. Central heating and air conditioning are provided for the entire building. Obviously, the cost to operate this type of facility is much lower than the cost for an equal number of separate theaters.

Advertising clout is the third example of an economy of scale that service businesses can use as a barrier to entry. Once it achieves a size that makes regional and/or national advertising economically feasible, a service business can use advertising as a competitive weapon to build and maintain market share. O.J. Simpson's advertisements for Hertz are an obvious example, but other companies such as Orkin, John Hancock, and FinanceAmerica also use advertising effectively. Smaller companies simply do not have the capital required to mount a competitive advertising campaign.

With the probable exception of advertising clout, the economies of scale that may provide a barrier to entry exist primarily in equipment-based, and not in people-based, service businesses. Where economies of scale cannot be developed easily, two other barriers to entry can be used: proprietary technology, and/or service differentiation.

Proprietary Technology

In equipment-based service businesses, proprietary technology is perhaps most commonly used as a barrier to entry. In the computer services industry the set of "canned" programs that a time-sharing company offers is crucial to the sales effort for the company's services. So-called raw computer time is a commodity product supplied by many vendors. The purchaser of time-sharing services is interested in knowing what other services the company has which are technologically advanced over the competition. The software provided by the time-sharing company must be technologically advanced in both what it will do and how efficient it is.

Less commonly, proprietary technologies have been developed by people-based service businesses, particularly those that provide professional services. The Boston Consulting Group has developed several proprietary technologies around its experience curve concept, including market segmentation and strategic portfolio analyses.

Service Differentiation

Product differentiation, or as I have called it, service differentiation, is another barrier to entry. In product-oriented companies, the product is developed and marketed in such a way that it attains a brand name identification in the market place. In the more successful efforts, the product's brand becomes an almost generic name for the class of products—Bic, Coke, and Xerox, for example. Very few services have developed a brand name identification. Instead, a service business develops a reputation for the type and quality of service it produces. The more abstract and complex the service is, the greater the need and potential for developing a reputation that will serve as a barrier to entry.

Consulting firms illustrate how a reputation can be a barrier to entry. There are many management problems that any one consulting firm could solve effectively. However, the large ones have unique reputations and thus each tends to be called in on

---

3. See W. Earl Sasser, "Matching Supply and Demand in Service Industries," HBR November-December, 1976, p. 133.

different kinds of problems. Such reputations provide some barrier to the entrance of other consulting firms.

Historically, the executive recruiting business, or "headhunting" as it is often called, has had a terrible reputation as a business. There are virtually no capital barriers to entry. All that is needed is a desk and a telephone. Recruiters work on a fee plus expenses basis, with the fee to the employer based on a percentage of the first year's total compensation to the person recruited. As a result, the business is highly fragmented and somewhat specialized by industry.

Building barriers to entry in service businesses is generally more difficult, or at least must be done in less traditional ways, than in product-oriented businesses. Managers must think less about brand identification and more about the reputation of the company. They must look for areas in which the advantages of economies of scale are available. Finally, they must seek ways to develop and protect proprietary technology.

Cutting Costs

A common misconception about service businesses is that it is almost impossible to obtain operating leverage and thus to improve profit margins. Operating leverage exists in a business when, through a change in operations, the relative cost per unit of the product or service decreases.

Substitution of capital for labor is the classic method of obtaining operating leverage in both product- and service-oriented businesses. Capital is used to purchase machinery which can produce a product or service at a faster rate with more consistent quality. Many service businesses have followed this path of development. Twenty years ago, virtually all car washes used unskilled labor; today, most are automated.

When the tasks cannot be automated because human judgment must be exercised, cheap labor can often be substituted for expensive labor as a means of obtaining operating leverage. This is often the case in people-based service businesses, and law firms are expert in the practice. A large percentage of the tasks are routine and require little legal expertise. For example, routine and time-consuming research and the preparation of briefs can, in many cases, be done by recent graduates of law school or by paralegal assistants, whose time is less expensive, while partners in the firm work on client relationships, develop legal strategies, and so on.

Other service businesses use the same basic technique in different ways. Consulting firms use teams of consultants who perform different tasks, depending on their skills. Many insurance companies break the sales task into its component parts of initial contact, presentation, and closing the deal, and have different people perform each function. In each case, the service is further broken down, and the aspects that can be performed by less expensive labor are identified. The expensive labor is then free to do those crucial tasks that bring profits to the company.

Value Engineering

The process of value engineering has become popular in many manufacturing companies in the last decade to determine what changes in design and/or manufacturing process can be made to reduce the cost of manufacturing a product without reducing its utility.

A similar process can be used for services. Once again, the service provided must be broken into its component parts. This time, however, the purpose is not to determine how the service is rendered, but rather what service is provided. The goals are to determine what parts of the service are essential, what parts can be eliminated, and what minor additions could greatly enhance the service.

Although they have not called it value engineering, a number of service businesses have used the technique. Perhaps the best current example is provided by Holiday Inns. This company has promoted the service as one that has no surprises. The quality of service has been set at a level that does not provide the extras that one would find at an expensive hotel. The service is guaranteed to be of consistent quality throughout the country. The company believes that consistent quality with no surprises is more important to its customers than swimming pools and other added services; therefore, the emphasis is on maintaining the quality of the primary service.

A second example is provided by first-class service on the airlines. The quality difference between first-class and coach service was significant ten years ago. Today, although the incremental fare is in excess of 50% for first class, the traveler receives a slightly larger seat, two free drinks, and marginally better food. Yet first-class seats still sell. First-class customers are apparently buying status, not personal service.

Value engineering is somewhat more difficult for a service than for a product, since the physical nature of a product allows a checking of its continued appearance and function. For a service, it is often difficult to know which attribute is most important to the customer's purchase decision.

In sum, it is probably more difficult to obtain operating leverage in service businesses, particularly those that are people-based. The opportunities for finding operating leverage are there, but they require different ways of thinking about operations.

Competing on Price

Virtually all product-oriented companies have ways of determining their product's cost per unit at various volumes. Part of their strategic game is to become the low-cost producer and use this position as a competitive weapon.[4] Other pricing strategies are of course available, such as the premium-price strategy for a premium-quality product.

In service-oriented businesses it is often difficult to determine what a unit of a given service is, much less its cost. In general, it is easier to determine costs in equipment-based service businesses than in people-based businesses. To be converted to an equipment-based service in the first place, the service usually has some routine character that can be analyzed. People-based service businesses, however, are much more complex. Until the theorists and practitioners who work with human resource accounting can refine the art sufficiently, it will be difficult to determine the cost of people-based services accurately on anything but an aggregate basis.

The pricing of services is thus often based on value rather than on cost. Value is generally determined by the customer and to some extent by competition. Customers tend to get a general feel for what they will have to pay for a particular service, but the source of this feeling is often unclear, because comparison shopping is often difficult. Customers will pay whatever they think the service is worth; thus pricing in many service businesses is based on whatever the market will bear.

An interesting game is played in the pricing arena. I have never heard a businessman brag that he had just hired the least expensive consultant available. People-based service businesses that rely on professionals to provide the service can, by pricing the service too low, create an image that is counter to that necessary for a professional operation that expects to remain competitive. Any good consultant knows that it is easier to sell a recommendation for which the customer has paid a significant amount than when the fee was quite low.

Prices can be set too low in equipment-based service businesses as well. At virtually every airport, one can find a fixed based operator (FBO) who performs one or several functions necessary to the operation of general aviation aircraft. One FBO at a busy municipal airport tried to increase the usage on the aircraft that he rented to local pilots by reducing prices by 5% to 7% throughout his fleet. The result was a decrease in volume. Somehow a rumor had started that the FBO had been able to reduce prices because he had cut back on the maintenance on the airplanes.

Probably less is known about the use of price as a strategic weapon in service businesses than about any of the other strategic variables. One fact, however, is clear. The general manager of a service business must use marketing methods that will enhance the perceived value of the service.

Developing New Services

Virtually all product-oriented companies have some form of research and development effort that is responsible for designing and testing new products and/or modifications to current products. The R&D task in service-oriented companies is different because it is complicated by the lack of a physical product. A service, especially in people-based businesses, can be a little bit different each time it is rendered.

The entire process of creating such services deals with concepts rather than physical objects. The testing process varies depending on whether the service is equipment-based or people-based, but in either case it is difficult to do test marketing or other types of market research on the new service. Customers must be enticed into experiencing the service, and this often requires major marketing efforts. Thus the cost of introducing a successful new service may be quite high because it is difficult to predict what service concepts will be understandable and attractive to the customer.

An example of a new-service development that most observers agree has stalled—at least for the next several years—is that of electronic funds transfer. Why has it faltered? The reasons are obviously complex and include political, legal, and economic factors. Perhaps most important, however, is consumer resistance rooted in fears about

4. See Patrick Conley, "Experience Curves as a Planning Tool," in *Corporate Strategy and Product Innovation,* ed. Robert R. Rothberg (New York Free Press, 1976), p. 307.

computer errors, invasion of privacy, and changes in life-styles. It should be made clear that the failure is not one of technology. The technology is available to create the so-called cashless society, but consumers to not want the service.

The example illustrates a major difference between R&D in product-oriented and in service-oriented companies. A product can be shown to a customer who can make some crucial decisions about whether he or she is interested in trying the product. But how do you test-market the concept of a cashless society?

The difficulty of test marketing can, however, be turned into an advantage. Service concepts, especially in people-based service businesses, are malleable and can be changed even after they have been introduced in the marketplace, and the cost of such a change is often quite low.

Any business must develop new services if it is to survive. This task is quite different from new-product development. It is highly abstract, and the services that are developed require difficult and expensive testing in the marketplace. Thus there is little real innovation, and a great deal of imitation of services. For example, airlines and banks are well known for their imitative practices.

Growing Through Acquisition

What is bought when a service business is acquired? There are several answers to this question, depending on the type of service business that is under consideration.

Many managers, particularly those with product-oriented experience, feel most comfortable when acquiring an equipment-based service business. Then the acquisition includes physical assets that can be quite valuable if bought for less than comparable new assets, if there is a limited supply of the assets, or if the business is in strategic locations (for example, a car rental business, or a string of self-service laundries). Unless one of these conditions exists, it is often less expensive to buy new assets than to buy those of an existing service business.

In people-based service businesses, the acquisition is more risky because people and their skills are the major purchase item. Regardless of the employment contracts and benefits that may be offered, there is always the risk that people will leave and take their skills with them. When physical assets are purchased, they are owned when the papers are signed. Decisions about their use and disposition can be made by the acquiring company.

The same is not true of people; they may decide to depart at any time after the purchase is completed.

This lesson was learned by a well-known consulting firm. The firm had been quite successful in the northeastern United States. Being an astute observer of current trends, its president noted that business activity was increasing rapidly in the southern half of the country. Rather than spend several years and a significant amount of money developing a field office, he decided to acquire a small consulting firm in Dallas that had an excellent client list. The acquisition was made, and the president and two vice presidents of the smaller firm were given employment contracts. Unfortunately, four of the better young consultants regarded the president of the new parent firm as a "Yankee carpetbagger." They left, formed their own firm, and within 18 months had acquired 40% of their former employer's clients as their own.

Whenever acquisition of a people-based service business is being contemplated, it is important to ask: "What is the business worth without the key people?" There are some instances where the "franchise" in a market is worth the price of the business. In other instances, the services provided have some proprietary characteristic that is valuable even without the people in the company. Often, however, the answer to the question is that all one is buying are people. When this is the case, it is usually less expensive simply to hire away the best of these people.

Growth through acquisition in service businesses is a risky proposition, but the risk varies. It is generally riskier as one moves down the spectrum toward people-based businesses, and within people-based businesses the risk increases when the service is provided by professionals or highly skilled persons. Any company that wants to acquire service businesses must make sure that it can attract and keep skilled service-oriented managers to run them.

Concluding Comment

Because manufacturing has been the dominant economic force of the last century, most managers have been educated through experience and/or formal education to think about strategic management in product-oriented terms. Unfortunately, a large part of this experience is irrelevant to the management of many service businesses. The general manager of a service business must develop a healthy skepticism about his and others' approaches to strategy.

One of the best ways to change managers' thinking patterns and thus to avoid the trap of force-fitting product-oriented management techniques into a service-oriented business is to change the language system in the company. If managers talk about services instead of products, they also think about services and those characteristics that make services unique.

Marketing Intangible Products and Product Intangibles

by Theodore Levitt

When you ask prospective customers to buy promises—as all service-oriented firms do—you must provide metaphorical reassurances of quality and "industrialize" the service-delivery process

Theodore Levitt, author of the well-known "Marketing Myopia," is the Edward W. Carter professor of business administration and head of the marketing area at the Harvard Business School.

Distinguishing between companies according to whether they market services or goods has only limited utility. A more useful way to make the same distinction is to change the words we use. Instead of speaking of *services* and *goods*, we should speak of *intangibles* and *tangibles*. Everybody sells intangibles in the marketplace, no matter what is produced in the factory.

The usefulness of the distinction becomes apparent when we consider the question of how the marketing of intangibles differs from the marketing of tangibles. While some of the differences might seem obvious, it is apparent that, along with their differences, there are important commonalities between the marketing of intangibles and the marketing of tangibles.

Put in terms of our new vocabulary, a key area of similarity in the marketing of intangibles and tangibles revolves around the degree of intangibility inherent in both. Marketing is concerned with getting and keeping customers. The degree of product intangibility has its greatest effect in the process of trying to get customers. When it comes to holding on to customers—to keeping them—highly intangible products run into very special problems.

First, this article identifies aspects of intangibility that affect the sales appeal of both intangible and tangible products. And, next, it considers the special difficulties sellers of intangibles face in retaining customers.

Intangibility of All Products

Intangible products—travel, freight forwarding, insurance, repair, consulting, computer software, investment banking, brokerage, education, health care, accounting—can seldom be tried out, inspected, or tested in advance. Prospective buyers are generally forced to depend on surrogates to assess what they're likely to get.

They can look at gloriously glossy pictures of elegant rooms in distant resort hotels set exotically by the shimmering sea. They can consult current users to see how well a software program performs and how well the investment banker or the oil-well drilling contractor performs. Or they can ask experienced customers regarding engineering firms, trust companies, lobbyists, professors, surgeons, prep schools, hair stylists, consultants, repair shops, industrial-maintenance firms, shippers, franchisers, general contractors, funeral directors, caterers, environmental-management firms, construction companies, and on and on.

Tangible products differ in that they can usually, or to some degree, be directly experienced—seen, touched, smelled, or tasted, as well as tested. Often this can be done in advance of buying. You can test drive a car, smell the perfume, work the numerical controls of a milling machine, inspect the seller's steam-generating installation, pretest an extruding machine.

In practice, though, even the most tangible of products can't be *reliably* tested or experienced in advance. To inspect a vendor's steam-generating plant or computer installation in advance at another location and to have thoroughly studied detailed proposals and designs are not enough. A great deal more is involved than product features and physical installation alone.

Though a customer may buy a product whose generic tangibility (like the computer or the steam plant) is as palpable as primeval rock — and though that customer may have agreed after great study and extensive negotiation to a cost that runs into millions of dollars — the process of getting it built on time, installed, and then running smoothly involves an awful lot more than the generic tangible product itself. Such intangibles can make or break the product's success, even with mature consumer goods like dishwashers, shampoos, and frozen pizza. If a shampoo is not used as prescribed, or a pizza not heated as intended, the results can be terrible.

Similarly, you commonly can't experience in advance moderate- to low-priced consumer goods such as canned sardines or purchased detergents. To make buyers more comfortable and confident about tangibles that can't be pretested, companies go beyond the literal promises of specifications, advertisements and labels to provide reassurance.

Packaging is one common tool. Pickles are put into reassuring see-through glass jars, cookies into cellophane-windowed boxes, canned goods get strong appetite-appealing pictures on the labels, architects make elaborately enticing renderings, and proposals to NASA are packaged in binders that match the craftsmanship of Tyrolean leather-workers. In all cases, the idea is to provide reassuring, tangible (in these examples, visual) surrogates for what's promised but can't be more directly experienced before the sale.

Hence, it's sensible to say that all products are in some important respects intangible — even giant turbine engines that weigh tons. No matter how diligently designed in advance and carefully constructed, they'll fail or disappoint if installed or used incorrectly. The significance of all this for marketing can be profound.

When prospective customers can't experience the product in advance, they are asked to buy what are essentially promises — promises of satisfaction. Even tangible, testable, feelable, smellable products are, before they're bought, largely just promises.

Buying Promises

Satisfaction in consumption or use can seldom be quite the same as earlier in trial or promise.

Some promises promise more than others, depending on product features, design, degree of tangibility, type of promotion, price, and differences in what customers hope to accomplish with what they buy.

Of some products less is expected than what is actually or symbolically promised. The right kind of eye shadow properly applied may promise to transform a woman into an irresistible tigress in the night. Not even the most eager buyer literally believes the metaphor. Yet the metaphor helps make the sale. Neither do you really expect the proposed new corporate headquarters, so artfully rendered by the winning architect, automatically to produce all those cheerfully productive employees lounging with casual elegance at lunch in the verdant courtyard. But the metaphor helps win the assignment.

Thus, when prospective customers can't properly try the promised product in advance, metaphorical reassurances become the amplified necessity of the marketing effort. Promises, being intangible, have to be "tangibilized" in their presentation — hence the tigress and the contented employees. Metaphors and similes become surrogates for the tangibility that cannot be provided or experienced in advance. [1]

This same thinking accounts for the solid, somber Edwardian decor of downtown law offices, the prudentially elegant and orderly public offices of investment banking houses, the confidently articulate consultants in dark vested suits, engineering and project proposals in "executive" typeset and leather bindings, and the elaborate pictorial documentation of the performance virtuosity of newly offered machine controls. It explains why insurance companies pictorially offer "a piece of the rock," put you under a "blanket of protection" or an "umbrella," or place you in "good hands."

Not even tangible products are exempt from the necessity of using symbol and metaphor. A computer terminal has to look right. It has to be packaged to convey an impression of reliable modernity — based on the assumption that prospective buyers will translate appearance into confidence about performance. In that respect, the marketing ideas behind the packaging of a $1-million computer, a $2-million jet engine, and a $0.5-million, numerically controlled milling machine are scarcely different from the marketing ideas behind the packaging of a $50 electric shaver or a $2.50 tube of lipstick.

1. For further discussion of this concept, see: Robert C. Lewis, "The Positioning Statement for Hotels," *The Cornell Hotel and Restaurant Administration Quarterly,* 22, No. 1 (May 1981), pp. 51-61.

Importance of Impressions

Common sense tells us, and research confirms, that people use appearances to make judgments about realities. It matters little whether the products are high-priced or low-priced, whether they are technically complex or simple, whether the buyers are supremely sophisticated in the technology of what's being considered or just plain ignorant, or whether they buy for themselves or for their employers. Everybody always depends to some extent on both appearances and external impressions.

Nor do impressions affect only the generic product itself — that is, the technical offering, such as the speed, versatility, and precision of the lathe; the color and creaminess of the lipstick; or the appearance and dimensions of the lobster thermidor. Consider, for example, investment banking. No matter how thorough and persuasive a firm's recommendations and assurances about a proposed underwriting, and no matter how pristine its reputation for integrity and performance, somehow the financial vice president of the billion-dollar client corporation would feel better had the bank's representative not been quite so youthfully apple-cheeked.

The product will be judged in part by who offers it — not just who the vendor corporation is, but also who the corporation's representative is. The vendor and the vendor's representative are both inextricably and inevitably part of the "product" that prospects must judge before they buy. The less tangible the generic product, the more powerfully and persistently the judgment about it gets shaped by the packaging — how it's presented, who presents it, and what's implied by metaphor, simile, symbol, and other surrogates for reality.

So, too, with tangible products. The sales engineers assigned to work with an electric utility company asking for competitive bids on a $100-million steam-boiler system for its new plant are as powerfully a part of the offered product (the promise) as is the investment-banking firm's partner.

The reason is easy to see. In neither case is there a product until it's delivered. And you won't know how well it performs until it's put to work.

The Ties That Bind

In both investment banking and big boilers, becoming the designated vendor requires successful passage through several consecutive gates, or stages, in the sales process. It is not unlike courtship. Both "customers" know that a rocky courtship spells trouble ahead. If the groom is not sufficiently solicitous during the courtship — if he's insensitive to moods and needs, unresponsive or wavering during stress or adversity — there will be problems in the marriage.

But unlike a real marriage, investment banking and installed boiler systems allow no room for divorce. Once the deal is made, marriage and gestation have simultaneously begun. After that, things are often irreversible. Investment banking may require months of close work with the client organization before the underwriting can be launched — that is, before the baby is born. And the construction of an electric power plant takes years, through sickness and in health. As with babies, birth of any kind presents new problems. Babies must be coddled to see them through early life. Illness or relapse must be conscientiously avoided or quickly corrected. Similarly, stocks or bonds should not go quickly to deep discounts. The boiler should not suddenly malfunction after several weeks or months. If it does, it should be rapidly restored to full use. Understandably, the prospective customer will, in courtship, note every nuance carefully, judging always what kind of a husband and father the eager groom is likely to make.

The way the product is packaged (how the promise is presented in brochure, letter, design, appearance), how it is personally presented, and by whom — all these become central to the product itself because they are elements of what the customer finally decides to buy or reject.

A product is more than a tangible thing, even a $100-million boiler system. From a buyer's viewpoint, the product is a promise, a cluster of value expectations of which its nontangible qualities are as integral as its tangible parts. Certain conditions must be satisfied before the prospect buys. If they are not satisfied, there is no sale. There would have been no sale in the cases of the investment banker and the boiler manufacturer if, during the prebidding (or courtship) stages of the relationship, their representatives had been improperly responsive to or insufficiently informed about the customers' special situations and problems.

In each case, the promised product — the whole product — would have been unsatisfactory. It is not that it would have been incomplete; it just would not have been right. Changing the salespeople in midstream would probably not have helped, since the selling organization would by then have already "said" the wrong thing about its "product." If, during the courtship, the prospective customer got the impression that there might be aftermarket problems — problems in execution, in timeliness, in the postsale support necessary for smooth and congenial relations — then the customer would have received a clear message that the delivered product would be faulty.

Special Problems for Intangibles

So much, briefly, for making a sale — for getting a customer. *Keeping* a customer is quite another thing, and on that score more pervasively intangible products encounter some distinct difficulties.

These difficulties stem largely from the fact that intangible products are highly people-intensive in their production and delivery methods. Corporate financial services of banks are, in this respect, not so different from hairdressing or consulting. The more people-intensive a product, the more room there is for personal discretion, idiosyncracy, error, and delay. Once a customer for an intangible product is sold, the customer can easily be unsold as a consequence of the underfulfillment of his expectations. Repeat buying suffers. Conversely, a tangible product, manufactured under close supervision in a factory and delivered through a planned and orderly network, is much more likely than an intangible product to fulfill the promised expectation. Repeat buying is therefore less easily jeopardized.

A tangible product is usually developed by design professionals working under conditions of benign isolation after receiving guidance from market-intelligence experts, scientists, and others. The product will be manufactured by another group of specialists under conditions of close supervision that facilitate reliable quality control. Even installation and use by the customer are determined by a relatively narrow range of possibilities dictated by the product itself.

Intangible products present an entirely different picture. Consider a computer software program. The programmer does the required research directly and generally on the customer's premises, trying to understand complex networks of interconnecting operations. Then that same person designs the system and the software, usually alone. The process of designing is, simultaneously, also the process of manufacturing. Design and manufacturing of intangible products are generally done by the same people — or by one person alone, like a craftsman at a bench.

Moreover, the manufacturing of an intangible product is generally indistinguishable from its actual delivery. In situations such as consulting, the delivery *is* the manufacturing from the client's viewpoint. Though the consulting study may have been excellent, if the delivery is poor, the study will be viewed as having been badly manufactured. It's a faulty product. So too with the work of all types of brokers, educators and trainers, accounting firms, engineering firms, architects, lawyers, transportation companies, hospitals and clinics, government agencies, banks, trust companies, mutual funds, car-rental companies, insurance companies, repair and maintenance operations, and on and on. For each, delivery and production are virtually indistinguishable. The whole difference is nicely summarized by Rathwell: "Goods are produced, services are performed." [2]

Minimizing the Human Factor

Because companies making intangible products are highly people-intensive operations, they have an enormous quality-control problem. Quality control on an automobile-assembly line is built into the system. If a yellow door is hung on a red car, somebody on the line will quickly ask whether that's what was intended. If the left front wheel is missing, the person next in line, whose task is to fasten the lug bolts, will stop the line. But if a commercial banker misses an important feature of a financing package or if he doesn't do it well, it may never be found — or found too late. If the ashtrays aren't cleaned on a rented car, that discovery will annoy or irritate the already-committed customer. Repeat business is jeopardized.

No matter how well trained or motivated they might be, people make mistakes, forget, commit indiscretions, and at times are uncongenial — hence the search for alternatives to dependence on people. I have previously suggested a variety of ways to reduce dependence on people in the so-called service industries. I called it the *industrialization of service*, which means substituting hard, soft, or hybrid technologies for totally people-intensive activities:

• *Hard* technologies include automatic telephone dialing for operator-assisted dialing, credit cards for repetitive credit checking, and computerized monitoring of industrial processes. And the benefits are considerable. Automatic telephone switching, for example, is not only cheaper than manual switching but far more reliable.

• *Soft* technologies are the substitution of division of labor for one-person craftsmanship in

---

2. John M. Rathwell, *Marketing in the Service Sector* (Cambridge, MA: Winthrop Publishers, 1974), p. 58.

production — as, for example, organizing the work force that cleans an office building so that each worker specializes in one or several limited tasks (dusting, waxing, vacuuming, window cleaning) rather than doing all these jobs alone. Insurance companies long ago went to extensive division of labor in their applications processing — registering, underwriting, performing actuarial functions, issuing policies.

• *Hybrid* **technologies** combine the soft and the hard. The floor is waxed by a machine rather than by hand. French fries are precut and portion-packed in a factory for finishing in a fast-food restaurant in specially designed deep fryers that signal when the food is ready. A computer automatically calculates and makes all entries in an Internal Revenue Service form 1040 after a moderately trained clerk has entered the raw data on a console.

The Managerial Revolution

Industrializing helps control quality and cut costs. Instead of depending on people to work *better,* industrialization redesigns the work so that people work *differently.* Thus, the same modes of managerial rationality are applied to service — the production, creation, and delivery of largely intangible products — that were first applied to production of goods in the 19th century. The real significance of the 19th century is not the industrial revolution, with its shift from animal to machine power, but rather the managerial revolution, with its shift from the craftsman's functional independence to the manager's rational routines.

In successive waves, the mechanical harvester, the sewing machine, and then the automobile epitomized the genius of that century. Each was rationally designed to become an assembled rather than a constructed machine, a machine that depended not on the idiosyncratic artistry of a single craftsman but on simple, standardized tasks performed on routine specifications by unskilled workers. This required detailed managerial planning to ensure proper design, manufacture, and assembly of interchangeable parts so that the right number of people would be at the right places at the right times to do the right simple jobs in the right ways. Then, with massive output, distribution, and after-market training and service, managers had to create and maintain systems to justify the massive output.

On Being Appreciated

What's been largely missing in intangible-goods production is the kind of managerial rationality that produced the industrial revolution. That is why the quality of intangibles tends to be less reliable than it might be, costs are higher than they should be, and customer satisfaction is lower than it need be.

While I have referred to the enormous progress that has in recent years been made on these matters, there is one characteristic of intangible products that requires special attention for holding customers. Unique to intangible products is the fact that the customer is seldom aware of being served well. This is especially so in the case of intangible products that have, for the duration of the contract, constant continuity — that is, you're buying or using or consuming them almost constantly. Such products include certain banking services, cleaning services, freight hauling, energy management, maintenance services, telephones, and the like.

Consider an international banking relationship, an insurance relationship, an industrial-cleaning relationship. If all goes well, the customer is virtually oblivious to what he's getting. Only when things don't go well (or a competitor says they don't) does the customer become aware of the product's existence or nonexistence — when a letter of credit is incorrectly drawn, when a competitive bank proposes better arrangements, when the annual insurance premium notice arrives or when a claim is disputed, when the ashtrays aren't cleaned, or when a favorite penholder is missing.

The most important thing to know about intangible products is that the *customers usually don't know what they're getting until they don't get it.* Only then do they become aware of what they bargained for; only on dissatisfaction do they dwell. Satisfaction is, as it should be, mute. Its existence is affirmed only by its absence.

And that's dangerous — because the customers will be aware only of failure and dissatisfaction, not of success or satisfaction. That makes them terribly vulnerable to the blandishments of competitive sellers. A competitor can always structure a more interesting corporate-financing deal, always propose a more imaginative insurance program, always find dust on top of the framed picture in the office, always cite small, visible failures that imply big, hidden ones.

In getting customers for intangibles it is important to create surrogates, or metaphors, for tangibility — how we dress; how we articulate, write, design, and present proposals; how we work with prospects, respond to inquiries, and initiate ideas; and how well we show we understand the prospect's business. But in keeping customers for intangibles, it becomes important regularly to remind and show them what they're getting so that occasional failures fade in relative importance. If that's not done, the customers will not know. They'll only know when they're *not* getting what they bought, and that's all that's likely to count.

To keep customers for regularly delivered and consumed intangible products, again, the customers must be reminded of what they're getting. Vendors must regularly reinstate the promises that were made to land the customer. Thus, when an insurance prospect finally gets "married," the subsequent silence and inattention can be deafening. Most customers seldom recall for long what kind of life-insurance package they bought, often forgetting as well the name of both underwriter and agent. To be reminded a year later via a premium notice often brings to mind the contrast between the loving attention of courtship and the cold reality of marriage. No wonder the lapse rate in personal life insurance is so high!

Once a relationship is cemented, the seller has created equity. He has a customer. To help keep the customer, the seller must regularly enhance the equity in that relationship lest it decline and become jeopardized by competitors.

There are innumerable ways to do that strengthening, and some of these can be systematized, or industrialized. Periodic letters or phone calls that remind the customer of how well things are going cost little and are surprisingly powerful equity maintainers. Newsletters or regular visits suggesting new, better, or augmented product features are useful. Even nonbusiness socializing has its value — as is affirmed by corporations struggling in recent years with the IRS about the deductibility of hunting lodges, yachts, clubs, and spouses attending conferences and customer meetings.

Here are some examples of how companies have strengthened their relationships with customers:

• An energy-management company sends out a periodic "Update Report" on conspicuous yellow paper, advising clients how to discover and correct energy leaks, install improved monitors, and accomplish cost savings.

• A computer service bureau organizes its account managers for a two-week series of blitz customer callbacks to "explain casually" the installation of new central-processing equipment that is expected to prevent cost increases next year while expanding the customers' interactive options.

• A long-distance hauler of high-value electronic equipment (computers, terminals, mail sorters, word processors, medical diagnostic instruments) has instituted quarterly performance reviews with its shippers, some of which include customers who are encouraged to talk about their experiences and expectations.

• An insurance company sends periodic one-page notices to policyholders *and* policy beneficiaries. These generally begin with a single-sentence congratulation that policy and coverage remain nicely intact and follow with brief views on recent tax rulings affecting insurance, new notions about personal financial planning, and special protection packages available with other types of insurance.

In all these ways, sellers of intangible products reinstate their presence and performance in the customers' minds, reminding them of their continuing presence and the value of what is constantly, and silently, being delivered.

Making Tangible the Intangible

It bears repeating that all products have elements of tangibility and intangibility. Companies that sell tangible products invariably promise more than the tangible products themselves. Indeed, enormous efforts often focus on the enhancement of the intangibles — promises of bountiful benefits conferred rather than on features offered. To the buyer of photographic film, Kodak promises with unremitting emphasis the satisfactions of enduring remembrance, of memories clearly preserved. Kodak says almost nothing about the superior luminescence of its pictures. The product is thus remembrance, not film or pictures.

The promoted products of the automobile, as everyone knows, are largely status, comfort, and power — intangible things of the mind, rather than tangible things from the factory. Auto dealers, on the other hand, assuming correctly that people's minds have already been reached by the manufacturers' ads, focus on the other considerations: deals, availability, and postpurchase servicing. Neither the dealers nor the manufacturers sell the tangible cars themselves. Rather, they sell the intangible benefits that are bundled into the entire package.

If tangible products must be intangibilized to add customer-getting appeal, then intangible products must be tangibilized — what Berry calls "managing the evidence."[3] Ideally, this should be done as a matter of routine on a systematic basis — that is, industrialized. For instance, hotels wrap their drinking glasses in fresh bags or film, put on the toilet seat a "sanitized" paper band, and neatly shape the end piece of the toilet tissue into a fresh-looking arrowhead. All these actions say with silent, affirmative clarity that "the room has been specially cleaned for your use and comfort" — yet no words are spoken to say it. Words, in any case, would be less convincing, nor could employees be reliably depended on to say them each time or to say them convincingly. Hotels have thus not only tangibilized their promise, they've also industrialized its delivery.

Or take the instructive case of purchasing house insulation, which most home owners approach with understandable apprehension. Suppose you call two companies to bid on installing insulation in your house. The first insulation installer arrives in a car. After pacing once around the house with measured self-assurance and after quick calculations on the back of an envelope, there comes a confident quote of $2,400 for six-inch fiberglass — total satisfaction guaranteed.

Another drives up in a clean white truck with clipboard in hand and proceeds scrupulously to measure the house dimensions, count the windows, crawl the attic, and consult records from a source book on the area's seasonal temperature ranges and wind velocities. The installer then asks a host of questions, meanwhile recording everything with obvious diligence. There follows a promise to return in three days, which happens at the appointed hour, with a typed proposal for six-inch fiberglass insulation at $2,800 — total satisfaction guaranteed. From which company will you buy?

The latter has tangibilized the intangible, made a promise into a credible expectation. Even more persuasive tangible evidence is provided by an insulation supplier whose representative types the relevant information into a portable intelligent printing terminal. The analysis and response are almost instant, causing one user to call it "the most powerful tool ever developed in the insulation industry." If the house owner is head of a project-buying team of an electric utility company, the treasurer of a mighty corporation, the materials-purchasing

agent of a ready-mixed cement company, the transportation manager of a fertilizer manufacturer, or the data processing director of an insurance company, it's almost certain this person will make vendor decisions at work in the same way as around the house. Everybody requires the risk-reducing reassurances of tangibilized intangibles.

Managers can use the practice of providing reassuring ways to render tangible the intangible's promises — even when the generic product is itself tangible. Laundry detergents that claim special whitening capabilities lend credibility to the promise by using "blue whitener beads" that are clearly visible to the user. In promoting its new decaffeinated instant coffee, High Point, Proctor & Gamble reinforces the notion of real coffee with luminescent "milled flakes for hearty, robust flavor." You can *see* what the claims promise.

Keeping customers for an intangible product requires constant reselling efforts while things go well, lest the customer be lost when things go badly. The reselling requires that tasks be industrialized. The relationship with the customer must be managed much more carefully and continuously in the case of intangibles than of tangible products, though it is vital in both. And it gets progressively more vital for tangible products that are new and especially complex. In such cases, "relationship management" becomes a special art — another topic all its own.

Meanwhile, the importance of what I've tried to say here is emphasized by one overriding fact: a customer is an asset usually more precious than the tangible assets on the balance sheet. Balance-sheet assets can generally be bought. There are lots of willing sellers. Customers cannot so easily be bought. Lots of eager sellers are offering them many choices. Moreover, a customer is a double asset. First, the customer is the direct source of cash from the sale and, second, the existence of a solid customer can be used to raise cash from bankers and investors—cash that can be converted into tangible assets.

The old chestnut "nothing happens till you make a sale" is awfully close to an important truth. What it increasingly takes to make and keep that sale is to tangibilize the intangible, restate the benefit and source to the customer, and industrialize the processes.

---

3. Leonard L. Berry, "Service Marketing Is Different," *Business,* May-June 1980, p. 24.

A New Marketing Mix for the Hospitality Industry

by Leo M. Renaghan

Traditional marketing-mix concepts have little utility for the service industries, because they reflect strategies for selling products, rather than services

Leo M. Renaghan, Ph.D., is head of the food-service and housing administration program at Pennsylvania State University. He holds an M.B.A. from Michigan State University and a doctorate in marketing from Pennsylvania State University.

Most hospitality firms use the same methods to market services as other firms do to market products, even though such traits as the following substantially differentiate services from products.

1. The intangible nature of services makes choosing a service more difficult than choosing a product, because the consumer cannot taste, touch, feel, or try the service before selecting it.

2. The simultaneity of production and consumption makes location paramount and limits the consumer's choice of alternatives (the number of service outlets in a given area is likely to be limited).

3. The perishability of services increases a firm's financial risks and aggravates demand problems because service cannot be inventoried.

4. The variability of output makes services hard to predict and control, for several reasons: service is inherently intangible; the consumer is nearly always present at the point of production; and services are often affected by the whims, idiosyncracies, and errors of the people who perform them.

5. The ease of duplicating services allows competitors to copy a service faster than they would a product, because there are few barriers to market entry.

6. The risk that consumers perceive in selecting services, in response to the foregoing factors is considerably higher than the perceived risk in selecting products. [1]

To prosper in the decades ahead, hospitality firms must develop competitive strategies based on a marketing mix that reflects all of these characteristics, and that also satisfies the needs of the target market. The process of identifying and determining profit potential in target markets follows the same general principles for both products and services. The differences between services and products, however, become problematic as a firm begins to develop a marketing mix.

The business executive who blends policies and procedures, searching for the mixture that will produce optimum profits, is designing a "marketing mix," a concept pioneered by Borden in the early 1960s. [2] The marketing-mix concept has been refined continually as its acceptance has grown. The adaptation applied most frequently to the hospitality industry is known as McCarthy's "Four Ps:"

• **Product:** A physical product or some combination of services that satisfies customer needs.

• **Place:** When, where, and by whom the goods and services are to be offered for sale.

• **Promotion:** Any method communicating information to the target market about the right product in the right place at the right time.

• **Price:** A price that makes the offering as attractive as possible. [3]

One problem with using this framework or similar product frameworks is that the traits that distinguish services from products have not been accounted for. Coffman mentions 12 "factors" in his

1. W. Earl Sasser, R. Paul Olsen, and Daryl Wyckoff, *Management of Service Operations,* (Boston: Allyn and Bacon, 1978), pp. 14-18.

2. Neil H. Borden, "The Concept of the Marketing Mix," *Managerial Marketing: Perspectives and Viewpoints,* ed. Eugene J. Kelley and William Lazar (Homewood, IL: Richard D. Irwin, 1968), pp. 109-118.

3. E. Jerome McCarthy, *Basic Marketing: A Managerial Approach,* (Homewood, IL: Richard D. Irwin, 1975), pp. 75-80.

marketing mix, ranging from product planning through display and marketing research. [4] Crissy, Boewadt, and Laudadio list the customer-service mix, the service mix, and the promotional mix. [5] Eison, on the other hand, offers no marketing mix at all. [6] Because a marketing strategy should be built on the framework of a well-defined marketing mix, hospitality operators without a marketing-mix concept applicable to services may grow confused when attempting to develop a strategy.

For those attempting to develop a strategy that reflects the differences between products and services, the author proposes a new hospitality marketing mix based on a set of clearly delineated but interrelated elements.

The mix contains three major sub-mixes:

1. The Product-Service Mix: The combination of products and services, whether free or for sale, aimed at satisfying the needs of the target market.

2. The Presentation Mix: All elements used by the firm to increase the tangibility of the product-service mix in the perception of the target market at the right place and time.

3. The Communications Mix: All communications between the firm and the target market that increase the tangibility of the product-service mix, that establish or monitor consumer expectations, or that persuade consumers to purchase.

The Product-Service Mix

The term "product-service mix" has been chosen because it explicitly reflects that hospitality firms offer a simultaneous blend of products and services. Generally, however, hospitality firms focus almost exclusively on selling products because most of the marketing-program mixes they employ are borrowed from product-strategy formulations, and because it is simpler to market products than to market services.

Products that can be seen and tasted can be described in concrete ways. Services can be described only in nebulous ways. Products can easily be test-marketed; services cannot. Furthermore, services are difficult to define in terms of the target market, hard to offer, and harder still to control. Numerous hotels and restaurants advertise friendly

service, for example, but even if operators and consumers agreed on what constituted friendliness, it would be difficult to determine what impact friendly service had on consumers' purchase decisions.

Consumers do not perceive the product and service elements of the mix separately; they perceive them instead as a unified whole. If the elements of the mix change, therefore, the consumer's perception of the entire mix changes, sometimes dramatically. Thus, when a firm develops a marketing strategy, the service elements of the mix should be an important part of that strategy, even though they may be difficult to understand or develop. Firms must also decide which services to sell, and should be aware that consumers measure service by performance rather than by possession. Firms promising elegant, friendly, adventurous, unique, or exciting service sometimes misunderstand this idea when they attempt to promote these intangible qualities as if they were products. Companies that market services should make sure that their promises are not isolated sales-promotion ploys but part of the total product-service mix. In his novel *Mother Night*, Kurt Vonnegut put the idea succinctly: "We are," he said, "what we pretend to be and must therefore be careful what we pretend to be." [7]

Deciding what to be (or pretend to be) has been rendered easier in recent years by the development of sophisticated statistical techniques. With conjoint analysis, for example, the operator can pinpoint the elements in the product-service offering that are important to consumers — as well as clarify consumer purchase intentions and determine how they correspond to combinations of elements in the offering. [8]

The Presentation Mix

The term "presentation mix" signifies an umbrella concept covering those elements under the firm's control that act in concert to make the total product-service offering more tangible to the consumer. The presentation mix is also the means by which the firm differentiates its product-service offering from competitive offerings.

Every restaurant sells food, of course, but not all restaurants are alike. Every hotel sells the use of a

4. C. DeWitt Coffman, *Marketing for a Full House* (Ithaca, NY: School of Hotel Administration, Cornell University, 1970), pp. 6-7.

5. W.J.E. Crissy, Robert J. Boewadt, and Dante M. Laudadio, *Marketing of Hospitality Services: Food, Travel, Lodging,* (East Lansing, MI: Educational Institute of the American Hotel and Motel Association, 1975), pp. 59-89.

6. Irwin I. Eison, *Strategic Marketing in Food Service: Planning for Change,* (New York: Chain Store Publishing, 1980).

7. Kurt Vonnegut, Jr., *Mother Night,* (New York: Avon Books, 1972).

8. James H. Myers and Edward Tauber, *Market Structure Analysis,* (Chicago: American Marketing Association, 1977).

room with a collection of furnishings, but not all hotels are alike. In each instance, the customer perceives the whole offering: the restaurant, not just the food; the hotel, not just the room. Differences in the elements of the presentation mix allow the consumer to distinguish one establishment from another.

Major elements of the presentation mix are the physical plant, location, atmospherics (light, sound, space, smell, accoutrements), price, and employees. Some of these elements are routinely included in product-strategy formulation, but they should be viewed differently by a firm planning a service-marketing strategy.

Physical Plant. Both the exterior of the physical plant and the location of profit centers within the building are part of the presentation mix. If a physical plant has been designed successfully, the customer should be able to tell what is happening inside a building simply by viewing its exterior. The physical structure should reflect the intangible service elements that are part of the total offering. Trader Vic's, for example, looks like not only a restaurant, but also a *Polynesian* restaurant. A hotel designed by John Portman is not only a hotel, but also a specific type of environment.

"Profit-center proximities" is a term that describes the relationship between a property's profit centers and its customer traffic. Profit-center proximities are important elements of a service-strategy formulation for numerous reasons. First, because services are intangible, it is difficult to communicate to customers what is being sold in a way that will entice them to buy. Advertisements, especially those that appear in print, may not fully describe the ambience of an "elegant" restaurant.

Second, because a service must be produced close to the point of consumption, a service outlet's proximity to the customer is important. Profit-center locations should correspond with a customer's normal movements through the property. An example of good profit-center proximity would be a layout that required hotel guests walking from the front desk to the elevator to pass and look into the cocktail lounge, the dining room, the game room, and the indoor pool. An example of poor profit-center proximity would be a cocktail lounge not visible from the hotel's lobby, and accessible only through the dining room.

Perceived risk is the third reason that profit-center proximities are important elements of a service-strategy formulation. All purchase decision-making involves some element of risk. Warranties, guarantees against defects, and tes-

timonials that assure consumers of a product's reliability are all elements of a product-marketing strategy intended to help consumers reduce perceived risk. These assurances are rarely available to someone buying services, and defects in services are not easily proven. For example, who advertises a money-back guarantee on a hotel room? How can a customer prove that a meal was unsatisfactory or the service unfriendly?

A recent study of consumer attitudes and behavior indicates that customers seek testimonials about service offerings. Consumers were asked which factors would influence their choice of a restaurant they had never patronized. Of the 13 factors mentioned, the two cited most frequently were friends' recommendations and the type of food offered. The appearance of a property and its location placed third and fourth. A favorable newspaper or magazine review was mentioned as the fifth most important factor.[9] In short, customers seek information that allows them to reduce the perceived risk of the purchase decision. If a customer is able to view the interior of a hotel before selecting it, or is given some clue as to the quality of a restaurant's food before electing to dine there, he reduces his risk because his choice is an informed one.

Location. Location is important for several reasons. Consumers are willing to travel a distance to locate the right offering if the cost of making the wrong decision is high enough. If the decision is less important, however, consumers will pick the most conveniently located offering. Fast-food restaurants are often clustered along one street, because consumers will not go far out of their way to find the right fast-food restaurant; the risk of making the wrong decision is slight. Location is therefore crucial to a fast-food operator. As one executive stated, "There's no such thing as a good secondary location in fast food."

Location can also act as a barrier to prevent competitors from entering a particular market. As part of its marketing strategy, every firm must consider how it can build and protect a strong competitive position. Product-oriented companies normally use capital and patents as barriers to their competition. For labor-intensive service businesses, multiple locations can serve as a barrier to entry.[10]

Atmospherics. A firm promising elegance can support its promises through such atmospherics as

9. *Consumer Attitudes and Behavior in the Foodservice Marketplace: A Report to the National Restaurant Association*, (Chicago: Market Facts, 1974), p. 20.

10. Dan R.E. Thomas, "Strategy is Different in Service Businesses," *Harvard Business Review*, July-August, 1978, p. 160.

furnishings, lighting, decor, music, and use of space. Atmospherics can act as cues to reinforce service offerings and make them more tangible to consumers. They can also affect purchase behavior by acting as attention-getting, message-creating, or emotion-creating media. [11]

Price. In product marketing, prices are commonly established on the basis of costs. In service marketing, however, this approach simply doesn't work. (What does friendliness cost, for example?) The value consumers place on services, and its effect on their purchase behavior, might determine the cost. For example, low price may affect purchase intent adversely. When consumers with little information must purchase something new or unfamiliar, they often make inferences about quality on the basis of price.

Employees. A firm's employees are the final element of the presentation mix. Because of the intangibility of services and the consumer's presence at the point of production, a firm may find it difficult to establish service standards and even harder to ensure that the standards are met each time service is delivered. One way that service firms can solve this problem is through training programs designed to recognize employees as an important element of the service-marketing strategy. "For services," William George notes, "employees are perceived to be the product; they become the physical representation of the product . . . The successful service company must first sell the job to its employees, before it can sell services to its customers." [12] For this reason, fast-food outlets dress all employees in stylish uniforms, and theme parks hire young, attractive "actors," even though they incur higher costs as a result. Such companies have realized that, to a consumer, the employee is the product.

The Communications Mix

In a service-marketing strategy, a communications mix serves two major purposes. First, it persuades the consumer — that is, it recreates the intangible qualities of a service and makes them more tangible to the consumer. An effective communications mix includes pictures that make the intangible more tangible. In some hotels, for example, slide shows and films that illustrate services can be viewed in guest rooms via closed-circuit television.

Second, a communications mix can both establish and monitor a consumer's expectations. Because of the intangibility of service and the variability of service output, operators may find it difficult to ensure that the meaning of "friendliness," for example, stays the same for the firm and the consumer, and that friendliness is delivered every time the consumer makes a purchase. Visual-communication techniques can help establish consumer expectations, but it is important to remember that communication is a two-way process, and that it involves more than the purchase persuasion we normally associate with advertising. Thus, the task of monitoring consumer expectations is also an essential part of a service-marketing strategy. Although many operators see this task as too difficult, new point-of-purchase computers that register guest attitudes and satisfaction levels will make it easier for firms to develop monitoring programs. [13] Some monitoring programs have already been tested at hotels, with positive results. [14]

Conclusion

A new marketing mix, one that reflects the differences between products and services, should be part of every hospitality firm's total marketing strategy for improving performance and for competing successfully in the marketplace. Firms that strive to develop specific service-marketing strategies rather than follow traditional product-marketing strategies are those most likely to succeed.

11. Philip Kotler, "Atmospherics as a Marketing Tool," *Journal of Retailing,* 49, No. 4 (Winter 1973-74), pp. 48-64.

12. William R. George, "The Retailing of Services — A Challenging Future," *Journal of Retailing,* 53, No. 3 (Fall 1977), p. 90.

13. Ernest R. Cadotte, "Tellus Computer Lets Retailers Conduct In-Store Marketing Research," *Marketing News,* December 12, 1980, p. 17.

14. Ernest R. Cadotte, "The Push-Button Questionnaire: A New Tool for Measuring Customer Satisfaction," *The Cornell Hotel and Restaurant Administration Quarterly,* 19, No. 4 (February 1979), pp. 70-79.

Strategic Planning: Part I

by Ram Capoor

*Ram Capoor is a management consultant with
Touche Ross & Co. Touche Ross provides general
management consulting assistance on a wide
range of strategic and business policy issues. This
is the first of a three-part series on strategic
planning for the restaurant industry by Touche
Ross, based on its presentation at the Restaurant
Business Roundtable, of which it was a
co-sponsor. In subsequent issues, Touche Ross
will discuss: In Part II, a strategic planning model
tailored specifically for foodservice businesses; and
in Part III, the implementation of strategic plans.*

The foodservice industry is an industry that is maturing. You are facing a softening consumer demand. You are facing rising prices and increased cost pressures. Many companies have curtailed expansion programs. You operate in a market of changing demographics, changing meal patterns, and intensive inter-segment competition.

To help business managers think through strategies for the restaurant industry, we at Touche Ross have developed a framework for the strategy development with nine major elements as shown in *Exhibit I.*

Now let us start with the first point in the strategic framework. We believe that it is very important to recognize the uniqueness of the service business that you are in. What do we mean when we say that service businesses are unique? To begin with, we need to recognize that most of our traditional planning vocabulary is manufacturing oriented.

"Because manufacturing has been the dominant economic force of the last century, most managers have been educated through experience or formal education to think about strategic management in product-oriented terms. Unfortunately, a large part of this experience is irrelevant to the management of many service businesses. The general manager of a service business must develop a healthy skep-

ticism about his and others' approaches to strategy." (From Dan R.E. Thomas, "Strategy is Different in Service Business," *Harvard Business Review*, July-August, 1978.)

We can identify the shortcomings of product concepts as they apply to the service business using the matrix in *Exhibit II.*

The key difference between a manufacturing and service business is that they have different components as shown in *Exhibit III.*

When talking about the service business most people tend to focus on the process component which in the foodservice industry is the process that results in the delivery of meals to customers. However, it is very important to recognize the interactive component and the customer component of the service business.

The interactive component in the foodservice business is, for example, the interaction between the waitress/waiter and the customer in the actual delivery of service, but also includes interactions of managers, bus-boys, cashiers, etc. with customers.

The customer component in foodservice is the customer's role in the transaction, his behavior relative to his expectations and needs. In a service business, every service occasion to each customer is a unique event.

The process component in the foodservice industry or any other service industry offers limited opportunities for innovation. Even when innovation occurs, like a new method of food preparation or storage, it is easily copied. The opportunity for differentiation lies in the interactive component of your service. It cannot be completely standardized because human beings cannot be standardized, both servers and customers have different moods and attitudes from one moment to another.

This is the area where a foodservice company can best create a perception of value-added, assuming it serves quality products. If the company succeeds in developing the right attitude among its servers — in a way that the customer perceives value-added — this will be a major differentiating factor, and will be difficult to copy.

From *Restaurant Business* (May 1, 1981) pp. 198-202. Reprinted by permission of *Restaurant Business.*

Exhibit 1.

Suggested Strategic Framework

1. Recognize service business uniqueness
2. Define business in terms of markets (not products)
3. Segment markets based on strengths and opportunities
4. Establish Strategic Business Units (SBUs) in terms of business and market segments
5. Formulate success model for each SBU
6. Develop strategies for execution
7. Organize to execute
8. Establish management controls
9. Monitor progress/variances, adapt

Exhibit 2

Shortcomings of Product Concepts When Applied to Service Businesses*

Product Concept	Application to Service Business
• Physical reality of product provides simple but powerful base on which to build a business description.	• Services are more abstract and more variable than products.
• Capital is the most common barrier to entry of competition.	• Building barriers to entry is generally more difficult, or at least must be done in less traditional ways.
• Operating leverage can be improved by purchasing faster, more reliable machinery.	• More difficult in service businesses, opportunities are there but required different ways of thinking about operations.
• All product oriented companies have ways of determining product cost.	• Difficult to determine what a unit of service is, much less its cost.
• Virtually all product companies have some form of R & D to design, develop, test new products.	• Complicated by lack of physical product; deals instead with people and concepts, difficult to test market.

*Summarized From Dan R.E. Thomas, "Strategy Is Different In Service Business", Harvard Business Review, July-August, 1978.

Exhibit 3

A Service Has Three Components:

1. Core—Basic Process—Finite Number of Variations
2. Interactive—Infinite Number of Variations *Delivered* in Partnership
3. Customer—Infinite Number of Needs/Expectations *Received* in Partnership

PROCESS COMPONENT

Core service/ Basic service Usually a process:	• Process component may be standardized, mechanized, etc.
• Airline flight • Loan transaction • Meal occasion • Audit process	■ Cannot be inventoried/stored ■ Little opportunity for perception of value-added by customer ■ Easily copied ■ Maybe capital intensive ■ Little opportunity for differentiation

INTERACTIVE COMPONENT DELIVERED BY PROVIDER

Interactive component: • Infinite variation	• Interactive component cannot be totally standardized • Great opportunity for perception of value-added by and with customer • Difficult to copy • Great opportunity for differentiation

CUSTOMER COMPONENT

■ Expectation ■ Need	• Customer component is infinite in terms of: ■ No. cust. x no. of services x no. of opportunities to serve ■ Expectations ■ Needs

Because of these unique features, we believe that foodservice companies should define the business in terms of markets and not products. One way to think of a company or a company's strategy is to do so in terms of the concept of the driving force. The driving force of a company is the primary factor which drives that company's management activities and strategies.

A product-driven company thinks in terms of products. They develop new products similar to old products. They look for new momentum for their products. Their ideas do not come from the definition of the market place. They start with the product idea and still live with the product definition of the market. Examples of product companies abound, a company that calls itself an office-products company — or a hamburger company or seafood restaurant, etc. — is product driven.

Companies can also be operationally driven, for example, a company which has as its major objective to be the least cost producer. This is common in commodity business like paper and carton producers. Companies where the motivation is to build a portfolio of businesses which satisfy certain established financial criteria — such as the achievement of a specified return — are financially driven. Conglomerates in many disparate businesses, like City Investing, are good examples of financially driven companies.

Companies are market driven when they say: "Here's a specific market we are trying to serve. What, therefore, should we offer to that market-place? What services should we provide?" Some of the premier consumer products companies, like Proctor & Gamble, and Norton Simon, are examples of market driven companies even though they sell products.

Based on our observations, we believe that in the past, foodservice industry participants have been largely product driven and have seen themselves as being in the hamburger business, the fish business, or the doughnut business, etc.

We would suggest that today, given what we have learned about the changing environment, given the fact that there is so much competition, you need to know who really is your customer. And you need to recognize that there are different customers, with different needs representing different markets. Is it families in the urban Northeast in certain age groups and certain income groups or is it an occupational group?

Most businesses have more than one customer set, the more there are the more important it is to understand who they are. Then, to understand why they come to you and when, as well as the reasons and times they don't think they need your service.

How should a foodservice company identify its markets and segment them? Market Segmentation must be based on strengths and opportunities. In the foodservice business there are many segmentation variables: age, sex, region, occupation, income, meal occasion, location, and activity.

There is no one right cut. You must start with the needs your business currently satisfies, and then define the customer sets you serve.

This should lead to the establishment of Strategic Business Units, preferably separate business units for each different major market you serve.

For a foodservice company with one concept, geography may be the major segmentation variable between markets. Thus each major geographical market area could become an SBU. What does that mean? It should mean that each SBU should be as stand-alone a business unit as possible with its own general manager and as full a complement of line and staff functions as feasible.

A SBU should be a self-contained mini-chain within a chain. Current practice in the industry by contrast is to organize functionally (operations, real estate, marketing, finance, etc.) at the top and then to break-out functions like operations regionally. Naturally, companies organized into SBUs will require each SBU to adhere to certain common guidelines and policies. The SBU concept is common-place in the manufacturing sector, pioneered by companies like G.E., but of relatively recent vintage in the service industry. Citibank has been a leader in the services sector.

Why organize by SBU? SBU management encourages entrepreneurial behavior. It provides the SBU general manager with most of the resources he needs to get the job done and he can be held accountable for the results. You can build pride, team spirit, and good people with the SBU concept.

Strategic Planning: Part II

by Ram Capoor

Following is the second of a three-part series on strategic planning for the restaurant industry compiled by Touche Ross, based on its presentation at the Restaurant Business *Roundtable I – Facing the Constraints on Growth. It analyzes a strategic planning model tailored specifically for foodservice businesses.*

The *first* article in this series introduced a framework for strategic planning in the foodservice industry, shown in *Exhibit I,* which addressed the first four elements of the nine-point framework. In brief, the article made the following major points:

• The foodservice business is a service business and as such is different from a manufacturing enterprise in many important respects. An understanding of these major differences will keep foodservice executives from making strategic errors.

• One of the first steps that any company must take in developing a strategic plan is to define clearly and concisely its specific business. All too often, as in the restaurant industry, a product definition is employed (e.g., we are in the hamburger business). For a service business, the better way to define your business is in terms of the market served or market planned to be served.

• Markets can be segmented in terms of several different variables, for example: age, sex, religion, occupation, income level, meal occasion, location, and activity. It is important to recognize that there is no single "right cut" of the market. Usually, the place to begin is with the needs of the market that the business currently satisfies, and to clearly define the different customer sets that are presently served by the foodservice business.

While a good starting point, this segmentation may or may not be the right approach to the marketplace in the future. What is right for the future in terms of segmentation depends upon the individual firm's unique strengths and opportunities in the evolving market environment.

From *Restaurant Business* (June 1, 1981) pp. 154-166. Reprinted by permission of *Restaurant Business.*

• Finally, the article discusses the establishment of strategic business units (SBUs). A strategic business unit is defined as being a segment of a foodservice business with a separate and distinct market and with the resources (in terms of organization, machinery, people, money, etc.) to be a self-contained business within a larger business.

Of course, in smaller foodservice enterprises, it is entirely possible that the entire business can be thought of as being one strategic business unit. A key test of whether or not a piece of the business is a strategic business unit is if it can be divested separately from the remainder of the business.

Planning Model

Having completed the above steps, the foodservice enterprise must then develop a strategic plan for each strategic business unit. The strategic planning process can be aided enormously by using a model appropriate to that particular business.

Unfortunately, most of the models currently available were developed largely for manufacturing businesses as opposed to service businesses like foodservice. The assembly line is a common model used to represent the manufacturing business whereby raw materials come to the enterprise, go through various pre-processing stages, through fabrication processes, and then to the assembly line, which essentially puts the parts of the product together. The finished products are then packaged and sent to a warehouse or to distributors and eventually reach the marketplace.

From the assembly line model have emanated several strategy-related concepts such as learning curves and price umbrellas. While similar activities occur in a service business (for example, in the foodservice industry, the preparation of a meal), there is limited value to using this model for strategic thinking.

We, at Touche Ross, prefer to use a different

Suggested Strategic Framework

Exhibit 1

1. Recognize Service Business Uniqueness
2. Define Business in Terms of Markets (Not Products)
3. Segment Markets Based on Strengths and Opportunities
4. Establish Strategic Business Units (SBUs) in Terms of Business and Market Segments
5. Formulate Success Model for Each SBU
6. Develop Strategies for Execution
7. Organize to Execute
8. Establish Management Controls
9. Monitor Progress/Variances, Adapt

**Strategies for a Service Business Should Flow From a
Model Which Embodies the Key Characteristics of Service Business**

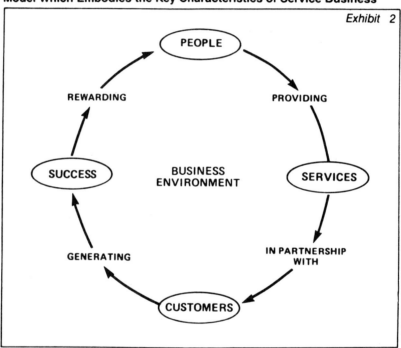

Exhibit 2

though simple model which better captures the essence of a service business. This model, shown in *Exhibit 2*, depicts a service business as being a cycle in which people provide services in partnership with customers and thereby generate success, which in turn rewards the people that provided the services to the customers.

The activities of providing services to customers occur in a business environment which is unique to each organization which in turn has its own set of values, codes of behavior and other organizational requirements. The environment is an essential part of this model.

This model suggests that the quality of the people in the organization is a key variable for success in a service business, like foodservice. Quality people providing value-added services in a spirit of partnership with their customers will inevitably generate success both for themselves as well as the organization of which they are a part.

Success can, and probably should, be measured more broadly than just in terms of profitability. Other important elements are recognition for the firm and its people and the firm's reputation for quality in the market. Success in a service business provides the fuel with which to reward good people, propelling this positive feedback cycle forward.

In a Service Business: Quality and Productivity—
Two Key Variables— Can Interact Synergistically and Lead to Success

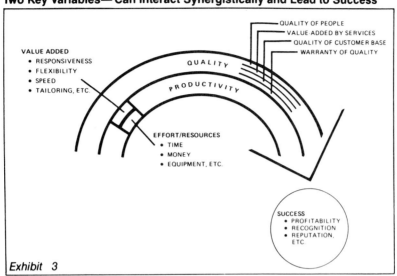

Exhibit 3

Further, a positive business environment that encourages teamwork develops an entrepreneurial spirit, builds people for the long term and will contribute significantly to the ongoing success of an organization.

On the other hand, poor quality people working in a harsh environment are unlikely to provide value-added services to customers, or to do so with a sense of partnership. Such an organization can at best hope for some short-term profits but is more than likely destined for an early grave.

Synergism

This "model for success" enables us to focus on the synergy among the key variables in a service business. It focuses on the interconnection of the key variables; it focuses on the feedback cycle of a service business.

The "customer-provider" interaction that is such a key part of the service business is also highlighted in this model. A worker in a manufacturing plant seldom sees the displeasure on the face of a customer upon receiving a poor quality product. However, an employee in the "plant" of a service business such as a restaurant sees this negative feedback instantly.

This model suggests that in a service business like foodservice, quality and productivity are two key variables, which can interact synergistically to lead to success.

By "quality" we mean: the quality of people; the value added by the services they provide to the customer; the quality of the customer base itself, and the warranty of quality for which the organization stands.

"Productivity," of course, is a much discussed subject today. We would suggest for a foodservice business that productivity be defined as being the value added per unit of effort or resources committed by the organization.

By "value added" we mean: responsiveness and sensitivity to customer needs; the flexibility with which customer needs are handled; the speed of service, and the extent to which the services are tailored to the customer's needs.

"Effort" or "resources" refers to time (i.e., the time committed by the organization of its people), money and equipment. This is shown in *Exhibit 3*. It is interesting to note that in his own way each participant in the *Restaurant Business* Roundtable from the foodservice industry highlighted the importance of these two variables.

The concept of "value added" addresses the issue of what value your particular foodservice enterprise provides to the customer. Of course the quality of the product itself is a key element of the value provided. However, the environment of the restaurant, the behavior and attitudes of the service providers are equally important elements of the value added to the customer.

Non-responsive behavior by restaurant personnel, sloppy service, the inflexibility to meet customer needs, such as insisting the customer adhere strictly to the service offerings provided by a particular restaurant, can all detract from the value added as perceived by the customer.

The Strategic Condition of a Service Business Can Be Established in Terms of the Model Using a Quality, Productivity Matrix

	LOW PRODUCTIVITY	HIGH PRODUCTIVITY
HIGH QUALITY	**TRADITIONAL** • GOOD MARKET REPUTATION • UNABLE TO GENERATE PROFIT GROWTH • INFLATION ERODING PRODUCTIVITY • ENCOUNTERING PEOPLE & CUSTOMER RETENTION PROBLEMS	**ATHLETE** *Exhibit 4* • PROFITABLE, GROWING • STRONG REPUTATION • WORLD-CLASS COMPETITOR • ATTRACTS BEST PEOPLE • PROSPECTIVE CUSTOMERS GO THERE FIRST
LOW QUALITY	**TROUBLED** • APPROACHING OR IN VIABILITY CRISIS • WEAK MANAGEMENT • POOR PEOPLE QUALITY • FORMERLY "TRADITIONAL" OR "MYOPIC"	**MYOPIC** • SHORT-TERM ORIENTED • COMPETES ON PRICE • DOES NOT HAVE BEST PEOPLE • HAS TROUBLE ATTRACTING QUALITY CUSTOMERS • LOSING GOOD BUSINESS TO ATHLETE

With regard to quality, the model also raises the issue of the quality of the customer base. What exactly do we mean by that? By the services it provides and the manner in which they are provided, a foodservice business exercises a fair degree of control over the quality of customers it attracts. The better the quality of your clientele, the higher the demands for service; however, the hard-won rewards are likely to be worth it.

Better customers have no difficulty paying for service; they perceive quality and value added. In the foodservice industry, we find that some companies do well even when the industry or their segment is "down." Their customer base quality is a factor in their resilience.

Neither productivity nor quality is easily measurable for a foodservice business; it is unlikely that you will find them measured on the financial statement of any foodservice enterprise. This, however, does not detract from their value as important variables in the strategic planning process.

Sophisticated companies in many industries are beginning to come to grips with the issue of measuring both quality and productivity. Measures of both quality and productivity *can* and *should* be developed by foodservice enterprises, even though they may be primitive at the outset.

Quality — Productivity

The "bottom line" of this model is that there is a direct relationship between the quality of services a business renders to its customers and the productivity of its people and other resources. High levels of quality and productivity can be expected to lead to profitability and other elements of success for the foodservice enterprise. It's called the Quality-Productivity Connection.

How can we use the Quality — Productivity Connection to advantage in strategic planning? To begin with, the strategic condition of the service business can be established in terms of this model by using the two key variables of quality and productivity. *Exhibit 4,* a simple matrix with quality and productivity as the two axes, can be effective in characterizing the current state of a food service business.

A business that scores low on the quality scale but works hard to maintain high levels of productivity is usually "myopic." A myopic foodservice

**Broad Strategy Implications Can Be Drawn
from the Quality Productivity Matrix**

Exhibit 5

	LOW PRODUCTIVITY	HIGH PRODUCTIVITY
HIGH QUALITY	**TRADITIONAL** ARREST PRODUCTIVITY DECLINE BEFORE LO P IMPACTS HI Q TO MAKE IT TROUBLED COMPANY	**ATHLETE** RETAIN/IMPROVE PREMIER POSITION, GUARD AGAINST • CHANGING ENVIRONMENT • COMPETITIVE ATTACK • COMPLACENCY
LOW QUALITY	**TROUBLED** DETERMINE MAGNITUDE OF VIABILITY CRISIS & DEVELOP BANKRUPTCY, DIVESTITURE OR TURNAROUND PLAN	**MYOPIC** INVEST PRODUCTIVITY GAINS IN A LONGER TERM ORIENTATION BEFORE LO Q IMPACTS HI P TO MAKE IT A TROUBLED COMPANY

enterprise is usually short-term oriented. It ends up competing mainly on price, seldom attracts the best people to work in its organization, has trouble attracting customers on a long-term basis and generally ends up losing business to the better firms in the industry.

Inevitably, the focus on productivity at the expense of quality shows in the marketplace. Many restaurant companies that were turnaround situations became myopic in their later stages: they failed to see past the short term, were unable to compete in terms of quality food and a quality environment, began to lose many of their better people and lost their franchise with their customers.

On the other hand, companies that enjoyed a reputation for high quality but failed to generate high productivity have also suffered over time. A "traditional" company, characterized by high quality and low productivity, becomes unable to generate profit growth. In this context, inflation often erodes productivity. The lack of growth begins, again, to drive the better quality people out of the organization. Prices continue to push upward and often the customer fails to see any additional value added.

Similar to the fate of the myopic company, the traditional company will also ultimately become a troubled company. It will approach a viability crisis, will become characterized by weak management and will generally show all the symptoms financially as well as from a marketplace point of view of a company without a future.

The "athlete" company offers a sharp contrast to the traditional company as well as the myopic company. A foodservice athlete is a profitable, growing company that enjoys a strong reputation and can be thought of as a world-class competitor. It has no trouble attracting the best people in the industry and, probably most importantly, prospective customers tend to go there first. It is important to recognize that what makes a company an athlete is its ability to maintain *both* high quality and high productivity.

An important step for a foodservice business to undertake in its strategic planning process is to determine where each of its strategic business units falls on the quality — productivity matrix. This will require a careful and insightful examination of the company's position both from within the company and from the outside looking in.

In addition to basic market research, a company will often benefit from a careful customer survey. Such a survey can reveal the customer's perception of quality in all of its elements. We have previously discussed both the difficulty and the necessity of measuring productivity. Without a fairly accurate understanding of the company's current strategic position, a strategic planning exercise cannot continue meaningfully.

Objectivity will also be important to a foodservice company in establishing its strategic condition; for example, existing management will find it difficult to arrive at conclusions that would lead to a characterization of myopia or traditionality for a strategic business unit.

While the strategic direction for each individual company will be unique, it is possible to draw some broad strategy implications from the quality — productivity matrix. This is shown in *Exhibit 5*.

**Market and Economic Pressures Exert
Downward Pull on Foodservice Companies**

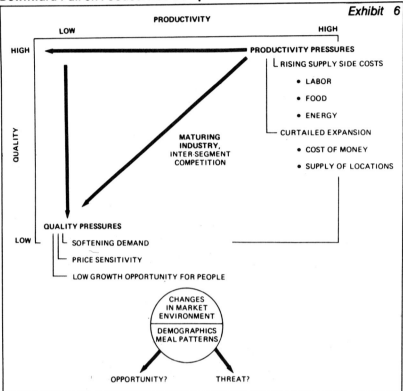

The Productivity Trap

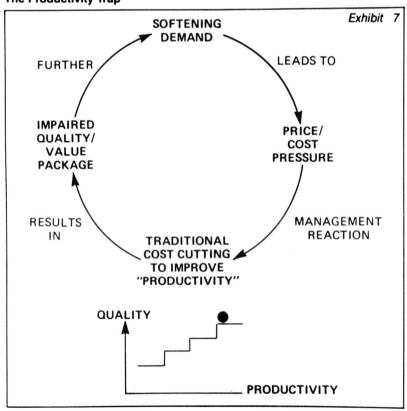

A strategic business unit characterized as currently being myopic needs to invest its productivity gains in a longer-term orientation; it needs to focus on its future viability before it becomes a troubled company. This will usually require a thorough evaluation of the marketplace and an assessment of where this particular strategic business unit fits on the value added spectrum. Organization and people will be important aspects of strategy for a myopic strategic business unit.

A traditional strategic business unit must seek strategies that will arrest the productivity decline before low productivity impacts high quality to make it a troubled company. The problem for such a strategic business unit is not likely to be found in the marketplace; the problem here is more likely to be the process of service delivery. Different kinds of people and new approaches to organization and systems may be appropriate.

An athlete, in turn, must guard against complacency. It must guard against a changing environment and be positioned to repel competitive attack. In other words, an athlete must seek strategies that will enable it to retain or improve its premier position.

Industry Pressures

It is also valuable to look at the current overall state of the industry as it relates to the quality—productivity matrix. This is graphically shown in *Exhibit 6.*

Overall, there are several pressures that exert a downward drag on almost any foodservice enterprise. These pressures were extensively discussed by the industry observers at the strategic planning roundtable.

Productivity pressures in terms of rising supply-side costs, curtailed expansion due to the high cost of money and the declining supply of quality locations are all pressures that show no sign of abatement.

The industry itself is maturing and competition both within segments and across segments is becoming more intense.

Productivity pressures and the pressure of a maturing industry are compounded by quality pressures. The factors impacting the disposable income of consumers are probably primarily responsible for the quality pressures that exist. This leads to concerns with regard to growth, traffic, frequency of eating out and increasing price sensitivity.

Furthermore, the maturity of the industry leads to concerns with regard to the growth opportunities available to the millions of people employed at the unit level. In addition to the above pressures, the market environment is rapidly changing, for example, in terms of demographics and in terms of meal patterns. This has been well established in the September 15, 1980 Restaurant Growth Index issue of *Restaurant Business* Magazine.

Are these changes in the market environment an opportunity or do they pose a threat to your particular foodservice enterprise? A well thought out strategic plan has the potential to convert threats into opportunities.

In the adverse economic and market environment that we face, it is worthwhile to caution foodservice companies against falling into the "productivity trap," illustrated graphically in *Exhibit 7.* Price and cost pressures that arise from softening demand often lead management to react instinctively to institute belt-tightening measures.

Traditional cost-cutting approaches for improving productivity, however, often result in an impaired quality/value package.

For example, service in the restaurant can deteriorate, cleanliness can suffer, renovation, refurbishments can be delayed leading to a decline in the atmosphere of a restaurant. Customers' negative reaction to the deteriorating quality of the service provided can lead to further softening in demand.

This, of course, sets up a vicious cycle where, with each iteration, both quality and *real* productivity decline. Unless management is enlightened enough to break the vicious cycle, a viability crisis is likely to be the result.

Strategies for Execution

Coming to step 6 in the strategic framework shown in Exhibit 1, the foodservice enterprise — in order to develop strategies for execution — should examine the success model for each strategic business unit.

The key questions that need answers include the following:

• What kind of people organized in what fashion should provide what services to which customers?

• How will this generate success and how will that, in turn, reward the people that made that success possible?

• What business environment will be most conducive to that success?

Answers to these questions will lead to the major

elements of strategy: market strategies, organization and people strategies, and financial strategies.

Quality and productivity will be the two variables that (a) link the strategies together and (b) provide the measures of success. In other words, the strategies that you generate are only meaningful to the extent that they enable you to improve the company's quality — productivity position.

For example, success for a foodservice company may no longer be about increasing the number of units or increasing volume. It may instead have to do with return on investment, enhancement of long-term competitive position and strengthening the "people balance sheet" of the organization. To accomplish these goals, the concept of what services the foodservice organization provides may expand.

A recent issue of *The New Yorker* Magazine carried a cartoon depicting a "Bank 'n Burger" in which a customer filling out a bank transaction form is shown next to a customer eating a sandwich. While tongue-in-cheek, it is also food for thought.

Strategic planning is all about charting the future course of an enterprise. The future course, given the changing environment, is likely to be substantially different from the present course of the enterprise. To be sure, the new course will be hard to chart, and once charted, will bring with it its own unique set of problems. However, with sound strategic planning, we can trade today's problems for a better set of problems.

New strategies always require change; change in the way that business is conducted by the existing organization, be it in terms of structure, policies, controls or systems.

Finally, the implementation of strategy and its monitoring and control are just as important as the formulation of strategy. We will discuss these in the final article in this series.

Strategic Planning: Part III
Alternatives to Managing by Objectives

by Ram Capoor

*The preceding two articles in this series
(See* Restaurant Business *May 1 and June 1, 1981)
addressed the first six points of a nine-point
framework (See* Exhibit 1) *designed for the
development of a strategic plan for a foodservice
company. In this article, compiled by Touche Ross
based on its presentation at the* Restaurant
Business *Roundtable I, the final three points
which deal with the implementation and monitoring
of strategy will be discussed.*

A strategic plan without an effective way to execute the strategies is almost a total waste of effort. Many organizations spend countless hours creating their own strategic plan. Others pay consultants considerable sums to develop strategic plans, only to have these documents shelved away in some executive's office. A typical comment with regard to strategic planning is "Wow, that was a great mind expanding exercise, but let's get back to the real world."

A strategic plan is a mere wish list if it cannot be applied to the executives' real world. The power of a strategic plan lies in its ability to provide overall direction for the day-to-day activities of managing a business. Moreover, management should compare the results of operating activity to goals and objectives.

For example, a foodservice company may establish objectives for renovating and refurbishing its restaurants as part of its "image enhancing" strategy, focus instead on generating short-term earnings and then fail to invest in the longer term. The first question here is did management consider its strategic objectives in its operating plans? And second, was the achievement of high short-term earnings really good news?

In other words, a foodservice company should establish a process of Strategic Management.

Strategic planning is a vital part of this process, but only a part. Strategy Execution and Strategy Monitoring (*See Exhibit 2*) are the other essential parts in the strategic management cycle.

The purpose of strategy monitoring is to determine how well the organization is doing on an *ongoing basis* in pursuit of its strategic goals and objectives. The result of strategic monitoring is a determination of what changes should be made either to the strategies themselves or to the means of execution and why.

For example, the foodservice company that invests a significant sum in renovation should also have a program to monitor its effectiveness through such methods as customer surveys and traffic analyses. If these measurements show no appreciable change in the preceived image, a review of the renovation problem would be in order.

The following options should be reviewed: Should the program be supported by more advertising dollars? Should it be modified? Or if it is scrapped, what should replace it to fully execute the image enhancement strategy?

While the concept of strategic management is relatively simple, it is much harder to make happen in "real life." On several occasions, we at Touche Ross have dissuaded our clients from having the consultants prepare "their" strategic plan *without* client participation. We believe that people within the company, especially the line managers, must "own" the plan, and be the architects. Otherwise, there is little interest in executing someone else's plan, much less monitor progress.

And so, we counsel our clients and assist them in building their own talent within the organization to plan and adopt a management style, organization structure and set of policies conducive to formalized planning. Vital to their success is also a system such that managers are rewarded for both long-term success and short-term success.

For example, a company that preaches long-range planning on the one hand but rewards managers solely on performance to budget is sending

From *Restaurant Business* (July 1, 1981) pp. 94-103. Reprinted by permission of *Restaurant Business.*

EXHIBIT I

SUGGESTED STRATEGIC FRAMEWORK

1. Recognize Service Business Uniqueness
2. Define Business in Terms of Markets (not products)
3. Segment Markets Based on Strengths & Opportunities
4. Establish Strategic Business Units (SBUs) in Terms of Business and Market Segments
5. Formulate Success Model For Each SBU
6. Develop Strategies For Execution
7. Organize To Execute
8. Establish Management Controls
9. Monitor Progress/Variances, Adapt

EXHIBIT II

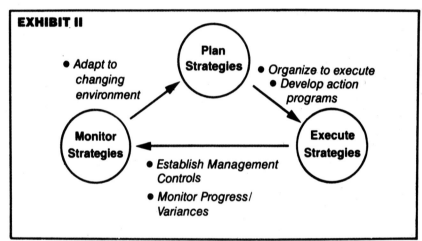

THE STRATEGIC MANAGEMENT PROCESS

signals that strategy is not important; tactics are.

Planning, to many entrepreneurs within the foodservice industry, is academic, esoteric, expensive and irrelevant. These line managers have what they consider to be a healthy dislike for strategic planning or strategic management. Usually the management process of these "gut-feel" managers/entrepreneurs falls into one of four categories explained by Steven Brandt of Stanford University in *Strategic Planning In Emerging Companies*, May 1981.

1. Managing by Extrapolation;
2. Managing by Crisis;
3. Managing by Subjectives;
4. Managing by Hope.

Review the descriptions of MBE, MBC, MBS and MBH and as you read it think about its relevance to your organization, and whether they are viable alternatives to strategic management.

"If you don't know where you are going any road will lead you there" is a big part of this message. The first step in positioning your organization to plan and manage strategically is to convince your people of the value and importance of it. Recognize that total acceptance will not be immediate; the rest will come only by doing.

Strategic management is also no panacea and no substitute for talent. The intrinsic talents and depth of the management team will dictate the quality of the strategic management process.

According to Bob Rosenberg, president of Dunkin' Donuts, "We believe a great deal of our sucess these past years is our commitment to building and keeping a high-quality organization. I believe it takes not only exceptional people to build an exceptional company, it also takes continuity."

To the extent that management quality and depth is lacking, it makes a lot of *sense* to update it *before* embarking on a strategic management program. Therefore, a foodservice company should critically evaluate its management team and its organization structure. Here are a few key questions that should be raised:

1. Do we have the people who can carry us through our next growth phase?

2. How strong are we in key skill areas such as marketing operations, finance and control and human resources management?

3. Do we have people who want to grow, who will be receptive to change?

Objectivity is of paramount importance in the evaluation of management depth and quality. Insiders have difficulty in being objective for obvious reasons of loyalty, vested interests, etc. Experienced general management consultants have a key role to play here because they are most likely to provide an objective, sensitive and pragmatic assessment.

The management style of an organization is also a key to effective strategic management. Imagine a spectrum with dictatorial styles on one end and "laissez-faire" styles on the other (see *Exhibit 4*).

What management style and behavior makes sense for your organization depends first on the size and complexity of your foodservice business. The answer is different for a one-concept foodser-vice operation with only a few units versus a multi-concept multi-state foodservice company. The answer will also be influenced by whether yours is a free-standing company or whether you are part of a larger corporation. More authoritarian styles of owner managers, with little delegation of authority or responsibility, work reasonably well when the business is smaller and less complex. This runs aground though as the business grows; the owner-managers can no longer cover all the bases.

Clearly, giving everyone in the organization complete freedom to do what he believes is right is also not the way to manage growth effectively. The appropriate management style as the foodservice operation grows is somewhere in between but probably "right-of-center."

The other key factor influencing management style is the stability/predictability of the market environment. *Roundtable I* clearly established that the restaurant industry environment is harsher and more uncertain than it's ever been. Centralized/authoritarian styles of management have difficulty coping with this kind of environment because the "central authority" has to obtain, track and absorb all the data and make all key decisions.

MANAGING BY OBJECTIVES*

MBE, Managing by Extrapolation	Users of this system keep on doing what they have always done. More is normally merrier, and all lines on the planning chart move upward and to the right over time. This essentially historical approach was adequate during the first half of this century . . . car companies and their suppliers produced and distributed cars; radio companies made radios; banks handled money; and so forth. Even after World War II, at least, business was in a relatively steady-state environment in which tomorrow could be reasonably expected to look a lot like yesterday, and the primary task for top managers was to do the same things right, i.e., more efficiently. A look at the national productivity curve during this period shows that in total, business managements succeeded in doing things right.
MBC, Managing by Crisis	This system, long the specialty of the entrepreneur, has picked up a larger following in recent times for two reasons. First, business life is much more complex than it used to be. So there are more crises to be handled; enough, in fact, to occupy everyone pretty much full time, if they are willing. Second, there are a great many more engineers in positions of management responsibility today, and as a group they tend to be great problem solvers. Give them a crisis and they will smother it with energy and innovation. And if there should be a gap in the flow of problems, chances are good that one can be invented — something nice and tangible that the manager can get his arms around — or teeth into. Management by crisis is popular, at the end of a given day no one can say the boss didn't earn his pay.
MBS, Managing by Subjectives	As the queen said to Alice as she hesitated along the path to Wonderland, if you don't know where you are going, any road will take you there. There are companies who operate successfully this way. Everyone does the best he or she can to accomplish what he or she thinks should be done. Somewhere up in the organization there is presumed to be a guiding star. And there could be well be. As long as the business lends itself to master minding (or central processing) by a single individual or a small team, implementation is relatively straight forward, and not much talent is needed below the top level, the mystery approach to managing has been and is a viable alternative. However, for an emerging company, the days are numbered for such an approach to managing.
MBH, Managing by Hope	Most readers over forty years of age recognize that the pace of living in the corporate world has increased markedly in recent years. Every business decision — staffing, capital investment, new services, etc. — has more ramifications than before. Certainties are hard to find. And the uncertainities of the times have led some managements into willy-nilly diversification . . . in hopes that it will work out . . . and other managements into paralysis by analysis . . . while they hope something will turn up to point the way for the enterprise. MBH is essentially a form of reacting, rather than acting, of letting events control you rather than vice versa.

*Excerpted from Strategic Planning In Emerging Companies, by Steven C. Brandt, Published by Addison Wesley, May 1981.

The environment may be changing too fast in too many areas for this to be humanly possible — again compounded by the size and growth of the company.

Says Phil Barksdale, president/CEO, Perkins' Cake & Steak, "Ideally, a successful foodservice company is able to retain the entrepreneurial spirit balanced with professional management."

"To be successful in the '80s, operators will also have to adopt a decentralizing management style — decentralizing operations and balancing that policy with centralized policy-making at the corpo-rate level," adds Joe Lee, president of the restaurant divison at General Mills.

Given this conceptual framework for thinking about management style, we suggest that a management style of Entrepreneurial Innovation can substantially add to the success of a growing food-service company with increasing complexity operating in today's uncertain environment. Enterpreneurial Innovation can significantly aid the effectiveness of strategic management, as indicated in *Exhibit 4*.

Using this management style, each SBU (SBUs

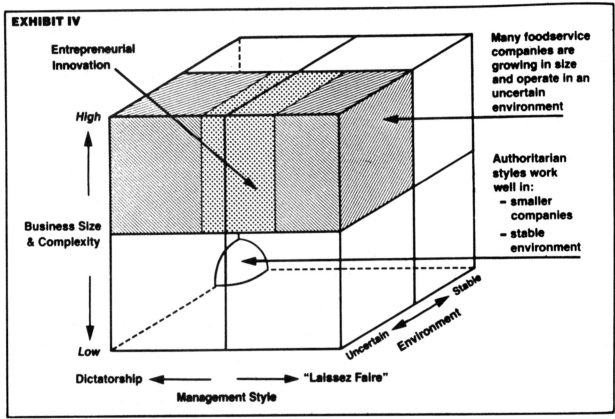

INCREASING BUSINESS COMPLEXITY AND UNCERTAINTY ARGUE FOR MORE DECENTRALIZED MANAGEMENT STYLES.

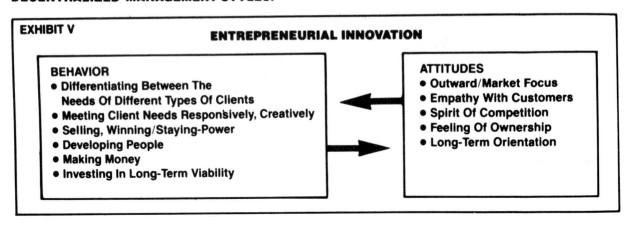

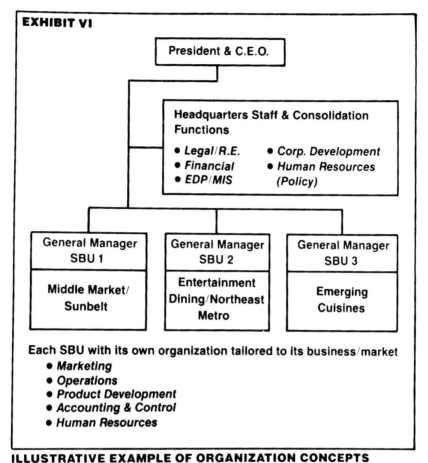

EXHIBIT VI

President & C.E.O.

Headquarters Staff & Consolidation Functions

- *Legal/R.E.*
- *Financial*
- *EDP/MIS*
- *Corp. Development*
- *Human Resources (Policy)*

General Manager SBU 1 — Middle Market/ Sunbelt

General Manager SBU 2 — Entertainment Dining/Northeast Metro

General Manager SBU 3 — Emerging Cuisines

Each SBU with its own organization tailored to its business/market
- *Marketing*
- *Operations*
- *Product Development*
- *Accounting & Control*
- *Human Resources*

ILLUSTRATIVE EXAMPLE OF ORGANIZATION CONCEPTS

were defined in Parts I and II) should be headed by a general manager who is motivated by an entrepreneurial reward system. By entrepreneurial rewards, we mean those consistent with "ownership" and long-term success. The attitudes and behavior patterns sought through this management style are shown in *Exhibit 5*.

A management style of entrepreneurial innovation requires that a set of management policies be established which provide an "out-side-in" orientation toward:

- Strategies for improving the productivity/quality position of the organization.
- Structure of the enterprise around the primary objective of providing services tailored to distinct market segments, with consistent decentralization of responsibility/accountability and resources.
- The implementation of a top-down management control system that establishes and monitors the measures of success in terms of quality and productivity.
- The establishment of operational controls that are responsive to the management control system

and linked with the organizational structure of the enterprise; and

- The establishment of an organizational framework and related skills which emphasize a team approach to: people development; customer service; problem solving as a means of conflict resolution; and implementation of projects.

To illustrate the organization concepts, consider a hypothetical foodservice company which, as a result of its strategic planning process, decided that it should organize around three SBUs defined as follows:

SBU 1: Dining and Related Services for Middle Market Consumers in the Sunbelt;

SBU 2: Entertainment Dining in Major Northeast Metro Suburbs;

SBU 3: Emerging Cuisines.

The company decided on the organizational structure illustrated in *Exhibit 6*. Each SBU is a relatively self-contained business organization. Centralized functions were limited to staff and consolidation functions. They decided that they did not have on-board the General Managers of SBU 1 and SBU 3 and initiated a search. The incentives offered to the General Managers were based on the Quality/Productivity model described in Part II of this series. As such, their targets were established in the following terms.

• Quality of their own organization;

• Customers' perception of value-added (based on a survey methodology);

• Productivity measures which include growth in real (deflated) sales per unit, return on investment and employee productivity;

• The quality of business environment (or "culture") that they build around them — as perceived by their subordinates and superiors;

• Competitive measures of success such as market position and competitive edge.

Admittedly, some of these targets are qualitative and somewhat subjective, i.e., the level of business is "in the eye of the beholder." But that's real life. Evaluations of people by people is, in the final analysis, subjective. Just because an accounting system does not or cannot measure a key variable of success, should you ignore the variable?

The final point we would make is that no matter how well a foodservice company plans its strategies and organizes to execute and executes, it needs to remember that its strategies were based on many, many assumptions — about the market, the economy, the people, etc. Without a crystal ball, some of these will turn out to be inaccurate, some slightly off-base and some totally wrong.

Says Joe Lee, "Today, the old strategies aren't working as well as they had in the past. Ultimately, the outcome for companies employing strategies that don't change will be lowered earnings."

Monitoring System

The point is that strategies must be "living things" — capable of growing and changing — adapting to changes in the environment, to new information. That is why the monitoring system is important. It should be an early warning system that tells you when your assumptions are on-target and when they are not.

As in poker, each additional card turned up is data to be used to stay, raise or fold and each hand is data on your competitor's strategies. This data can be used or disregarded. The wise foodservice competitor pays close attention to what's happening because he uses this information to decide what strategies he will keep pursuing, which ones he will discard and which new ones should be explored. This updating should be an ongoing process. Periodic strategic review cycles will aid in adapting strategies to a changing environment.

In closing, it would be worthwhile to remember that in order to succeed, one must begin and learn by doing. This is just as true for strategic planning as it is for learning to ride a bicycle.

Part II

Strategic Marketing Planning — The Process

Part II outlines the process of strategic marketing planning and describes the general anatomy of a strategic marketing plan. The articles that follow emphasize the "how to" of strategic marketing planning, which is an orderly process composed of several separate, but closely related parts. The articles examine those sections of the plan.

Business Definition

The first step in strategic marketing planning is to define what the business is and what it is not. It is often a time consuming task, yet it is essential to the balance of the plan. Business definitions, also called statements of business purpose or business mission statements, decide the direction the business will take.

Business definitions answer questions such as: What is our business? What should our business be? Who is the customer? What do customers perceive value to be? To summarize, business mission statements answer the question: For whom are we trying to do what? This is probably the most difficult question to answer.

The Situation Analysis

The second step in the strategic marketing planning process is a situation analysis. It consists of the following sections:
1. Background—analysis of the firm that includes summaries of revenues, occupancies and customer counts, costs, profits, and other similar analyses.
2. Forces in macroenvironment—six major forces in which hospitality firms must operate. Changes in these forces may create new opportunities or threats. These forces are: demographic, economic, ecological, technological, political, and cultural.
3. Normal forecast—forecasts market sizes and composition, cost factors and revenues, assuming no major changes in the macroenvironment.
4. Analysis of competitors—analysis of who and where competitors are and their strengths and weaknesses.
5. Analysis of the firm's strengths and weaknesses—includes, among other things, location, physical property, access, image, reputation, financial structure, and strength and labor market.
6. Statements of opportunities and threats—based on the previous analyses. The purpose of this section is to define strategic windows (opportunities). It is the place where changing forces in the marketing environment are translated into practical meaning for the hospitality firm. It suggests future directions and activities for the firm.

Goals and Objectives

Strategy development presupposes objectives. Hence, the third step in the strategic marketing planning process is the formulation, in writing, of the company's goals for a specific period of time. General managers typically define the overall objectives for the hospitality firms. Within this framework, department heads develop goals for their departments.

Marketing Strategy

Developing specific marketing strategies and reducing these strategies to written statements is the fourth step in the strategic marketing planning process. This step is the "game plan." It is the marketing logic by which the firm hopes to win the competitive battle. It is concerned with what should be done to reach the firm's objectives. All preceding steps, while essential, only provide background for the actual marketing strategy. The steps following the strategy statements, while also vital, are largely devoted to the way strategies will be carried out and to determining whether or not they have been successful.

Marketing strategy is composed of three parts; positioning, identifying target markets, and developing strategies for each element of the marketing mix (product, price, place, and promotion). Product positioning is a term used to describe the ranking that consumers give to a product or service in comparison to other similar products or services that are available. Positioning is the attempt by management to establish, in the minds of the customers, a certain image of the company's product or service. It is one thing for management to say, "We're number one" and quite another for consumers to say, "You're number one." Therefore, strategies must be developed that will create and maintain the image and ranking (comparison with competitors) that is desired.

Positioning strategies are based on answers to the question: For whom are we trying to do what? Consequently, it is essential to know as much as possible about the target market that is to be attracted and served. A target market is a segment of the total potential market that offers the greatest opportunities. It is a combination of consumers who have reasonably homogeneous characteristics. That is, the people who comprise a market segment are alike in more ways than they are different. They have basically the same needs and wants and the same resources with which to satisfy their wants. In other words, target markets are those segments that offer a strategic fit between the capabilities of the firm and the needs, wants, and buying abilities of the group of people who make them up.

Hospitality firms cannot be all things to all people. Choices must be made concerning which target market or markets are to be served. A variety of information is useful in understanding the characteristics of market segments. Such information can be separated into four general categories.
1. Geographic—groups of people by region, state, county or SMSA, density, climate, etc.
2. Demographic—includes groupings by factors such as age, sex, family size, income, occupation, religion, race, and nationality.
3. Psychographic—incorporates information about social class, lifestyle, and personality.
4. Behavioristic—groups people by purchase occasion, benefits sought, user status, user rate, and loyalty status.

Using this information consumers can be separated into homogeneous groups and a great deal can be learned about the group to be served; i.e., who they are, where they are, and their needs and wants.

MODEL FOR
STRATEGIC MARKETING PLANNING

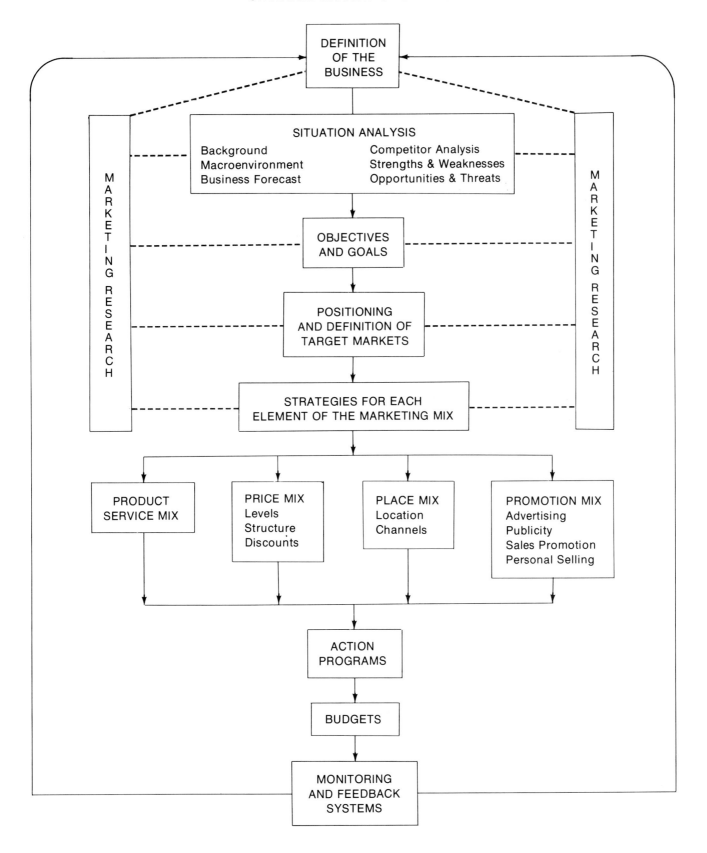

Based upon knowledge about the target market, strategies can be developed for each element of the marketing mix, i.e., product, price, place, and promotion. Product strategies are decisions about the number and level of products and services to be offered. Pricing strategies require decisions about price levels, pricing structure, and discounts. Place strategy considers location strategy and decisions about channels of distribution. Promotion strategy is concerned with how best to reach consumers through a mix of advertising, publicity, personal selling, and sales promotion.

Marketing Research

Marketing research is not really a separate step in the strategic marketing planning process, but rather an integral part that permeates the whole process. Marketing research should be both internal and external. Collection and analysis of internal data indicates where the business has been and how well it has done in the past. It reveals strengths and weaknesses. External data, on the other hand, provides information about opportunities and threats, and suggests directions the business should take in the future. Consumer research is especially important because it reveals guests' and potential guests' opinions of the firm, their needs, and the services and products they seek.

Action Programs

Marketing strategy must be implemented if company objectives are to be reached. Action programs spell out how strategies are to be implemented by establishing the specific activities that must be performed. They dictate when and where these activities will take place and who will perform them.

Budgets

Strategic marketing planning implies change. New strategies are expected to yield greater profits than old strategies. New strategies, however, require expenditures of resources. Management must know what the return for the expenditures will be.

A strategic marketing budget is essentially a projected profit and loss statement. On the revenue side it projects the revenue to be realized. On the expense side it shows the expenses required to implement the strategy. The difference or projected profit is determined and, once approved, the budget becomes the guide to strategy implementation.

Feedback and Control System

The last section of strategic marketing planning deals with tracking the progress of the plan. It is the link that completes the process and provides the basis for continued strategic planning. Feedback systems tell whether or not objectives have been achieved. The success or failure of one set of strategies establishes guides to future strategy development. Some common feedback systems are sales and revenue analysis, market share analysis, marketing expense to sales analysis, and customer attitude tracking.

How to Develop Marketing Strategies

by Michael Leven

Michael Leven, senior vice president, Americana Hotels, New York, is a recent past president of Hotel Sales Management Association International. Formerly with Dunfey Hotels, Hampton, New Hampshire, he is one of the most respected authorities on marketing in the lodging industry.

The objective of this article is to increase your awareness and understanding of the term, "Marketing Strategy." By the time you have read what follows, you should be able to (1) see your own marketing universe and (2) see that universe as fragmented to its most important finality; the strategies you need to achieve desired results.

What is "Strategy?"

A strategy is an action you decide to take to initiate activity that will achieve a specific result. A strategy is not an objective; a strategy is a tactic by which you propose to achieve an objective. Here are some examples of the difference:

Objective: Lower percentage of payroll to 32% of dollars of sales.

Strategy: Re-do staffing guides to effect a 10% reduction in fixed payroll.

Objective: To increase penetration of the corporate meeting market, resulting in 10,000 additional room nights a year.

Strategy: Redecorate and rehabilitate present meeting facilities by June 1, 1980.

Do not mix up objectives and strategies. Objectives don't create change. Strategies do create change; they are actions that must be tracked and measured, road maps to results. Objectives are well thought out; they should be inflexible. Strategies are flexible, elastic, malleable. Our problem in the hotel business is that we focus more on objectives and then when things go wrong, assume that our

objectives were wrong. We therefore change objectives that were right in the first place. Our failure is not as often in the choice of incorrect objectives as in the choice of incorrect strategies or the failure to change strategies when strategies fail to get us where we want to go.

All strategies generate sub-strategies. In the example above where the strategy calls for "redecoration of meeting rooms," the sub-strategies might be (1) have designs by March 1; (2) select plan by March 30; (3) enter order by April 20—etc. Sub-strategies are planned steps for implementing key strategies.

Why "Marketing Strategy"

As the lodging industry has matured, it has become a common practice for hotels and motels—chain, franchise or independent properties—to come up with marketing plans. In some cases, as with any planning process—financial, marketing, personnel, etc.—the planning process is personalized by the producer of plans. Most formalized claims standardize planning processes and create shelves of annual and revised documents.

The purpose of a plan is to outline the end results to be achieved; i.e., (A) the annual and 3-year objectives of the unit; (B) the strategic action steps to achieve the objectives; and, (C) ways to measure success or failure or to judge progress.

Frequently, our industry falls into the pattern of simply writing the plan, putting it into the appropriate "in-box" and pulling it out again only when formulating next year's plan.

We must avoid this. A "living plan" should be created with the focus on marketing strategy. Why? Because marketing strategy sets up a frequency for accountability in areas that are trackable. The beautifully typed and bound objectives can be left on the shelf, but the strategies and their measuring apparati can be daily put into the hands of both the executors and the monitors.

Without strategies there are no directions to

From *Lodging* (March 1980) pp. 12-16. Reprinted by permission of *Lodging.*

work with; there is a place to go to (objective) but no road map for getting there. So—how many strategies do we need? How extensive should they be? Is there a general rule?

The number of strategies depends on the diminishing return of each succeeding strategy. Your strategies should start with the *key ones; e.g.,* what must be done to achieve the greatest percentage of the objectives? What then can be done to generate the remainder of the desired result, and at what strategy investment, financial and human?

Virtually all hotels fall into the trap of setting down too many strategies. Hence, none get strength in terms of financial and human investment. The successful market strategist simply works more efficiently on fewer strategies and thereby generates the greatest possible progress toward his objective.

How to Develop Strategy

Ideally, marketing strategy development begins before a hotel is built; it begins with the first meeting of the developer of the project and the architect. Marketing strategy is endemic to the successful result of the overall planning process.

Let's look at an example. Last year, when a developer was going to construct a hotel in Cancun, Mexico, marketing people were called in to review the competitive environment, the location as a destination, the area market condition and the preliminary architectural plan. After the review, decisions were reached on the major positioning objectives of the hotel; i.e., ". . . the liveliest and most exciting hotel on the island, a unit known for activity and entertainment capability; a hotel that would attract other hotel guests in the evening . . . "

To achieve that positioning, a major marketing objective, required a product capable of delivering that objective. The key product strategy stated: ". . . the hotel must create an entertainment lounge environment featuring live show groups attractive to both singles and couples." Up to that point in the planning, no lounge had been contemplated. Now that a marketing strategy was agreed on—to implement a marketing objective—the owner did not hesitate to revise the plan to insure compliance.

Unfortunately, this example of preconstruction strategy development is not typical. Most marketing strategy is created after the hotel has been constructed or while it is being constructed. Let's deal next with strategy development in such instances.

Strategy delineation begins after clear, concise and agreed-upon objectives are established in the

marketing plan. Jon Canas, executive vice president of Dunfey Hotels, developed the term, "Mission Statement." A Mission Statement for every hotel and motel should document succinctly the description, the location and the position of the establishment, and what is required for the hotel or motel to be successful in finance, operations and marketing.

The Mission Statement tightens the unit management into a neat framework from which one can draw objectives for all the elements in the planning process. Although Mission Statements vary from company to company, depending on the input of those around the planning table, a sample for the Ala Moana Americana in Honolulu is presented on these pages.

The Mission Statement

Mission statement work is the key point of annual marketing review meetings. After this statement is complete, objectives are developed for:
1. Positioning the unit
2. Room revenue
3. Food and beverage revenue
4. Other income

Financial objectives are usually spread to three years to help create product development strategies far enough in advance to anticipate capital spending requirements.

Strategy development takes place when your team agrees on objectives (goals) in each of the revenue categories: occupancy, average rate, covers, average checks, number of drinks to be served, etc. It might surprise you when the greater part of the marketing planning process takes place before strategy development. It takes more time to agree on mission, positioning and objectives than on how to achieve goals. Don't let it worry you if strategies take little time to put on paper. You'll spend plenty of time making them work.

When objectives for all elements in the marketing plan are complete, you can begin strategy planning. Determine for each objective which of the elements of the marketing mix can effect the objective; then, for each element, develop the key strategies to achieve. For example:

Objective: Increase occupancy by 2 points over 1979.

A discussion now takes place on what markets or segments are desirable or available to generate that increase. The group reaches the decision that the increase should come from the corporate meeting business segment to improve Sunday night or

Thursday night occupancy. Once that decision is reached, the checklist works this way:

Applicable marketing elements to obtain objectives:
    a. Direct Sales   Yes
    b. Advertising   Yes
    c. Public Relations   No
    d. Sales Promotion   Yes
    e. Research   No

Following each—if they are applicable—strategy development takes place at the team level. When each strategy is completed, a measurement and benchmark tracking system is set up. If a strategy can't be tracked, it shouldn't be there.

A Case Example

When at the Dunfey Hotel Company, I found a difficult marketing problem with Dunfey's resort at Hyannis, a 200-plus-room unit located in Cape Cod, Massachusetts. The unit had meeting room facilities far greater than sleeping rooms could utilize. For years, occupancy was lower than required because trade associations and transients came at the same time. This left wide mid-week gaps in the seven shoulder season months and the three off-season months.

The marketing objective developed from the mission statement read: "To be successful, the unit must be known as catering to individual vacationers on weekends and during the height of the season. But it must establish itself as a corporate meeting center in New England. Occupancy objectives were set at the low 70's (from the high 50's a year previously). Strategic development began:

I. POSITIONING OBJECTIVE

Strategy: Change name to Dunfey's Hyannis Resort and Conference Center. Elements of marketing mix applicable: advertising, sales promotion and public relations.

Strategy: Advertising
a) Name to be on all media advertising to impress reader that resort and conference center caters to both markets.
b) Small space campaign to be developed in meetings trade magazines so regional meeting planner awareness will be created.
c) All in-house and external sales collateral material to be redone with new name (rack brochures, directory of services, meeting brochure, calendars, etc.)

Strategy: Public Relations
a) Writers from meetings publications, business

and newspapers to be invited to resort to generate business oriented articles.
Note: Direct sales, research and sales promotion are not applicable to promoting this objective.

II. OCCUPANCY-INCREASE: OBJECTIVE

Objective is to sell 20,000 midweek corporate meeting room nights to be booked and consumed in the next 12 months.

Strategy: Direct Sales
a) Increase sales force from two to four and change location of outside representatives to four district territories.
b) Free up director of sales to sell the business by establishing convention service department to handle site inspections and group details.
c) Set up incentive program based on the 20,000 room-night target.

Strategy: Advertising
a) Meeting magazine campaign

Strategy: Sales promotion
a) Set up complimentary weekend stay package for New England area site planners; target three per weekend, "Be Our Guest" theme.
b) Set up two familiarization weekends for meeting planners.
Note: Public relations and research strategies not necessary in this case.

Obviously, the entire strategic plan developed for the hotel in the case example is not exposed here. What you need to understand is how and why objectives were stated and strategies developed. Strategies were executed and monitored and success, in meeting objectives, achieved. A year later, strategies were once again changed to meet the changing needs of the unit.

Strategy Execution & Measurement

Surprisingly, the lodging industry seems to handle the marketing planning function fairly well. Few hotels stand out as marketing white elephants or Edsels. Interestingly enough, most people in our industry are capable of adequate strategy development, even if we don't follow a process as comprehensive as the one discussed above.

So where do we fail? I feel that where we fail is in the execution of plans. Thus, we find an inordinate number of aborted marketing plans. Advertising agencies with hotel accounts confirm this judgment. What happens is this: the failure to adequately execute a strategy causes more often than not—a change in objective and premature denial of what might have been a progressive step. Besides the wasted dollars we have wasted human resources. People blame themselves for the wrong reason—for poor planning instead of poor execution. The hotel does not make its fiscal goals.

If nothing else, we should insure that strategies are being worked prior to changing anything. This requires monitoring on a regular, scheduled basis. We need to monitor to insure measurement of what is happening today, not just what happened last month.

Case Example

MISSION STATEMENT
ALA MOANA AMERICANA, HONOLULU

The Ala Moana Americana is a first-class hotel located between Honolulu's business section and the Waikiki tourist area. There is no first-class hotel closer to the business section and Honolulu's special event areas. The hotel is adjacent to Hawaii's largest shopping center with 155 stores.

To be successful, the hotel must be No. 1 to Honolulu's business traveler, airline crews, Japanese special campaigns, Kamaaina individuals, and Kamaaina groups. These markets should be supplemented by Japanese package series business, government employees, special events, and one-shot group business.

The Ala Moana must have authentic Hawaiian atmosphere, entrance, decor, and uniformity. It should be known for its Hawaiian style service (language, dress, fruit, flowers, and special touches).

When Japanese and U.S. F.I.T. demand slackens in the Waikiki area, the hotel is vulnerable to competition and loses significant business to the first-class Waikiki hotels. During these periods, it must depend on its major market segments and get one-shot group business. The hotel's rooms product must be designed and maintained to meet the needs of its four major market segments. There is a potential F.I.T. market of frequent Hawaii visitors and stopover business.

Because of the hotel's difficult competitive position for tourist room business and its high vulnerability to tourist fall-off, the food and beverage outlets offer the only major opportunity for revenue growth. These outlets must appeal to its local community; however, they must be flexible enough to meet its room guest requirements as well.

The Ala Moana must be known by its employees as the "best hotel in Honolulu to work in." Its employees should have the Aloha Spirit and should communicate that spirit to each other and to the guest.

Financial Goals

	Occupancy	Avg. Rate	Room Revenue
'79	86.4%	$30.16	$11,357,300
'80	87.0%	32.14	12,186,000
'81	87.0%	35.00	13,270,400

	Food Revenue	Beverage Revenue
'79	$5,757,000	$2,194,000
'80	6,670,000	2,632,800
'81	7,670,000	3,036,000

Assumptions:

1. **Major Market Segments**—The sales and marketing efforts of the hotel are geared toward the following market segments:
    a. Airline Crews
    b. Japanese Special Campaigns
    c. Yes We Cana
    d. Government
    e. Kamaaina
2. **Rooms Rehab Program** will continue as planned.
3. **Food & Beverage Department**—A master plan to reconceptualize total Food and Beverage outlets is being prepared in order to update and gear the operation toward the markets identified. This effort in connection with increased sales and marketing efforts, will increase the growth in the Food & Beverage Department over the next several years.
4. **Room Supply**—Additional hotel rooms in the area are planned as follows:

1978	
440 Rooms	Cinerama Reef Hotel-Waikiki Tower
1979	
650 Rooms	Hawaiian Regent
360 Rooms	Ala Wai Sunset Seaside Towers
630 Rooms	Hawaiian Princess
495 Rooms	Pacific Beach Hotel

The Ala Moana

Consider, for example, the Mission Statement of the Ala Moana Hotel in Honolulu. The hotel previously had a significant occupancy problem. Occupancy objectives were set and strategies were developed to radically change the mix of business from a resort to a commercial base. The result was to be a commercial hotel located in a resort area.

This approach involved commitment to a new marketing position. One of the key strategies involved increasing the semi-permanent airline crew room base. A monitoring system was set up to test strategy execution and results on a weekly, then monthly, basis where call reports on the segment decision makers, proposals and decisions were reviewed by the general manager and his director of sales. This system continued until long after the strategy had been fully executed and was successful.

Follow-up strategies to insure that the hotel keeps business are developed annually in a similar way. A combination of monthly written reports and weekly sales meetings review all segments to guarantee execution of this or other key account strategies.

Had no one monitored execution, the strategy might not have been successful. The business would surely not have showed up on its own. Failing in the new approach, management might have changed objectives. They might even have returned to the resort marketing approach where the product had had little competitive strength. Marketing dollars committed to that endeavor would have failed and the hotel would have operated at a significant dollar loss.

Strategy execution is the primary responsibility of the executor. But as managers, our primary responsibility is to monitor that execution. Systematic strategy monitoring is essential all through the marketing disciplines.

No strategy should be created, agreed upon and put in any plan without the ability to monitor its execution. The best way to do that is to have the measurement system already in place in the plan. (See insert story on Ala Moana.)

The measurement system I recommend forces the responder to write in, on a scheduled basis, performance results vs. goals—either daily, weekly or monthly, whichever is applicable. Let's return to the Hyannis example (above) for a moment. You'll recall that an objective was 20,000 corporate meeting room nights over a 12-month period and that one strategy was to increase the sales force to four

people. What had to be monitored was:

1. Number of sales people in the field.
2. Number of leads generated.
3. Number of site inspections.
4. Room nights booked.
5. Room nights consumed.

There is no way the strategy could work without this monitoring. Forms (for reporting) were divided so that each key area was reported in the appropriate time frame. The 20,000 room nights were divided into target dates. By each date, sales people entered statistics that measured performance against ideal performance goal. This "paper work" was execution insurance. No attempt would be made to change anything until we knew a strategy wasn't working due to lack of response rather than lack of execution.

Changes in Strategy

Two circumstances warrant a change in strategy:

1. The strategy has been executed according to a prescribed plan, monitored for results, given time to grow and mature—and then has failed. Failure under these conditions gives you the right to sit down and create new strategies, or

2. The strategy has achieved the desired result and continuation is not necessary to maintain the result.

As a matter of policy, we review marketing strategies at least twice a year at formal meetings. In resorts with multiple seasons, we review more often. Once at a resort strategy review in Acapulco, we determined that food and beverage revenue objectives had been met at the expense of guest satisfaction. A projected decline in repeat business resulted. Specifically, forecasts indicated that our February and March occupancy projections would not be met. Since our occupancy plan represented our major objective, a number of strategies were discussed to beef up advance room sales; strategies that included:

1. Advertising in major markets.
2. Cooperative promotions with carriers and suppliers.
3. Direct sales programs.
4. Rate policy changes.

After full analysis, we decided on the key one: to change compulsory Modified American Plan to optional M.A.P. Sub-strategies chosen related to execution, mailgrams, telephone calls, sales calls, etc. Due to the timing, the new strategy gave us several advantages: a three-week lead time before

---

Case Example

STRATEGIES AND OBJECTIVES
Rooms Business, Ala Moana
1980

Market Segment: *Special Events*

DEFINITION: Any one-shot event taking place in Honolulu in a city, state or public facility or area; i.e., state fair, high school/college or professional athletic events and trade shows that create a demand for lodging for either the participant or spectator.

OBJECTIVE: The Ala Moana Americana will be first choice because of location, facilities, service and price.

PERSON RESPONSIBLE: Group Sales Manager.

QUOTA: 3,100 Room Nights

Jan.	300	July	500
Feb.	200	Aug.	450
Mar.	250	Sep.	150
Apr.	150	Oct.	450
May	150	Nov.	150
June	150	Dec.	200

KEY STRATEGIES

1. Develop leads through the following facilities:
   a. Aloha Stadium
   b. Blaisdell Center
   c. University of Hawaii
   d. Department of Planning & Economics
2. Maintain list of special events in the city. Source: Newspapers, HVB (Hawaii Visitors Bureau), monthly activities at Blaisdell Center.
3. Cultivate key personnel within these facilities to insure that we get the leads.
4. Identify and work the five key promoters using these facilities:
   (In the Strategies worksheet, names of five key promoters are listed at this point, with affiliations and telephone numbers.)
5. Identify and solicit the major studios and producers filming in Hawaii:
   (In the Strategies worksheet, the names of five producers are listed at this point, with major movie studio affiliations.)
   Use other sources—newspaper (close)in business).

MEASUREMENTS

1. Source of Business Report.
2. Site inspection quotas met.

---

competitors could react; a better chance to reach the occupancy objective in February or March; and a higher degree of guest satisfaction, which we know was a trade-off for food and beverage revenue. Benefits of the trade-off were minor compared to the potential damage to profit from lower occupancy.

Incidentally, this strategy was for 1980. At this writing, our measurements and benchmarks (daily reservations over the 800 number, weekly forward occupancy forecasts) have improved dramatically. Apparently, we are reaching goal. Here is an example of a planned review of a strategy creating a change because the strategy—which had worked—developed new circumstances not anticipated at the time of creation.

Although I do not recommend rapid changes to well-thought-out tactics, I do think it wise to set up a formalized, frequent review of marketing strategies due to rapidly occurring market changes and demands. Even annual marketing budgets should have contingency provisions to allow the flexibility to spend or hold back expenditure if objectives are not being met. The only way to know your strategy is correct is to note that the objective is being achieved. There is no law against reinforcing your commitment to a working strategy. The risk is to change for change's sake. This could result in the destruction of what is an already-sound foundation.

Conclusion and Summary

1. Marketing strategy begins as early as the purchase of the site for a hotel. Objectives set then create strategies in the product directly related to later financial and product success.

2. Normally, however, marketing strategies take place after the unit is built, or during construction. Strategies should never be agreed on until tight marketing objectives are fixed. A "mission statement" for every entity is necessary to help focus objectives.

3. Objectives are always set before strategies. No strategy can exist without an objective.

4. A strategy is an action/decision designed to initiate activity to achieve a specific marketing objective. Strategies are not objectives; objectives are ends, strategies are means.

5. Strategies are flexible. They should be reviewed periodically with corrections or additions in mind. Objectives should be in cement. They should be adjusted only when major changes in the product or the environment take place.

6. Strategies create sub-strategies. Sub-strategies are tactics to insure that the strategy is executed.

7. Strategies are living things. They involve daily work. Objectives are shelved — that is, looked at in longer time frames, and rarely reviewed. Strategies put life into the corporate or unit planning process.

8. The number of strategies depends on the diminishing financial return and human investment necessary to achieve results. Too many strategies result in dispersion of effort over non-key areas and minimized capability of achievement.

9. Objectives are changed and plans fail more often than not because strategies are not properly executed, not because the objectives were wrong or the plans faulty in the original.

10. Monitoring systems should not only be regarded as a device for measuring results but also as a necessity for measuring strategy execution; they are vital to insure compliance.

11. The key results expected from a strategic success and the key steps to implement the strategy should both be measured and reported.

12. Changes should take place only when strategies fail after execution, or when, even though they are successful, better or different results need to be obtained.

In addition to the 12 points listed, there is another ingredient—an elusive ingredient—to marketing success; that is, marketing intuition. Some people sense more, or feel more, than others. But in all cases, the successful strategist has, either by written design or mental past experience, logged a carefully organized path to strategy development.

He or she creates first the unit objectives. The rest has to do with understanding the unit capability, the competitive environment, the location conditions, the economic factors, the elements of the marketing mix—these and countless other input data. This data bank solidifies the objective planning and provides the foundation for strategic development.

But let there be no mistake about this: no intuitive genius ever achieved marketing objectives without a systematic approach to the execution of his strategies and measurement of their results. Creativity and intuition are no guarantees of success. Careful plodding, on the other hand, often sounds less exciting—less dramatic—but produces more effective results.

A Management System for the 1980s: Part I

This is the first of a three-part series about strategic planning in the foodservice industry prepared by Robert L. Sirkis and Stephen M. Race of Arthur D. Little, Inc. Sirkis is a consultant in the Food Service Group. The Food Service Group has been involved in a broad range of projects for clients in all segments of the industry. Race is a consultant in the Strategic Management Unit where he has been involved in strategy planning for clients in a variety of businesses.

During the past year, a number of foodservice companies have been unable to maintain the levels of successful performance they achieved in the past.

In many cases, the strategies and tactics that have been successful have not been modified. However, since the operating environment has changed, some of these past strategies are no longer appropriate.

Strategic planning is a technique adopted by numerous companies to anticipate and respond to changing business conditions.

In light of fundamental changes in the industry, market, customers and competitors, foodservice companies will need to review their strategies. For profits in the future, foodservice management will have to focus on developing realistic objectives and appropriate plans for the long-term success of their operations.

Strategic planning is an orderly process for determing the direction and management systems of a business or corporation. Planning implies looking into the future and developing projections for the economic, social, and political environments.

Within this context of the future, the business then sets objectives, develops strategies, and allocates skills and resources in support of selected strategies.

Strategic planning is based on five principles:

- Planning centers can be identified.
- Business is not random.
- There is a limited set of strategies from which a planning center chooses those it will pursue.
- The conditions a planning center faces, not the ambitions of the individual managers, should be paramount in choice of strategy.

Identification of Planning Centers: All corporations have at least one business planning center. These business units or planning centers are the entities for which strategies need to be determined. Very often strategy centers are not synonymous with existing divisions, cost, or profit centers.

Cost and profit centers have often been defined around the historical development of the business, the location of facilities or by geographic scope. Consequently, there frequently is a bias against examining the company in terms of planning centers. However, the correct identification of business units is fundamental to strategy formulation.

A strategic business unit is a business area with an external marketplace for its goods or services. It is an area of the company that can develop and execute strategies independent of other business areas, and one that could probably stand alone if divested from the corporation.

Managers should determine if their organizational unit is:

- An independent business;
- More than one business;
- A part of some larger business unit within the corporation or,
- A functional activity (such as research and development) that is part of several other business units.

A set of clues can be utilized to help make this determination. The clues focus on conditions in the marketplace rather than current corporation configuration.

These clues include:

- Competitors—A single set implies one business unit, while multiple sets imply multiple strategy centers.

From *Restaurant Business* (August 1, 1980) pp. 84-90, 202. Reprinted by permission of *Restaurant Business*.

• Prices—Do price changes in one organizational unit mandate price changes in another?

• Customers—Do they represent a single set or multiple set?

• Divestment/liquidation—Can one area of business be dropped without materially affecting other businesses?

Let's examine why the identification of strategy centers is important.

As an example, we might look at the foodservice organization of a university responsible for contract feeding of resident students and for a la carte sales to commuting students, staff and faculty.

In planning for the future, it would be helpful for the organization to understand that these are two separate business units. Since they serve different groups of customers with different needs, the programs executed in one area are largely independent of those programs in the other.

Students on board depend on the foodservice program to provide most of their meals and require nutritionally balanced selections at a reasonable price. Because meals are an integral part of dormitory living, the foodservice experience must be developed to facilitate interaction and generally enhance the quality of student life.

On the other hand, non-resident students, faculty, and staff have different foodservice needs: quick and convenient meals and snacks, primarily during luncheon periods.

The key point is that the university foodservice organization engages in these two types of activities. It must consider each separately because different strategies are required for each to be successful.

Another example may be helpful. As reported by *Restaurant Business* in its May 1, 1980 issue, General Mills has a number of separate business strategy centers in food products, toys, retailing, fashion, and restaurants.

Within the restaurant group, Red Lobster and York Steak House are separate planning centers. It is clear that they are separate business units operating largely independent of each other.

They differ from the third strategy center that manages test concepts: Casa Gallardo, Hannahan's and Fennimore's.

In addition to these three foodservice strategy centers, there are two other entities to consider: a shrimp aquaculture project and a construction company.

At this point, the shrimp farm is being developed to supply Red Lobster units. It is not a separate strategy center because it does not have an exter-

nal market for its goods and cannot execute strategies independent of the Red Lobster restaurants. If the shrimp operation developed significant sales to companies other than Red Lobster or other General Mills operations, it would have to be considered a separate strategy center.

The construction company is best classified as a separate strategy center. While it began as the Red Lobster construction division, it now builds a variety of restaurants and other types of buildings for outside companies, competing with other construction firms.

Thus, the General Mills restaurant group would need to develop plans for four separate strategy centers.

Planning is a Data-Based Activity: The second principle of planning is that it is a data-based activity. By data-based, we mean based on facts.

Information needs to be gathered on several levels: the planning center itself, the foodservice industry, and the political, social and economic environment.

To illustrate the need to collect and analyze information, let's look at some national trends. Significant changes are going on in the U.S. that will impact the foodservice industry over the next few decades.

One example, often written about, is the aging of the U.S. population. In 1970, over 46 percent of the U.S. population was under the age of 24; by 1990 less than 37 percent of the population will be under 24. Between 1980 and 1990, the number of 18-24 year olds will decline by over 4.2 million.

This group has traditionally been the target customer for major segments of the foodservice industry (such as fast food, school and college foodservice facilities). Companies in these segments of the foodservice industry can anticipate increasing competition for their traditional client. They will need to develop adaptive strategies to meet increasing competition and to broaden their appeal.

Additionally, this 18-24 age group has represented a major labor pool for most foodservice operations. Competitors in the foodservice industry will need to plan for this future constraint.

Other underlying social changes will further impact the foodservice industry. While the domestic population will grow at a compound rate of 0.9 percent over the next 10 years, household formations will increase at almost two percent per year. The households of the 1990's will devote an increased proportion of their disposable income to durable goods and services and a smaller proportion to non-durable goods and away-from-home dining.

The foodservice corporation or business must also plan for such changes as:

• Geographic shifts in the population to the sunbelt states;

• Dietary changes, including the gradual decrease in the consumption of fats and increases in the consumption of fish, poultry, fruits, and vegetables;

• Increasing consumer interest in nutrition;

• Differing rates of inflation for key food products and labor; and

• Continuing increases in energy costs.

Those businesses that can anticipate these changes, analyze the implications of these changes on their businesses, and create strategies to adapt to a new future will be in a better position than those firms that continue doing business as usual.

In most corporations, both good and bad news is discovered in collecting data. It is critical to evaluate all data in an honest, frank, and realistic manner since the data collected provides direction for strategy selection.

If the data collected is insufficient or interpreted incorrectly, the foundation for strategy selection is weak. Good strategic planning requires superior information.

Business is Not Random: If business was random, there would be no need for planning. However, it is not random; there are reasons some competitors succeed and others fail. It is therefore necessary to identify the critical factors necessary for success.

In order to understand these critical success variables and to develop plans for success, a business needs to be evaluated in terms of its strategic condition. An inventory of a particular strategy center's strengths and weaknesses must be taken and compared against the critical factors necessary for success in that business.

Two factors must be examined in detail to determine a planning center's strategic condition; industry maturity and competitive position.

Industries, like products, experience life cycles. *Figure I* shows a curve representative of a normative industry life cycle and some examples of the maturity of selected industries.

Maturity can be characterized by four phases: embryonic, growth, mature, and vintage. A number of factors provide clues in determining maturity including: sales growth rate, growth potential, breadth of product line, number of competitors, share distribution, and stability.

Industries generally start in embryonic, pass through growth and maturity, and can eventually be characterized as vintage. These four phases are generally of unequal duration; an industry may be embryonic for a long period of time, pass quickly through growth, experience a protracted mature stage and age rapidly if replaced by a new technology. The entire maturation process can take many decades or simply a few years, depending upon the industry.

In *Figure I,* we have plotted the foodservice industry in the late growth phase, approaching maturity. While individual segments of the industry will be in earlier and later stages of the life cycle, the overall foodservice industry can best be categorized in late growth. Sales are growing but the growth rate is slowing. The number of competitors is declining slowly as chains continue to replace inde-

Industry Maturity

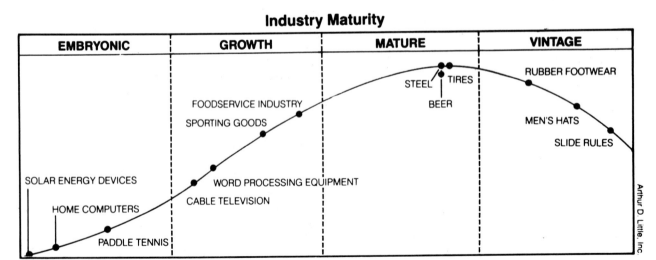

The curve indicates the maturity of various industries or products.

pendent operators. Market share is shifting but only slowly, and major new participants are not likely to emerge.

There are no good or bad maturity positions.

While most managers like to think of their businesses as participating in growth industries, the fact is that most industries in the U.S. can be characterized as mature.

A particular stage of maturity becomes "bad" only if the expectations or strategies adopted by a business are inappropriate for that stage of maturity.

The second factor analyzed in determining a business is strategic condition in its competitive position. Competitive position is a summary of a strategy center's strengths and weaknesses relative to those of its competitors. Businesses can be characterized as dominant, strong, favorable, tenable or weak.

To understand competitive positioning, it is necessary to understand the basis of competition in the industry: What critical actions must a company perform well to succeed in this business?

For example, in the national fast food hamburger segment, the primary basis of competition is penetration—the competitor with the most units can generate the greatest awareness and trial.

Greater penetration implies high market share, greater buying power and an increased ability to finance projects and functions like advertising, training, and product development.

The immediate response to the question of the basis of competition is often "quality, service, cleanliness" and "operating margins." We agree that these are important. In fact, we believe they are essential. A fast food restaurant cannot compete without them.

Thus, rather than being bases of competition, these belong in a category we refer to as requisites. They are required simply to be in business.

Perhaps the best method for determining the bases of competition is to answer the question: "In my business, what must I do to be the most successful company?"

By combining industry maturity and competitive position into a matrix *(Figure 2),* the relative posi-

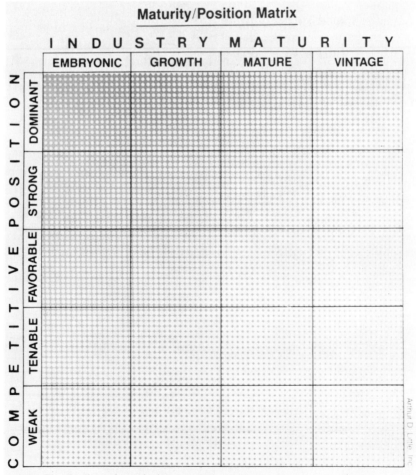

The shading relates the industry's maturity with its competitive position.

tion of a business unit can be compared to that of its competitors. An analysis of a business unit in terms of its industry maturity and the unit's competitive position has implications for strategy determination, risks, financial expectations, objectives, and likely competitor actions and strategies.

For every strategy selected, managers can anticipate certain levels of investment, return and risk. These expected results must be carefully evaluated so that management can be certain that the selected strategies can be executed, that they will have complementary results, and that the risk and reward potential is balanced.

A Limited Set of Strategies Exist: Most business managers have an innate sense of the range of possible business strategies. However, for each position in the *industry maturity/competitive position matrix* some strategies are more appropriate than others. We call these natural strategies.

In general, a stronger competitor has more natural strategic alternatives than a weaker competitor—McDonald's has a wider range of strategy options than its smaller competitors.

Similarly, the strategies employed by a business in a vintage industry are likely to be different from the strategies pursued by a business in a growth industry.

However, a planning center is not always free to select a natural strategy. The business may be precluded from choosing natural strategies by competitor actions or by an inability to fund, staff or support these strategies.

Thus, a unit may pursue other strategies which, though "unnatural" for its maturity and competitive position, are appropriate because of its limited options.

An excellent example of an operator with limited strategic options is Jack-in-the-Box.

In discussing Principle 3, we indicated that the primary basis of competition in the national fast food hamburger business is penetration—the strongest competitor has the most units.

Thus, a natural strategy for any competitor would be to build more units as quickly as possible. To achieve significant penetration across the country, Jack-in-the-Box would be required to open a large number of new units; however, they recently chose to close and sell off a number of their Eastern U.S. stores.

With McDonald's, Burger King and Wendy's trying to further increase their market penetration, it is clear that Jack-in-the-Box was unwilling to take the risks involved in a nationwide penetration effort.

A regional market rationalization strategy, calling for the closing off of all units in the East, would generate significant amounts of cash which then could be used to more fully penetrate the remainder of the country.

In this case, the natural strategy called for greater capital requirements and risk than management was willing to accept. The rationalization strategy better fit Jack-in-the-Box's ability to finance reasonable growth and its parameters of acceptable risk.

Strategy Selection Should be Condition, Not Ambition, Driven: The conditions in which a business finds itself (external environment, industry maturity and competitive position) are paramount in setting strategies.

Other factors, including ambitions, need to be considered but are of secondary importance.

For example, regardless of ambition, American Motors would not be expected to achieve a dominant role in North American automobile production and sales.

Similarly, it is unlikely that a 10-unit hamburger chain would achieve leadership in the national fast food market, in spite of its management's desire to accomplish such a feat.

In setting objectives and charting strategies, the realities of the operating environment and the strengths and weaknesses of the business unit define the boundaries of possible actions. Management discretion can only be exercised to select options within these limits.

Determining the best direction for a business and developing appropriate systems are not easy tasks. Considering the pressures expected in the years ahead, it will become increasingly difficult to achieve success in the foodservice industry. Strategic planning is one tool that can enhance a business's chances for profitable, long-term success.

By rigorously applying the five principles introduced in this article, a corporation or business can anticipate and respond to changes in the political, economic and social environment. Since competitive circumstances and the industry maturity are factors also subject to change, they must be taken into consideration.

In the next article of this series, we will show an example of how a business applies these principles in developing a strategic plan.

A Management System for the 1980s: Part II

This is the second of a three-part series about strategic planning in the foodservice industry, prepared by Robert L. Sirkis and Stephen M. Race of Arthur D. Little, Inc., Cambridge, Mass.

In the first installment of this series, we introduced strategic planning and discussed the five principles upon which planning is based.

Having set the stage with this background information, we are now going to share an example of how a business applies these principles in developing a strategic plan. In using this disguised example based upon actual past work for clients, we will go beyond just listing abstractions or prescriptions for installing a management system.

Our case study deals with a hypothetical regional fast food hamburger chain, Burgeria, Inc. Although the Burgeria story is based on actual experience with a number of clients in recent years, we have deliberately simplified the example to focus on the principles of planning and clarify the process.

The reader is cautioned that we have presented both real and illustrative information to make the example relevant yet manageable.

While we have chosen a fast food chain as an example, these principles can be applied to other segments of the foodservice industry.

Burgeria, Inc.

Let us share some history on Burgeria. The company was started by Joe Block in Dallas, Texas. Upon graduating from college in 1965, Block was employed by a leading national fast food hamburger chain, where he worked his way up from assistant manager to regional manager.

In 1972, he invested all his savings and leased and remodeled a closed unit of a national chain. Based on his belief that he knew the hamburger business and was ready to go into business for himself, he opened the first Burgeria.

The first Burgeria was a success. Because the unit was located across the street from a large university, Block had modified the existing building and concept to appeal more to college students.

Over several years, the menu evolved to include a salad bar, one-third pound hamburgers and a variety of deli sandwiches. Additionally, Block obtained a beer and wine license, installed comfortable tables and chairs, and added a music system that played "golden oldies."

In 1975, Burgeria enjoyed annual sales of $900,000 and Joe opened a second unit in Dallas patterned after the first. He sold a 30 percent share of the business to Ken Dietz, a college classmate and former olympic discus thrower who had become a successful commercial builder in the Ft. Worth area. Together they developed plans and built the first prototype free-standing unit.

By early 1980, Burgeria had expanded to 38 units in the Dallas-Ft. Worth area, with all but two operating very profitably.

The company also included two other divisions: distribution and construction. The distribution commissary, opened in 1976, purchased and delivered all food and supplies to units in the expanding Burgeria chain. The construction division was kept busy building new Burgeria units.

By 1980, the company had reached a level of $24 million in annual sales. Joe Block and Ken Dietz had begun to wonder if their intuitive approach to planning and management would still be effective. A number of issues had arisen, and Block and Dietz had trouble finding the time to back away from day-to-day decision-making to resolve them. Among the issues they faced were these:

- Block had recently received a letter from an entrepreneur who was prepared to open as many as 18 franchised Burgeria units in the Oklahoma City area if suitable arrangements could be made.

- The real estate buyer was telling Block that there were few good sites left in Dallas-Ft. Worth

From *Restaurant Business* (September 15, 1980) pp. 103-114, 133. Reprinted by permission of *Restaurant Business*.

and recommended opening units in Houston, which happened to be Block's hometown.

• Burgeria's bank had raised the interest rate on loans for new units to 18 percent.

• Customer counts were falling in the units.

• The construction division had been approached by a regional clothing store chain and was investigating a program of building stores for that chain.

It was the combined weight of these concerns that led Block to seek outside help. He felt strategic planning might help him put his problems and opportunities into perspective.

Strategic Planning

When Burgeria initiated its strategic planning effort early in 1980, Joe Block and Ken Dietz asked a consulting firm to guide them through the development of their first strategic plan and to train the Burgeria management to be able to develop successive strategic plans on their own. Let's look at the process they used.

To begin with, a case team was established including Block, Dietz and four additional members of Burgeria management, along with specialists in strategic planning for the foodservice industry from the consulting firm. The specialists were used to familiarize the key managers of the business unit with strategic planning philosophy, then assist them to analyze their own business situation and to select logical strategies to attain selected goals.

Among the advantages of this method are:

• Strategies and supporting plans are developed by the managers who must execute them.

• The process is learned by participants over a few cycles.

• Business unit management develops a better understanding of the dynamics of its industry and the competition.

• Differences of opinion among peers over key assumptions, alternate strategies and related risks are resolved so that the entire organization is able to move forward together toward common goals.

Identification of Planning Centers

The first principle of strategic planning is that strategic business units, or strategy centers, can be identified within a corporation.

In the first installment of this series, we defined a strategic business unit as a "business area with an external marketplace for goods or services for which one can determine objectives and execute strategies independent of other business areas."

It amounts to a business that probably could stand alone if divested by the corporation. These are the entities for which strategies need to be developed.

In determining the strategy centers for Burgeria, the planning team jointly evaluated several clues: competitors, prices, customers, and divestment/liquidation. By using these clues, Burgeria was able to identify a single business within the corporation—the building, supplying and operating of a regional chain of fast food restaurants.

As in most corporations, the conclusion that Burgeria was in only one business was not reached without some difficulty. In Burgeria's case, the issue was whether the construction and distribution functions represented separate businesses.

The conclusion was that these were not separate businesses, but rather represented important components of a single business operation. Since neither division had any sales outside of Burgeria and both were dependent on the continuing operations and expansion of the units for their success, both of them were actually part of the hamburger business unit.

Early in the process, Block and Dietz felt they could already resolve one of the issues that had been troubling them. They realized that if the construction division began a significant building program for the clothing store chain, the company would be starting a second strategic business unit.

At this point they felt it was best not to divert their attention from their primary business—operating a chain of fast food hamburger restaurants.

Having determined that strategies needed to be developed for a single business unit, the managers of Burgeria started analyzing data to chart a direction for the future.

Planning: A Data-Based Activity

When we say that planning is data-based (second principle), we mean based upon facts. These facts are gathered on several levels:

First, there is information on the general market, political, economic and social conditions affecting the business;

Next, more specific data on the particular industry in which the business participates;

Finally, data and trends internal to the business unit.

The data from all these inputs then needs to be analyzed and evaluated.

The Burgeria planners began their data gathering by looking at relevant demographic, economic and lifestyle trends. The findings can be summarized as follows:

Demographic: Foodservice sales are correlated with population, personal income and penetration of women in the workforce.

The U.S. population is expected to grow slightly faster between now and 1990 than it has for the last decade.

The Southeast, Southwest, Far West and Rocky Mountain states will grow faster than the U.S. average, while the Mideast, Great Lakes, Plains and New England areas will grow at a slower rate.

The age distribution of the population will change dramatically as the 18-24 and 13-17 categories decline and the 35-44 and over-65 categories grow.

Economic: Personal income will continue to be squeezed in 1980. After 1980, real growth is expected to return slowly to levels of 3-4 percent.

Inflation will affect away-from-home eating more than at-home eating through the mid-1980s. After 1985, the two segments will be affected about equally.

Lifestyle: Risk will be avoided; quality will become even more critical.

Nutrition will be a bigger factor in deciding where and what to eat.

Speed of service will remain important for some eating occasions.

Shortages and high prices of oil will reduce automobile usage.

Next, the planners looked at the entire U.S. foodservice industry and, after much discussion, concluded that the relevant area for analysis was the fast food hamburger segment.

While other parts of the foodservice industry (including other fast food segments and other types of restaurants) would be monitored in the future, the principal area of focus would be the hamburger segment.

Burgeria obviously competed with other types of restaurants; however, the managers felt its primary competition came from national and regional hamburger chains operating in the Texas area. Among the data gathered on the foodservice industry were the following:

• Between 1973 and 1979, foodservice industry sales grew at an 11.3 percent annual compound growth rate.

• The fast food category was the fastest growing during that period, with a 20 percent growth rate.

• The hamburger segment of the fast food category remained the largest, with 51 percent of the

category's sales; its share had declined from 59 percent in 1971, due primarily to even faster growth in the seafood, pizza and Mexican segments.

• The average store volume for fast food hamburger units grew at a 12 percent annual rate from 1971.

The last step in analyzing data was to examine the strengths and weaknesses of Burgeria.

Among the relevant findings were the following:

Strengths: Average unit volume of $700,000 annually, second only to McDonald's;

Guest check of $2.12 highest of segment;

Good market share in Dallas-Ft. Worth;

High top-of-mind awareness among target audience in market research studies in Dallas-Ft. Worth;

All units relatively new and all but two of the same design.

Weaknesses: Customer counts per store among the lowest in the industry and falling;

Existing Dallas-Ft. Worth market nearing saturation;

Debt service at an all-time high and interest rates still climbing.

Business is Not Random

If business was random, there would be no need for planning. However, it is not random (third principle); there are reasons some competitors succeed and others fail. It is therefore necessary to identify the critical factors necessary for success.

In order to understand these critical success variables, analyze the data and determine strategies for success, Burgeria needed to be evaluated in terms of its strategic condition. Two factors were examined in detail: industry maturity and competitive position.

Industry Maturity

Let's look first at industry maturity. In determining the maturity of the fast food hamburger industry, the planning team jointly studied a number of clues, among them: sales . . . breadth of product line . . . number of competitors . . . market shares . . . technology . . . ease of entry.

Industries, like products or restaurant concepts, experience lifecycles. The lifecycle has four segments—embryonic, growth, mature, and vintage. Each segment has different characteristics and implications for business strategy selection.

Burgeria's management found it difficult to reach a consensus on the maturity of the fast food ham-

Exhibit 1

	Penetration	Product Pricing
McDonald's	+	+
Burger King	+	+
Wendy's	−	0
Longhorn Burger	−	−

burger industry. But, after analyzing the data, the following observations were made:

- *Sales growth rate*—Real sales growth is slightly faster than GNP, but the rate is declining from that of the early and mid-1970s. Growth is anticipated to slow as inflationary pressures squeeze disposable income. Most markets, including Dallas-Ft. Worth, are approaching saturation.

- *Breadth of product line*—While many companies will continue to experiment with new products, the capabilities of most existing facilities will limit menu expansion. By 1985, most chains will have finished major new item experimentation and will have rationalized their menus and production systems.

- *Number of competitors*—The number of hamburger competitors has been declining and will continue to do so. Major chains will continue to force independents out of business.

- *Market share stability*—Major chains have become relatively stronger at the expense of independents; overall market share in the hamburger segment will remain fairly stable despite aggressive marketing tactics.

- *Ease of entry*—It is becoming increasingly difficult to start a successful large-scale fast food operation. Economies of scale in purchasing and advertising represent major hurdles.

- *Technology*—Technology has been fairly unimportant in the past but will become increasingly important as labor cost pressures escalate and the availability of labor decreases.

After much discussion, the planning group agreed that the fast food hamburger industry was in the late stages of the growth phase and was quickly moving toward maturity.

Several of the managers had expressed opinions that the industry was in the early growth or even embryonic stage. It should be noted that this is a fairly common stumbling block—managers often would like to believe their industry is earlier in its lifecycle than the data suggests.

However, we should reiterate that there are no good or bad stages of maturity. A particular maturity position becomes "bad" only if the strategies adopted by a business are inappropriate for the actual stage of maturity.

Competitive Position

The second factor analyzed in determining a business' strategic condition is its competitive position. Competitive position is a summary of a strategy center's strengths and weaknesses relative to those of its competitors. Businesses can be characterized as: dominant, strong, favorable, tenable, or weak.

To develop Burgeria's competitive position, the group first had to determine the bases of competition: What critical actions must a fast food company perform well to succeed?

Burgeria management threw out a number of elements of the business that the group decided were not bases of competition, but rather were prerequisites and thus should already be established in order to be in business.

These prerequisites were: good locations, profitability, and the quality of unit operations—food quality, service, and cleanliness.

The planning group agreed that there are six major bases upon which firms in the fast food business compete. In order to keep this example manageable, let's look at two:

- *Penetration*—The total number of units and the number of units in each market.

- *Product Pricing*—The breadth of price points and the price/value relationship compared to other fast food operators.

Market research indicated that Burgeria competes in Texas with McDonald's, Burger King, Wendy's and a local chain, Longhorn Burger. Against each of these competitors, the Burgeria planning team evaluated its own performance on each of the bases of competition.

Exhibit 1 demonstrates their findings.

McDonald's was perceived as better in both penetration and product pricing. In the Dallas-Ft. Worth market, McDonald's has 56 units while Burgeria has 32. McDonald's units are generally either newly constructed or recently remodeled. Burgeria has no drive-thru windows; about half the McDonald's units have them. Additionally, McDonald's has a variety of products priced from 40 cents for a hamburger to $1.20 for a ¼-pound hamburger with cheese.

The Burger King franchisee in this market had built a number of units in the late 1960s and had continued developing the market slowly, with a total of 40 units. While some of the units needed to be remodeled, in general the planning group felt the Burger King menu and price points were better than Burgeria's.

Wendy's had just entered the market. While the planning group felt the Wendy's units were very appealing to the adult market, they concluded Wendy's was vulnerable to high beef prices and had a limited menu with marginal appeal to children. Wendy's drive-thru windows and labor efficiencies earned it a high evaluation, but a relatively limited number of units (8), poor geographic distribution in the area, and a rather highpriced and limited menu were seen as making it somewhat less competitive. Burgeria's management, however, anticipated Wendy's becoming a bigger factor in the market in the future.

Longhorn Burger is an old chain, with most of its units built in the 1950s and 1960s. The planning group concluded that Longhorn's curb service and menu were out of date and that the company would not be able to expand beyond its existing 16 units. It was seen as weaker in both penetration and concept, yet was still a viable competitor in this market.

Based on this evaluation, the Burgeria planning team then classified each of the competitors, along with themselves in the Dallas-Ft. Worth market as shown in **Exhibit 2** below:

The consensus was that Burgeria could be classified as favorable because of the following reasons:

• Its concept had unique strengths. No other competitor had deli sandwiches, and Wendy's was only beginning to test salad bars in its units.

• The Burgeria chain had momentum. In each of the past two years, it had opened up 9 new stores.

• Some concept problems were noted. For example, Burgeria's prices are higher than the major chains, yet margins are lower due to less efficient buying and poorer labor utilization.

After completing the situation analysis, Joe Block and Ken Dietz felt they finally had their arms around their business. However, a number of

Exhibit 2

Competitive Position

	EMBRYONIC	GROWTH	MATURE	VINTAGE
DOMINANT				
STRONG		• McDonald's • Burger King		
FAVORABLE		• Burgeria • Wendy's		
TENABLE		• Longhorn		
WEAK				

Arthur D. Little, Inc.

Exhibit 3

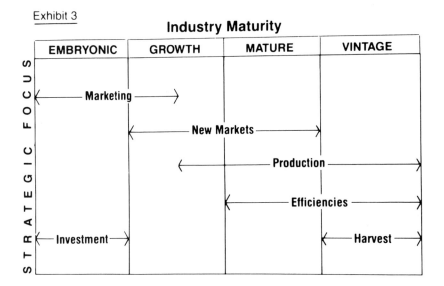

questions remained and a plan for the future still needed to be developed.

A Limited Set of Strategies

Having reached a consensus on the strategic condition of its business, Burgeria was ready to consider appropriate strategies. To do this, Burgeria's managers applied the fourth principle in strategic planning—"recognizing that a limited set of strategies exist."

Generally we have found that strategies can be grouped into the following five clusters:

1. *Marketing strategies*—Increasing sales of current products and the development of new products or new concepts.

2. *New-market development strategies*—Rolling new or existing concepts into new markets.

3. *Production rationalization strategies*—Improvements and standardization of design, equipment, and production processes as a means of lowering production costs.

4. *Methods and functions efficiencies*—Cost reduction techniques through "soft" technology; for example, improved production planning and inventory control or computerized labor scheduling.

5. *Investment or harvest strategies*—The input or extraction of cash from the business. One harvesting approach is stripping down a business to its most profitable pieces and reinvesting the proceeds of divestments in other businesses having greater potential.

These five clusters of strategies tend to fall into periods of execution which relate to the stages of industry maturity. This relationship is illustrated in

Exhibit 3:

For example, strategies that focus on marketing tend to be more appropriate in the earlier stages of industry maturity where the name of the game is to establish market position.

Production and efficient management strategies are more appropriate in later stages when the emphasis is on being the lowest cost producer.

After becoming familiar with this concept, Burgeria's management was ready to begin its strategy selection. With characterization of its industry as late growth and an understanding of its favorable competitive position, Burgeria looked at those strategies identified as most appropriate or natural.

Based on the data available to Burgeria's management, it was decided the first priority would be to strengthen Burgeria's penetration in the existing market.

Management felt it to be extremely important to increase and then maintain the current share of the Dallas-Ft. Worth market. This market would become the source of cash flow to fund subsequent growth.

However, Block and Dietz felt that the Dallas-Ft. Worth area could not provide sufficient potential to maintain growth at the company's historical levels. Consequently, management felt it was necessary to penetrate new markets.

Burgeria management reviewed the real estate buyer's suggestion of opening units in Houston.

The commissary manager felt it would be difficult to service this market from the existing warehouse.

The marketing manager pointed out that Houston was in a separate and expensive media market and recommended additional units in small cities that would enjoy spill-over from the Dallas-Ft. Worth area.

After the Vice-President of Finance estimated what it might cost to build enough units in Houston to achieve acceptable penetration, management opted for San Antonio and Oklahoma City as targets for expansion. An aggressive plan was developed to enter these markets.

Thus, the company selected as its first two strategies:

- Market penetration in existing markets.
- Expansion into the new markets of San Antonio and Oklahoma City.

It should be noted that these strategies fall within the cluster of strategies we labeled "marketing strategies."

Earlier we indicated that the majority of marketing strategies are executed during the embryonic and early growth stages. Burgeria agreed that they were probably late in executing this strategy and realized they were going to have to play "catch-up" with the larger competitors.

It was also agreed that additional penetration had to be accomplished quickly. As the industry entered the mature stage, additional growth would be more difficult and costly to achieve.

As an adjunct to these first two strategies, Burgeria selected excess capacity as its third strategy—to provide additional pre-emptive capacity beyond current needs.

Management felt it was important to maintain a very strong presence in the existing market and wanted to be aggressive in seeking the best available sites in the growing section of the Dallas-Ft. Worth area—sites that might not really be ready to support a mature unit for several years. Burgeria wanted to be the first chain to open units in these areas so that it would make it difficult for competitors to penetrate or gain predominance in the market.

In addressing the second basis of competition—product pricing—Burgeria realized it was at a competitive disadvantage.

Although research indicated that customers felt product quality was quite good, it also ind cated that Burgeria was perceived as somewhat high priced. Because they are ⅓ pound, the least expensive ham¹ gers were priced above competition at $1.4 and deli sandwiches ranged from $1.89 to $2.49. While the check average had re-ained high, customer counts were falling.

on reviewing the available research, the man-

agers decided that more price points were needed and the appeal of the concept had to be broadened beyond the existing base of primarily young (18-34) males.

After much discussion, the company concluded that new products were needed and smaller portions with lower prices were necessary for Burgeria to broaden its appeal to children and women.

Once the appropriate strategies were recognized, the company began an intensive study of the menu, portions and prices to help determine key price points and the feasibility and direction for new product development and implementation.

Be Condition, Not Ambition, Driven

At this point, the planning team paused in its plan development to see if sufficient capital was available to fund additional growth in new markets. The fifth principle of planning applied: the conditions a planning center faces, not the ambitions of the individual managers, are paramount in strategy selection.

While management had the ambition of becoming a major regional chain, it could only develop plans based on actual conditions, including its financial strength. It became clear that after building already-planned units in the existing markets and adding the pre-emptive additional new units, Burgeria's capital funds would be depleted.

It was at this point that the idea of a franchising program was seriously considered.

If suitable agreements could be made with the interested developer to assure quality control in Oklahoma City, and a similar arrangement of company-owned and franchised stores could be developed for San Antonio, franchising would allow regional penetration for Burgeria with significantly reduced capital outlays.

Although there would be costs involved with developing the franchise agreement, training and quality assurance programs, management felt that franchise fees would more than cover these expenses. At the same time, the chain would be developing the necessary size to achieve greater economies of scale in both purchasing of food and regional advertising.

After reviewing its strategic condition, Burgeria identified a total of six strategies for a five-year plan.

A detailed discussion of each of Burgeria's strategies and associated programs is beyond the scope of this article, however, it should be noted that just six strategic directions were identified.

It is our belief that a company can implement only a few strategies well at any given time. If a business attempts to pursue a variety of strategies and directions simultaneously, the result is more often than not poor execution and unmet expectations.

At the conclusion of this portion of the strategic planning process, Joe Block and Ken Dietz felt, for the first time, that they had developed a thorough plan for their burgeoning business for the next five to seven years.

They would solidify and defend their market share in Dallas-Ft. Worth and penetrate new markets. With the regional fast food hamburger segment approaching maturity, Block and Dietz realized it was necessary to reach a large enough size by 1985 to allow Burgeria to compete effectively.

One final point: Block and Dietz wondered how the management of Burgeria would monitor and track the chain's progress against the newly developed plan. That topic will be the subject of the final installment of our series.

A Management System for the 1980s:
Part III

This is the last of a three-part series about strategic planning in the foodservice industry, prepared by Robert L. Sirkis and Stephen M. Race of Arthur D. Little, Inc., Cambridge, Mass.

In the first article of this series, we introduced the five principles of planning. In the second, we shared an example of how a business applies these principles in developing strategic plans.

The second article focused on a hypothetical company, Burgeria, and how that company was guided through the planning process to develop future plans for a regional fast food hamburger business. At the end of the planning process, Joe Block and Ken Dietz, Burgeria's managers, felt they had developed a thorough plan for the next five years. They would solidify and defend their market share in Dallas-Ft. Worth and penetrate new markets. With the regional fast food hamburger segment approaching maturity, Block and Dietz realized it would be necessary to reach a sufficient size by 1985 to allow Burgeria to compete effectively. With the strategic plan in place, Block and Dietz wondered how they would monitor and track Burgeria's progress against their newly developed plan.

This final installment of our series addresses that issue.

Measuring Performance

The performance measurement system we recommended is not revolutionary. Rather, we are suggesting a change in focus and perspective from the "actual versus budget" systems presently used in most companies.

Performance measurement reports will not replace profit-and-loss statements, but will supplement them as effective management tools. Just as

From *Restaurant Business* (October 1, 1980) pp. 92-102. Reprinted by permission of *Restaurant Business*.

unit managers use P&L's to monitor their performance, corporate managers should use strategic measurement reports to monitor their performance.

P&L's are very important to unit and multi-unit managers, i.e. profit center managers. These managers are not particularly concerned with strategic performance and should not review the strategic performance reports.

On the other hand, heads of strategic business units, or the president of a single-business unit company, must be concerned about performance against strategic plans. The strategic performance report is for these top managers.

There are three basic considerations in putting together a performance measurement system:

1. In selecting performance measures, only those measures that are relevant to the strategies adopted by each business unit should be chosen.

2. The established performance standards, or targets, should be realistic. They should be consistent with both the strategic position of the business units and the strategies selected.

3. Reports should be designed to focus management attention on variances in key performance measures.

The performance measurement system is designed to focus attention on the execution of strategies chosen for each strategic business unit, not necessarily on existing profit or cost centers. To properly monitor the strategic performance of a business unit, some companies will find it necessary to redefine corporate divisions or restate financial results based on business unit reporting centers.

First Principle

Performance measures are determined by the strategies selected. We should monitor those measures which indicate whether the strategies selected are being properly executed. Some examples may be helpful.

In our previous installments, we indicated that a

Strategic Performance Measures

Exhibit 1

STRATEGY GROUP	PERFORMANCE MEASURES	Total Sales	Sales Per Unit	Administrative Costs	Food Cost	Profit	Return on Assets	Fixed Asset Investment
1. Marketing		↑	↑	↑	✓	✓	✓	
2. New Market Development		↑	↓	↑	✓	✓		↑
3. Production								
4. Efficient Management								
5. Harvest								

limited set of strategies exists. We grouped strategies into five clusters: marketing, market development, production rationalization, methods and functions efficiencies, and harvesting.

In *Exhibit 1,* we show these five strategy groups and a few typical performance measures. However, there are many other financial as well as nonfinancial performance measures that might be relevant, depending on the strategy selected. Let's see what we might expect from the strategies which Burgeria chose.

The strategies Burgeria selected were consistent with its favorable competitive position in a late-growth business. They included:

1. Improve penetration in existing markets.
2. Expand into new markets.
3. Develop new products for the existing concept.
4. Develop pre-emptive capacity beyond current needs.

The first and third strategies apply to marketing, while the second and fourth concern new market development.

As a result of the marketing strategies Burgeria selected, we would expect total sales and sales per unit to increase, as indicated by the arrows in *Exhibit 1.* Administrative expenses would increase as a result of additional staff necessary for menu development, stimulated real estate and construction activity, and larger marketing budget. We would want to monitor food costs to see the impact of new menu additions. There is likely to be an impact on profits which we would want to monitor closely.

Since profit is likely to be changing, we would also expect return on assets to change. These measures to be monitored are flagged with check marks.

The marketing strategies should not cause a significant change in the rate of fixed asset investment, so we leave that column blank.

The new market development strategies provide another example. Total sales would be expected to increase as before, but sales per unit should be lower in the pre-emptive stores and in the first units in new markets.

As Burgeria began to achieve sufficient penetration in new markets, we would expect sales per unit to increase. But this would not be the case in the first few years.

Administrative expenses would be high due to the start-up expenses associated with the new units and the development of a franchising program.

Burgeria would want to monitor food and labor costs closely in the new and pre-emptive units. The introductory period in a new neighborhood or in a new city is not a good time to cut costs. An over-zealous operations manager cou__ __uin the development program by cutting too many corners.

Profits should be closely checked as a general measure of the success of the new market development strategies. Fixed assets investment would be expected to increase with the addition of company-owned units.

Different results can be anticipated for each group of strategies. It is important to remember that the measures selected to monitor performance are determined by the strategies selected.

Second Principle

The second key element in developing a performance measurement system is setting realistic standards. A standard is the expected or budgeted value against which the measured actual value is compared.

Strategies chosen for each business unit indicate which performance measures are to be monitored and in what direction we expect them to move.

For setting actual numerical standards, it is also important to consider the strategic position of each business unit in order to have a realistic expectation of what standards can be achieved. *Exhibit 2,* using several examples, illustrates what we mean.

We would expect to see dollar sales vary over the four stages of industry maturity.

In an embryonic industry, we would expect low but rapidly growing sales. In the growth phase, sales would continue to increase rapidly, until the

mature phase when they would tend to level out. In the vintage phase, we would expect them to begin to drop off.

A business unit's competitive position affects both the amplitude and the rate of change of this sales curve. For example, a strong competitor would experience much faster sales growth in the embryonic and growth stages than would a tenable competitor. Similarly, a company in a strong competitive position would become profitable earlier and would earn higher profits than a weaker competitor.

Let's look at profit after tax as another example. We would expect profits to be negative in an embryonic industry, but then increase rapidly to the positive side in the growth state. In the later stages, mature and vintage, we would expect profitability to remain high as the business capitalizes on its market position.

Exhibit 2 also shows what we might expect to see in net assets of the business unit in each stage of industry maturity. We would expect rapid building of fixed assets in the early years, but then a tapering off as new investment is decreased and depreciation lowers net asset values.

Finally, a company with several business units might take cash out of some businesses and invest more heavily in others. Businesses in embryonic and growth industries often have negative cash flows. In the later stages of growth and on into the mature and vintage stages, cash flow turns positive,

Exhibit 2

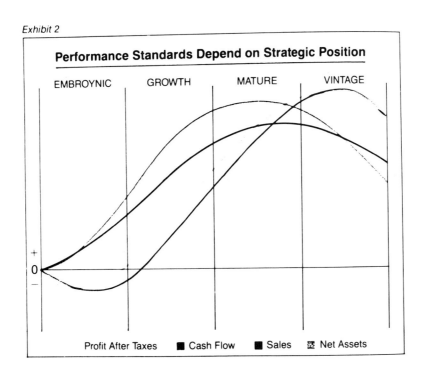

Performance Standards Depend on Strategic Position

EMBROYNIC GROWTH MATURE VINTAGE

+
0
−

Profit After Taxes ■ Cash Flow ■ Sales ▨ Net Assets

Burgeria, Inc.
Strategic Performance Report

Exhibit 3

\multicolumn{4}{YEAR-TO-DATE}		THIS MONTH			
VARIANCE	ACTUAL	PLAN	LAST YEAR*	FINANCIAL HIGHLIGHTS	VARIANCE	ACTUAL	PLAN	LAST YEAR*
61	14,698	14,637	12,126	Sales ($000)	50	2,450	2,440	2,020
—	42.0	42.0	42.5	Food Cost (%)	0.1	41.6	41.5	42.6
0.7	2.9	3.6	3.1	Administrative Cost (%)	0.8	2.8	3.6	3.1
121	1,121	1,000	942	Operating Profit ($000)	19	186	167	157
1,258	2,396	3,654	2,260	Capital Investment ($000)	210	400	610	377
1,179	(75)	(1,254)	118	Cash Flow ($000)	210	—	(210)	32
				STRATEGIC INDICATORS				
7.5	367.5	360.0	350.0	Sales/Unit ($000)	1.4	61.3	59.9	58.4
2	4	6	4	New Units Opened	—	1	1	1
.15	2.30	2.15	2.12	Guest Check Average ($)	17	2.32	2.15	2.10
42	878	920	907	Daily Unit Customer Count	42	890	932	919
0.4	4.6	5.0	—	Sales From New Products (%)	0.2	5.2	5.0	—

*Note: Last year's data are adjusted for inflation.

often reaching its height in the vintage stage.

These ideas can be summarized by returning to Burgeria and examining some of the performance standards we might apply.

While Burgeria plans to increase the rate of new unit openings, we would expect sales to grow faster than the GNP but slower than their growth rate during Burgeria's embryonic years. Profits would be expected to increase. Net assets would continue to grow rapidly for the next several years, causing a drain on cash flow. But as the segment reaches maturity, growth of net assets would slow and cash flow would increase.

Here, we have described the performance standards in general terms. Actual companies would establish a numerical value for the standards based on two factors.

• The actual current or prior year figure, and

• The direction and amount of change expected based upon the chosen strategic course and the business unit's strategic position.

For example, in 1979 Burgeria's system-wide sales were $23.9 million. Based upon the plans for more rapid unit development than in the past, Burgeria projected an annual compound sales growth rate of 38 percent for the period 1980-1983, 17 percent from 1984 to 1986, and a lower rate thereafter as the opportunity is reduced for additional market penetration.

A new unit opening standard would also be developed. Whereas the company had opened nine units during each of the past two years, management set the following goals for new unit openings through 1985.

1980: *12 new units (12 company, 0 franchised);*
1981: *20 new units (14 company, 6 franchised);*
1982: *20 new units (14 company, 6 franchised);*
1983: *18 new units (12 company, 6 franchised);*
1984: *13 new units (10 company, 3 franchised);*
1985: *9 new units (8 company, 1 franchised);*
At this rate Burgeria would grow from 50 units at the end of 1980 to 130 units by the end of 1985.

Similarly, specific standards were developed for each performance measure. All of the standards were based on Burgeria's favorable competitive position in a late-growth industry.

Third Principle

The final consideration in performance measurement is designing the actual reports. Management information reports should include both financial highlights and what we call strategic indicators. *Exhibit 3* shows the report Burgeria developed for monitoring performance.

Note that this is a one-page report containing both year-to-date and monthly data. We have indicated two major sections within the report, with the middle column listing the performance measures selected.

Key financial highlights make up the first section. This section usually includes sales, profits, and funds flow information.

The second section displays the strategic indicators for the business unit. These are the particular performance measures, in addition to the financial highlights, that we want to monitor—for example, product development expenditures or market share.

Within each section we typically show last year's information (adjusted for inflation) for historical comparison.

The "plan" column contains the standards we've been talking about, and the "actual" column measures the business unit's performance.

We also included an additional column to show variance from plan. By highlighting variances, management is able to use the report for exception-oriented action.

Utilization of reports such as these allows top management to monitor the business unit's performance against the standards set and take appropriate actions if actual results begin to vary from the plan.

There are three possible reasons for a strategic business unit's failing to achieve standards set.

The first could very well be improper execution of the strategies.

On the other hand, the standards may have been set too high or too low. The development of standards, especially the first time strategic planning is done, should be a repetitive process, with adjustments made as necessary.

A third possibility for failure is that some external factors may have changed so that it is no longer possible to achieve the standards set.

In general, variances from key performance standards provide an early warning if strategies are not working and allow the business unit to make adjustments in execution or, as the case may be, change the strategies.

Let's look at the results for Burgeria to see how the report works.

Financial Highlights

Burgeria was focusing on marketing and new market development strategies.

Therefore, in the financial highlights area, the first section of *Exhibit 3,* we have chosen to look at sales, operating profit, capital investment and cash flow. We want to look at administrative cost to see what is the impact of additional staffing and heavier advertising and development expenditures. Food cost is monitored to help evaluate the effectiveness of the new menu item development program.

Sales were expected to grow, reflecting additional units, and, in fact, they did. Food costs were lower than last year as planned. This reflects the successful introduction of a family of new dessert items with low food costs.

What might ordinarily be looked upon as good news—the fact that administrative costs are lower and profits higher than planned—actually reflects an unhealthy situation.

Capital investment is lower than planned because only four units have been opened while plans called for six by this point in the year. Moreover, although the plan included the purchase of eight additional pieces of property for subsequent development, only five have been obtained. This will make it difficult to open the twelve units planned for 1980 and begins to jeopardize the 1981 schedule.

The negative cash flow is much less than anticipated, reflecting the delayed development program.

There are significant variances from these financial standards. If we were looking at just a profit-and-loss statement, we might think that everything was running better than planned.

We identify any variance, positive or negative, with a strategic performance variance report. It is then up to management to determine if that variance is good or bad. A well-designed strategic performance report will include enough data to allow top management to explain variances and problems before they get out of control.

Let's see if we can figure out what is going on at Burgeria.

Strategic Indicators

While we saw in the financial section that sales were ahead of plan, this is misleading. Sales per unit are 5 percent ahead of last year on a real basis. Since a 2.9 percent increase had been budgeted, the better-than-planned sales per unit have offset the unit opening shortcoming. Sales increases can be traced to increases in the guest check average. The negative trend in customer count is continuing.

When Burgeria's managers, Block and Dietz, reviewed these results with the director of marketing, the facts behind these figures became clear.

The marketing department had focused its efforts on the introduction of new desserts. Point-of-sale materials, bounce-back coupons for customers purchasing the new items, and a dessert dish giveaway had all been targeted against existing customers.

The programs were successful in that the guest check average increased, but no programs had been aimed at bringing new customers into the units.

Management agreed to shift the focus of the marketing program primarily towards that goal while redirecting the new product development program towards lower cost sandwich items. A broader range of price points was considered important in broadening the customer base.

In a meeting with the director of development, Block and Dietz explored the new unit opening variance. Only four units had been opened and five land parcels purchased versus plans for six and eight, respectively. The construction department was getting the units built in the scheduled period of time but was just not getting enough sites.

Two problems were identified.

• The real estate department had planned on hiring a second buyer but had not done so, and

• Several extremely desirable sites that had been purchased were facing extended delays for permits and zoning which, in turn, were inhibiting development.

Block and Dietz agreed with the director of development's suggestion of creating a new position of project manager to provide for someone to expedite the process of getting a new site ready for construction. They also urged the real estate department to bring the additional buyer on board quickly.

The strategic performance report identified variances. Burgeria's management determined that these variances represented problems in the execution of the strategies selected. By addressing the problems with the responsible managers, Joe Block and Ken Dietz were able to diagnose and resolve the problems before they got out of control. By redirecting the marketing effort and addressing staffing problems in the development group, Burgeria should be able to achieve its planned results.

Summary

In the three articles in this series, we have introduced the principles of a strategic planning system for foodservice companies. The approach outlined in our simplified Burgeria example has illustrated the key concepts of such a system.

The first of these key concepts is that strategic planning should be an orderly process for determining the direction of a business.

It involves classifying the business's current strategic position and looking into the future to develop projections for the operating environment. The business then sets objectives, develops strategies and allocates skills and resources to execute these strategies.

The second key concept is that strategic planning should be more than a one-time process; it should be a system.

This requires an ongoing control or feedback system that enables management to track performance relative to the plan. Such a control system often represents a departure from the financial reporting systems we know today. These measures that are relevant to the strategies selected are monitored closely, with variances "red flagged."

Reports should include enough information to allow management to determine the cause of any variances.

We introduced this series with the title, "A Management System for the 1980s," because we feel foodservice companies more and more will need to adopt strategic planning to remain competitive. As the industry matures and the social, political, and economic environment continues to evolve, fundamental changes will occur in the marketplace.

In the future, foodservice management will have to focus on developing realistic objectives and appropriate plans for the long-term profitability of their businesses.

A Guide to Long-Range Planning for Hotel Management

The great success stories in American enterprise are based more on strategic planning (direction setting) than on operating effectiveness

Byron Brady has become the lodging industry's most respected spokesman on performance planning—often called long-range planning—because of his work with Westin Hotels, the American Hotel & Motel Association, and AH&MA's several affiliates. This article is based on his presentations.

Effective planning requires you to use both sides of your brain. You use the intuitive side to fly by the seat of your pants. You use the logical side to put method into your plan.

The following pages set forth guidelines for effective hotel planning. You need first to know how the author of these guidelines, Byron Brady of Westin Hotels, defines planning. Here are his concepts:

Planning is a process. It is necessary, for effectiveness in using these guidelines, to move consecutively from step one through step six. A common cause of failure is to fail to take steps in the proper order.

Planning is visualizing your future. Unless you can see clearly where you are going it is unlikely that you will get there.

Planning is the first and most important responsibility of management. The manager who does not plan does not manage.

Planning is a process that requires team involvement to succeed. Final decisions are always made by management. But unless management involves staff in the planning process management cannot expect staff commitment.

Planning takes time. The higher your rank on the management team the greater the proportion of your time spent in planning.

Planning is more of an art than a science. It requires greater dexterity in human relations than in technical knowledge or skills.

Finally, planning is a process through which in-dividuals working as a team come to a common understanding of where they are and where they would like to go and how to get there.

Underscore and capitalize two words in the above sentence: *COMMON UNDERSTANDING.* Just as in planning, the process (taking the steps in the proper order) is more important than the plan, the common understanding (moving in the same direction) is more important than the management staff's brilliance.

Nothing sidetracks performance quicker than for the general manager and department managers to move in different directions.

The planning process outlined here can be applied at any management level—company, division, hotel/motel, department or other identifiable unit. The six essential steps are:

1. Analyze your situation. Take a hard look at your property, performance (operating results), people, position in the market and prospects. Stop saying, "We're the best in the world," and ask, "What's the truth about our situation?"

2. Formulate your strategy. Decide what your position will be in the market. Where are you going? How can you set directions?

3. Identify priorities. How will you commit human, financial and physical resources? What comes first, second, third, fourth and fifth?

4. Set objectives. Set your goals in measurable terms. For example, a strategy might be: "To have the highest occupancy in the trade area." An objective might be: "To run a 73% occupancy with a $67 average rate."

5. Plan actions. State each goal in terms of a breakdown of actions needed to achieve goal.

6. Budget. The mechanics of budgeting will not be discussed here. What is important to state is this: budget after, not before, completing the other steps in the planning process.

1. Situation Analysis

Performance planning may be ongoing (prefera-

From *Lodging* (February 1982) pp. 15-18. Reprinted by permission of *Lodging*.

bly) or for a period, short-range or long-range. Situation analysis is, however, a present analysis of the (1) past, (2) present and (3) possible future of:

a) Business performance

b) The market and the hotel's position in it

c) The economy and the direction it is taking

Management calls the planning session; management conducts it. The best yardstick of management's success is the degree to which participants speak out on the situation as they see it.

Who participates? Whoever can contribute vital information. The only restriction is that nobody should be brought in whose presence will inhibit free discussion.

Where are planning sessions held? Wherever you can be free of interruptions and get down to shirt-sleeve work.

What about timing? There are five phases in situation analysis. Sufficient time should be allowed for the completion of each phase. But the time lapse before moving from a completed phase to the next phase should be minimal. Here are the phases:

1. Preparation. Management prepares background information and distributes it (their home work) to participants prior to situation analysis sessions. Background data includes information for study on business performance, the market and the economy.

2. Presentation. Staff members present the type of information that falls within their purview. They use audio and visual resources as available. Questions and answers are encouraged at this stage, but not challenges.

3. Contribution. In this phase, challenges are encouraged. Participants comment on whatever has been said. More important, they comment on anything pertinent that seems to them to have been left out of the presentations. Their comment is unrestricted. The general manager sits by, primarily in the role of psychiatrist: LISTENING.

4. Discussion. To this point, two things have happened. Participants have presented information. Participants have had their information challenged. Now comes the discussion phase—a phase that moves in the direction of decision-making. Items considered irrelevant are eliminated. Duplication is eliminated. Remaining items are sorted and recorded (put in writing) so that all participants may make constant reference.

In a word, the remaining items are called "findings." They are categorized and arranged in logical sequence. Thus they become a set of findings about a hotel's (or other unit's) situation.

5. Conclusions and assumptions. At one hotel the "remaining items" after a situation analysis reflected 123 strengths and weaknesses of (1) business performance; (2) market penetration, and (3) response to economic realities.

Space will not permit a case example of this hotel's conclusions. But let us consider the conclusions in one category—the market. Here are the conclusions reached:

• Convention and group business accounts for 65% of all revenue at first class hotels in our trade area

• Convention and group business is increasing in this competitive area at the rate of 10% a year

• Convention and group business at our hotel accounts for only 45% of total business

• Five other first class hotels in our competitive area have greater banquet and meeting space.

2. Strategy Formulation

Strategy formulation means deciding what direction to take in light of the situation analysis. Where do we go from here? What do we want to be? What will be our positioning in the market?

Let's take our case study example a step further. Two options seemed open:

Option 1: To remain competitive, it is essential for our hotel to increase its strength in the convention and group market by expanding physical facilities; that is—enlarging the ballroom, adding a smaller ballroom, creating three new meeting rooms.

Option 2: It would be to our advantage, economically, to leave the convention market (large groups) to the competition and to concentrate on personalized services to the individual business traveler and the elite small groups.

The second option was chosen. Thus the positioning became: we will be the number one choice of the upscale individual business traveler and the elite small group.

3. Priority Identification

Priorities are identified by stating what has precedence in the allocation of financial, material and human resources.

Priorities are easy to list but agonizing to narrow down to a workable number—say five.

Priorities should be listed in a separate statement and attached to any budget submitted.

No manager (of a company, hotel, departments, etc.) should be allowed to get by with (1) ignoring the priority step altogether; (2) saying it doesn't apply to his or her unit; or, (3) making up a priority list so long that it diffuses.

The hotel in the case study example above might have listed these bases for a priorities list to implement its new positioning on group and individual business traveler marketing:

1. Do a market study of meeting planners for small elite groups to find out what they would consider ideal in equipment and special services.

2. Create small meeting rooms, train service staff, and purchase special equipment to provide ideal appeal to small elite groups.

3. Do a market study to ascertain the needs of upscale, individual business travelers in terms of facility, equipment and service.

4. Provide executive floors with special facilities, equipment and trained personnel to provide ideal lodging to the upscale, individual business traveler.

5. Develop and implement advertising and promotion programs targeted at small elite groups and upscale individual business travelers.

The repetition of terms in the above—small, elite, upscale, individual, business—is not to annoy the reader but to emphasize the need to be specific. To pinpoint targets in formulating strategy and identifying priorities is to promote common understanding. Participants prepare to move in the same direction.

4. Objective Setting

Objectives are measurable and attainable goals. They mainly fit into these categories: financial, marketing, operating (human resources, systems development, etc.) and capital investment.

Management effectiveness may be measured by management's ability to "deliver" on objectives that are in harmony with the strategies and priorities of the enterprise. Examples of objectives:

• With marketing emphasis on the small elite group, average banquet check should increase by 14% in the next year.

• Fifty percent of the advertising budget (overall) of the hotel will be allocated to promoting individual business travel patronage. 25% to promoting small elite group business.

• Six-week employee training programs will be completed as follows: for small elite group service, by April 15; for upscale individual business traveler service, by May 30.

• Secretarial offices for individual business travelers on the 11th floor will be completed by June 1.

• With increased marketing emphasis on the upscale individual business traveler, average rate should be $73.25 by July 15.

5. Action Planning

Action planning means translating each objective into a breakdown of jobs that have to be done to meet the objective. It is highly significant because a single objective can involve several departments.

Take, for example, staff training to render special services to small elite groups. An action plan would include:

1. Obtain training materials; revise to fit needs of special project.

2. Select trainers; train trainers.

3. Establish place of training, time frame for training; frequency and length of sessions.

Similar breakdowns would be needed for projects to implement objectives such as: (1) survey of meeting planners; (2) physical upgrading of meeting rooms for small elite groups; (3) purchase of improved audio-visual equipment for small meeting rooms; (4) structural changes in guest floor redesigned for business executives; (5) purchase of special business equipment for executive floors; (6) staff training in VIP services for upscale individual business travelers.

Budgeting

As stated earlier, this presentation will not cover the technicalities of budgeting. Our concern with budgeting in this guideline can be summarized as follows:

Budgeting must follow all other steps in the planning process, and must relate directly to the priorities stipulated in the plan.

We come now to plan approval. This is management's job, of course. It requires knowledge of the entire plan—not just the financial figures—and how elements in the plan relate to each other.

We come finally to the questions of when may a plan be changed and how, and how often is a plan evaluated and by whom.

Changes should not be made except for good reasons. When necessary, changes will be found easier to make with a plan than without one. It is easier to change something than nothing. Changes should be made, however, in an atmosphere of discussion. Remember that the key to effectiveness is COMMON UNDERSTANDING.

Evaluation should be on-going. But perhaps that is too vague; evaluation of a long-range plan with annual revision during the period of forecasting and budgeting may be scheduled—roughly—as follows:

January-March. All management units (departments) review last year's performance. They evaluate plans in terms of results produced.

April-June. Top management evaluates long-range objectives in light of changing conditions and needs. Remember, top management is responsible for providing "home work" reports to department management.

July-September. All management reevaluates plans during the forecasting period. This is the time of the year for a situation analysis.

October-December. All management is involved in performance planning for the year ahead with top management making final decisions.

In summary, here are some thoughts on planning:

- The planning process is even more important than the plan itself. Take the steps in order.
- The formulation of strategy is even more important than operating effectiveness. Determining what direction to move has been the basis for the success of all giant American enterprises in the periods of their success.
- A statement of priorities—a separate statement—should be submitted along with a budget.
- Objectives should be both attainable and measurable.
- One function of a breakdown of jobs to be done to meet each objective is to show the need for cooperation among departments.
- Budget-making should follow completion of all other steps in planning. Only the completion of a plan for performance justifies consideration of a budget.

Strategic Planning:
How to Hold a Market Profitably

by William C. Hale

In the first article of this series, we focused on the results of an executive survey concerning strategic planning. The survey identified the five most important strategic issues facing the industry in the 1980s:

1. Improving cost controls.
2. Attracting an adequate labor force;
3. Improving productivity;
4. Managing in an intensified competitive environment; and
5. Responding to market saturation.

This article explores how management might approach resolution of these Market Share/Penetration issues, or *How can our chain hold a market profitability in a highly competitive environment?*

The reason for linking the requirement for holding a market with market penetration is quite simple. As a market becomes highly competitive (normally a symptom of a mature industry), management must make a basic decision. Do we:

Abandon the market because it is unprofitable; we have a very weak position; and, long term it does not fit our development scheme;

Trim back the number of units to the most profitable units or niche, and reinvest capital in the remaining units;

Maintain the current level of effort, i.e., same number of units, marketing efforts, etc.; or

Penetrate market so as to increase share of market and improve overall operating efficiencies.

In or Out

In most of the geographic markets Technomic has evaluated over the past few years, maintenance has not been a viable strategy. The question comes down to, are we *in* or *out* of the market. If we are *in,* then we either implement a niche penetration (trim back to few most profitable); or implement a broad market penetration. This is a principal way to hold a market in a highly competitive environment.

The basis for gaining a strong market position through a market penetration strategy is tied to economics. The chains with the high-market-share positions will tend to be the most efficient operators, and generally, the efficiencies realized increase with share. The economics come in the form of more efficient marketing and advertising; better utilization of supervisor management; lower costs of distribution, among other efficiencies. Also, most chains can point to a sizable increase in average unit sales as the overall market share increases, since per unit sales are significantly lower in a low share market than in a high share market.

Define Market

The first step in deciding whether to penetrate or abandon (let's not consider maintenance as a viable option) is to define the market. How do we want to define our markets; by the way operations has structured its field management?; or by the way consumers' life patterns, and purchasing patterns are structured and defined?

We would strongly suggest that consumers provide the clues to how markets are described. In fact, one convenient way to describe a market is by an Area of Dominant Influence (ADI) of a TV signal. Each ADI is defined by the configuration of the beamed TV signal. Each ADI can be further defined by demographic characteristics, growth, and most important, by expenditure patterns. (For example, *Restaurant Business* tracks the eating and drinking sales for each of the 212 ADIs in the U.S.)

As we move forward, it is important that we have a means to measure effort-input against results. ADIs will allow us to do that.

The next step is to develop a good understanding of the market. Most management teams do not know their markets well! For example, how many

From *Restaurant Business* (January 1, 1982) pp. 80-88. Reprinted by permission of *Restaurant Business.*

of these questions could you answer for your major competitors? (See *Figure 1* for checklist of competitive factors.)

Competition

How many units do your competitors have in each of your ADIs?

What is their average unit volume in your market area?

What is their share of the market?

What is their menu/pricing strategy?

What is their cost structure (operating costs)?

Where are the units located (location strategy); how old are the units?

What has been the expansion or renewal activity over the last four years? Cost of new unit construction?

How is their management organized and what are their strengths and weaknesses?

What is known about the competitors' supply system?; operational systems?

What is their marketing thrust in terms of: new products, new services, consumers targeted, and profile of users, advertising budget?

What is the competitors' overall strategic direction in this market?

What does the consumer like and dislike about the competitors?

Answers to the above questions are among the major factors that should be mapped out for each of the major competitors. The information can be readily assembled for analysis. Some of the information sources are shown in Figure 2.

Consumers

What do you know about the consumers in your markets?

How many are there in the market and what is their: age distribution, household structure, consumer expenditure patterns, income levels, employment status, and labor force composition?

What are the dynamics of the population in terms of: growth, movement, life style shifts and other shifts?

What do your customers as well as nonconsumers think about your concept and execution?

What are the consumer trends operating in your markets that will have an adverse or positive impact?

What can be done to minimize or accentuate those impacts?

Industry Trends

The last set of questions that management should be able to answer concern the industry structure and other institutional factors. For example:

What are the trends within the foodservice industry that will impact my business in terms of: new concepts or competitors; new products/service or

Figure 1.

CHECKLIST OF COMPETITIVE FACTORS	
☐ LOCAL MARKET PENETRATION	☐ G&A STRUCTURE AND COSTS
☐ CONSUMER IMAGE/PREFERENCES	☐ UNIT MANAGER TRAINING & EXPERIENCE
☐ SALES PER UNIT	☐ BACKWARD/HORIZONTAL INTEGRATION
☐ CHECK AVERAGE	
☐ FOOD COST RATIOS	☐ FRANCHISEE STRENGTHS
☐ LABOR COST RATIOS	☐ AVAILABLE CAPITAL FOR EXPANSION/RENEWAL
☐ UNIT GROSS MARGINS (%)	
☐ UNIT CONTRIBUTIONS ($)	☐ MARKETING
☐ AGE OF UNITS	☐ "SECRET WEAPONS"
☐ LIFE CYCLE OF CATEGORY	
☐ LIFE CYCLE OF CONCEPT	

technology; procurement practices and raw material market trend; labor practices; and unit design?

What are the institutional factors that will impact the business in terms of: cost and availability of capital; government regulations; and economic situation?

Business Review

In addition to market information on the competition, and the state of the industry, management should take an *objective* look at their business:

What has been the unit sales, traffic count, and operating margin history?

What has been the return on capital employed?

What is the market share by ADI (company and licensed)?

What is the product sales mix and contribution by item?

What is the pricing history and relationship/effect on customer traffic counts?

What is the consumer profile of user and non-user?

What has been the marketing thrust and its effectiveness?

What is your cost of unit construction?

What has been your expansion history?; renovation history?; and its payback?

What is your cost of raw material?

What is the status of your franchising program (if appropriate)?

What are your human resource programs—recruiting, training, promoting?

How effective is your research and development effort?

What is your real estate situation and strategy?

What are the strengths and weaknesses of your

concept, management and operations?

Depending on the specific chain and its unique characteristics, there will be other questions that need answers. However, the key point is, managers should base the *in* or *out* decision on facts, not feel—facts about the competition, market conditions, industry dynamics, institutional factors and your own business situation.

Penetration Strategy

With the above information in hand, business managers should perform an *objective* analysis to see how their chain stacks up to competitors in each of the ADIs.

Let's assume that a fairly rigorous analysis of the chain's strategic position relative to competition, the industry's development, the market/consumer perceptions was conducted. The results of that analysis suggest that in the core ADIs, management believes the market should be retained and, in fact, penetrated. The steps to implement a penetration strategy are:

Step 1. Rank ADIs—Establish a ranking of ADI in terms of the order they are to be developed/penetrated.

• It is difficult to focus on all ADIs at once, focusing on a few at a time may be easier to manage and more effective.

• Do not necessarily attack the most difficult or largest ADIs first, since that may be frustrating to management. Take the ones that are most likely to succeed first. This develops a track record and moves management along the learning curve faster.

Step 2. Develop share measurement mechanism—Develop a means to determine and

Figure 2.

COMPETITIVE ANALYSIS INFORMATION SOURCE CHECKLIST	
☐ ANNUAL REPORTS	☐ TIME SERIES OF PRINTED MENUS
☐ 10-K	☐ DIRECTORIES
☐ D&B, CREDIT AND OTHER PURCHASED REPORTS	☐ TELEPHONE BOOKS
☐ TRADE PUBLICATIONS/FINANCIAL PAGES	☐ RESEARCH REPORTS
☐ ANALYSTS' REPORTS	☐ SUPPLIERS
☐ TRACKING SERVICES	☐ PERSONAL OBSERVATION
	☐ COMMISSIONED RESEARCH

track share of market trends for your chain and major competitors.

• Before you attempt to *gain* share, make sure you know your current share and have a way to monitor changes in share over time. This can be done with published data—such as the *Restaurant Business* Restaurant Growth Index. Data (*See Restaurant Business,* September 15, 1981) on ADIs might be based on number of units and traffic surveys as well as Crest (Consumer Reports on Eating Share Trends) data on a regional basis, or some other scheme.

• The tracking mechanism will be important in monitoring and managing the strategy.

Step 3. Establish share target and determine the share gap for each ADI—Analyze the current share information and determine what share is required to place you among the top three chain operators. The share target should be for each ADI, and the competitive set you should compare your chain with might be described as "close-in competitors" (same menu and service).

• In mature markets, there will be two or three major players and a few other niche players. Other chains will tend to shake-out. Therefore, to hold a market, the chain should be aiming at the 1, 2 and 3 position.

• If management thinks that it will be impossible to be in the top three, then a niche-strategy should be considered.

• Given the chains *current share* and *targeted share,* management can readily determine the difference, or *gap.* If the market is mature and the share gap is quite large, management may want to consider a niche strategy.

Step 4. Delineate a market development plan for each ADI—For each ADI, a specific detailed plan of action describing how the share gap will be filled should be established. In most cases, this will be a multiple year plan. The plan should address the role each marketing element will play:

Product/service features—Will new menu items be needed? Will new service be offered? Can the current menu items and services be improved?; differentiated?; expanded? Can the quality image be enhanced? Will remodeling help build traffic?

Price—What should be the pricing strategy?; premium?; or discount? Can new pricing points be added to make the overall package more attractive?

Promotions—What will be the promotion strategy?—games, premiums, tie-in, cents-off? Are special promotions needed to attract non-current users? What promotions can be employed to increase usage by current users?

Distribution—How many new units are needed to achieve better market coverage, i.e. more convenient for customers? Where should these be located? Can existing buildings be purchased/leased and converted to your chain's image?

Communications—Is there a need to alter signage? What will be the advertising strategy and level? What other publicity campaigns must be employed? Can other instore/point of purchase displays add to sales?

The market development plan should say what is to be done; who is to do it/be responsible for implementation: when it is to be done; the estimated budget; and the expected results.

Step 5. Management review—The ADI market development plans should be reviewed by management and accepted or modified. The review should include:

1. Completeness;
2. Cost of implementation versus expected results/return;
3. Resource needs people, capital, outside services;
4. Reasonableness, i.e. ability of planned actions to fill the share gap; and
5. Assurance that the individual in charge is aware of responsibilities and expectations.

Step 6: Implementation and monitoring—The implementation calls for the orderly roll out of the actions delineated in the plan. This should be coordinated by one individual. This individual would have management's support and be able to call upon all the impact functional areas, i.e. research and development, marketing, operations, personal, financial.

Management reports should be established specifically to review the implementation and results. Otherwise, the experience gained in the early ADIs targeted for penetration will be lost. Also, without a monitoring system, management will not know how it is progressing toward its share object.

Managing the Strategy

Once the planning is completed and the decision to implement given, the successful penetration of the market will be the result of *good, solid blocking and tackling.* While there is a need for creativity in the design of the strategy, a steady competent management team is required to make it happen.

Marketing for the Eighties: Marketing a New Hotel

by William Q. Dowling

Bill Dowling is a marketing consultant to the hospitality and tourism industries and is president of Dowling Marketing, Inc.

There are only two things you have to know about marketing a new hotel.

1. You can never start early enough.
2. You may have to wear a name tag home so your wife and kids (or husband and same) will remember who you are.

In spite of all this, quite a few hotels open every year—many of them successfully—and there are a few pointers you can pick up which might mean the difference between success and failure.

One of the most professionally marketed chains in the world is Marriott Hotels. In this article, you will see, step by step, how they successfully opened the Washington Marriott March 3 of this year.

"Marriott has developed a successful formula for opening its new hotels," said Elizabeth D. (Biffie) Meyers, vice president advertising and market research for the chain. The basic plan:
- Research
- Positioning
- Advertising strategy
  - Objective
  - Target Market
  - Basic Selling Proposition
  - Support for Selling Proposition
  - Tone (of the advertising)
- Media Plan
  - Media Objectives
  - Strategy and Rationale
  - Budget
  - Media Flow Chart

From *Lodging* (July 1981) pp. 24-31. Reprinted by permission of *Lodging.*

- Sales Strategy
- Public Relations Strategy
- Promotion Strategy
- Total Marketing Budget

The opening of the new 350-room Washington Marriott provides a case study of how the planning process works and how the corporate marketing department works with the hotel's director of marketing. When the Washington Marriott opened, the hotel's director of marketing was John J. Hyland. He is now off to open another new hotel. Hyland reported to the hotel's general manager, Hugh Walsh. The advertising agency is Ogilvy & Mather. Their vice president and (Marriott) account supervisor is Henry (Hank) Ferris, who is based in the New York Office.

Research and Positioning

Marriott had six other properties in the Washington area. "So we had a lot of market data available to us," said Meyers. "We were able to quickly identify the customer mix we should go after and how to reach them. We knew the transient business traveler was our single most important market segment and we set our priorities accordingly."

The Washington Marriott was being built at 22nd and M Streets in the heart of Washington. Therefore the positioning agreed upon by Meyers, Ferris and Hyland was:

". . . the most convenient quality hotel in the Washington area for the business traveler."

The sales effort followed directly from this positioning. Said Hyland: "We secured office space next to the site nine months in advance and hired four sales people. One person concentrated exclusively on transient business travelers. . . "

Hyland set up sales coverage of all offices in the downtown area. The sales team signed up secretaries and travel department managers in the Marriott 100 Club, which offers swimming privileges, discounts in the gift shop, and many other benefits for those who book executives into the Washington Marriott. The goal was to set up 80 top-volume bookers, but the sales team hit 100. Members were given a special reservations number which bypasses the switchboard and rings in the hotel's reservations department.

Developing Advertising Strategy

Once the positioning was determined, the agency and client worked together to develop the advertising objective and strategy. First, the objective was agreed upon:

"To convince the target market that the new Washington Marriott is the finest hotel in the heart of town."

They defined the target market as the transient individual business traveler in the northeast and the middle income local professional. The business travelers were important for obvious reasons. The local professionals were important for these two reasons: (1) they book incoming clients and corporate executives; and (2) they are primary customers for the dining room—the Atrium—the lounges—the Court Lounge and Gambits and the function rooms and ballrooms.

A "basic selling proposition" was then prepared to set forth the reason why a customer should select the hotel. Note that while the objective was stated in terms of what the advertising hopes to achieve, the selling proposition is stated in terms of consumer benefits:

"The Washington Marriott is the most convenient quality hotel in the Washington area."

When a benefit is promised, it must be supported by facts. The support for this selling proposition is as follows:

- the reputation of the Marriott Hotels
- excellent location
- deluxe facilities including an indoor pool, hydrotherapy pool and sauna.

The tone of the ads, it was agreed, should reinforce the quality image of the hotel.

Creating the First Ad

Once the account team at Ogilvy and Mather had the preceding information, they turned it over to the writer and art director team. The creative team was also given basic guidelines regarding media selection. For the Washington Marriott, it was decided to use a 600-line ad in local newspapers and one-page black and white ads in business magazines. The writer and the art direc-

tor, said Ferris, decided four things:

1. The campaign must be consistent with the corporation's national campaign, which features President Bill Marriott as spokesman.

2. They would trade on the fact that the Marriott has six other hotels in the D.C. area and has gained a reputation for quality.

3. They would emphasize location, since this is one of the most important factors in a business traveler's decision.

4. They agreed that two separate ads were needed: one for the business traveler in the Northeastern United States, and the second for the local D.C. market.

They wrote the following headline for use in both ads:

"I'm proud to announce the opening of my seventh Washington Marriott Hotel—the first to be squarely in the middle of town.'
  —Bill Marriott, President,
    Marriott Corporation

But the body copy differed greatly. For the business traveler, the copy said:

"When the people at Marriott do it, they do it right. They knew Washington, D.C. already offered a large selection of convention hotels. So they built a luxurious 'personal' hotel."

(The rest of the ad features location, dining facilities, a special floor, and both local and toll-free reservations numbers.)

The ad for the Washington resident, by contrast, began as follows:

"A large part of the new 350 room Marriott at 22nd and M Streets was built for out-of-towners. But the rest was built for the residents of greater Washington—for you."

(The rest of the ad mentions the dining room, lounges, meeting rooms and weekend packages. The only telephone number listed is the local one.)

Pre-opening Media Plan

Because Marriott has a substantial corporate advertising campaign, the budget for each hotel's own media plan is usually set at about 1% of estimated room sales. For most hotels, especially independent properties, the advertising budget runs 2% to 3% the first year.

The media planner at Ogilvy & Mather was provided with three types of information by Hank Ferris and the account group: the target market including the cities where the target customers live; the opening budget (determined by the client), and the creative considerations (advertising objectives and strategy). From this, the media planner decided the most efficient and effective way to deliver the advertising message.

To reach the business traveler, it was decided to use the *Wall Street Journal's* eastern edition; *Business Week; Nation's Business* in the New England and Middle Atlantic Regions; and *Dun's Review,* the eastern edition.

In order to afford a two-month introductory campaign to build quick awareness, it was decided to use a quarter page ad in the *Wall Street Journal* for three consecutive weeks in March (the month of the opening) and full-page black and white ads in the business magazines for March and April.

Said Meyers: "We identified this as a 60-day announcement program to be followed by an ongoing advertising program."

For the association market, advertising was placed in *Association Trends,* and for the travel trade, advertising was used in joint participation with other Marriotts in directories and meetings publications.

For the local market, the original plan called for three ads each in the *Washington Post* and the *Washington Star.* This would have given the hotel coverage of 77% of the metro area. But the agency and client agreed that most of the target customers were covered by the *Post.* Therefore they decided to drop the *Star* and add an additional insertion in the *Post.* The resulting schedule was one ad each week for the first four weeks in March, thereby building frequency against the local prime prospects.

Pre-opening Sales Program

John Hyland's sales team had been marketing the Marriott 100 Club nine months prior to the introductory advertising. They did so by a combination of direct mail and the sales calls discussed earlier. Hyland sent a letter, application form, and a color rendering of the new hotel to the prospect list. A newsletter was sent to the Marriott 100 Club members periodically and a party was thrown for them at the hotel the day after opening.

Next, Hyland targeted efforts toward the tour brokers, to develop much-needed weekend business. "We sent over a thousand letters which I personally signed, mentioning features that would be of interest to a tour broker: special weekend rates, parking for buses, indoor pool and sauna, and the fact that the hotel is adjacent to Blackie's House of Beef. I know it's a bit unusual to mention a com-

petitive restaurant, but Blackie's has been a favorite of the tour operators for years," said Hyland, "and we saw it as a strong attraction." Lists for the mailing were culled from NTBA (National Tour Brokers Association) and sources from within the Marriott organization.

Once the primary prospects for midweek and weekend business had been covered by direct mail and follow-up phone calls, the sales team concentrated on association business. Said Hyland, "Our national sales director, Skip Boyd, came up with an idea for a 'hardhat luncheon' next door to the construction site. Association executives were invited. After lunch, our general manager, Hugh Walsh, conducted a tour. The involvement of Walsh is one of the reasons for our success. Customers want to meet the general manager."

The "hardhat luncheon" idea was so successful it resulted in about 4,000 room nights being booked prior to opening. Forty-nine percent of all group bookings into the hotel came from associations.

Hyland's sales team also sent letters to all tourist inquiries received by the Washington Convention and Visitors Bureau, promoting a 50% discount off the rack rate for weekends and holiday periods. A return reply card was enclosed along with a color rendering of the new hotel.

Hyland became active in the Washington Society of Association Executives (ASAE), Meeting Planners International (MPI) and other local group-producing organizations. He also enlisted the support of all available Marriott sales people in the Washington area for a three-day sales blitz of the area.

Other sales efforts included:
* mailings to chambers of commerce in major cities throughout the U.S., informing them of the hotel opening
* sales trip to London to tap the inbound British traveler
* familiarization trips in conjunction with airlines, following the hotel opening,
* promotion through direct mail to existing Marriott accounts, of the "Marquis Level" floor with special services at a premium price.

Pre-opening PR Program

There are six times during the construction of a new hotel that publicity can be obtained to generate awareness prior to the first ad running. They are:
* when construction plans are announced

- at the groundbreaking ceremonies
- at the topping-off of the building
- when the management and sales teams are hired

MARKETING CHECKLIST FOR OPENING A HOTEL

Designed Specifically for an Independent Hotel Located in a City

12 months in advance

—hire Director of Marketing

—retain advertising agency & public relations firm

—establish tentative rate structures

—affiliate with rep firm, international reservations systems, etc.

—begin market research on sources of business, competition

—submit listings to all directories which close prior to opening of the hotel (examples: Hotel & Motel Redbook, Hotel and Travel Index, Yellow Pages and White Pages of local telephone directory, Convention & Visitor's Bureau publications, Chamber of Commerce publications, tourist map companies, meetings and association magazines annual directory issues, inplant agency and corporate travel association directories)

—join local ASAE, MPI and other organizations for client contacts

—enter into agreements with any tour brokers or wholesalers whose programs/brochures you want to be in.

—obtain mailing lists for all corporate, association and tour/travel clients who produce business for the area.

—send press release to media to update them on progress of hotel and staffing

9 months in advance

—finalize Positioning, Advertising, Media, Sales and P.R. Strategies

—finalize pre-opening marketing budget

—have full sales team in place

—begin sales coverage of accounts which are top priority for your hotel (such as corporations' travel departments and secretaries who book incoming business)

—place heavy concentration on advance booking of association and corporate group business into the first three-six months the hotel will be open

—schedule advertising in the meetings and association magazines

—print all pre-opening sales material including 4-color architects rendering

—make any necessary revisions in rate structure

6 months in advance

—intensify sales coverage of corporate transient accounts

—adjust rates if necessary

—continue direct mail to corporate accounts, meeting planners and tour operators; update them on hotel progress

—continue press releases to local media, travel trade and meetings magazines

3 months in advance

—release advertising to consumer magazines and trade magazines to meet closing deadlines

—begin sales and direct mail blitz of travel trade

—continue updating corporate and association customers, giving them "hardhat" tours of hotel, including sample furnished room

—begin local, regional and (if appropriate) national publicity effort for hotel, including tours of hotel, personal interviews with general manager or owner

—finalize hotel rates for next 15 months

The last 30 days up to opening day

—release advertising to local media for introduction beginning the week prior to opening

—finalize plans for Grand Opening party, ceremony, etc.

—hold opening press conference

—intense telephone sales blitz of all corporations in area for inbound business

—continue sales blitz of travel agents

—increase inspection tours by meeting planners who can book short term business

—hold receptions opening week for top corporate accounts and, separately, for local travel agents

• at a pre-opening press party, a week or two before opening

• at the grand opening party

The objective of the publicity should be to communicate the same points agreed upon in the advertising "basic selling proposition."

How Much to Spend

There are no industry averages to compare for pre-opening budgets, as there are with on-going marketing budgets. Because the expenses are generally capitalized along with construction costs, they don't usually show up on an operating statement.

Hotel pre-opening marketing budgets will range generally from 50% of an on-going year's marketing budget to as low as 25%. But the best way to budget for the pre-opening period is to use the zero-based budget. In other words, decide what is needed to open the hotel, don't just arbitrarily spend a fixed amount.

The first expense will be a director of marketing. Then the sales team will be added. Advertising in the group or meetings publications will begin as much as a year prior to opening. But advertising to the consumer/business traveler will not begin until

the month before opening. Temporary brochures, from the architect's renderings, should be produced as far in advance as possible, along with the hotel's logo, stationery, mailing labels, business cards, meeting planner fact sheet, press kit covers or news release paper, rate cards, flyers, etc.

Chain hotels can rely on the national and regional sales offices for much of the pre-opening sales effort, and will therefore have relatively low pre-opening expenses. An independent hotel, on the other hand, has a much bigger task.

The Marriott Formula

The Marriott formula, as indicated by their advertising, is, "If Marriott does it, they do it right." So it is with their marketing a new hotel. They have the advantage, of course, of the national sales department, Biffie Meyers' corporate marketing department, and Hank Ferris and his colleagues at the agency.

But if you are general manager or marketing director of an independent hotel, you might have to do more yourself than you would at a chain hotel. Thus, we have included in this article a checklist designed for the independent.

A Guide to Planning the Marketing Budget

Edited by William Q. Dowling

When Art Tauder found himself in charge of budgets for the world's largest advertising agency, Interpublic, he was given some advice by an executive of a client company, Coca Cola. The executive of the giant company told him that all he had to worry about, in planning budgets, was that there is only one problem in all business: "Revenues are too low; expenses are too high."

The hotel executive who develops a marketing department budget probably encounters a similar attitude from the general manager; too little money coming in and too much going out. One of the best tools for achieving a better balance of income and expense, however, is to prepare a marketing budget that is as simple as possible—and as well thought out.

The marketing budget for a typical hotel should include at least the following items:
- advertising, printing and production
- sales promotion, trade shows and special events
- sales/marketing departmental wages and benefits
- departmental overhead, including telephone
- travel and entertainment

You can prepare a marketing budget on a more sophisticated level by including more of the items on the accompanying "Outline for a Marketing Budget."

The marketing department's organization and its budget should be an outgrowth of the overall marketing strategy. The development of the budget, whether aggressive or conservative, large or small, should use the same kind of process used by the large marketing companies.

Art Tauder suggests seven steps in budget development:

From *Lodging* (October 1980) pp. 66-68. Reprinted by permission of *Lodging*.

1. Plan = Budget + Text

"To understand the relationship between the Plan and the Budget," says Tauder, "I must first define how I see the Plan. The operating plan is a communication of goals (objectives), allocation of resources (strategy), actions to be taken, and standards for evaluating performance over a given time.

"I look at the Budget as the stripped-down basics," he says. "The text is the qualitative expression that adds nuances of meaning to the bare numbers of the budget."

2. Plan Backwards

The old adage of "plan ahead" should be reversed when developing budgets. Interpublic establishes a backwards calendar which begins with an action date or target due date for budget submission. Then the agency's division heads back up from that due date to determine what action must precede it and when that action must begin. By continuing to do this, Interpublic executives end up with a 12-month planning cycle that alleviates the typical last minute "budget crunch."

For example, let's suppose the budget for your hotel's marketing department is due December 15th. Working backwards, you can set certain check dates. The first draft should be typed for your review by November 15th. To do this, you must decide on all wage increases and personnel changes by November 1. The advertising agency must have their first draft of an advertising budget to you by October 1st so you will have time to review it, suggest changes and receive a revised plan by November 1st. And you continue to work backwards on the calendar to set key due dates for every action that must be taken to complete the budgeting process. It is important to understand the continuous nature of the process and the interrelationship of events. "This understanding," according to Tauder, "can end the 'dog days' of plans and budgets."

3. Peddle the Cycle

Once you have established your backwards calendar, make copies for everyone involved. The Ad agency, the P.R. firm, the sales force, your administrative personnel and anyone else who must contribute to the process of meeting a due date. It will help everyone to do a better job.

Have you ever had your ad agency come to you with a great idea only to find out that the budget was closed the week before and there was no money available for this new idea? You will be a better client for your agency, and will get more out of them, if you involve them. "Peddle the planning cycle," says Tauder, "to keep reminding everyone of key due dates."

4. Plan-A-Plan

Hold a planning meeting two or three months before your budget is due. Review the following:
- status report on year-to-date sales and costs
- report on action plan for remainder of year
- discuss the main thrust of next year's marketing effort
- review the format for next year's Plan
- establish budget guidelines for next year.

5. Decide What to Spend

How much should you spend on marketing? There are a number of ways to determine the answer, but Tauder warns "You should not get locked into one approach."

There are three basic approaches. One is the *Empirical Approach*, where you produce your own hypotheses from marketplace experience. This means starting from scratch, i.e., zero-based, and developing a media plan based on marketing goals without budget restrictions, then seeing what the resulting plan will cost. You may be surprised to know that one of the most prominent and successful hotel companies in the U.S. uses this method. The only instruction the chief executive officer gives his marketing team is: "Tell me what it will take to get the job done."

A second, more conventional method, is to arrive at a budget which is within *Industry Guidelines* based on the ratio of marketing budget to room sales. Two major accounting firms, Pannell Kerr

Forster and Laventhol & Horwath, issue reports to their clients with summaries of costs as a ratio to sales for all sizes and configurations of hotels and resorts.

Over the years, however, some guidelines have emerged. See "Range in Marketing Budgets from Conservative to Aggressive."

Within the overall marketing budget, the split between Sales costs and Advertising costs can range anywhere from 60/40 to 40/60, depending upon the importance of each to the market you are concentrating on. For example, a hotel that depends primarily upon convention business would skew towards a larger sales budget, because those prospects can be more easily identified and called on by the sales force. However, a hotel that depends primarily on transient business or individuals booked through travel agents, will have a smaller sales force and will spend more on advertising to build awareness among individual prospects. Only you can make the determination as to what works best for your hotel.

Once your advertising budget is determined, you and your agency must allocate budgets for printing, production, fees if any, and other related costs. The amount remaining is your media budget. If it is not enough, then you may want to reverse the process and first determine the media budget, then allocate the remainder to printing, production, etc.

A third approach, which relates strictly to advertising and is too complex to discuss here, is the *Theoretical Approach* using the Hendry Analysis. There is an excellent short book on this subject called *How Much to Spend For Advertising*, edited by Malcolm McNiven. You can obtain a copy by sending **$7.50** to the publisher.

The Association of National Advertisers
155 East 44th Street
New York, NY

6. Segment Your Budget

You should construct a marketing budget just like you lay a foundation for a building: one block at a time. You should have specific budgets for each step of the marketing plan. In media, for example, there should be a separate budget for each season if you operate a seasonal hotel, or for each type of business, or both. There should be separate budgets for travel trade advertising, for convention publications, for directories. There should be separate budgets for trade shows, familiarization trips, and other sales promotion efforts.

Outline for a marketing budget

Sales
Payroll and related
Operating Supplies
Other operating expenses
Postage, telegrams
Trade shows
Travel and entertainment

Advertising
Payroll and related
Exchange advertising (due bill)
Other operating expenses
Outdoor
Print:
   Magazines: conventions, travel
   Magazines: consumer
   Newspapers
Production
Radio/TV

Merchandising
Payroll and related
In-House graphics
Other selling aids
Point of sale material

Public Relations
Payroll and related
Community projects
Fees for outside services
Other operating expenses
Photography

Research
Payroll and related
Guest history
Other operating expenses
Outside services

Fees and Commissions
Advertising agency
Franchise fees
Hotel representatives
Marketing fees
Other operating expenses

Other Selling, Promotion Exp.
Association dues
Complimentary guests
Credit card costs—internal
Direct Mail

The above is adapted from "A Uniform System of Accounts for Hotels,"
Seventh Revised Edition

Calendar for a marketing plan

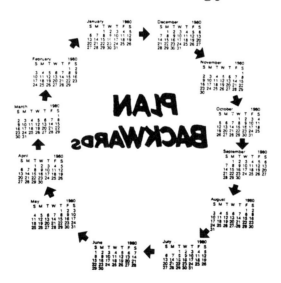

Sample range in marketing budgets

Total Marketing Budgets
Ratio of Costs to Gross Rooms Revenue

	Smaller Property	**Larger Property**
Resort Hotel*	8-9%	7-8%
City Hotel	5.5-6.5%	6-7%
Suburban Hotel/Inn	5-6%	6-7%

*In certain regions of the U.S. and Caribbean, marketing costs can run as high as 14-15% of
rooms sales for resort hotels, 7-8% for city hotels, and 7-8% for subruban inns.

Budgeting by specific marketing programs is a step towards increased accountability for marketing plans. It is also a technique to prevent arbitrary budget cuts. When large pockets of money appear in a budget under broad categories such as "media," these funds become a target for budget cuts. By breaking the budget into each of its components, management will have a better understanding of the consequences of taking $50- or $100,000 out of your proposed budget.

7. Adopt a Computer

The current generation of corporate executives received their formal education in a period before EDP was being taught in the colleges and universities. Many people in top management today are insecure about the new technology and its new vocabulary.

If your hotel is using a computer for its front or back office work, make a friend as soon as you can with someone who is in that department. If you can use your computer for even a portion of your budgeting or monitoring process, it will rid your life of the many tedious and repetitive tasks that must be done every week.

Finally, there is one more point that Tauder stresses that is perhaps the most important of all.

• Present your Plan and Budget in a brief and actionable format.

All of us have been guilty in the past of turning out budgets and plans that are judged by weight rather than substance. But we are all overwhelmed today by too much paperwork. Your marketing plan will be more effective (and read more often) if you will limit it to a statement of the objective and strategies, and concise statements of action that will be taken during the year with the name of the person who will take that action and the due date for that action to be taken. Next should be a summary of the media budget, on one page, and a media flow chart followed by a very brief rationale for media selected. This should be followed by a well-organized presentation of the total budget for your marketing department. This Plan and Budget should be in a format that will allow for monthly updating to show plans vs. actual.

A simple, condensed approach to budgets and plans has worked for the world's largest advertising agency and will work for you. Art Tauder calls these budget disciplines the ". . . universal language of planning."

Menu Engineering

by Donald Smith

What to do with plowhorses, stars, puzzles, and dogs on your menu

Don Smith, head of the School of Hotel, Restaurant & Institutional Management at Michigan State University, published a book titled, "MENU ENGINEERING." It reflects his experience as owner of specialty restaurants, president of a chain of (500) fast-food operations, and professor of foodservice administration.

A menu is a portfolio of items. The way you manage this portfolio determines what your consumer demand and profit contribution margin will be. The key to any menu's success is whether or not it produces more customers and more contribution dollars.

Menu engineering is a tool foodservice operators can use to evaluate one menu against another. It requires that the operator know each menu item's total product cost, selling price, and quantity sold over a specific period of time. A menu item's revenue contribution margin and sales activity is categorized as either relatively high or low. Each menu item is classified and evaluated for both its marketing (popularity) and pricing (profit) success.

By categorizing and classifying menu items through logical mathematical procedures, menu engineering enables the operator to make the right decisions.

Food Cost Percentages

Most foodservice operators have been conditioned to judge profitability by cost of goods percentages. To establish a total product cost in a foodservice operation, management must know three key pricing factors: standard recipe cost, garnish cost, and supplementary food cost.

Standard recipe cost. The cost of all products used to produce one standard portion of a menu item. For example, New York Strip Steak may be served as a 10 oz. portion of 180A strip loin extra short. At $6 per pound, the cost of the standard 10 oz. portion would be $3.75 ($6 lb./10 oz. equals ⅝ lb. x $6 equals $3.75).

Garnish cost. Products used in garnishing the standard recipe for each item to enhance eye appeal and flavor. For example, parsley, fruit, lobster butter, mushroom caps, and onion rings. The New York Strip Steak might be garnished with onion rings and mushroom caps.

Supplementary food cost. Foods that are included with menu items regardless of selection or sales price. Many restaurants offer bread, butter, salad (including salad dressing) and potato with all menu items. Supplementary foods can account for a substantial cost factor.

The total product cost for a standard portion of New York Strip Steak might be as follows:

Standard recipe cost	$3.75
Garnish cost	.18
Supplementary food cost	.57
	$4.50

Once management analyzes the total cost of each menu item, the menu's potential cost of goods can be determined. The potential cost of goods is the total cost if all items purchased are sold, and if no foods are incorrectly portioned, stolen, or otherwise wasted. Obviously, potential cost of goods sold and actual costs will vary. Variance—usually from one to three percent—depends on the type of restaurant and the effectiveness of management control. Actual food costs are determined by purchases and inventory at the end of an accounting period.

As a rule of thumb, the variance in potential and actual cost of goods at fast food operations is one half to one percentage point; at table service and specialty restaurants, it is two to two and a half percentage points. Any larger variance should signal management that a problem exists.

From *Lodging* (March 1982) pp. 46-50. Reprinted by permission of *Lodging.*

1. Items Ranked by Contribution Margin

	(A) CM Classification	(B) Menu Item	(C) CM	(D) Food Cost%
1	HIGH	Lobster Tail	4.65	41%
2	HIGH	Prime Rib (20 oz)	4.30	46%
3	HIGH	NY Strip Steak	4.00	41%
4	HIGH	Top Sirloin Steak	3.65	39%
5	LOW	Shrimp	3.05	41%
6	LOW	Red Snapper	3.00	39%
7	LOW	Prime Rib (12 oz)	3.00	45%
8	LOW	Chicken	2.74	31%
9	LOW	Chopped Sirloin	2.55	41%
10	LOW	Tenderloin Tips	2.45	42%

2. Menu A: When Chicken Is Most Popular Item

	Menu Mix	Cost	Income
Chicken	1000	$1500	$ 4,500
Steak	400	1200	2,800
Lobster	300	1350	2,700
	1700	$4050	$10,000

Potential Food Cost: $\frac{4050}{10,000} = 40.5\%$

Contribution Margin: $5,950

Average C.M. per Guest $3.50

3. Menu B: When Steak is Most Popular Item

	Menu Mix	Cost	Income
Chicken	300	$450	$ 1,350
Steak	800	2400	5,600
Lobster	600	2700	5,400
	1700	$5550	$12,350

Potential Food Cost: $\frac{5550}{12350} = 44.9\%$

Contribution Margin: $6,850

Average C.M. per Guest $4.03

A Menu Item	B Menu Mix	C MM%	C
Shrimp	210	7	
Chicken	420	14	
Chop Sirloin	90	3	
Prime Ribs/12 oz.	600	20	
Prime Ribs/20 oz.	60	2	
New York Strip	360	12	
Top Sirloin	510	17	
Red Snapper	240	8	
Lobster Tail	150	5	
Tenderloin Tips	360	12	
TOTALS	3,000	100%	

To determine each menu item's food cost percentage, the item's total product cost for a standard portion is divided by its selling price. The food cost percentage for the entire menu is determined by dividing the menu's total food cost by total revenues.

Cost percentages, however, should not be the sole means of evaluating food profitability. Illustration I ranks the menu items at Johny's Grill, a hypothetical restaurant that we will use as a case study. The menu items are ranked from highest to lowest contribution margin. For our purposes, contribution margin is the amount left over after subtracting the item's total standard portion cost from its selling price.

As you can see, low food cost percentages do not necessarily indicate profitability. The chicken entree has the lowest food cost percentage, 31%, but yields only a $2.74 contribution margin. The lobster tail entree produces the highest contribution margin—$4.65—and has a food cost percentage of 41%.

Illustrations 2 and 3 show the importance of tracking the effects of varied consumer demand—menu mix—on contribution margin and potential food cost. Each menu contains the same three entrees prepared with similar standard recipe and product costs. The total number of covers sold is the same for each menu—1,700—but the consumer purchase pattern, menu mix, is different.

In Illustration 2, Menu A, the chicken entree is the most popular item. It produces, however, only $4,500 in income when 1,000 covers are sold. Menu A's food cost percentage is 40.5%, its average contribution margin per guest is $3.50 and it generates a total contribution margin of $5,950.

In Illustration 3, Menu B, the steak entree is the most popular item. With only 800 covers sold, it produces income of $5,600. Menu B's food cost percentage is 44.9%, but its average contribution

How Menu Engineering Was Used to Analyze a Menu for a 30-Day Period

E Menu Price	F Food Cost	G CM	H Total Menu Revenues	I Menu Food Cost	J Menu CM	K CM%	L CM Category	M Class.	N Action Taken
.95	$4.90	3.05	$1,669,50	$1,029.00	$640.50	6.6	L	Plowhorse	Carefully increase price
.95	2.21	2.74	2,079.00	928.20	1150.80	11.9	L	Plowhorse	Retain as low price leader
.50	1.95	2.55	405.00	175.50	229.50	2.4	L	Dog	Eliminate
.95	4.95	3.00	4,770.00	2,970.00	1800.00	18.6	L	Plowhorse	Retain
.95	5.65	4.30	597.00	339.00	258.00	2.7	H	Puzzle	Increase price
.50	4.50	4.00	3,060.00	1,620.00	1440.00	14.9	H	Star	Increase price
.95	4.30	3.65	4,054.50	2,193.00	1861.50	19.3	H	Star	Retain
.95	3.95	3.00	1,668.00	948.00	720.00	7.4	L	Plowhorse	Increase price
.50	4.95	4.55	1,425.00	742.50	682.50	7.1	H	Puzzle	Test by lowering price as special to see if demand increases
.45	4.00	2.45	2,322.00	1,440.00	882.00	9.1	L	Plowhorse	Increaes price in stages
			$22,050.00	$12,385.20	$9,664.80	100%			

Potential Food cost: 56.17%   Average Contribution Margin: $3.22

margin per guest is $4.03. It generates a total contribution margin—$6,850—higher than Menu A.

The menu with the lowest cost of goods percentage is the least profitable as a result of menu mix. The more a foodservice operator can shift demand to higher contribution margin items, the greater the menu's total contribution margin will be.

Gathering Information

Every attempt to improve your menu begins with a statistical evaluation of your current situation. A foodservice operator's objective is to make the next menu more profitable and appealing to the guest. In order to do this, management must consider:
- The wants and needs of the target market
- What menu items to offer
- How to describe menu items
- How and where to place each item on the menu
- How to graphically design the complete menu.

Management needs accurate information to answer these questions. Hence, the first step in menu engineering is to systematically gather information about each current menu item. This should include standard recipe cost and direct labor cost.

All recipes require lesser or greater time and skill depending on the product recipe and stage of raw or readiness of the ingredients. For our purposes in this article, we will treat direct labor, a semi-variable cost, as a fixed cost. The subject of direct labor input to each menu item will not be discussed.

Using Menu Engineering

Let's see how menu engineering works in actual practice. Johny's Grill is a table specialty restaurant with ten items on its dinner menu. Illustration 4 shows how menu engineering was used to analyze Johny's menu for a 30-day period.

1. First, the operator lists all menu entrees in column A. Only entree items are listed. Do not list appetizers, desserts or other side items. Do not list alcoholic beverage sales on this list. The ratio of food to beverage sales is a key to successful merchandising in most restaurants. The analysis of beverage sales, however, should be done separately. While we separate purchases for the purposes of our menu analysis, the successful operator is always concerned with the guests' total expenditure.

Daily specials must also be analyzed separately.

By listing purchases of daily specials separately, their impact on the menu is more easily identified. If the operator's suggestive selling program is effective, daily specials should become popular with relatively high contribution margins.

2. The total number of purchases for each item is listed in Column B, menu mix. All purchases are listed on a per person basis.

3. Each item's sales is divided by the total number of purchases—3,000 in this case—to determine that item's menu mix percentage, column C.

4. In column D, each item's menu mix percentage is categorized as either high or low. Any menu item that is lower than 70% of the menu mix average percentage is considered low. Any item that is 70% or above the average is considered high. On a ten-item menu, for example, each item would theoretically get 10% of the mix. On a 20-item menu the average would be 5%. For Johny's ten-item menu, we multiply 10% times 70% to get the desired menu mix percentage rate of .07, or 7%. Any item 7% or higher is considered high. Any item less than 7% is low.

5. Each item's published menu selling price is listed in Column E.

6. Each item's standard food cost is listed in column F. An item's standard portion cost is composed of standard recipe costs, garnish cost, and supplemental food cost. Not all items, however, will have all three cost components.

7. The contribution margin for each item is listed in column G. Contribution margins are determined by subtracting the item's standard food cost (column F) from its selling price (column E).

8. In column H we determine the total menu revenues by multiplying the number of purchases of each item (column B) by its selling price (column E).

9. In column I we determine the total menu food cost by multiplying each item's standard food cost (column F) by the number of items purchased (column B).

10. The total menu contribution margin is listed in column J. This is determined by multiplying each item's contribution margin (column G) times the item's total number of purchases (column B).

11. In column K we list the contribution margin percentage for each item. This is determined by dividing each item's contribution margin by the total menu contribution margin which is the total of column J, $9,664.80.

12. Each item's contribution margin is categorized as either high or low in column L, depending upon whether or not the item exceeds the

menu's average contribution margin. The menu's average contribution margin is determined by dividing the total contribution margin—$9,664.80—column J, by the total number of items sold, 3,000. The average contribution margin for Johny's Grill is $3.22.

13. We use all the data we have gathered to classify each item into categories in column M. Each menu item is classified as either a Star, Plow Horse, Puzzle, or Dog. These classifications are

Average CM Line

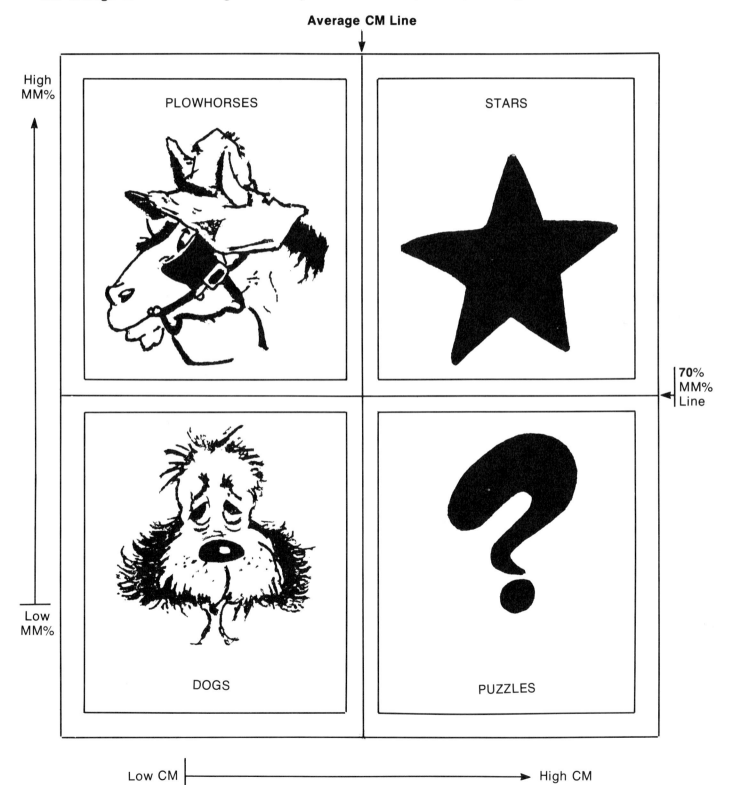

High MM%

PLOWHORSES

STARS

70% MM% Line

Low MM%

DOGS

PUZZLES

Low CM

High CM

standard marketing theory terms (see below).

14. In column N we list the decisions made on each item. Should the item be retained, repositioned, replaced, or repriced?

The Four Key Menu Categories

When accurate information has been gathered and analyzed for each menu item as we have done in Illustration 4, the items are then categorized for decision making. All menu items can be grouped into four categories: Stars, Plow Horses, Puzzles, and Dogs.

Stars. Menu items high in both popularity and contribution margin. Stars are the most popular items on your menu. They may be your signature items.

Plow Horses. Menu items high in popularity but low in contribution margin. Plow horses are demand generators. They may be the lead item on your menu or your signature item. They are often sigificant to the restaurant's popularity with price-conscious buyers.

Puzzles. Menu items low in popularity but high in contribution margin. In other words, Puzzles yield a high profit per item sold, but they are hard to sell.

Dogs. Menu items low in popularity and low in contribution margin. These are your losers. They are unpopular, and they generate little profit.

Developing Strategies for the Categories

Once you have grouped your menu into the four key categories you are ready to formulate strategies for dealing with them. Each category must be evaluated separately and separate strategies must be formulated for each.

Strategies for Stars. You must maintain rigid specifications for quality, quantity, and presentation of all Star items. Locate them in a highly visible position on the menu. Test them occasionally for price inelasticity. Are guests willing to pay more for these items, and still buy them in significant quantity? The Super Stars of your menu—highest priced Stars—may be less price sensitive than any other items on the menu. If so, these items may be able to carry a larger portion of any increase in cost of goods and labor.

Strategies for Plow Horses. These items are often an important reason for a restaurant's popularity. Increase their prices carefully. If Plow Horses are highly price sensitive, attempt to pass only the

cost of goods increase on to the menu price. Or, consider placing the increase on to a Super Star item. Test for a negative effect on demand (elasticity). Make any price increase in stages (from $4.55 to $4.75 then $4.95). If it is necessary to increase prices, pass through only the additional cost. Do not add more. Relocate non-signature and low contribution margin Plow Horses to a lower profile position on the menu. Attempt to shift demand to more profitable items by merchandising and menu positioning. If the item is an image maker or signature item hold its current price as long as possible in periods of high price sensitivity.

Determine the direct labor cost of each Plow Horse to establish its labor and skill intensiveness. If the item requires high skills or is labor intensive, consider a price increase or substitution. Also, consider reducing the item's standard portion without making the difference noticeable. Merchandise the Plow Horse by packaging it with side items to increase its contribution margin. Another option is to use the item to create a "better value alternative." For example, prime ribs can be sold by the inch, and steaks can be sold by the ounce. This offers guests an opportunity to spend more, and get more value.

Strategies for Puzzles. Take them off the menu. Particularly if a Puzzle is low in popularity, requires costly or additional inventory, has poor shelf life, requires skilled or labor intensive preparation, and is of inconsistent quality. Another option is to reposition the Puzzle and feature it in a more popular location on the menu. You can try adding value to the item through Table D'Hote packaging. Rename it. A Puzzle's popularity can be affected by what it is called, especially if the name can be made to sound familiar.

Decrease the Puzzle's price. The item may have a contribution margin that is too high and is facing price resistance. Care must be taken, however, not to lower the contribution margin to a point where the Puzzle draws menu share from a Star. Increase the item's price and test for inelasticity. A Puzzle that has relative high popularity may be inelastic.

Limit the number of Puzzles you allow on your menu. Puzzles can create difficulties in quality consistency, slow production down, and cause inventory and cost problems. You must accurately evaluate the effect Puzzle items have on your image. Do they enhance your image?

Strategies for Dogs. Eliminate all Dog items if possible. Foodservice operators are often intimidated by influential guests to carry a Dog on the menu. The way to solve this problem is to carry the item in inventory (assuming it has a shelf life) but not on the menu. The special guest is offered the opportunity to have the item made to order upon request. Charge extra for this service. Raise the Dog's price to Puzzle status. Some items in the Dog category may have market potential. These tend to be the more popular Dogs, and may be converted to Puzzles.

Whenever possible, replace Dogs with more popular items. You may have too many items. It is not unusual to discover a number of highly unpopular menu items with little, if any, relation to other more popular and profitable items held in inventory. Do not be afraid to terminate Dogs, especially when demand is not satisfactory.

Strategies for New Menu Items

There are three reasons to add new menu items: to increase demand, to increase contribution margin, and to create greater market share for your property. And there are strategies to make these things happen.

Each new menu item should be carefully considered and pretested as a special before adding it to the menu. When adding new items, attempt to build off of products already in inventory. Try to develop new items that require low skills, and are not labor intensive. Add items that have the growth potential to become highly popular. Items not easily prepared at home—roasts and fish, for example—have good potential. Make sure food cost for the new item is relatively stable. And finally, aim for items with low food cost and good plate coverage. This will allow you to give the item a lower price and still maintain a high contribution margin.

Strategies for increasing demand. Add a menu item with already proven popularity to increase frequency or broaden your market. For example, salad bars have high appeal to light eaters, and have proven their effectiveness in both fast food and specialty restaurants. Eggs and omelettes are also items with high popularity. Another way to increase demand is by adding a signature item that cannot be found anywhere else.

Strategies for increasing contribution margin. Try to add new items with high contribution margins, especially if they do not require additional inventory. For example, 20 oz. prime rib is a particularly good item to add when smaller cuts are already being served.

Strategies for signature items. Signature items, like Plow Horses, may be the most important reason for your restaurant's popularity. These are items found only at your operation, the specialty of the house. Properly developed and merchandised, they can create greater market share, and bring prestige and visibility to your operation. Add signature items with the utmost care.

Summary and Conclusion

Menu engineering provides management with a tool to evaluate the effectiveness of its current menu, and to make decisions on menu pricing, content and design. It is a step-by-step process that helps management develop a menu with both popularity and profits.

Every attempt to improve your menu must begin with a statistical analysis of your current situation. By categorizing and classifying menu items through logical mathematical procedures, menu engineering enables the operator to make the right decisions.

The key to any menu's success is whether or not it produces more customers and more contribution dollars. A foodservice operator's objective must always be to make the next menu more profitable and appealing to the guest.

Part III

Research For Strategic Marketing Planning

The long-run success of any hospitality firm depends upon how well managers make decisions about the future. There is an old saying that successes of today are products of the past and successes of the future will be products of today. Decisions to build more rooms or add meeting and convention facilities and services to a hotel are based upon management's expectations of the size and characteristics of future markets. So are decisions to build new hotels, buy more airplanes, open new restaurants, or enlarge existing restaurants.

To make decisions about today's action requires that management have relevant information available. Marion Harper stated it well when he said, "To manage a business well is to manage its future; and to manage the future is to manage information." [1] As markets for hospitality products and services become increasingly complex, management has an increasing need for information. Several things have happened in the hospitality industry that have created a need for more and better information about both present and potential markets.

First is the growth in the markets served. Fifty or sixty years ago hotels served primarily one group of customers and managers often knew many guests personally. Managers knew their guests' needs and wants firsthand. Also geographical market areas were often restricted; people were not as mobile as they are today. But as people became more mobile, markets expanded. Hotels began to serve a variety of market segments. Consequently, today's managers typically have little firsthand knowledge about guests. They must turn elsewhere for information about present guests and potential guests.

Second, as more people travel and use hospitality products and services, and as incomes increase, guests become more demanding and selective. It is more difficult today to predict guests' expectations and their ideas of value. Thus, managers today feel a greater need for information concerning guests' preferences than at any time in the past.

The third factor is the increased usage by hospitality firms of marketing tools such as advertising and sales promotions. Managers need to know the effectiveness of the tools they use, but information must be gathered and analyzed to learn results.

Most hospitality managers agree that there is great need for more and better marketing information. And they are right. Good strategic marketing planning requires useful information. Information obtained from market research and other sources surrounds the process of strategic marketing planning (as the model in Part II shows) and is the foundation for planning. Intelligent planning cannot go forward without information.

1.Marion Harper Jr., "A New Profession to Aid Management," *Journal of Marketing,* January, 1961, p. 1.

So where does the information come from? Many progressive companies are developing marketing information systems (MIS) to meet the needs of management for marketing information. Complete marketing information systems generally consist of at least three subsystems—an internal reports system, a marketing intelligence system, and a marketing research system.

Every hospitality firm produces internal reports to supply management with information relating to daily revenues, occupancy rates, payroll costs, and guest mix. Many of these reports provide timely marketing information. Reservation files, for example, are a ready source of information about future levels of business and can quickly alert managers to soft periods.

Computerized systems have become a major tool in providing timely marketing information. Large volumes of data can be processed rapidly, thus producing needed reports at the time they are useful. Properly implemented, computerized systems can furnish managers with more and better internal information than has heretofore been possible. They can do it faster and at less cost.

A second major source of information is a marketing intelligence system. Marketing intelligence is information about what is happening in the marketing environment in which the firm operates. Managers gather marketing intelligence through routine activities such as reading newspapers and trade publications, listening to news broadcasts, talking to guests, attending trade association meetings, talking to outsiders, and talking to subordinates.

While these intelligence-gathering activities are somewhat casual and tend to occur in the normal course of events, more formal methods of intelligence gathering are available. One is to train salespeople and other employees to be alert for information relating to activities of competitors, general market conditions, and guests' changing needs. Comparison shopping also provides knowledge about what competitors are or are not doing. Marketing intelligence can also be purchased from outside sources.

Marketing research is a third source of marketing information. Managers often need specific information upon which to base decisions. This means deciding what information is required and determining how that information will be obtained; in short, researching the market. Marketing research consists of systematically collecting data, analyzing it, and then reporting it in usable form.

There are two types of data used in marketing research. One type is secondary data. The other type is primary data. Secondary data are data that already exist. Usually they have been gathered for purposes other than the problem at hand. Primary data are original data collected specifically to provide answers to the question being considered.

Large quantities of secondary data are available from a variety of sources. Some sources of secondary data are listed below.

- Internal records. Records such as occupancy rates, guest history files, and similar records often provide useful information.
- Government. Federal and state governments are major sources of marketing information. State travel bureaus often collect and publish large quantities of information.
- Trade associations. Trade associations such as the American Hotel & Motel Association and the National Restaurant Association collect quantities of useful marketing data. Other associations such as the Air Transport Association of America and the National Association of Motor Bus Operators are often excellent sources of information.
- Private business firms. Two major sources of information are the firms of Pannell Kerr Forster and Laventhol and Horwath.
- Marketing firms. Firms specializing in marketing research have large quantities of data, as do advertising and other media firms.

- Universities and research foundations. Universities and research foundations often are sources of secondary information.
- Professional journals. Professional journals and specialized business publications often provide useful information.

Although secondary data are fairly abundant and available at relatively reasonable costs, they have limited value and should be used with caution. Remember, they were collected for purposes other than the problem at hand.

Primary data are much more useful because they are gathered specifically to provide information about a well-defined question or problem. They are also more expensive to obtain. Primary data are gathered by using one or more of the four research methods that follow:

- Observation. Researchers might circulate in a hotel lobby and listen to comments made by guests, or they might stay as guests in competing hotels to observe facilities and services and listen to guests' comments.
- Casual interviewing. Researchers might talk to guests, travel agents or airline employees, and previous hotel customers.
- Focus group interviewing. Small groups of people (ideally, six to ten) are gathered to discuss a hotel, restaurant, airline, or some other kind of firm. Or they may be asked to discuss how they go about doing something; how they choose a hotel, their needs, their expectations, and their dislikes. Comments are recorded and analyzed for answers to marketing questions.
- Formal survey research. Good formal research doesn't just happen; it is a job for trained professional researchers. Consequently, few hotel managers are qualified to conduct formal research and, even if they are, they seldom have the time for such projects. The wise choice is to employ professionals (in-house if it is economically feasible to do so). Otherwise, many excellent research firms are available.

Strategic marketing planning, then, is based upon information. Without information there can be no planning. The articles in this section emphasize the need for marketing data and suggest techniques that hospitality managers may use.

What You Need to Know Before You Spend Money on Marketing

by Dr. Peter C. Yesawich

Peter Yesawich, Ph.D., received his doctorate from Cornell University's School of Hotel Administration where his areas of concentration were psychology, marketing, and communication theory. He is vice president and director of marketing research for Robinson's, Inc. This article is an adaptation of his presentation at an AH&MA convention.

The components of a successful marketing plan are the same for all lodging establishments regardless of size, location and configuration. They are:

1. Timeliness, in the sense that the program acts on what is occurring;

2. Cohesiveness, in the sense that every component of the plan should complement every other component; and

3. Focus, in that the plan should be targeted against specific groups of prospects.

If marketing decisions are made outside the framework of a total marketing plan, the result is a haphazard program that achieves little in proportion to the costs.

Robinson's recommends seven steps in formulating a marketing plan: (1) profile your property; (2) profile your competition; (3) identify your prospects; (4) establish marketing objectives; (5) formulate strategy; (6) execute plan, and (7) establish means of measuring results.

Property Profile. A property profile should include both physical and intangible features. Physical features include, among others, sizes and types of guest rooms; number and types of restaurants; location and availability of meeting facilities; extent of recreational facilities such as tennis, golf and swimming. Intangible features include the sort of information you get from intensive guest reaction surveys on promptness of service and courtesy of personnel, and also include whatever information you can put together on the image your property has in the public mind due to media and word of mouth advertising. An intangible feature might also be chain affiliation.

Profile of Competition. Within most market areas, there are several properties that compete for the same business. You must find out what properties constitute your competition, and what are their strengths and weaknesses in location, physical features and, insofar as possible, intangible features. Without this knowledge, it is impossible to establish what is unique about your appeal.

Prime Prospects. Within your market area, certain travelers represent prospect groups that are most likely to produce business for you. They may be defined demographically as to residence age, income level and level of educational attainment. They may be identified psychographically in terms of life style and travel behavior. The latter includes mode of travel, purpose of hotel/motel stay, length of stay, range of acceptable rates and interest in special packages.

Marketing Objectives. Marketing objectives should be based on realistic occupancy goals. They must also relate to how much you can budget to attain what goals. You shouldn't expect to budget the same amount to produce an additional 6,000 room nights that you would budget to produce an additional 3,000.

Marketing Strategy. The nucleus of your marketing plan is the strategy you formulate once you have profiled your own and competitive properties, identified prime prospect groups and set occupancy goals. Strategy formulation is the matching of prime prospects with your property profile.

Plan Execution. The marketing plan should be executed over a predetermined period that usually covers a 12-month period. Execution must employ a graphic, thematic approach to what you have to sell.

Measurement. Once you have related the above components in a marketing plan to each other—the profiles, the prospects, the objectives, the strategy and the execution—you must establish

From *Lodging* (January 1978) pp. 7-9. Reprinted by permission of *Lodging*.

Seven Interrelated Steps in Formulating Marketing Plan
Research Information Gleaned from Three Guest Records

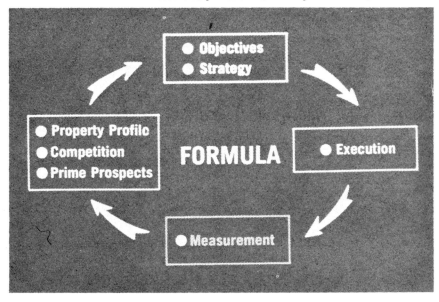

procedures for measuring results of your expenditures on marketing.

Let us approach the question of how to measure results against expenditures by discussing how to research guest records to identify prime targets and how to analyze information attained.

Research

Marketing plans should not be structured around intuitive beliefs about the tangible and intangible appeals of your property or assumptions about the characteristics or prime prospects. Rely on fact uncovered by research.

Researching the physical and intangible attributes of your property requires a checklist. Use the same checklist for inventorying the strengths and weaknesses of your competition as you use for your own property. (Editor's note: the reader might find help in formulating checklists by studying the LODGING series in June, July, September and November 1976, titled "Marketing for Motor Hotels." See especially, checklists on Position—including location; Product—meaning physical facilities; People—implying human assets; and Price—meaning just what it says.)

Researching prime prospects is a more crucial task. You need to think of travelers to a market area as comprising a prospect pie and yourself as deserving a slice.

Begin by considering secondary sources. Among them, federal, regional, and local reports on travel movement; previous surveys that map trends in

consumer travel patterns and attitudes. These secondary sources are usually available free of charge.

Continue by considering primary sources: (1) reservation requests; (2) registration cards and (3) guest folio forms. From these sources, you can get 12 critical pieces of information for analysis leading to the identity of your prime markets:

1. Where guests come from (name and address).
2. Date of reservation.
3. Method of reservation (WATS line; mail; personal call; through a representative, etc.).
4. Date of arrival.
5. Length of stay.
6. Number in party, broken down by adults and children, etc.
7. Room rate paid.
8. Package plan purchased.
9. Type of guest (identifying purpose of trip—commercial, corporate, recreational).
10. Group affiliation.
11. Total charge (and details that reflect spending type).
12. Method of payment (cash, check, credit card, billing).

Marketers of consumer goods spend tens of thousands of dollars on research to obtain the type of information that is routine to the lodging industry. Analysis of that information, however, is not as simple as that statement infers. Smaller properties usually analyze information manually; larger hotels, by electronic computing.

Data Analysis Provides Guides for Budgeting Expenditures
Advertising Tools are Usually Used in Combinations

ADI	Population Base*	% Budget	% Share	Action
New York	38%	25%	16%	—
Miami	10%	3%	6%	+
Tampa/ St. Pete	5%	0%	2%	+

*INCLUDES ADJUSTMENT FOR HOUSEHOLD DISCRETIONARY INCOME.

Computer technology is now advanced to the point where market data analysis is very rapid. For example, guest records at a 250-room hotel for an entire year can be electronically analyzed in 10 minutes, provided, of course, that data are collected and formatted properly. The same analysis conducted manually would take at least four persons a minimum of six weeks.

Analysis

The advantage of computer analysis is evident. For instance, you can get instant analysis of zip code of residence. You can get analysis per geographic market area, or Area of Dominant Influence (ADI). What this means is an area covered by major media emanating from a specific city. (ADIs, incidentally, are not restricted by legal boundaries such as city or state limits; they present a precise picture of actual prospect concentrations.)

Guest registrations, per ADI, may be analyzed in terms of absolute frequency or adjusted frequency. Absolute frequency is the actual number of registrations from the area. Adjusted frequency is the percentage of total registrations represented by registrations from the specific ADI.

Assume, for example, that a hotel had 200 registrations from the New York ADI during a 30-day period, and a total of 1270 registrations from all areas. The New York ADI would have an absolute frequency of 200 and an adjusted frequency of 15.9%.

In one of the illustrations shown here, three ADIs are listed—New York, Miami and Tampa/St. Petersburg—and the adjusted frequency is shown as a percentage share of total business represented by each of these ADIs.

Budgeting

The illustration helps us understand how specific market action may be based on an analysis of data. Two types of market information are added: the population base of each ADI adjusted for household discretionary income, and the percentage of the marketing budget allocated to the three ADIs during the reporting period.

Note that the New York ADI represents 38% of the population base from which the hotel received business during the period (or 38% of families of four with effective incomes exceeding $15,000 in the market areas currently producing business for the hotel). Further, note that during the period the hotel spent 25% of its market budget on the New York ADI but got only 16% of its business from the area.

This would indicate that the New York ADI is a saturated market at the time under study. The amount of business attracted is not proportionate to the amount budgeted to get that business. Consequently, it would appear that the budget for the New York ADI should be decreased and reallocated elsewhere.

Look now at Miami. This ADI represents 10% of

the case-in-point hotel's effective population base; 3% of its marketing budget for the period; and 6% of business produced. This time, it appears that the relationship is disproportionate in favor of arrivals. This indicates considerable potential for additional business from this area and that intensified marketing efforts would be justified.

Finally, note the Tampa/St. Petersburg ADI. This area represents about 5% of the population base in the hotel's market. During the reporting period, none of the marketing budget was invested in this ADI, yet it produced 2% of the hotel's business. On the basis of these data, Tampa/St. Petersburg represents a potentially lucrative source of new business and should become a target area for a marketing program.

Area of residence (zip code, ADI) represents only one item that may be analyzed to construct guest profiles. In fact, "Where guests come from" is only one of 12 items (see above) that may be taken from registration-related documents that should be analyzed in relation to each other. When combined, they yield a rich picture of who your prospects are and what patterns characterize their travel behavior.

Having established guest profiles and identified prime prospects, you are better prepared to (1) allocate marketing budget both by media and by geography, and (2) set the parameters for a graphic and thematic approach that will appeal to your prospective audience.

As you approach final decisions on how to spend your marketing money, remember to be realistic in relating objectives to marketing dollars available, and in setting occupancy and sales objectives that are capable of measurement. At this point, these questions must be considered:

1. What message will be delivered?
2. To which prospects?
3. With what intended effect (room nights, length of stay, weekend or midweek arrival, seasonal or offseason)?
4. And measurable by what devices?

In the selection of tools, consider (1) print or broadcast advertising; (2) outdoor advertising; (3) collateral material; and (4) direct mail and special promotions.

Tools chosen will vary by prime prospect. To reach traveling businessmen you might choose direct mail supported by a limited but well-targeted consumer-media campaign. To reach social guest prospects traveling by auto you might lean heavily on outdoor advertising supported by a direct mail campaign to the travel trade that could presell the social guest before he or she leaves home.

A later article will cover planned creativity in target marketing.

This article, hopefully, has convinced you that before you spend money on marketing—the innkeeping activity most susceptible to guesswork and waste—you should profile your property, profile your competition, and profile your guest.

In sum, research before you spend.

Protecting Service Markets With Consumer Feedback

by Arthur J. Daltas

Arthur J. Daltas, a 1973 Boston University MBA valedictorian, is currently a consultant with Cambridge Communications Group, Inc., a marketing and management consulting firm located in Cambridge, Massachusetts. He wishes to acknowledge Professors Lawrence Wortzel and Gerald Leader, both of Boston University, who aided in the preparation of this article.

Most organizations are vulnerable to service deficiencies but the best examples are found among those that must maintain very decentralized operations and that depend on repeat business. Many of these companies have well-defined marketing efforts supporting their businesses. They may have a nationally accepted image and the policies, procedures, and products to reinforce that image. Unfortunately, the final translation of all these elements into daily behavior by employees is seldom perfect. Compounding the problem are customer attitudes and expectations that change with time and location. Because of these factors, service is always a locally manufactured item, even though it may be backed by a national organization.

In marketing consumer packaged goods, the key factors inducing both trial and repeat patronage are advertising and product quality or features, respectively. It is realistic to think of advertising's function as one of telling consumers what to expect about the product in order to induce product trial. The functions of product quality and product features are to encourage patronage by providing a pleasant experience. Both the advertising dimensions and the product quality and feature dimensions are controllable centrally, by the product manufacturer.

The marketer whose "product" is a service or whose "product" includes service is in a much different position. Such a marketer can control advertising, and thus, can control consumers' desire to try the service "product," but the marketer of services does not have the same control as a product manufacturer over what is actually delivered to the consumer. Moreover, the quality of the service consumers receive is likely to be the key determinant of their willingness to use the service again.

The nature of consumers' experience with a service is under even less management control where the service is offered at multiple sites, since important dimensions of the service "product" are usually "manufactured" at the site at which the service is offered to consumers. It is the local manager and employees who must translate the policies and procedures—the service package—and the advertising message into daily problem-solving behavior in order to retain the customers who have been attracted to the service. For example, a fast food provider can advertise "Have it your way" until he is very hoarse indeed, but his advertising will soon lose its effect if the sites that provide the food appear unwilling or unable to provide the specific combination of condiments requested by individual customers.

Our experience with a variety of service firms in several industries as diverse as fast food chains, hotels, bank branches, and automobile service centers has convinced us that service "product" providers are generally experiencing a problem that is chronic and severe. All too often the service actually "produced" for a consumer is not at all what the advertising promises.

Because a clientele is made up of many individual customers, determining what particular customers dislike (and like) about an individual store compared to what they expected, and then having the local manager act quickly on that information, is critical. To avoid losing the future stream of purchases from these customers, these tasks must be accomplished before the customers decide not to return.

This article was originally published in the May 1977 issue of *The Cornell Hotel and Restaurant Administration Quarterly*, pp. 73-77, and is reprinted here with the permission of the Cornell University School of Hotel Administration. 1977.

Inadequate Information at the Local Level

In most cases, service businesses rely on inadequate means of assessing and responding to consumer behavior at the local level. These methods typically include financial control measures and complaint or suggestion programs. Each falls far short of fulfilling the need, as a brief review will demonstrate.

Traditional financial control methods are important for the long-run success of the operations. They help all levels of management to track the activity that goes on below them, but this control information is inadequate for evaluating the relationship between the local stores and its customers. Sales revenues, inventory levels, turnover, and profit are summary performance measures and, as such, suffer from three major shortcomings. First, they only indicate *that* something is wrong, not what is wrong. Second, they provide information long after the fact. It is not unlikely that, by the time higher management discovers through traditional financial reports that one of its stores is operating below its potential or is actually losing business, many customers already may have been completely alienated. Thus, while traditional methods are important for the overall control of the organization, they do little for the local manager in terms of pinpointing the problems affecting his customers. Even when they do act as signals, they lag well behind the attitudes and actions of the buyers that produce them.

Complaint or suggestion programs are inadequate because they only tap the opinion of the most flagrantly abused or the most highly satisfied customers. Typically, real complaints are often the final contact with a particular customer. Complaint systems also tend to produce negative information with "halo" effects, i.e., "everything's wrong." Thus, the complaint may be only the culmination of other issues which remain hidden, and the relative importance of the issues may also remain unknown. Conversely, suggestion programs can produce innovative ideas but seldom point out real weaknesses. Neither type of program puts the true strengths of the business in perspective with what may be going wrong (or where opportunities for improvement lie) in a positive, comprehensive way. Even local consumer panels, though helpful, are often unrepresentative and provide subjective feedback, usually only to managers. In short, no adequate forum of information exchange is created for the employee, the consumer, or the service organization.

Finally, while market research provides companies with a far better means of understanding their customers than ever before, it does not fulfill all the marketing needs at the local level. It tends to deal with the broad issues of stimulating demand and defining the common characteristics of its buyers, while overlooking local differences. Like financial measures, programs and policies resulting from market research tend to lag well behind the attitudes and action of the buyers. Moreover, the opinions of local managers and employees are not solicited when market research is conducted. Local management and staff are therefore likely to view subsequent marketing efforts or policy changes only as a reflection of the wishes of higher management, rather than a response to the perceptions of their own customers. Rightly or wrongly, those who work in the decentralized units often view higher management's directives as ivory tower theory. But if customers provide information to those units, thus reinforcing policies and procedures, the field personnel are likely to follow them more enthusiastically.

Each of the above activities falls short of creating the most useful connection between customer information and the actions of the organization. There is a way, though, by which a strong relationship can be built and which augments the other activities.

Rx: Link Local Customer Feedback With Local Action

Using specialized materials, it is now possible to diagnose some of the major causes of gaps between product promise and customer experience. More important, it is possible to implement a new type of solution for closing the gaps: a consumer-survey feedback system.

Given the right feedback tools, customers, local managers, and employees can effectively work together to create and maintain a mutually beneficial environment. In turn, this will help ensure longer-lasting customer satisfaction and can help expand as well as preserve the market share of the local unit. These goals may be achieved through the establishment of a consumer-survey feedback system, as shown in Figure 1. In such a system, the actions of the local manager and employees are linked to the opinions of the customers. These actions and opinions are then regularly fine-tuned as time passes. This same link can be used to provide information to higher levels of the organization where other adjustments can be made. In effect, the customer becomes part of the internal information system of the local operations and of the entire organization.

Basically, a consumer-feedback system consists of specifically developed questionnaires and a defined analytical process for use by lower-level managers. In final form, local managers (or a special team) are able to administer a relatively brief questionnaire to customers periodically. The questionnaire can be designed for local hand-tabulation or for centralized computer processing. With results in hand, the local manager, either alone or with assistance, determines weak areas and initiates corrective action within established guidelines. Periodic questionnaire administrations are used subsequently to determine the effectiveness of action taken and to identify new areas of concern.

A consumer-feedback system for the local level of a service organization provides two important problem-solving elements; speed of response and direct relevance of the information. The swiftness is provided by a built-in ability to act on problems promptly without working through hierarchical

channels. By addressing customer attitudes and perceptions regularly, the manager can deal with "live" information on which he can take specific, timely action. Because the data are directly relevant to the local level, immediate and often minor corrections avoid both prolonged diagnostic procedures and broad corrective programs, which take time to design and implement and which are likely to be far more costly.

A Consumer-Survey Feedback System That Works

Experience with these systems has shown those aspects which are of particular importance to their successful design and use. In capsule form, the characteristics are as follows:

1. The instrument (the questionnaire) must be carefully tailored to the customer attitudes which will best indicate the degree of success in delivering the critical elements of the service. In other words, the attitudes should be demonstrably related to maintaining or improving *revenue and profit*. This ensures that the system is not just maximizing positive attitudes but also resulting in tangible benefits

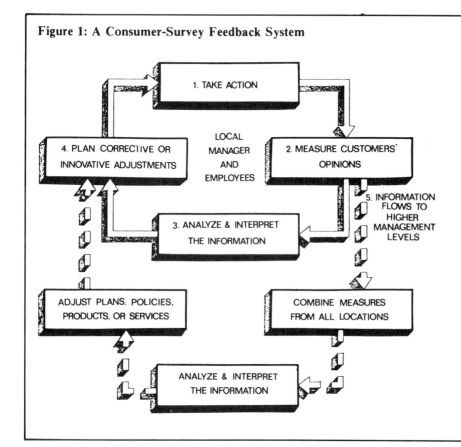

Figure 1: A Consumer-Survey Feedback System

1. TAKE ACTION

4. PLAN CORRECTIVE OR INNOVATIVE ADJUSTMENTS

LOCAL MANAGER AND EMPLOYEES

2. MEASURE CUSTOMERS' OPINIONS

3. ANALYZE & INTERPRET THE INFORMATION

5. INFORMATION FLOWS TO HIGHER MANAGEMENT LEVELS

ADJUST PLANS, POLICIES, PRODUCTS, OR SERVICES

COMBINE MEASURES FROM ALL LOCATIONS

ANALYZE & INTERPRET THE INFORMATION

1. LOCAL MANAGERS AND EMPLOYEES SERVE CUSTOMERS' NEEDS ON A DAILY BASIS, USING LOCALLY MODIFIED PROCEDURES ALONG WITH GENERAL CORPORATE POLICIES AND PROCEDURES.

2. BY MEANS OF A STANDARDIZED AND LOCALLY SENSITIVE QUESTIONNAIRE, DETERMINE THE NEEDS AND ATTITUDES OF CUSTOMERS ON A REGULAR BASIS.

3. COMPARING FINANCIAL DATA, EXPECTATIONS, AND PAST ATTITUDE INFORMATION, DETERMINE STRENGTHS AND WEAKNESSES AND THEIR PROBABLE CAUSES.

4. DETERMINE WHERE AND HOW EFFORT SHOULD BE APPLIED TO CORRECT WEAKNESSES AND PRESERVE STRENGTHS. REPEAT THE PROCESS BY TAKING ACTION — STEP 1 — AND MAINTAIN IT TO ATTAIN A STEADY STATE OR TO EVOLVE IN TERMS OF CUSTOMER CHANGES.

5. A SIMILAR PROCESS CAN TAKE PLACE AT HIGHER LEVELS, USING AGGREGATED DATA FROM THE FIELD AND THE EXISTING POLICY FLOWS OF THE ORGANIZATION.

to the company. If the survey instrument is not useful, the system will show this very quickly.

2. The survey items are categorized into attitude dimensions that lend themselves to managerial action. There are, of course, some issues which are outside the purview of the local manager and employees. Distinctions must be made between the problem areas that are not controllable (or only partially controllable) at the local level and those that are. This helps focus problem-solving efforts at the most appropriate levels in the organization.

3. The items must be tailored to capture regional or local differences. The aim is to use the information to develop the appropriate managerial emphasis so that service coincides with actual customer expectations. Otherwise, only the rules get satisfied, not necessarily the customer.

4. The items should lend themselves to aggregation so that higher management can track broad patterns in comparison with overall programs and policies. The instrument should also be flexible, permitting higher management to explore the newly emerging attitudes and needs of its customers.

5. The information must be useful as soon as possible at the location from which it is gathered. Whether hand-tabulated or computer-processed, it must be quickly and inexpensively converted into meaningful indicators. By doing this, local managers are encouraged to use their initiative instead of constantly checking with management. Such checking typically forces distant, higher managers to set the daily priorities for local managers—a situation in which real, pressing problems are often overlooked.

6. The information must not be used punitively against the managers or employees, for to do so is the surest way of receiving misinformation. Instead, they should be measured only on their profit-performance indicators, perferably in the context of an MBO program. The consumer-feedback system is a tool to aid performance, a tool by which learning and self-correction take place. The information from the system can be used to measure the effectiveness of the system and to indicate where managerial attention should be focused, but to do this properly, it must not be used as an evaluation tool of one person by another.

7. The system can be used as often as necessary for a "quick snapshot" or a comprehensive tracking of the consumer situation. Although regular use is recommended, as few as two surveys a year can yield significant trend information and can identify gray areas needing corrective action.

Hallmark Hotels: An Example

In the fall of 1974, the management of Hallmark Hotels, Inc., faced some unhappy facts.* A detailed physical review of its facilities showed that eight out of the firm's twelve hotels would require major renovations to maintain the high standards set in the past. However, the long-term debt position of the corporation could only support renovations for perhaps two of the hotels. In addition, the company's overall profits had declined for the second year in a row.

The executives decided to use a temporary retrenchment strategy, allowing the physical quality of many of their hotels to decline and concentrating renovation investment on one hotel at a time over the next few years. For the hotels where only maintenance would be performed, it was decided that service instead of physical attributes would be emphasized.

The decisions required that a number of questions be answered. For example:

• What would be the net effect on occupancy if the physical plant were allowed to decline and the emphasis were placed on service?

• How could a tighter balance be established between what guests anticipated and what they actually experienced? (Management felt it was an unnecessary expenditure to exceed customer expectations to any large extent, just as it was a loss of future revenue to disappoint those expectations.)

• Since increasing all of the services at all of the hotels would be overly expensive, which services at which hotels should be accented?

• Since service depends a great deal on the motivation of the employees, what should be done to improve their cooperation?

To answer these and other questions, a highly specialized study was conducted. Interviews were conducted with many of Hallmark's corporate managers, hotel managers, employees, and customers. Characteristics of critical importance to the Hallmark hotels in general and to specific Hallmark hotels were identified. These were then used to devise over 200 carefully worded questions, from which 55 were selected for use in the final questionnaire. For example:

• To what extent do you feel the desk clerks were friendly and helpful to you?

---

*this is a hypothetical case example, based in part on a composite of actual work conducted by Cambridge Communications Group, Inc. for three organizations.

- To what extent was your room a relaxing and comfortable place?
- To what extent did the waiters and waitresses seem to know their jobs?
- To what extent did the waiters and waitresses seem friendly?
- To what extent was the food itself satisfying?
- All in all, to what extent were you satisfied with our food service?
- All in all, to what extent were you satisfied with our facilities?
- All in all, to what extent were you satisfied with our staff?

About 40 of the 55 questions were identical for all the Hallmark hotels, and about 15 were unique to each hotel. These latter 15 questions allowed measurement of customer attitudes toward unique aspects of each hotel, since different services were featured in different locations. For example, at the Miami Hallmark, guests tended to stay longer and were thus more interested in food service and room service than guests at other Hallmark hotels. In contrast, guests at the Atlanta Hallmark wanted efficient, personal desk service, probably because of their shorter but more frequent visits. Management at the Chicago Hallmark had a particular interest in how well it was satisfying its convention guests, so the variable part of its questionnaire was oriented accordingly.

The complete consumer-feedback system was then initiated in all hotels. First, virtually all of Hallmark's employees and managers were introduced to the system. They learned that, every four months, Hallmark would survey a sample of its customers' attitudes regarding their current visit. The results were displayed as numerical indices for each question and for groups of questions which described a particular Hallmark characteristic. Indices were computed for individual hotels and for all of the hotels together. An example of the feedback received by each hotel manager is shown in Figure 2.

The managers were encouraged to review the information in terms of what the guests were reporting compared to what they, the managers, expected for their hotels (indicated under "goal" in the numerical report). Managers were then encouraged to share the information with their employees, pointing out the strengths that needed to be preserved and the weaknesses requiring additional attention. Specific courses of action to accomplish these adjustments were then developed by and for each hotel. To augment these efforts, managers were encouraged to conduct additional

Figure 2: Sample Survey Feedback

| | Miami Hallmark | | | All Hotels | |
Question	This Period	Last Period	Goal	This Period	Last Period
Facilities in general	2.5	2.6	2.5	2.9	3.0
Staff in general	4.3	3.9	4.1	4.0	4.0
Visit in general	3.8	3.8	3.8	3.8	3.8
Characteristic A*	4.1	4.0	4.5	4.2	4.1
Characteristic B**	4.7	4.7	4.0	3.1	3.1

* Based on three related questions.
** Based on four related questions.

customer surveys using the same questionnaire during the time between the regular survey periods.

The performance rating and rewards system of the hotel was not dependent on the consumer data. As in the past, such evaluations were based only on the profit performance of the hotel and each person's ability to live up to other standards described in a detailed job description. The survey was an information tool to hone performance using customer opinion as a guide. This purpose would have been defeated if the report were directly linked to rewards and punishments.

Local managers were not allowed to see the data gathered at other Hallmark hotels. However, higher management received detailed information in many different formats appropriate to the more complex analyses they needed to perform.

Results of the consumer-feedback system were very gratifying to all levels of the organization. The manager of the Atlanta Hallmark, for example, discovered that unusually low ratings for his Hallmark facilities were due to a poorly designed maintenance program. Top management, working closely with its advertising agency, adjusted its general and local advertising messages to present the hotel's strengths more accurately without unduly raising expectations, which could ultimately produce customer dissatisfaction. At many of the hotels, another benefit came in the form of a slight decline in employee turnover.

While Hallmark Hotel earnings did not rise dramatically, by the summer of 1976 the decline in profits had been arrested and a slight gain registered. Hallmark's renovation program, although a major cash flow headache, was proceeding ahead of schedule, and the very positive effects of solid occupancy rates coupled with premium prices in the renovated facilities were being felt throughout the Hallmark corporation.

Valuable Side Effects

There are some intangible benefits which can also result from a consumer-survey feedback system. For example, even if ameliorative efforts are not completely on target, the attitudes of customers are likely to be improved to some degree if only because it appears that the store cares enough to ask their opinion. Similarly, it is a positive message from management to employees in the field that management is interested in the customer's opinion. As a kind of internal checklist, it also indicates which opinions are considered important in general and which ones the employees may be overlooking.

Besides tracking the delivery of current services, the consumer-survey feedback instrument can be used to test consumer opinions about new or different services. And with customers involved in the process of improvement, a new kind of motivated customer can result—one who is not just satisfied but who also actively encourages others to patronize the service.

Finally, the strengthening of the relationship between customer and company through consumer-survey feedback can serve the finest ideals of the discipline of marketing. Aiding the human problem solving that goes on at the local level helps bring business action closer to the individual needs and desires of the customer. The successful matching of those needs and desires with what is actually delivered is the heart of a profitable consumer business.

How to Apply the Principles of Marketing To Motels and Small Hotels

by Joyce Wilson

Joyce Wilson, who headquarters in Dallas, is vice-chairman of AH&MA's Public Relations Committee and a holder of an AH&MA Gold Key Award for excellence in public relations. Wilson is also vice president of marketing, La Quinta Motor Inns.

People who manufacture and distribute cars or cereal or soap find it easier to apply the traditional principles of marketing than do we in the lodging business. They can evaluate need for a product, create a product, test it on the market, and revise it to match supply to demand.

But those of us who devote our lives to hotels and motels deal with a less tangible product. Hopefully, we provide a good night's sleep; perhaps a meal. Most of all, however, we provide personal attention to human needs.

The guest leaves us not with a product in his or her hand but with an impression. A memory. And that, my friends, is more difficult to evaluate and revise than a tangible product.

I nonetheless think that to apply the traditional principles of good marketing to the lodging business—even to the small hotel and motel — makes dollars and cents. We have found that at La Quinta, which operates about 75 motor inns. So here are the principles of marketing I recommend:

1. Identify the need for the product.
2. Identify the competition, if any.
3. Develop the product.
4. Package the product.
5. Price the product.
6. Pre-test with its target market.
7. Revise the product and plan, if necessary.
8. Distribute the product.
9. Promote and sell the product.
10. Reinforce brand preference.

From *Lodging* (September 1978) pp. 56-59. Reprinted by permission of *Lodging*.

Identify the Product

Step one is identify what you have to offer. Ask yourself:

1. When is business good and why?
2. What kind of property do I run now? (Commercial, pleasure, combination?)
3. What are my rates?
4. Who am I in a convenient location to serve? (Business travelers, tourists, seasonal groups, conventioners?)
5. What facilities or services do I have to offer?
6. What kind of physical shape is my property in? (Need renovating, remodeling or just cleaning up?)

Chart your occupancy by the week and the month like the example shown here. If figures are available, chart volume for three years so you can note trends by day of week and time of year. Use this graph to determine your peaks and valleys.

Ask yourself why you have peaks. What is attracting customers at that particular time? Then ask what happens to your community when you have slack times.

La Quinta Motor Inns concentrate on the business traveler. We see on the charts of most of our inns dips on the weekend and during the season extending from November into February. A few of our properties, however, surprise us with peaks at these very times.

I talked with one manager who reminded me that his inn is located in the whitewing dove hunting country. So his Novembers run high. Another manager said that although he's located 52 miles from the race track, his business hits a peak during the winter racing season. Both these motels are commercials, with good weekly business. When attractions pull their weekend business up, they show unusually good occupancy for the month.

If you offer special rates (such as commercial),

your daily income statement will show the extent of your business resulting from a special offer.

Guest history files on regular guests (name, address, company, specific needs, dates of visits) are sure indicators of commercial business and can be used for research. More on that later.

Then there's your location (question 4). Take a city map and draw a 5-mile radius around your property like the illustration shown here. Then get out and familiarize yourself with business opportunities you have been missing because you neglected to look under your own nose.

Next, make two lists of your services and facilities. On one, list your appeals to commercial guests; on the other, your appeals to the pleasure traveler. Don't say to yourself, "I already know what I offer." A written list will help you remember what you know so well that you forgot to tell the customer. It will also remind you where you need to strengthen your appeal—perhaps by improving laundry service for commercials and playground equipment for travelers with children.

Study the Competition

Gathering information on your own property is not enough. You must do the same for your competition. Ask the same questions about competitive hotels and motels that you asked about your own.

Make an on-site investigation at competitive properties. Spend a little time in the lobby. Check the key and mail racks. Observe how many people are on the desk and how busy they are. How much phone activity is there? Listen to what they say to their guests. You can learn a lot!

You might inquire if you would have trouble getting a room that night if you find you must stay over and what the rates are. If it's a Wednesday, for example, and there is plenty of room, it is doubtful that they attract much commercial business.

Check the lobby, restrooms and restaurant for an evaluation of housekeeping. Spot check the parking lot. From 5 to 6 p.m., watch for check-in activity; at 7 a.m., count the cars. While you're counting, do a survey of the license plates to help you determine the points of origin of the guests. CB antennas on cars usually indicate a driving traveler and rental cars may indicate those who fly in.

If the desk clerks indicate they are full, ask what other properties they have nearby to which they could refer you. You'll learn about other competitors in your area.

Make a separate evaluation sheet on each of the other hotels/motels in your immediate area. What you learn about their operations and sources of business can help you improve your own.

Get Your House in Order

You have been gathering a lot of information during this evaluation process. You should be very close to preparing a sales plan.

But first, do whatever is necessary to improve your own property. It's hard to look at yourself with the objective eye you turn on the competition. But do your best.

Drive into the parking lot and pretend you've never seen it before. How is the general condition of the landscaping? What about the exterior of the building? Are the grounds free of trash? First impressions count. Get an honest one.

Just as you played detective when you checked the competition, you must now play award-winning actor as you walk into the lobby and pretend you've never seen it before. Is it clean? Warm? Inviting? Is the front desk uncluttered? Efficient? Is there a conversation piece in the lobby?

Watch and listen to your own front desk people as if you were going to grade them on a report card. Are they courteous? Do they recognize regular guests? Do they smile? How do they respond to complaints? Is this the kind of hospitality committee you want to represent you?

Check your rooms. Make a list of repairs that are necessary. This time, as you walk the property, look for missing light bulbs, peeling paint and worn out room furnishings. Some of us spend years congratulating ourselves. Why not spend a few moments taking a hard look at our housekeeping.

Spend some time on the front desk yourself. Take reservations, register guests, answer the phone. Talk to and listen to—everyone. Some of what you'll hear will be less than significant, but you need all the input. The front desk is an excellent place to learn what guests think about your property, where they come from, what brings them to your city, and whether there are other members of their company whose business you might get.

Survey Guest Reaction

If you are chain affiliated, you probably have a guest comment card for your rooms addressed to corporate headquarters. Unless you get to see the card—not just a tabulation of compliments and complaints—you will need to do spot checks of guest reaction yourself.

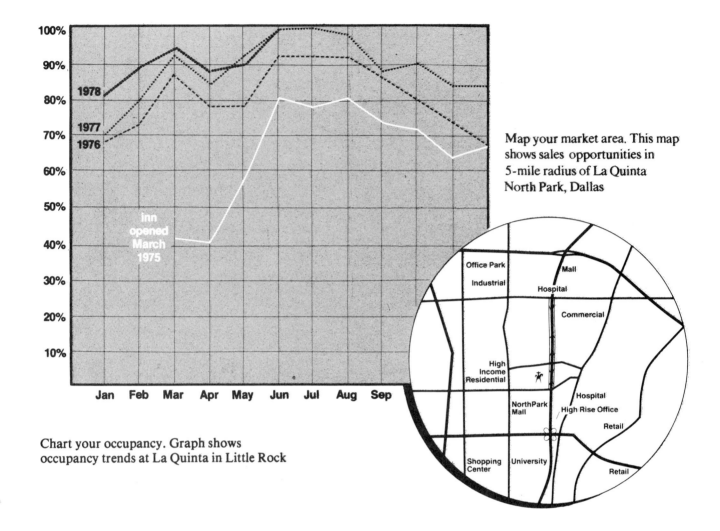

Map your market area. This map
shows sales opportunities in
5-mile radius of La Quinta
North Park, Dallas

Chart your occupancy. Graph shows
occupancy trends at La Quinta in Little Rock

La Quinta Motor Inns runs a survey on all properties periodically. In the interim, our properties do individual spot checks. A quick-print place can reproduce survey sheets inexpensively.

We either hand survey sheets out at the desk, leave them in the room, or mail them to guests. About 20 questions are asked, the most important being why they chose the property. For example, they might be asked to check one of the following:
- Close to next day's activities
- Saw it when ready to stop
- Recommended by a friend, relative, business associate, etc.
- Specified by your company
- Personal preference based on previous experience
- Price
- Stayed here before
- Friendly/courteous personnel
- Other motels full
- Saw billboard
- Called our reservation service

- Advertising, directory, yellow pages, (or however else they could have found you)
- Other

In our experience, the best response is to the mailed questionnaires. We enclose a self-addressed envelope to the inn. Guests, who frequently say "Thanks for asking," are given the option as to whether to sign their names.

Guest history files and guest survey responses will tell you where guests come from and why and guide you in locating highway billboards and making other advertising decisions.

Identify the Market

By now you should be able to make a written statement on what brings you business and when and how much.

What brings people to town? Business? Which ones? Tourist attractions? Industry? Training seminars? Sports activities? Colleges? High school activities? Conventions?

Which of these sources of business are within a 5-mile radius? Hit every source of business in your area with a personal visit. Tell them you want their business, no matter how little, and leave your business card and brochure (or a card with a simple summary of your facilities and services).

Here are a dozen sources of business, some good for weekends, others for weekdays:

1. Schools: High schools, colleges, universities
   A. Interscholastic and intercollegiate sports events
   B. Interscholastic tournaments (drama and speech competition)
   C. Music competition (band and vocal)
   D. Guest speakers, seminars
   E. Visits from prospective students
   F. Family days, homecoming (alumni association)
   G. Sororities, fraternities, departmental and scholastic club activities
2. Hospitals, medical offices, health centers
   A. Pharmaceutical and medical equipment sales reps
   B. Patients or their families needing housing
3. Funeral homes with out-of-town visitors
4. Guest relations offices at local tourist attractions. Be sure your facility is on their recommended list.
5. Sports Centers
   A. Bowling lanes which host tournaments.
   B. Sports arenas, racing tracks, etc. which attract both spectators and participants. (tennis, golf, motorcycle or car racing, basketball, etc.)
6. Churches, synagogues
   A. Visiting religious leaders and/or choral groups.
   B. Educational seminars and study groups
7. Airports
   A. Private—small craft pilot and passengers
   B Municipal—major airlines which may need daily housing for crews, and sometimes, weathered-in-passengers
8. Industry
   A. Training or sales seminars. This may mean housing and/or meeting space.
   B. Vender reps make calls on these people
9. Realtors, home builders have contact with people moving to city in need of temporary housing.
10. Gas station attendants, restaurant personnel, car dealers and mechanics.
11. Large shopping centers
    A. Manufacturer and distributor reps

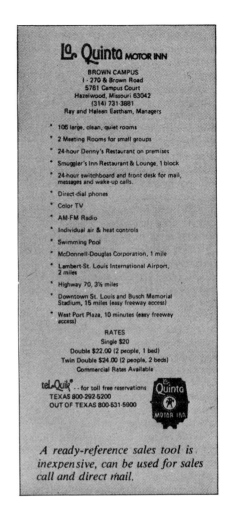

A ready-reference sales tool is inexpensive, can be used for sales call and direct mail.

    B. Out-of-towners who come to shop
12. Fairgrounds, civic or convention centers
    A. During fairs or conventions there are visitors and exhibitors. Check administrative office for names of persons who will recommend or coordinate housing.
    B. Entertainment sponsors (concerts, plays, etc.)

If you don't have a color brochure, a ready-reference card (approximately the size of an envelope or postal card) can be used to list your facilities and service on one side—pool, bar, restaurant, rates, location, television, etc. If attractively printed—one-color and inexpensive—this will serve as ready reference if left with people you visit on sales calls. They often prefer it to a color brochure because it is simpler to use and can be more explicit.

On the other side of the ready-reference card, you can type in addresses, if you use it for direct mail, or you can rubber stamp your own address and such messages as you want to convey ("Under new management," "Newly remodeled," "weekend rates," etc.)

Advertise Selectively

Some fairs or conventions mail out programs well in advance to promote attendance. If so, program advertising can be worthwhile. But be wary of advertising in programs distributed only at the convention or fair.

Outdoor advertising should be based on research and made as simple as possible—for example, "Take next exit" or "Exit 12th Street for 2 miles."

The best public relations advice I can give you is (1) get active in community affairs and stay that way (2) read Ron LaRue's article on public relations in the June 1978 issue of LODGING.

In sum, marketing is not just for the larger properties. It is for all hotels and motels, even the smaller ones. Perhaps they need most of all to research their product, find out what it has to offer and to whom, sell it personally, and promote it through advertising and public relations.

Use all your resources to spread the word about your property. Never relax your efforts. Don't let the competition out-distance you. But do learn what the competition is doing to find out what you can do better. That's the competitive system working at a creative level.

Trends change. So be alert to changes. It is far easier to revise and maintain a program than to start anew.

Productivity: The Marketing Function

by Robert M. Champlin

Robert M. Champlin is Director of Human Resource Development for Hilton Hotels Corporation.

Someone has said that "nothing happens until somebody sells something." The statement was modified to read that for hotel management ". . . nothing happens until somebody sells something to the satisfaction of a guest and at a profit to the establishment."

In the first article in this series on management productivity, we discussed the management process; that is, how management, with reference to a plan for the year ahead, organizes, controls, and measures results to assure productivity.

Marketing is our major tool for producing revenue; financial control is our major tool for assuring profit. Thus, this article, Part II of the series, is on the marketing function. Part III will be on the financial function.

Human resource development is, I believe, the key to implementation of all management productivity programs in the lodging industry. Communications is, in my opinion, what turns the key. Thus, Part IV and V of this series will represent the author's best efforts to provide guidelines on human resources development and communications for lodging establishments.

A hotel's success or failure in the market place depends on the degree of commitment to a marketing concept. The concept should permeate every department and motivate every employee.

Each department must support each other department—each individual must support each other individual—in commitment to marketing as one of the major tools to insure the hotel's survival (. . . something must be sold, it must satisfy the customer, it must produce a profit).

I am going to discuss two aspects of this subject:
1. Development of a Marketing Concept
2. Management of the Marketing Function
Developing a marketing concept requires:

From *Lodging* (July 1978) pp. 36-43. Reprinted by permission of *Lodging*.

A. Product knowledge (what is the hotel or motel selling?)

B. Understanding of the significance of product delivery (how is the sale serviced?)

Marketing management requires:

MARKET RESEARCH PLANNING
Forecasts
Objectives
Programs
Policy Reviews
Schedules
Budgets
ORGANIZING
CONTROLLING
MEASURING RESULTS

Product knowledge and the delivery system will be discussed conceptually. I have known hotels to increase revenue as much as 30% in relatively short time by better conceptual understanding of the hotel product and delivery system.

Market research will be treated both conceptually (theoretically) and specifically.

Marketing management, which includes the traditional elements of all management (plan, organize, control, measure), will be treated both conceptually and specifically. To achieve this, we will consider a case in point: How one 204-room motor hotel developed a marketing program—excerpts from its market research data; forecasts of business; objectives and programs; schedules for marketing achievement; organization plans, controls and measures.

The hotel in the case study is hypothetical. The input, however, is from persons experienced in actual operations. So figures are, in a sense, composite.

The Marketing Concept

Productivity Knowledge and the Delivery System

Ford and General Motors do not think of their

product as cars and trucks. They think of it as transportation. We should not think of our product as rooms and food. We should think of it as space and service.

Mere semantics? I don't think so. How we perceive of our challenge—how we conceive of what we are doing—has an almost immediate influence on the effectiveness of our marketing.

Our frequent mistake is to over-emphasize certain attributes of our properties and to under-emphasize the service aspects. Without question, location, size, age and decor are important attributes of a lodging establishment. But what we are selling, primarily, is space; and how we are making space a desirable product is—by certain levels of service.

Think for a moment of levels of service. Before space is occupied, it is serviced by a variety of people (housekeeping, engineering, etc.). In order that space may be occupied, several departments are involved in service (marketing/sales, reservations, front office).

While the space is being occupied, an even larger number of departments are influencing the RESALE of space. And an important group of people are influencing the PROCESS OF RE-SALE.

Before delving into the Cycle Concept of Selling (Sell, Serve, Resell), let us examine a "distinction" of our business that underscores the significance of our (1) product knowledge and (2) understanding of the delivery system concept of hotel marketing.

Our product—space/service—cannot be inventoried in the traditional sense. You can't inventory yesterday's unsold rooms or idle people and put them on "sale" at a special price. Nor can you order a quick delivery of additional guest rooms from a supplier if you run short.

Room-Selling Cycle

The Cycle Concept of Selling which applies to guest rooms or to other space is: Sell, Service, Resell. The selling cycle begins each day when there is one vacant room. Imagine the following as a drawing that runs in a circle from vacant room to vacant room:

VACANT ROOM

to sale of space
to occupancy of space (or use)
to service of occupants of space
to checkout from space to
VACANT ROOM

The common concept is that we move from "vacant room" to "sale of space" by one or more of these marketing tools: rack brochures, comprehensive brochures, sales/advertising/promotion efforts, letters of commendation, etc.

This is true. But a more effective marketing concept (for every department and every individual employee) is to think not only of sale but also of sale/service/resale as the Selling Cycle. Let me illustrate.

A major hotel experienced reversals in its normal business. Complaint letters increased. More guests seemed "miffed" when they checked out. Sales decreased, and profits went to pot.

The operators called consultants in—financial, marketing, operations, others. Capital expenditures were recommended; sales programs suggested. Finally, the consultant who probably charged the least for his counsel reported that he had registered at the hotel himself and what he didn't like about it was the following: (1) the doorman; (2) the bell staff; (3) the guest registration people; (4) the maid; and (5) food and beverage service personnel.

A subsequent guest survey revealed that a lot of customers didn't like the doorman, bellmen, room clerks, maids, waitresses and waiters. And yet—up to this point, not a single analyst of the marketing scheme at the hotel had addressed the subject of personnel attitudes.

By a program of involving every department and every employee in a new marketing concept—sell, service, resell—the management turned the situation around.

The Delivery System

The entire staff—management and the employees—constitute a hotel's delivery system. The system depends not only on warm and friendly employees but perhaps even more on competent and committed employees.

In carrying through the Space Selling Cycle—the Sell, Serve, Resell concept of marketing—consider the impact of the employees of all departments on the delivery system:

SPACE (ROOM)	Delivery System
VACANT	Housekeeping Engineering
AVAILABLE	Marketing/Sales Reservations/Front Third Party Sales
SOLD	Housekeeping Engineering

Doorman
Guest Registration
Bell Staff
Mail and Information
Room Service
PBX Personnel
F&B Service Personnel
CHECKOUT Bell Staff
Cashier
Doorman
Follow-up Communication
VACANT Housekeeping
Engineering

In a typical situation, the hotel guest is served by up to 10 employees directly and up to 30 indirectly. The total house count is served by the total staff. If they know that the hotel product is space/service, and that the delivery system—sell, serve, resell—is in the hands of the employees, you have a sturdy conceptual base on which to build a successful marketing management program.

Market Research

Between marketing concept and marketing management, there is an interim step—Market Research. Jerome B. Temple, in four articles on "Marketing for Motor Hotels" published in 1976, suggested that marketing research (as prerequisite to a marketing program) should include these components:

POSITION | Analysis of property's location in relation to its market and its competition
PRODUCT | Study of physical facilities in relation to market demand, trends, and competition
PEOPLE | Evaluation of human resources for the implementation of marketing programs
PRICES | Analysis of rate and price structure with reference to ability to market space/services
PROMOTION | Review of effectiveness of present sales and advertising programs
PERFOR-MANCE | Analysis of profitability of types of revenue produced.

Temple's articles on marketing have significantly influenced hotel companies. He reminded us that market research is finding and analyzing facts to assist in making rational marketing decisions. I would add to the categories for analysis:

• Evaluation of best-producing trade areas now served
• Analysis of general economic environment
• Study of current consumer interests; that is, trends in likes and dislikes

Market Evaluation By Trade Area

You will recall that I said we would discuss market research both theoretically and specifically—the latter in terms of a case study of a motor hotel. The hotel (hypothetical) has these characteristics:

Luxury Commercial
204 guest rooms
8 parlors, 3 meeting rooms
Divisible ballroom, seats 520
Grand ballroom, seats 800
Coffee shop, 200
Dining room, 125; lounge, 185

A room night analysis report shows this breakdown for the hotel's five top-producing trade areas (standard metropolitan statistical areas):

CITY I: 26% | 15% local and state conventions /corporate groups
| 8% individual business traveler
| 2% rate programs
| 1% pleasure travelers
CITY II: 9% | 7.5% individual business traveler
| 1.5% pleasure traveler
CITY III: 8% | 4% tour market
| 2.5% pleasure traveler
| 1.5% individual business traveler
CITY IV: 4% | 1.5% convention business
| 1.5% individual business traveler
| 1% pleasure traveler
CITY V: 3.5% | 2% convention business
| 1% individual business traveler
| .5% pleasure traveler

Let us call our case-in-point property The Cityville Hotel. We can then observe that 50.5% of the Cityville's room nights came from five best-producing trade areas (metropolitan).

To establish trends, the person in charge of marketing at the Cityville will compare these percentages, for each area, to percentages for the previous year and the year before that. I do not need to tell professional hotel/motel operators how essential this information is to preparing an effective marketing program for the year ahead.

Cityville Hotel Room Night Occupancy Forecast (annual)

Total Available Room Nights	**74,460**	
Total Occupied Room Nights	**53,611**	
% of Occupancy	**72.0**	
Average Room Rate	**31.50**	

SPECIFIC MARKETS	Room Nights	Percent
Convention		
National, Regional, State, Local	3,723	5.0
Corporate Group	14,519	19.5
Total Convention & Group Business	18,242	24.5
Tour & Travel		
Domestic		
Individual	373	.5
Group	2,233	3.0
Visit U.S.A.		
Individual		
Group		
Total Tour & Travel	2,605	3.5
PERMANENT		
Airline		
Permanent Crew		
Extra Crew		
Distressed/Interrupted Passengers		
Airline Personnel (Pleasure)		
Total Airline		
Individual		
Rate Program	8,936	12.0
Company Rate	5,957	8.0
Buyers Rate		
Speed Check	3,723	5.0
Others (Walk-ins, Unidentified, etc)	3,723	5.0
Total Individual Business	22,338	30.0
Vacation/Pleasure		
Family Plan	5,212	7.0
Hotel Market Plans (Packages, etc.)	3,723	5.0
Travel Agency Personnel	373	.5
Total Vacation/Pleasure	9,308	12.5
Government/Military	744	1.0
Student/Faculty	372	.5
TOTAL OCCUPIED	53,611	72.0

Marketing Management Planning

Forecasts

The first step in management is planning; the first step in planning is forecasting.

Marketing expenses are forecast on a departmental basis. General headings are: Sales, Advertising, Merchandising, Public Relations and Publicity, Research, Fees and Commissions, and Other Selling and Promotion Expenses. For itemization of expenses under these general headings, see the illustration on page 41—taken from pages 66-67 of "A Uniform System of Accounts for Hotels—Seventh Revised Edition." This same format is used for marketing department forecasts and budgets. Initial forecasts reflect changes in the cost of continuing present programs; budgets reflect deletions from and additions to marketing programs to implement revised objectives.

Revenue forecasts are for the hotel as a whole, and include all items shown on a statement of income—rooms, food, beverage, casino, telephone, garage and parking, other operating revenues, rentals and other income—with appropriate breakdowns (food by restaurant and by banquet operations, etc.).

Revenue is forecast by units of volume (room nights, food covers) and then converted to dollars (reflecting changes in rate and price). Guidelines for forecasting volume and revenue may be found in the first article in this series: LODGING, June 1978 issue, pages 20-24; and in "The Radisson South—An Operational Study," LODGING, November 1977, pages 30-36.

The Cityville Hotel marketing department uses the breakout shown here of forecast room nights by type of market: convention, tour, individual business traveler, vacation travelers, government/military and student/faculty.

The Cityville uses the same format—forecast by type of market—for forecasts of volume each month for the year ahead.

Objectives

The Cityville Hotel marketing management writes down objectives of the marketing function in three categories:

ROUTINE: Looking at the items on the forecast, what are our objectives for improving the cost picture and the revenue picture with reference to routine, continuing business?

PROBLEM SOLVING: What is costing too much or producing too little to the extent of posing a real problem? What trends need reversing? How can it be done? What is realistic?

INNOVATIVE: What new programs would improve the productivity of the operation? What innovations in marketing mix, sales technique, advertising and promotion, special packages, level of service to type of market?

A statement of objectives should amount to a statement of goals based on market research facts. Here are some examples—excerpts from the Cityville Hotel's statements of objectives:

Individual Business-Commercial: "Will generate approximately 30% occupancy, or 22,338 room nights for year. This market is year round, with less on weekends and summers (vacation period). We get some corporate travelers off the highway, and as a result of well placed highway signs. An objective should be to increase pre-made reservations for these corporate travelers, so we can forecast more accurately with resultant tighter controls over occupancy."

Conventions-Regional, State, Local: "Will generate 5% occupancy or 3,723 room nights, according to a review of bookings, and historical records (trends). Convention business good in city. But our facilities limit size of convention we can solicit. Objectives should be increased selectivity in solicitation list, more depth in solicitations, more emphasis on summer bookings."

Conventions-Corporate Groups: "Will generate 19.5% occupancy, or 14,519 room nights, thus is hotel's second most important market. Local companies responsible for our getting this business. But problem is developing: there is a slackening of sales—even though slight. Objective: increase depth of continuing study of service needs of corporate groups holding training schools, sales seminars, and company meetings."

Tour Market: "Will generate 3.5% occupancy, or 2,605 room nights. Hotel's location hinders its competitive appeal as a destination for tours. It is not near attractions. But it is ideal for stopover tours (en route to another destination). Objective: To work through two tour management organizations (specified under "Programs") to generate from .5% to 1% occupancy from stopover tour business."

Vacation-Pleasure Market: "Will generate 12.5% occupancy, or 9,308 room nights. Ours is not a vacation hotel. But it has what could be called 'stop-over recreational facilities.' Objectives should be: (1) to program new tennis courts to exploit a trend; (2) to compete more strongly for some of the business now going to low-budget hotels by telling them that for a little more they can get 'stopover vacations' and (3) to develop mini-vacation programs to improve occupancy on Christmas, New Year's, Easter, right after school closes, the 4th of July, Labor Day and Thanksgiving.''

Space limitation forbids a full report on the Cityville Hotel's statement of objectives. But it included a statement covering business from military personnel, government employees, sports teams and student-faculty personnel. In each case, management decided whether to (1) continue marketing as-is; (2) try to solve any apparent problems; and, (3) introduce innovative programs.

Programs

Marketing management at the Cityville Hotel, as a part of plan development, records all programs designed to accomplish marketing objectives. This includes all programs related to improvement of the product (space/service) and of the delivery system (sale/service/resale).

But marketing management is not directly responsible (budgeting, implementation) for such marketing-related programs as (1) upgrading of physical facilities and (2) development of human resources in all departments. Marketing concerns itself with the development and progress of these programs through:

• September, October and November meetings of the overall management to plan for the year ahead.

• Monthly meetings of the management staff (departmental managers and top management).

• Quarterly reviews of departmental progress with top management.

Marketing management is directly responsible for programs relating to market research, sales, advertising, merchandising, public relations and publicity—whether these programs be routine, problem solving or innovative.

*Format from "A Uniform System of Accounts for Hotels." Certain costs of obtaining business are not included; e.g., fees to travel agents and tour operators, expenses of reservations system

While the Cityville uses this format, it does not necessarily have this number of marketing expenses.

MARKETING EXPENSES
Costs Associated with Obtaining Business for Cityville Hotel*

Sales
   Salaries and wages
   Employee benefits
   Operating supplies
   Other operating expenses
   Postage and telegrams
   Trade shows
   Travel and entertainment

Advertising
   Salaries and wages
   Employee benefits
   Exchange (due bills)
   Other operating expenses
   Outdoor
   Print:
      Magazines—group, travel
      Magazines—other
      Newspapers
   Production
   Radio and television

Merchandising
   Salaries and wages
   Employee benefits
   In-house graphics
   Other selling aids
   Point of sale material

Public relations, publicity
   Salaries and wages
   Employee benefits
   Civic and community projects
   Fees for outside services
   Other operating expenses
   Photography

Research
   Salaries and wages
   Employee benefits
   Guest history
   Other operating expenses
   Outside services

Fees and commissions
   Advertising agency
   Franchise fees
   Hotel representatives
   Marketing fees
   Other operating expenses

Other selling & promotion exp.
   Association dues
   Complimentary guests
   Credit card costs, internal
   Direct mail

Routine sales tools at the Cityville Hotel reviewed constantly by marketing with reference to objectives are:

Convention Meeting Packet
  Convention folder
  Fact sheet
  Room diagrams and capacity charts
  Meeting-planners package plan
  Floor plan set-up diagrams
  Banquet menu

Rack Brochure

Package Plan Brochures
  Weekend package
  Honeymoon package
  Meeting-planners package

Reservation Cards (for group return)

Stuffers

Highway Billboards

Company Published Rate Brochures

Here are samples of the Cityville's written plans to alter routine programs for problem solving or innovative reasons:

Newspaper Advertising: "Budget for advertising in five selected cities, located in our five top-producing trade areas, 1,200 column inches. Allocation to be in direct relation to percentage of business from the market. Copy to be directed to meeting planners and vacation travelers."

Billboards: "Continue with two presently being rented. Same location. Add two: one at I-XY South just before the I-YZ perimeter (northbound, right hand reader) and one on I-AB just south of Townsboro."

Magazine Advertising: "Budget for six quarter-page insertions, black and white, three for Eastern Living, three for Western Living. Promote weekend package; meeting planners package."

Tennis Package: "Budget for reprint, twice a year instead of once, of stuffer describing our tennis courts. Budget for brochure to promote new tennis package plan:
2-hour adult tennis clinic (1-day lesson)
2-hour reserved court time (private) for two days
Complimentary tennis balls
Complimentary rental of rackets for court time
Breakfast each morning in Emperor Room
Dinner each night in Empress Room

Daily rate
$38.50 per person double occupancy
$43.50 per person single occupancy

Variety of packages
3-day, 2-night; 4-day, 3-night."

(The marketing program included the building of two new tennis courts, but implementation was not up to the marketing department).

Policy Reviews

Before the Cityville Hotel's programs are scheduled and budgeted they are reviewed against (1) company policy and (2) sales policy.

Company policy relates to credit, travel expenses and legal considerations. Sales policy at the Cityville includes:

• Required statement to the customer of cut-off dates for conventions (14 days prior to arrival of the group).

• Rate ranges that may be sold to conventions and group bookings without the approval of management (they are printed in the Marketing Plan).

• Rate ranges that may be sold with the approval of management.

• Rules governing reference to Convention Calendar for clear listing by date of maximum number of group rooms allowed for sale.

• Rules governing confirmation of banquet function (other than banquets included with a group also reserving room nights) more than 90 days prior to the event.

Schedules, Budgets

Scheduling is the allocation of time resources to achieve each objective through the selected programs.

The marketing manager first makes a list of programs and schedules them with three aims in mind: (1) to limit overlapping to the extent that staff can be scheduled; (2) to activate programs when appropriate rather than to postpone them due to brush fires; and, (3) to show the general manager what can logically be expected at what time.

The Cityville Hotel marketing manager follows this up with a scheduling by calendar which he can post for review by staff. A sample is shown here.

Budgeting is the allocation of money resources to achieve each objective through the selected programs.

The budget is prepared by taking the initial expense forecast for the department, and revising it to reflect changes in program during the development of the plan for the year ahead.

Among the principles of budgeting discussed in this series (Productivity: The Management Process), the most important to remember is this: at the point where money is committed to a program,

Sample of Scheduling of Cityville Hotel's Marketing Management

OCTOBER 1978

MONDAY	TUESDAY	WEDNESDAY	THURSDAY	FRIDAY
2 ROSH HASHANAH SALES MEETING-REVIEW PROGRESS REPORT	**3** Develop in-house Halloween Promotion.	**4** Develop Secys' Halloween Party Invitations. and have printed.	**5** Management Staff Meeting	**6** Develop ad copy Western Living Eastern Living
9 COLUMBUS DAY OBSERVED Prepare Thanksgiving Special Promotion, including newspaper ads.	**10** REVIEW 3rd QUARTER PROGRESS REPORT WITH MANAGEMENT.	**11** YOM KIPPUR	**12** COLUMBUS DAY (continue preparation of 1979 Marketing Plan)	**13**
16 SALES MEETING-REVIEW LEADS.	**17** Direct mail of Halloween Party Invitations to secys.	**18** Prepare mailing list for Christmas wine-tasting party for Corporate Accts.	**19** Make out list, in-depth promotion, summer conventions	**20** Develop invitation for secretaries' luncheon in Novemb and have printed.
23 Develop invitations for wine-tasting Christmas party and have printed, for top Corporate accts.	**24** Preliminary copy, tennis brochure	**25** (continue preparation of 1979 Marketing Plan)	**26**	**27**
30 Prepare mailing list for Christmas cards from hotel. SECRETARIES' HALLOWEEN PARTY	**31** Final plans, Nov. 1 meeting programs, schedules, budgets			

responsibility for the program is fixed. In other words, when the general manager approves a budgeted marketing program, this action fixes responsibility for organizing, controlling and measuring results of the program on the marketing manager.

Organizing

As previously stated, marketing management is concerned with, but not responsible for, implementation of programs to improve physical facilities and personnel performance (space/service).

Marketing management is, however, directly concerned with and responsible for initiating the selling cycle (sell/serve/resell).

Organizing—step two in the management process—requires identification and grouping of work to be done so that it can be accomplished effectively by people.

At the Cityville Hotel, which has projected a 72% occupancy at an average rate per occupied room of $31.50—or $1.7 million rooms revenue—and a food and beverage business (statistics not shown here) of almost the same dollar volume, the organization for direct sales is as follows:

1 Director of Sales
1 Sales Representatives
1 Sales Secretary
2 Convention Coordinators

The sales director will handle specific markets:

association convention market, tour business and pleasure traveler market. In addition, the sales director will provide back-up, training, guidance and supervision to the staff with emphasis on:

Orientation training
Written job description (updated for new programs)
On-the-job training

The sales representative will be responsible for direct personal solicitation of potential corporate and commercial prospects in assigned market areas. In addition, he will be assigned to the Cityville metropolitan area to solicit local and state association business.

The sales secretary will handle secretarial work for the sales director and sales representative, and manage the clerical aspects of the sales operation.

Convention coordinators will handle in-coming calls and group servicing. They will handle groups from the point of booking: telephone communications, visits from convention (association) managers, arrangements in-house.

At no place else in hotel operation is organization design to match objectives and programs to goals more critical than in organizing staff for direct sales and follow through.

Controlling & Measuring

Steps three and four in the management process are controlling and measuring results (the principles of which were defined in the first installment of this series). Essentially, this means that the sequential steps of the plan are examined something like this:

Controlling
What is supposed to happen?
What are the limits of tolerance?
What is happening?

Measuring
What was supposed to happen?
What were the limits of tolerance?
What did happen?

You will recall that controls are mechanical (measurable) and self (acceptance of individual responsibility). In no other hotel activity is the result of controls more obvious than in marketing. Either we have booked the business or we haven't.

At the Cityville Hotel, time is budgeted in terms of number of calls per sales person per period, and results are measured in terms of number of calls per dollars of sale or dollars of sale per call.

You will note on the Cityville marketing man-

agement calendar for October that there are two monthly meetings relating to the control and measurement of the direct sales effort: a sales progress report on the first Monday of the month, and a sales meeting to review leads on the third Monday. This is where actual is measured against forecast (what was supposed to happen? et al) and prospects are reviewed.

Note also that on Tuesday, October 10, marketing management is scheduled to make a regular, quarterly report to top management. This is the type of meeting where marketing management joins general management in concern with the stated profit goal of the operation. Jointly, they are concerned with:

Sales
Occupancy, number of meals served, etc.
Pricing structures
Sales mix
Costs and selling expenses

This is important—unless these relationships are known, there can be no assurance that plans and subsequent actions to control activities according to plan will lead to the anticipated profit. General management must know, not only the amount of sale, but the profitability of sale; marketing management must respond with attention, where appropriate, to the sales mix.

Marketing management's overall goal is that something must be sold to the satisfaction of guests and at a profit.

The Information Flow

A major (if not the major) responsibility of marketing management is to make sure that each and every employee of the hotel is made aware of:

1. the types and volume of business that has been booked;
2. the advertising and promotion materials being used by all the media;
3. the unique qualities and differences that each guest brings to the hotel;
4. the types of markets served and the special qualities that guests from each market place bring to the hotel; and
5. the significance of the sell/serve/resell concept of total-staff marketing.

The success of hotel marketing is to recruit the entire staff for the marketing function. The key to productivity in this process is communications.

Pre-Opening Marketing Analysis for Hotels

by Clarence H. Peters

Clarence H. ("Pete") Peters is a manager in the San Francisco office of Laventhol and Horwath. He earned a bachelor's degree from the University of Pittsburgh before taking an M.B.A. in hotel administration at Michigan State's School of Hotel, Restaurant and Institutional Management. Following work in the management of food service operations, Peters joined L&H, where his present areas of specialization include economic feasibility, valuation, and service as a liaison between developers and lending information.

To the uninitiated, identifying and quantifying the market for a proposed lodging facility might appear to be a reasonably straightforward task. Exhibit 1 shows eight major identifiable market segments. Four of those segments appear to be concerned only with seeking shelter en route to a destination, and will probably accept the most convenient product that meets capacity and price requirements. The terminal visitors, who also represent four segments, need shelter, but as an adjunct to the real purpose of the visit that keeps them overnight in the community. Except, perhaps, for the price variable, the market analyst expects these two categories of consumers to consider all products as quite similar, so that it is not necessary to make fine discriminations between the determining factors required for the products' selection. The local resident segment, which is not represented in the diagram, is the only one that actively seeks out the product. Since those customers are primarily interested in food service and entertainment, they are more easily identifiable and quantifiable.

Unfortunately, the above categorizations of the market for lodging facilities are much too simplistic. For instance, only the current transient visitors to the area have been considered. There is another group that must be identified: the potential visitor who may come because of growth, changes in the transportation network, new commercial, industrial, or recreational developments, or even new lodging facilities. Surprising as it may seem, a new hotel in a community regularly visited by commercial travelers can change the travel pattern for a great many people. Add to these complexities another perpetual concern: a hotel is a single-purpose structure requiring a significant capital investment. Unless its design enables it to serve the major available markets, the property's economic performance will suffer. In view of all these interrelated factors, hotelmen and investors realize that pre-opening marketing analysis can be a critical ingredient in determining the ultimate success of a lodging facility.

The Community Profile

The first step in quantifying the market for overnight lodging in an area is to identify the essential reason for existence of the community or communities that make up the area. There are two major reasons to perform this step. First, it is necessary to determine the extent to which the location of the community is convenient as a stopover for persons traveling to another destination, and, second, one must identify the attractions that exist or may be developed which make the area a destination. It is important to remember that very few travelers visit a community for the purpose of staying in a hotel. Even when they are on a pleasure trip, the primary product being purchased is recreation: shelter, food, drink, and other commodities may be required, but they are secondary to the purpose of the visit. The analyst must therefore isolate and evaluate the characteristics of the community that help to create the need for overnight accommodations.

Some obvious and standard research techniques are used to obtain preliminary information. Before

This article was originally published in the May 1978 issue of *The Cornell Hotel and Restaurant Administration Quarterly*, pp. 15-22, and is reprinted here with the permission of the Cornell University School of Hotel Administration. ©1978.

visiting the community, for example, a good atlas, an almanac, an encyclopedia, and various trade journals—particularly those relating to real estate—should be consulted. Once in the community, the researcher will use observation and personal-interview techniques to obtain the information necessary. Checklists can be very helpful at this stage, and some examples are presented in Exhibits 2 and 3.

The checklist shown in Exhibit 2 is intended primarily as a reminder of likely information sources; it is not necessarily an all-inclusive list of the alternatives available in every urban center. The community profile (Exhibit 3) is used to identify the essential reasons for the existence of the population center. For example, the purpose may be industrial—that is, an urban center that has developed around one or more basic industries reliant on some essential resource. On the other hand, it could be a commercial center that has developed because it is a natural transportation hub for both products and people; or it could be an educational center, containing one or more institutions of higher learning, possibly surrounded by research and scientific organizations or health-care distribution facilities. Some communities owe their existence to recreational attractions, natural or man-made, but most communities are supported by a combination of two or more of the different attribute sets identified above.

Physical Size and Scope

The size and scope of the market seeking accommodations in a community may range from local to national. Las Vegas, for example, is generally recognized as one of the primary recreation destinations in the United States, and attracts people from all over the world. In 1975, however, more than 47 percent of the people accommodated in Las Vegas by the reservation office of the

Las Vegas Convention and Visitors Authority came from California, and a majority of these probably came from the Los Angeles metropolitan area, a reasonable driving time from Las Vegas. The developer of a property in Las Vegas could not afford to ignore the local market.

The analyst must attempt to answer the question, "where does the community draw from?" A definition of the geographic area of influence of the community is an essential step in identifying the market—and that for a suburb of San Francisco will differ substantially from that for a city in Hawaii or a community in Alaska. It is also important that the population of the area be considered, especially growth trends and demographic characteristics. There are approximately 10 guest rooms per 1,000 population in the United States, but the ratio varies substantially from one community to the next. Exhibit 4 provides a comparison of the number of rooms to population for selected commercial-industrial centers and major resort areas. Although population does not create a need for hotel rooms, the size of a community and its growth patterns, in combination with other economic indicators, bear a relationship to the market for lodging facilities.

Accessibility of the Area

The accessibility of the area must be evaluated when identifying the market. Analysis of the capacity of the transportation network is the starting point for this evaluation. Since a majority of travelers use the automobile as their major means of transport, the adequacy of the highway system should be assessed first. The local office of the state Department of Transportation should be able to provide the information necessary to answer the following questions:

• How many federal and state highways serve the area?

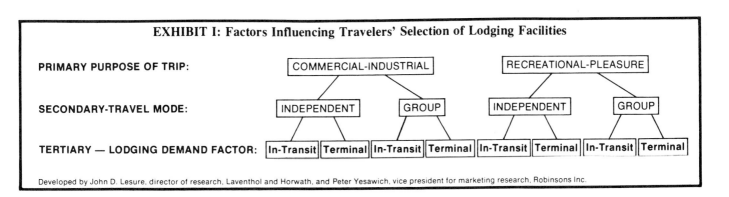

EXHIBIT I: Factors Influencing Travelers' Selection of Lodging Facilities

PRIMARY PURPOSE OF TRIP: COMMERCIAL-INDUSTRIAL | RECREATIONAL-PLEASURE

SECONDARY-TRAVEL MODE: INDEPENDENT | GROUP | INDEPENDENT | GROUP

TERTIARY — LODGING DEMAND FACTOR: In-Transit | Terminal | In-Transit | Terminal | In-Transit | Terminal | In-Transit | Terminal

Developed by John D. Lesure, director of research, Laventhol and Horwath, and Peter Yesawich, vice president for marketing research, Robinsons Inc.

EXHIBIT 2: Checklist of Information Sources

GENERAL INFORMATION
Airport, highway, and port authorities
Building owners and managers' association
Chamber of Commerce
Department of Transportation — city, county, state
Municipal officials
Newspaper publishers

NUMBER OF VISITORS
Convention and visitors bureau
Customs and immigration
Industrial board
Officers of major industrial and commercial companies
Prominent bankers, realtors, attorneys
Transportation companies
Deans of universities and colleges
Administrators of health-care distribution centers
Managers of amusement, recreational, and sports centers

COMPETITIVE SERVICES AND FACILITIES
Local hotel and restaurant associations
Operators of competitive lodging and food service facilities

• What is the condition of the highways? Are there plans for improvement, relocation, or expansion?

• What is the present highway usage, including both toll and non-toll roads?

A similar study should be made of airline service to the area, if any. The local airport authority is generally a good source of information concerning: the passenger capacity of the airport; the major airlines providing service; the frequency of domestic and international flights; and records of arriving and departing passengers. If possible, the analyst should arrange personal interviews with representatives of the major airlines serving the area to obtain information about present load factors on their flights, the number of direct and stopover flights to the area, and the carrier's plans for the future. In addition, the extent to which the community is a stopover point for airline crews should be determined, because this activity can be a good source of rooms demand.

Other available modes of transportation should be evaluated, including rail, bus, ferry systems, and ocean or inland waterway transport. When the capacity of the various systems has been determined, the information should be evaluated in relation to the proximity of the community to other major metropolitan areas, and the access times to each should be computed. From these data, the analyst can construct a matrix showing the essential information on preferred travel modes of the various market segments from the major metropolitan areas, travel time, and potential demand for overnight lodging.

Evaluation of Attractions

The features of a community that give rise to visits by non-residents can be classifed into the two major groups discussed in Exhibit 1, recreational-personal and commercial-industrial. Each major group can in turn be divided into two subsets— man-made or natural attractions in the personal-recreational group, and basic or sustaining developments in the commercial-industrial group. The major purpose for this disaggregation is to help the analyst identify the market. For example, a *basic* industry such as automobile assembly not only employs local residents; it also creates products for export so that funds are brought into the community and traffic is generated. A sustaining development, like a retail store, provides employment but only recirculates funds already in the

---

EXHIBIT 3:
Guidelines for Preparing a Community Profile

DEMOGRAPHICS
1. Prepare a complete analysis of the trends in population in the area for the past five years.
2. For the past two years, show how the population breaks down in terms of age, sex, professions or occupations, education, income.

HOUSING
1. List the type, number of units, and capacity of single family and multi-family dwellings.
2. Obtain representative price ranges and occupancy percentages for each type and note trends.
3. Pinpoint new housing developments and growth areas.

TRANSPORTATION
1. List types available to the area.
2. For each type, determine capacity and volume of passengers and freight.
3. Obtain data on proposed expansion, if any, from reliable sources.

INDUSTRIAL AND COMMERCIAL ACTIVITY
1. Prepare a list of major employers by type of activity, employment, and value of activity.
2. Determine plans for expansion of existing facilities and potential for new developments.
3. List the source and volume of visitors.

HEALTH AND EDUCATION
1. List the major health and educational institutions by type, capacity, and volume of activity.
2. Obtain information on expansion plans from authoritative sources.

RECREATIONAL
1. List the amusement, recreation, and sports facilities that attract visitors from outside the community.
2. Obtain information on source, volume, and seasonality of use.
3. Obtain information on expansion plans, if any.

UNUSUAL AREA ACTIVITIES
1. List all special events of a recurring nature that attract visitors.
2. Obtain data on volume.

community, and it generates very little traffic and attendant lodging demand. When the sustaining development is the central office of a major national chain, or when a retail outlet is part of a large, regional shopping complex, its status is upgraded because of the traffic generated by those features.

Evaluation of the attractions should be based on data obtained by observation, personal interview, and mail survey (if the number of attractions requiring analysis warrants the expenditure).

The information needed includes:

- Present physical condition and capacity.
- Planned expansion or retraction.
- New or proposed developments.
- Number of visitors by month (or other appropriate period) for the past five years.
- Number of visitors (or an estimate) requiring lodging.

The information obtained may be verified by discussing the attractions of the community with those citizens and representatives of municipal government who are most interested in the progress of the area. For example, the Chamber of Commerce and the industrial Development Board or its equivalent (if one exists) should be contacted, as should the heads of the major commercial banks and savings and loan associations. Many local business-support organizations are also good sources of published information concerning the economic and demographic characteristics of the community.

In the evaluation of the commercial-industrial base of the community, some indication of the influence that the companies may have on the market for lodging facilities can be obtained from the list in Exhibit 5. Using the 1967 Input-Output tables prepared by the U.S. Department of Com-

---

EXHIBIT 5: Major Purchasers of Lodging

RANK	INDUSTRY	TYPICAL REPRESENTATIVES
1.	Wholesale trade	Salesmen for industrial products
2.	Finance and insurance	Agents; brokers; bank examiners
3.	Miscellaneous professional services	Lawyers; accountants; engineers
4.	New construction	Contractors; buyers, workers
5.	Retail trade	Buyers; salesmen
6.	Health-care services	Doctors; patients; salesmen of medical equipment and pharmaceuticals
7.	Food processors	Buyers; salesmen to the trade
8.	Motion picture production, amusement, recreation services, and commercial sports	Production companies; artists and entertainers; professional teams
9.	Nonprofit organizations	Members of business and professional associations
10.	Miscellaneous business services	Agents and employees of advertising companies; credit and computer services; news syndicates

Source: U.S. Department of Commerce, "Input-Output Structure of the U.S. Economy: 1967."

---

merce, one can identify those industries that are the major purchasers of overnight accommodations nationally. In any community the analyst can expect that representatives of those industries will require lodging facilities if they have adequate reason to contact the companies in the local commercial-industrial base.

Factors That May Change the Market

When obtaining information on existing attractions and historical data concerning the traffic they have generated, it is imperative that the researcher be alert for evidence of plans that may alter the size and scope of the market. All avenues of growth and expansion or contraction of the commercial, industrial, or recreational development of the community should be explored as fully as possible, including the following:

- Urban renewal.
- New industrial development.
- Proposed government projects.
- Expansion of transportation modes.
- Construction of commercial office space and shopping centers.
- Proposed convention and civic centers.
- Regionalization of health-care delivery systems.

EXHIBIT 4

Number of hotel, motor-hotel, and tourist-court rooms per 1,000 population in selected standard metropolitan statistical areas in 1972

COMMERCIAL-INDUSTRIAL		RECREATIONAL-PLEASURE	
Chicago	8	Atlantic City	69
Cleveland	6	Daytona Beach	71
Los Angeles	7	Honolulu	35
New York	6	Las Vegas	75
Philadelphia	5	Miami	40
Pittsburgh	6	Orlando	36

Source: 1972 Census of Business; 1970 Census of Population.

- New institutions of higher learning, or additions to existing institutions.
- Proposed amusement parks, stadium development or expansion, or planned recreational services.
- Elimination or contraction of any of the activities listed above.

Information obtained should be verified whenever possible by consulting with municipal and other officials, and all available data pertaining to expected completion dates and capacities should be recorded.

Market Characteristics

The information obtained for the evaluation of the existing attractions must next be analyzed to determine the following characteristics of the market:

- The primary, secondary, and tertiary (if applicable) purpose of visits to the community.
- The duration of visits (overnight or in-transit; if terminal, number of days at destination).
- The seasonality of visits (percentage of annual visits that occur in each month).
- The demographic characteristics of the visitors.

When these characteristics have been determined, the analyst should prepare, on a monthly basis if possible, a projected schedule of the visitors to the community during a typical year, broken down by the market segments delineated in Exhibit 1.

Analysis of Existing Lodging Facilities

The ability of existing facilities to meet the need for overnight accommodations, as estimated by the analysis above, is calculated next. To perform this calculation, it is necessary to obtain, through observation and personal interview, the following information for each existing lodging facility:

1. Number of rooms
2. Occupancy levels (monthly)
3. Double occupancy levels (monthly)
4. Guest market segmentation
5. Rate structure
6. Average length of stay
7. Age and condition of property
8. Food and beverage facilities
   a) number of seats
   b) menu prices
   c) decor
   d) service standards

e) type of food served
f) ratio of food and beverage sales to total departmental sales
9. Additional amenities and facilities
   a) reservation system, if any
   b) recreational facilities
   c) store rentals; other guest services

The data should be confirmed, to the extent possible, by discussion with competing operators and representatives of convention and tourist bureaus with possible knowledge of occupancy trends. The analyst should then prepare a schedule of the number of rooms occupied monthly, based upon the data obtained.

The schedule of number of monthly visitors should be compared with the number of rooms occupied and number of guest nights developed from the accumulated data concerning existing lodging accommodations. There are four ways in which this can be accomplished:

- By visual verification. There should be a clearly visible relationship between the number of visitors and the number of occupied rooms or number of guest nights.
- By preparing a chart in which number of visitors is the variable or x axis and number of rooms occupied (or guest nights) is the y axis. It should be possible to draw a trend line connecting the points.
- By linear regression. Many of the more sophisticated pocket calculators are preprogrammed for computing the trend line.
- By computing and comparing the seasonality indices for the number of visitors and the occupancy or number of guest nights.

An Example

An illustration of the schedules that might be prepared for a feasibility study of a proposed lodging facility is presented in Exhibit 6. We have assumed that the site is in the central business district of a metropolitan area with a population of 300,000. Although mostly commercial-industrial, the fictitious city also contains a major regional health-care facility and a small college. It is a transportation hub and, because of location and facilities (a relatively new civic center), receives a good share of regional conventions. Let us also assume that it is a logical stopover point on the route to several well-known recreational resort areas.

At the time of the study, there are 12 lodging facilities in the area with a total of 1,860 rooms considered competitive by the analyst. Using occupancy statistics obtained as a result of personal interviews and verified by observation and discussion with community officials, the number of rooms occupied and number of guest nights for the most recent 12-month period are computed.

The estimated number of visitors has been compiled from the data obtained by evaluating the various attractions in the area. From personal interviews, some telephone contacts, a mail questionnaire, and observations, the number of visitors to the commercial-industrial complex, the health-care center, and the college is computed. A discussion with the convention bureau provides data on conventions. The number of visitors who were en route to the resort area has been estimated on the basis of discussions with the Department of Transportation, analysis of traffic counts provided by that department, and observation. The aggregate of those sources is shown in Exhibit 6. Scanning the data shows some correlation, but if we assume that the analyst elects to prepare a linear regression for verification, the result of the computation, based on the formula **y** (guest nights) = **a** + **bx** (number of visitors) is: *The number of guest nights monthly equals 31,570 plus 58 percent of the number of monthly visitors.*

The correlation coefficient (r) is a fairly high .83 and shows that variations in the number of visitors accounts for about 70 percent (r^2 = .6889) of the variation in guest nights. The large value of the **a**, or y-intercept, constant (31,570) would seem to indicate that a significant percentage of the visitors to the community stay more than one night—and, in fact, the average duration of stay for the community is 1.7 days, a figure typical of a commercial-industrial base with a high volume of intransit visitors.

The arithmetic means of the number of guest nights and number of visitors monthly were computed and used as a basis for computing the seasonality factors (see calculations, Exhibit 6). The major variations in these indices might be interpreted as follows:

EXHIBIT 6: Comparison of Number of Visitors and Number of Guest Nights

MONTH	PERCENTAGE: ROOM OCCUPANCY	PERCENTAGE: DOUBLE OCCUPANCY	NUMBER OF ROOMS OCCUPIED	NUMBER OF GUEST NIGHTS	NUMBER OF VISITORS	SEASONALITY INDEX: GUEST NIGHTS*	SEASONALITY INDEX: VISITORS**
JANUARY	62%	31%	35,749	46,831	37,500	78.10	76.99
FEBRUARY	67	33	34,894	46,408	40,000	77.39	82.12
MARCH	73	48	42,092	62,296	31,000	103.89	63.64
APRIL	72	52	40,176	61,068	38,000	101.84	78.02
MAY	72	38	41,515	57,291	43,000	95.54	88.28
JUNE	79	45	44,082	63,919	70,000	106.60	143.71
JULY	80	67	46,128	77,034	82,000	128.47	168.35
AUGUST	85	75	49,011	85,769	80,000	143.04	164.24
SEPTEMBER	74	45	41,292	59,873	51,000	99.85	104.70
OCTOBER	77	55	44,398	68,817	49,000	114.76	100.60
NOVEMBER	67	32	37,386	49,350	35,000	82.30	71.86
DECEMBER	55	29	31,713	40,910	28,000	68.22	57.49
TOTAL			488,436	719,566	584,500	1,200.00	1,200.00
MEAN VALUES	72%	47%	40,703	59,964	48,708	100.00	100.00

*Calculated: $\dfrac{\text{NUMBER OF GUEST NIGHTS FOR MONTH}}{\text{MEAN NUMBER OF GUEST NIGHTS EACH MONTH}}$ = GUEST NIGHTS SEASONALITY INDEX   e.g., $\dfrac{46,831}{59,964}$ = .78099

**Calculated: $\dfrac{\text{NUMBER OF VISITORS FOR MONTH}}{\text{MEAN NUMBER OF VISITORS EACH MONTH}}$ = VISITORS SEASONALITY INDEX   e.g., $\dfrac{37,500}{48,708}$ = .76989

Source: Competitive operations; Convention and Visitors Bureau; Airport Authority; Laventhol and Horwath estimates.

1. Extended stays by convention guests in March, April, and October provide more guest nights from fewer visitors. Those months were seasonal lows for in-transit visits.

2. Heavy travel to the recreational areas increased overnight stops in the summer months. Other lodging facilities not analyzed attracted more of the market, probably because of price.

The general conclusion would probably be that the number of guest nights and related occupancy figures are realistic estimates, and form a reasonable basis for future market projections.

Future Demand

When the data have been verified to the extent possible, the analyst has a basis for projecting future demand. The size and composition of the present transient market have been established. It now remains to determine the probable growth factors and to project the demand into the appropriate

future period. By also projecting the extent to which existing lodging facilities and known additions to the capacity will satisfy that market, it will be possible to show the gap—if any—that would be filled by the proposed operation. An illustration of this calculation, prepared using a computer, is shown in Exhibit 7.

It is the final projection that will influence the design and scope of the food and beverage facilities recommended as part of the proposed property. The basic seating capacity required for transient guests can be computed based upon standard, well-established relationships, but the additional capacity for local residents is more difficult to quantify. An evaluation of that market is made primarily by observation and by polling those interviewed during the course of the study to determine their personal dining-out preferences. The analyst can also obtain some insight by visiting competing restaurants and estimating their activity during meal periods on different days during the week. If the capacity of the food service facilities is an essential

EXHIBIT 7

PROJECTED AVERAGE OCCUPANCY – FUTURE MARKET COMPOSITION

YEAR	COMMERCIAL	CONVENTION	TOURIST	ROOM NIGHTS DEMAND	ROOM NIGHTS AVAILABLE	AVERAGE GROWTH (PERCENT)	AVERAGE OCCUPANCY
1978	163,300	82,100	72,500	317,900	441,700	—	.72
1979	168,199	84,563	74,675	327,437	441,700	3	.74
1980	173,245	87,100	76,915	337,260	474,900	3	.71
1981	178,442	89,713	79,223	347,378	508,100	3	.68
1982	183,796	92,404	81,599	357,799	617,600	3	.58
1983	189,309	95,176	84,047	368,532	617,600	3	.60
1984	194,989	98,032	86,569	379,590	617,600	3	.61
1985	200,838	100,973	89,166	390,977	617,600	3	.63
1986	206,864	104,002	91,841	402,707	617,600	3	.65
1987	213,069	107,122	94,596	414,787	617,600	3	.67

PROJECTED OCCUPANCY OF PROPOSED HOTEL

YEAR	COMMERCIAL	CONVENTION	TOURIST	ROOM NIGHTS DEMAND	ROOM NIGHTS AVAILABLE	EXPECTED OCCUPANCY
1978	—	—	—	—	66,430	—
1979	—	—	—	—	66,430	—
1980	19,084	10,877	9,614	39,585	66,430	.60
1981	19,656	1,214	9,903	40,773	66,430	.61
1982	18,404	9,240	8,568	36,212	66,430	.55
1983	18,955	9,518	8,825	37,298	66,430	.56
1984	20,500	10,783	9,523	40,806	66,430	.61
1985	21,115	11,107	9,808	42,030	66,430	.63
1986	21,749	11,440	10,102	43,291	66,430	.65
1987	22,401	11,783	10,406	44,590	66,430	.67

Source: Analysis of competitive properties; Laventhol and Horwath estimates of growth rates.

EXHIBIT 8: Development and Design Criteria Matrix

MARKET SEGMENTS

GUEST REQUIREMENTS	COMMERCIAL-INDUSTRIAL				RECREATIONAL-PLEASURE					
	INDEPENDENT		GROUP		INDEPENDENT		GROUP		LOCAL	
	In-Transit	Terminal	In-Transit	Terminal	In-Transit	Terminal	In-Transit	Terminal	Independent	Group
LOCATION										
Accessibility	X		X		X		X			
Parking	X	X	X	X	X	X	X	X	X	X
Proximity	X	X	X	X	X	X	X	X	X	X
Visibility	X		X		X		X			
APPEARANCE										
Decor		X		X		X		X		
Design		X		X		X		X		
Landscaping						X		X		
Structure	X		X	X		X		X		
LODGING										
Capacity				X			X	X		
Equipment		X	X	X		X		X		
Rates	X	X	X	X	X	X	X	X		
Room Size	X	X		X		X		X		
RESTAURANTS										
Capacity	X		X	X			X	X		X
Diversity		X		X	X			X	X	X
Function Space				X				X		X
Hours of Operation	X		X	X	X	X	X	X	X	X
OTHER GUEST SERVICES										
Laundry		X		X		X		X		
Shops		X		X		X		X	X	
Valet		X						X		
ENTERTAINMENT AND RECREATION FACILITIES										
Active		X		X		X		X	X	X
Sedentary		X		X		X		X		

element in the property's planning and design, a more elaborate study and analysis may be required.

Relating Market Demand to Design

Once the market for the proposed facility has been identified, the analyst's findings should be related to the site of the proposed facility and to the design of the building and interior space. Assuming that the economics of the project justify the development, and the decision is made to proceed, the architects and engineers will need general specifications concerning the following:

- The number, size, and type of guest rooms and food and beverage facilities, including function space.
- The space to be allocated for administrative, control, and general support purposes.
- The size, type, and scope of recreational facilities.
- The type of vehicle housing required and the necessary space.
- The space allocated for shops and other guest services.
- The suggested visibility of the proposed project.

The characteristics and requirements of the various market segments are the basis for judgment in developing design specifications and space allocations. Guests will fit into three standard categories: those who use the facility largely because it is convenient; those who select it after comparing the price and quality of competing facilities; and those who select it because of particular aspects of structural design, interior decor, and quality of product and services. Exhibit 8 presents a development and design criteria matrix, relating the requirements of potential customers by groups to the factors that will influence the final structural design, interior design, and space allocations.

Summary

Except for the local resident who generally selects the services of a lodging facility for some special attribute, guests are most often guided in their selection by convenience (which includes proximity) or else accept lodging services as part of a travel package. For example, the primary motivation for the member of a group is attendance at a function, not the purchase of the lodging services. Since the demand is derived from the real purpose, most customers feel that all lodging facilities are similar and will differentiate only on the basis of a bad past experience—seldom on a good one. For those reasons, the marketing thrust of the lodging industry has been based primarily upon location, brand identification, price, architectural design, or status. Little effort has been made to identify the market and to determine how the needs of the customer can best be met. Even less effort has been expended to promote the use of lodging facilites by the millions who travel, but who stay with friends and relatives or in their own vacation shelters.

My firm's analysts do not foresee that the traveler will change his habits drastically in the future, although demographic data point to a significant increase in the segment of the population that provides the best market for lodging facilities. We do believe, however, that the lodging industry can capture a greater share of the market for overnight accommodations. An important part of striving toward this goal is the recognition of the need for a more thorough market analysis early in the development of a lodging facility.

Post-Opening Marketing Analysis for Hotels

by Dr. Peter C. Yesawich

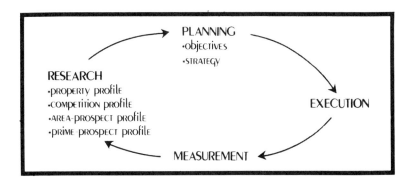

Peter Yesawich, Ph.D., received his doctorate from Cornell University's School of Hotel Administration where his areas of concentration were psychology, marketing, and communication theory. He is vice president and director of marketing research for Robinson's, Inc.

In a recent issue of *The Quarterly,* Clarence Peters discussed the considerations that should govern a pre-opening marketing analysis—in brief, how to identify and quantify the market for a proposed lodging facility.[1] For most hoteliers, however, the marketing problem is not that of determining the feasibility of additional rooms, but rather one of cultivating established markets to fill *existing* rooms.

Basic Components of the Marketing Process

Through the 1960s and early 1970s, the demand for lodging facilities generally kept pace with

supply, and most hoteliers therefore concentrated more heavily on operations than on marketing. Today, however, the proliferation of guest rooms has created a competitive atmosphere in many areas throughout the world, and hoteliers must place greater emphasis on marketing to remain competitive.

Although there is no universally accepted approach to marketing in the hospitality industry, most hoteliers agree that judgments regarding the objectives of the marketing program, the appropriate creative strategy, and the mix of marketing tools that will reach the target audience most effectively should be based on the following considerations:

- The attributes, services, and amenities the establishment has to offer guests;
- The attributes, services, and amenities competing establishments have to offer the same guests;
- The origins and characteristics of existing guests; and
- The amount of money available to spend on marketing.

Although it should be modified to reflect environmental or operational factors unique to a given property, a proven marketing process that may be applied by any lodging establishment (regardless of size or type) is depicted in the figure above. Summarized, this marketing process takes the following sequence: research, plan, execute,

This article was originally published in the November 1978 issue of *The Cornell Hotel and Restaurant Administration Quarterly,* pp. 70-81, and is reprinted here with the permission of the Cornell University School of Hotel Administration. ©1981.

1. Clarence H. Peters, "Pre-Opening Marketing Analysis for Hotels," *The Cornell Hotel and Restaurant Administration Quarterly,* 19, No. 1 (May 1978); pp. 15-22.

EXHIBIT 1:
Lodging Profile Checklist

I) **LOCATION:**
_____ Downtown
_____ Suburban
_____ Rural
_____ Beachfront
_____ Airport
_____ Other (_____)

II) **CLASSIFICATION:**
_____ Commercial Hotel
_____ Conference-Convention Hotel
_____ Resort Hotel
_____ Other (_____)

III) **OPERATING STATUS:**
_____ Independent
_____ Chain-Affiliated, Chain-Operated
_____ Chain-Affiliated, Franchised
_____ Other (_____)

IV) **GUEST COMPOSITION**
(Room-Nights — 12 months):
_____% — Commercial
_____% — Commercial-group affiliated
_____% — Social
_____% — Social-group affiliated
100%

V) **PROPERTY ON MAJOR TRAFFIC ARTERY?**
_____ Yes
_____ No

VI) **DISTANCES:**
A) From major commercial center _____
B) From major recreation center _____
C) From airport _____

VII) **FACILITIES:**
A) **Guest Rooms**
1) Number of single rooms _____
2) Number of double rooms _____
3) Number of suites _____
4) Total rentable units _____
5) Comments: _____

B) **Meeting Rooms**
1) Total number of meeting rooms _____
2) Maximum single room accommodation, theater configuration _____
3) Maximum accommodation all rooms, theater configuration _____
4) Audiovisual facilities _____
_____
5) Comments: _____

C) **Food and Beverage**
1) Number of food outlets _____
2) Number of beverage outlets _____
3) Maximum single room banquet accommodation _____
4) Maximum banquet accommodation _____
5) Specialty restaurants, lounges _____
6) Comments: _____

D) **Recreation**
1) Golf _____
2) Tennis _____
3) Swimming _____
4) Sailing _____
5) Riding _____
6) Fishing _____
7) Diving _____
8) Health Club _____
9) Other _____

VIII) **RATES:**
A) **High Season** (Dates: _____)

	EP	CP	MAP	FAP
Single				
Double				
Extra				
Suites				

B) **Low Season** (Dates: _____)

	EP	CP	MAP	FAP
Single				
Double				
Extra				
Suites				

IX) **SPECIAL PACKAGES:**
(list and describe)
_____
_____

X) **MARKETABLE GUEST SERVICES:**
(list and describe from guest services directory)
_____
_____

XI) **RESERVATIONS SYSTEMS AND/OR REPRESENTATION:** (list and describe)
_____
_____

XII) **SPECIAL COMMENTS:**
_____
_____
_____
_____
_____

---

measure, and—responding to the results of program measurement—begin again.

As indicated in the figure, marketing planning must begin with: (1) a *property profile*—an evaluation of the tangible and intangible features the establishment offers guests; (2) a *competition profile*—an evaluation of the tangible and intangible features offered to guests by competing establishments; (3) a *prime-prospect profile*—an investigation of the origins and characteristics of current guests; and (4) an *area-prospect profile*—an investigation of the origins and characteristics of other visitors to the area.

Property and Competition Profiles

Although developing a profile of one's lodging establishment may appear a rudimentary exercise,

it is the keystone of judicious market planning. Without a clear definition of the lodging products and services you intend to market, you cannot achieve a desirable level of program efficiency.

As noted previously, the profile of a lodging establishment should incorporate both tangible and intangible features. The tangible features encompass such characteristics as location, operating status, number of guest rooms, meeting facilities, number and type of food and beverage outlets, recreational facilities, and so on. The intangible features include perceived quality of service, existing reputation, popularity of the destination, and area attractions. Perhaps the most convenient way to evaluate all of the relevant features is through use of a checklist. A sample profile checklist is provided in Exhibit 1.

Different portions of the checklist should be

EXHIBIT 2:
Synopsis of Property Profiles

Attribute	(Own Establishment) Property A	(Competitive Establishments) Property B	Property C
Downtown location	X	X	X
King-size beds	X		X
Meeting facilities	X	X	X
Audiovisual equipment			X
Free guest parking	X	X	
24-hour room service	X		X
$26 commercial rate		X	X
"800" number			
Express checkout procedure		X	
Guaranteed reservations	X	X	X

completed by the general manager, sales manager, marketing manager, food and beverage manager, and comptroller, as appropriate. These individuals should also complete checklists on operations deemed competitive. When the results have been compiled, a synopsis should be prepared: a sample format is depicted in Exhibit 2. Differences among the property profiles are readily discerned when a recording procedure of this type is used. These distinguishing characteristics may be used as a foundation for developing advertising and sales-promotion strategies. It is particularly useful when the attributes listed on the left side of the profile sheet are ranked in terms of their perceived importance to the markets that will be aggressively sought in promotional efforts. This ranking procedure will indicate the best candidates for emphasis in advertising and promotion.

Area-Prospect Profile

After the tangible and intangible features of the establishment have been profiled, it is necessary to study the characteristics of guests who have patronized the establishment, as well as those who have patronized competitive establishments in the area.

There are generally several sources of secondary information on visitors who patronize lodging establishments in a given area. For example, many area chambers of commerce maintain records of the origin of inquiries they receive concerning cultural events, lodging facilities, and area attractions. Moreover, in areas where tourism contributes substantial jobs and revenue, chambers of commerce often conduct periodic surveys of the origins, characteristics, and lodging preferences of visitors. Larger metropolitan areas and areas that attract sizable numbers of visitors may also support an office of tourism that routinely collects information on visitor travel patterns. Other possible sources of information on area prospects include the local hotel association and the visitors and convention bureau.

Several additional sources of information may be tapped to round out the area-prospect profile—for example, studies and reports issued by such organizations as the United States Travel Data Center, the Travel Research Association, and publications directed toward the traveling public. Operators interested in air traffic to an area may wish to consult sections of the Civil Aeronautics Board's *Origin-Destination Survey of Airline Passenger Traffic,* which provides data on the routings of air travelers to a specific city and thus passenger counts by specific points of origin. Offshore establishments interested in traffic from the United States may obtain copies of *U.S. International Air Travel Statistics,* published monthly by the U.S. Department of Transportation and listing passenger counts of both American citizens and aliens by port of embarkation and first port of disembarkation. Data are provided on both air and sea passengers, with air departures listed by carrier and flight status (scheduled versus nonscheduled).

The information gleaned from the sources enumerated above should be sufficient for the development of an area-prospect profile. They represent a particularly good starting point for a prospect analysis because the research has already been performed, the results are available at a nominal—if any—charge, and the data are generally valid. The two major deficiencies of secondary-source information: the data apply only to an area, not to the specific lodging establishment; and they are rarely categorized by identifiable segments of the traveling public (e.g., recreational travelers, commercial travelers, etc.). Consequently, it is incumbent on the operator to conduct a prospect analysis for his own establishment.

Prime-Prospect Profile

Many lodging properties rely on in-room questionnaires (guest surveys) as a primary source of market information, but these will receive little mention here because the data they generate are, more often than not, unreliable and statistically invalid. Their inherent deficiency, simply stated, is that data are not gathered in such a way that each guest has an equal probability of completing the survey form. For example, the manager of a 200-room establishment running at 100-percent occupancy might receive 10 completed survey forms every day, each of which was completed by a guest who felt compelled to respond because of an exceptionally positive or negative experience. Obviously, these 10 respondents may not be representative of the entire population of guests on the property at the time; thus, operators must be cautious when interpreting in-room survey results.

There are three primary sources of information available to the operator attempting to profile his own prospects: reservation requests, reservation cards, and folio forms. When gathered and analyzed properly, the data available in these documents provide a clear picture of current room-night (market) composition; they also indicate which segments of the market are most lucrative and which should be sought in future promotions.

These three sources can be used to isolate the travel patterns and preferences of previous guests in each market segment. For example, the documents can yield the following information on every registrant:

Reservation Requests
1. Date of reservation
2. Method of reservation
3. Source of reservation
4. Type of guest (commercial, conference, etc.)
5. Special package or plan requested

Registration Cards
6. Name of guest
7. Address
8. Zip or postal code
9. Date of arrival
10. Number in party (adults, children)
11. Room rate

Folio Forms
12. Length of stay
13. Total of folio charges
14. Method of payment.

Data Analysis

Myriad techniques are available for compiling and analyzing the data, ranging from manual procedures to the application of computers. Because the quality of the results varies from one technique to the next, the selection of technique should be based upon the frequency and speed with which market data are required as well as the availability of competent staff members to conduct the analysis. For all practical purposes, properties with up to 100 rooms will generally find manual procedures adequate to the task, while properties with more than 100 rooms should either use in-house data-processing equipment or commission the services of a qualified consulting firm.

The exact procedures followed in conducting the prospect analysis will vary from property to property because each has its own established front-office and accounting procedures, but the general steps of the process are common to all establishments regardless of their size and type:

• **Reservation request and confirmation procedures.** As much information as possible should be recorded at the time the reservation is made to minimize the time required for registration.

• **Registration.** Guests holding reservations and pre-registered guests should be asked to confirm the accuracy of the information transcribed to their registration cards. Information that has been omitted should be requested cordially by the desk clerk. (Naturally, all information on walk-in guests must be recorded at the time of registration.)

• **Checkout.** If all the information has not been transcribed to one document (usually the folio), all of the separate source documents should be collated in preparation for processing.

• **Editing and data entry.** The source documents should be edited visually and all errors corrected prior to data entry. The data are then ready for recording, whether in the form of a document prepared manually, punched cards, magnetic tape, magnetic discs, or optical-scanning forms. (Properties with their own data-processing equipment may elect to key data directly to a system file.)

• **Analysis and report preparation.** The data are analyzed and market reports are generated in accordance with a predetermined schedule.

It should be noted that the competence of the analyst and the flexibility of the computer software (assuming a computer is used) are limiting factors in the degree of analytic sophistication that can be achieved. Ironically, deficiencies in computer software currently outweigh human deficiencies in marketing applications; this is presumably because most hotel computing systems in use were designed to satisfy the requirements of accounting and general management rather than marketing needs.

EXHIBIT 3

Market Area	Registrations*	Percentage of Total Registrations	(Average Stay)	Room-Nights	Percentage of Total Room-Nights
New York	850	34%	1.2	1,020	25%
Philadelphia	620	25%	1.3	806	20%
Boston	540	22%	2.0	1,080	26%
Chicago	290	12%	2.3	667	16%
Houston	200	7%	2.8	560	13%
Total	2,500	100%		4,133	100%

*Assumes only 1 registration per room.

Note that the percentage distribution of registrations differs significantly from the distribution of room-nights. If registrations were used as the criterion unit of analysis, New York would be ranked the number-one market (34%). When room-nights are used as the criterion unit of analysis, Boston appears to represent the number-one market (26%).

When the preceding steps have been executed, the market planner must turn his attention to (1) the criterion unit of analysis, (2) the type-of-guest classifications, and (3) the origin-market definitions.

Market planners generally use room-nights as the **criterion unit of analysis.** Although the distribution of room-nights at a property will bear a relationship to the number of registrations over time, the latter should not be used as the criterion unit because it does not reflect variances in market composition caused by disparate lengths of stay. An example of the results received when analyzing registrations, and those produced by analyzing room-nights, is provided in Exhibit 3.

One of the more difficult issues to be addressed in the analysis is that of classifying guests with reference to established **market segments.** Although marketing managers display considerable creativity in embellishing upon and refining them, there are for all practical purposes only eight lodging market segments, as outlined in Exhibit 4. As indicated in that figure, all market segments may be defined on the basis of three criteria: the traveler's principal reason for journeying from home (commerce or recreation); whether the traveler is part of an identifiable group (individual or group travel); and (3) whether the traveler is en route or has reached his final destination (in transit versus terminal). (The

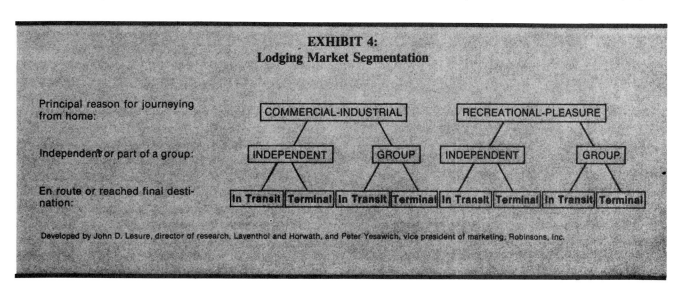

EXHIBIT 4:
Lodging Market Segmentation

Principal reason for journeying from home: COMMERCIAL-INDUSTRIAL RECREATIONAL-PLEASURE

Independent or part of a group: INDEPENDENT GROUP INDEPENDENT GROUP

En route or reached final destination: In Transit | Terminal | In Transit | Terminal | In Transit | Terminal | In Transit | Terminal

Developed by John D. Lesure, director of research, Laventhol and Horwath, and Peter Yesawich, vice president of marketing, Robinsons, Inc.

local market—i.e., individuals living near the property—is outside the purview of Exhibit 4, and is omitted from this discussion, because its contribution to gross revenue is generally limited to food and beverage sales.)

Each of the three criteria may be subdivided further, as deemed appropriate by the market planner in light of the property's marketing objectives. For example, in the general category of recreation, the market planner may wish to isolate the honeymoon, tennis, golf, or diving sub-segments; in the area of group travelers, he may wish to identify the corporate-meeting, association, or tour sub-segments.

Without a means of discriminating between the market segments that constitute a property's business, the analyst will find that the guest-history data are nothing more than a mass of confusing, even meaningless, output—because the segments differ in respect to how they purchase accommodations. For example, assume the analyst intends to base advertising decisions on the distribution of room-nights by origin market. Lacking sorting criteria, he might obtain distribution figures like those in column 1 of Exhibit 5. On the other hand, by applying appropriate segmentation criteria, he may obtain the more useful distribution figures shown in columns 2 and 3 of that exhibit, using the same data base. Clearly, the analyst concerned with advertising decisions would be more interested in the distribution for individual guests, because most group sales are consummated through personal selling. Thus, the analysis must incorporate useful segmentation criteria if it is to be used as a foundation for making sensible decisions.

Another task that warrants thought in the market analysis is that of defining **origin markets.** Several techniques have been developed to define origin markets, most of them relying on zip codes for the establishment of geographic perimeters. In their crudest form, origin markets may be defined with reference to state boundaries, but this perimeter is not specific enough to facilitate efficient market planning. For example, knowing that 35 percent of a property's room-nights are attributable to guests from the state of New York is of little value to the market planner because New York comprises several widely dispersed and economically disparate metropolitan market areas, each served by its own group of media. Consequently, more precise origin markets must be defined.

Marketers of consumer goods have adopted a variety of market definitions, all of them applicable to hospitality marketing. Perhaps most commonly known is the *Standard Metropolitan Statistical Area* (SMSA). SMSAs are geographic areas defined by the federal government in terms of economic rather than political boundaries, although political considerations occasionally distort the way they reflect economic realities. (For example, northern New Jersey communities are technically not part of the New York SMSA even though they clearly fall within the confines of its effective marketing area.) For the most part, SMSAs represent an excellent device for defining origin markets. Planners using SMSAs have an added advantage in the availability of voluminous amounts of secondary data on the origin markets under examination, because most federal reports relating to such things as population, income, and economic activity are prepared with reference to SMSAs.

A second origin-market definition, developed under the aegis of the A.C. Nielson Company, is the *Designated Market Area,* or DMA. DMAs reflect the geographic area served by clusters of television stations, and are used as the referent for data on the size and characteristics of television audiences. Thus, planners contemplating the use of television advertising might consider analyzing their room-night composition by DMAs.

A third and perhaps more useful origin-market definition is that known as the *Area of Dominant Influence,* or ADI. Developed by Arbitron, Inc., ADIs reflect the geographic area within which the majority of television households are served by a given cluster of television stations. A portion of the U.S. map divided by ADI plots is shown in Exhibit 6. Similar to the DMA in that it is defined in respect to television coverage, the ADI is a more flexible market measure because several newspapers and magazines have aligned their regional editions to correspond to these geographic boundaries. Thus,

EXHIBIT 5:
Distribution of Room-Nights

Market Area	I All Guests	II Group Guests	III Individual Guests
Chicago	31%	42%	20%
Cleveland	26%	18%	34%
St. Louis	23%	18%	28%
Milwaukee	12%	8%	16%
Detroit	8%	14%	2%
TOTAL	100%	100%	100%

NOTE: Example assumes distribution of *total* room-nights to be 50% group and 50% social.

it is possible to use ADIs as a referent for both print- and broadcast-media decisions. As with most origin-market measures, ADIs have specific zip-code correlates (defined in terms of the first three digits of the code; for example, the New York City ADI zip-code correlates are 100-119, 124-127, 068-079, and 087-089).

In sum, there are numerous techniques available to define origin markets, and the advantages and disadvantages of each are relative to the anticipated media mix to be used in the marketing program of the property. Generally, operators who expect to use several media to address their target markets will find that some combination of the

origin-market definitions discussed here serves their purposes best.

The Analysis

With units of analysis properly specified, guest segments classified, and origin markets defined, the planner may begin the analysis. Except where there are unusual requirements, frequency distributors and cross-tabulations—as shown in Exhibits 7 and 8—should provide the analyst with most of the information necessary for market planning. Of course, it may be necessary to assess the relationship between two or more items (e.g., ex-

EXHIBIT 6: ADI Plots

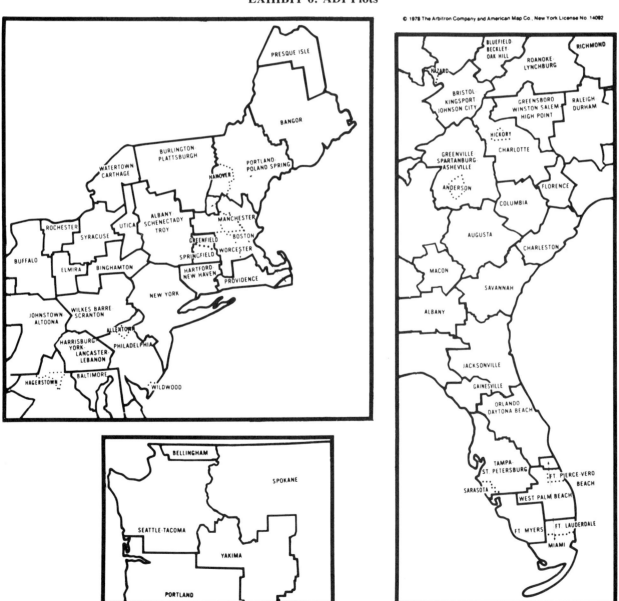

CATEGORY LABEL	CODE	ABSOLUTE FREQ.	RELATIVE FREQ (PCT)	ADJUSTED FREQ (PCT)	CUM FREQ (PCT)
PLAN STAY PLAN					
EP	1.	1238	66.4	66.5	66.5
FAP	2.	10	0.5	0.5	67.0
MAP	3.	7	0.4	0.4	67.4
SUMMER SAFARI	4.	178	9.5	9.6	76.9
GOLF SAFARI	5.	74	4.0	4.0	80.9
FAMILY SAFARI	6.	14	0.8	0.8	81.6
WINTER SAFARI	7.	32	1.7	1.7	83.4
WINTER AFFAIR	8.	29	1.6	1.6	84.9
HONEYMOON	9.	171	9.2	9.2	94.1
MEMORIAL DAY	11.	73	3.9	3.9	98.0
THANKSGIVING	14.	1	0.1	0.1	98.1
CHRISTMAS	15.	1	0.1	0.1	98.1
NEW YEARS	16.	1	0.1	0.1	98.2
SPECIAL PACKAGE	17.	29	1.6	1.6	99.7
OTHER	18.	3	0.2	0.2	99.9
	19.	2	0.1	0.1	100.0
	0.	1	0.1	MISSING	100.0
TOTAL		1864	100.0	100.0	

EXHIBIT 7: The output file for a frequency distribution may include several statistics, two of which are fundamental to the market analysis: the absolute frequency and the adjusted frequency percentage. The absolute frequency is the number of registrations in each of the "category label" classifications listed in the left-hand column of the table. The adjusted frequency percentage (second column from the right) is the absolute frequency expressed as a percentage, with registrations on which no information was available deleted from the computation. In this example, the data indicate that 1,238 of the 1,864 registering parties during the period purchased their accommodations on the European Plan (EP); 178 purchased the summer-safari package; 171 bought the honeymoon package; and so forth. These figures are converted to percentages in the adjusted-frequency column (EP, 67%; summer safari, 10%; honeymoon, 9%).

penditures for advertising and market share of room nights), for which more sophisticated statistical procedures, such as regression analysis, would be appropriate.

Regardless of the time period under study (e.g., the entire year, a particular season, a given month, or even days of the week), the registration records processed in the analysis should be representative of all registrations during the period. Obviously, the most accurate picture of what transpired during the period would be obtained by processing every registration record—but, because this is not always feasible, the analyst may find he can process only a sample of registrations. It should be emphasized that it is possible to process only a sample of records without compromising the accuracy of the results as long as the sample is drawn properly. Without delving into the nuances of sampling theory here, let us state that a stratified random sample with proportional allocation (where the cri-

```
* * * * * * * * * * * * * * * * * * * * * * * * * * * * * * * * * *
* * *   ZIP    ZIP CODE OF RESIDENCE   * * *   C R O S S T A B U L A T I O N   * * *   * * *   * * *
* * *   ZIP                   BY ARRIVAL   DATE OF ARRIVAL   * * *   PAGE  1 OF  2
* * * * * * * * * * * * * * * * * * * * * * * * * * * * * * * * * *
```

ARRIVAL		JULY 77	AUGUST 77	SEPTEMBER 77	OCTOBER 77	NOVEMBER 77	DECEMBER 77	JANUARY 78	FEBRUARY 78	MARCH 78	UNCLASSIFIED	ROW TOTAL
ZIP	COUNT / ROW PCT / COL PCT	1.I	2.I	3.I	4.I	5.I	6.I	7.I	8.I	9.I	10.I	
JACKSONVILLE ADI 1.	COUNT	14	6	1	1	4	5	6	14	5	0	56
	ROW PCT	25.0	10.7	1.8	1.8	7.1	8.9	10.7	25.0	8.9	0.0	1.1
	COL PCT	2.8	1.4	0.5	0.3	0.8	0.9	1.1	1.4	0.4	0.0	
ORLANDO ADI 2.	COUNT	15	4	7	6	15	7	2	9	4	1	70
	ROW PCT	21.4	5.7	10.0	8.6	21.4	10.0	2.9	12.9	5.7	1.4	1.3
	COL PCT	2.9	0.9	3.8	1.9	2.9	1.3	0.4	0.9	0.3	2.4	
MIAMI ADI 3.	COUNT	85	54	16	85	45	76	80	82	126	6	655
	ROW PCT	13.0	8.2	2.4	13.0	6.9	11.6	12.2	12.5	19.2	0.9	12.5
	COL PCT	16.7	12.2	8.7	26.7	8.8	14.2	14.1	8.2	11.0	14.6	
TAMPA ST PETE AD 4.	COUNT	26	26	35	22	11	8	22	22	46	1	219
	ROW PCT	11.9	11.9	16.0	10.0	5.0	3.7	10.0	10.0	21.0	0.5	4.2
	COL PCT	5.1	5.9	19.1	6.9	2.1	1.5	3.9	2.2	4.0	2.4	
NEW YORK ADI 5.	COUNT	39	13	3	14	31	43	52	106	87	2	390
	ROW PCT	10.0	3.3	0.8	3.6	7.9	11.0	13.3	27.2	22.3	0.5	7.4
	COL PCT	7.7	2.9	1.6	4.4	6.1	8.0	9.2	10.6	7.6	4.9	
LOS ANGELES ADI 6.	COUNT	4	4	1	3	13	8	7	8	12	3	63
	ROW PCT	6.4	6.3	1.6	4.8	20.6	12.7	11.1	12.7	19.0	4.8	1.2
	COL PCT	0.8	0.9	0.5	0.9	2.5	1.5	1.2	0.8	1.0	7.3	
CHICAGO ADI 7.	COUNT	8	7	3	1	18	26	34	37	66	1	201
	ROW PCT	4.0	3.5	1.5	0.5	9.0	12.9	16.9	18.4	32.8	0.5	3.8
	COL PCT	1.6	1.6	1.6	0.3	3.5	4.9	6.0	3.7	5.8	2.4	
PHILADELPHIA ADI 8.	COUNT	4	6	3	3	19	10	12	42	37	1	137
	ROW PCT	2.9	4.4	2.2	2.2	13.9	7.3	8.8	30.7	27.0	0.7	2.6
	COL PCT	0.8	1.4	1.6	0.9	3.7	1.9	2.1	4.2	3.2	2.4	
COLUMN TOTAL		509	443	183	318	512	535	568	997	1144	41	5250
		9.7	8.4	3.5	6.1	9.8	10.2	10.8	19.0	21.8	0.8	100.0

EXHIBIT 8: In this figure, the ADI origins of guests have been cross-tabulated by date of arrival (month). Each "cell" of the cross-tabulation contains three items: 1) the number of room-nights (top item); 2) the "row percentage room-nights" (middle item) — the room-nights expressed as a percentage of all room-nights traceable to the specific ADI during the 12-month period; and 3) the "column room-nights" (bottom item) — the room-nights expressed as a percentage of all room-nights booked on the property during the month. Because the tabulation runs both vertically and horizontally, the table may be read in either direction. For example, the table reveals that 12.2 percent of all room-nights traceable to the Miami ADI over the 12-month period were realized during the month of January; 12.5 percent during the month of February, 19.2 percent during the month of March, and so on. However, guests from Miami accounted for 14.1 percent of all room-nights during the month of January, 0.4 percent were accounted for by guests from Orlando, 3.9 percent by guests from Tampa-St. Petersburg, 9.2 percent by guests from New York, and so on. Thus, reading down the column percentages will reveal the share of room-nights contributed by the various ADIs during any given month. Reading across the row percentages will reveal how each ADI "moves" by month of the year.

terion for stratification is month of arrival) will yield an accurate picture of current guest composition. A systematic sample (i.e., one comprising *every nth* registration) will also suffice if the records are filed chronologically by date of arrival. In short, planners interested exclusively in a statistical profile of their guests have no reason to work with a complete set of registration records because all of the information they require can be obtained accurately—and less expensively—from a sample. The primary advantage to processing all registration records is that guests' names and addresses may be recorded at the time statistical information is obtained and used at a later date for direct-mail promotion.

The planner must next compare the profile of the property's guests to all information available from the area-prospect profile. A sample profile for independent commercial guests is provided in Exhibit 9. Profiles of this sort should be prepared for all market segments identified.

Once the guest profiles have been constructed, the planner can proceed to establish reasonable objectives for the marketing program and adopt an appropriate marketing strategy.

Objectives

The overall objective of the marketing program is, of course, to increase the dollar volume of business. But as the operative goals necessary to achieve this larger objective, the planner may wish to specify his expectations in terms of two significant measures of activity that contribute to gross dollar volume: (1) guest-room occupancy, and (2) market mix of room-nights. Objectives should also be stated with reference to the time period over which the marketing funds will be expended and the time required for the volume and composition of room nights to reflect the marketing efforts. Generally, these two temporal periods should be designed to fall within the same 12 months, but shorter (seasonal) and longer (biennial) periods may be appropriate, depending on the nature of the program.

For most operators, determining the amount of money to spend on marketing is a fairly routine task because budgets are generally established with reference to either past or projected sales. A less scientific approach still extant is the "whatever's-left-over method"—a technique that does little to facilitate long-term growth. More astute operators have adopted a zero-base approach, whereby the budget is established as a function of program need and not in terms of what has been expended in the past.

When the budget has been established, the objectives of the program may be made final. Whether the projected increase in gross dollar volume is to be achieved through an increase in guest-room occupancy, a more lucrative market mix, or both, is a decision left to management. This decision should be based on management's evaluation of its own strengths and weaknesses, as well as the competitive atmosphere within which the property must be marketed.

The market planner frequently finds that he must bridle his enthusiasm to insure the objectives he establishes are reasonable. Perhaps the most common error at this stage of planning is that of setting overly ambitious objectives, particularly for guest-room occupancy. It has been the experience of

---

EXHIBIT 9:
Profile of Commercial (Independent) Guests
(30-Day Period)

	Property	Area*
1) Percentage of Total Room-Nights	55%	47%
2) Average Reservation Lead Time (Days)	9	N/A
3) Percentage Reservations Through "800" Number	78%	N/A
4) Percentage of Reservations Made By Guest or Representative Thereof	95%	N/A
5) Percentage of Reservations Made By Travel Agents	5%	3%
6) Percentage of Walk-Ins	8%	15%
7) Percentage Staying EP	100%	N/A
8) Percentage of Room-Nights From Top 3 ADIs:		
New York	32%	28%
Washington, D.C.	21%	30%
Boston	15%	17%
9) Average Number in Party	1.2	N/A
10) Average Room Rate	$42.50	$38.00
11) Average Length of Stay (Nights)	2.3	2.0
12) Average Total of Folio Charges	$112.40	N/A
13) Percentage Settling Account With Credit Card:		
American Express	40%	N/A
Visa	21%	N/A
Master Charge	18%	N/A
Diners Club	8%	N/A
14) Estimated Total Revenue Contribution	$162,000.00	N/A

*Estimated from secondary sources.
N/A: Not available.

FIGURE A   **FIGURE B**

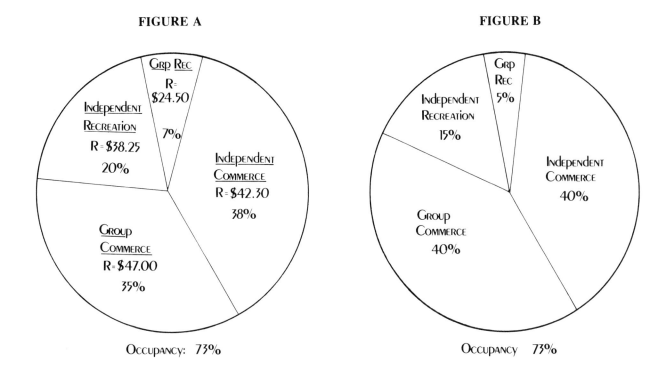

R = Estimated revenue per registrant per room-night, including personal food and beverage expenditures for all guests, and meeting room, banquet, and beverage revenues from functions for group guests.

most properties that annual increments in occupancy resulting from a concerted marketing effort are not likely to exceed six to nine percent annually, assuming relatively stable market conditions (e.g., no major increase in the number of available guest rooms; no significant depression of local, regional, or national economic activity; no major alterations in transportation access to the destination), and may be far lower, depending on the amount of the marketing investment.

The composition of room-nights that will yield the highest gross dollar volume (even if total occupancy remains unchanged) will become evident subsequent to the prime-prospect analysis. Examination of the revenue contributed by each market segment per registrant per room-night will indicate to the market planner what the most desirable mix of business is. For example, assume the prime-prospect analysis of a given establishment yields the room-night composition depicted in Figure A. (Note that only two segmentation criteria have

been used in this example: commerce versus recreation, and independent versus group.) Group commercial guests accounted for the highest revenue ($47.00) per registration per room-night, followed by independent commercial guests ($42.30), independent recreational guests ($38.25), and group recreational guests ($24.50). It is evident that the two commercial segments of the market contribute substantially more revenue than the others; thus, the market planner might establish the room-night mix depicted in Figure B as the establishment's objective for the next fiscal year.

Strategy

The next step in the development of the marketing program is the adoption of a strategy for achieving the objectives. There are three fundamental strategies from which the market planner may select: (1) differentiation, (2) segmentation, and (3) a differentiation-segmentation combination. [2]

As its name implies, a differentiation strategy is one in which the differences between competitive establishments are emphasized. This strategy may be appropriate where prospective guests can perceive a discernible difference between one property (or group) and its competitors. The source of differentiation may be either real or "manufactured," but it is worth noting that a differentiation strategy based on relatively elusive qualities (e.g., quality of guest service) runs a higher risk of failure than one based on tangible differences like location. Furthermore, differentiation stragegies are most effective when the individuals defined as constituting the market exhibit a high degree of demographic, geographic, and psychographic homogeneity. As most market planners will attest, this is not typically the case in the lodging industry.

The second strategy alternative, market segmentation, has gained considerable favor among practitioners in recent years and is generally regarded as more efficient than differentiation. Segmentation is based on the premise that the market comprises several demand-specific sub-markets: for example, some guests may be interested primarily in recreational facilities, others in rates, and still others in location. When the total market may be divided into several subsegments, each with a dominant affinity—and this is generally the case for lodging establishments—a segmentation strategy will typically prove most effective.

The third alternative is to adopt both the differentiation and segmentation approaches, either simultaneously or in a predetermined sequence designed to accommodate market changes. Assuming the total market is segmentable, it is likely that several properties are in direct competition for the same subsegments; as a result, differentiation with the subsegments may be required. This is generally the case where a number of lodging establishments in an area offer essentially the same services and amenities to guests.

Strategy selection should be based upon six considerations: (1) the size of the total market, (2) market sensitivity to differences between establishments, (3) the number of years the establishment has been in operation, (4) the distinctiveness of the establishment, (5) the number of competitors, and (6) competitors' marketing strategies.

A differentiation strategy will generally prove most appropriate where the following can be demonstrated:

1. The total market is demographically, geographically, and psychologically homogeneous;
2. Market sensitivity to differences between establishments is high;
3. The establishment is relatively new;
4. The establishment is distinctive;
5. There are few competing establishments; and
6. Most competitors employ a differentiation strategy.

A segmentation strategy is most appropriate when the following conditions prevail:

1. The total market is demographically, geographically, and psychologically diffuse;
2. Market sensitivity to differences between establishments is low;
3. The establishment has been in operation for several years;
4. The establishment is not distinctive;
5. There are several competing establishments; and
6. Most competitors employ a segmentation strategy.

When the establishment in question cannot be classified definitively as belonging to one of these two categories, a combination of differentiation and segmentation strategies is probably called for.

Conclusion

In summary, the development of a successful marketing plan must begin with the preparation of both property and prospect profiles. Having established which lodging services will be marketed to whom, the planner can proceed with the determination of objectives and the selection of a strategy. The next two steps of the marketing process—program execution and measurement—will be the subject of an article appearing in Part VI of this book.

2. B. W. Kotrba, "The Strategy Selection Chart," *Journal of Marketing*, 30 (1966), pp. 22-25.

Guest Surveys: A Missed Opportunity

by Robert C. Lewis and
Abraham Pizam

Effective management depends on information. Guest surveys could offer crucial information for evaluating current policies and making management decisions, but many surveys in use today obscure as much as they reveal. This article shows how traditional surveys fail and outlines a new method for getting the facts.

Robert C. Lewis, Ph.D., is an associate professor of marketing and managment in the department of hotel, restaurant, and travel administration at the University of Massachusetts. Abraham Pizam, Ph.D., is a professor in the same department and is currently on sabbatical leave at the University of Surrey, England.

Most hospitality enterprises use some form of in-house guest survey. A recent national survey of hotel executives revealed that 92 percent of the respondents use guest surveys either continually or sporadically.[1] Hoteliers use the comment cards placed in hotel rooms, restaurants, coffee shops, and cocktail lounges to measure their properties' performance and guest satisfaction. Some companies also use them to "grade" management and to compare properties.

These uses of guest-survey responses mandate that the data-collection method yield an accurate measurement of guest satisfaction that is statistically valid and readily interpreted. When surveys meet these requirements, they can indeed be powerful tools for management action and planning, as well as for measuring management performance. Unfortunately, most guest-survey methods now used fail in these respects. This article describes the inadequacies of present methods and proposes a new method of measuring guest satisfaction and management performance to overcome most of these shortcomings.

Present Methods

The numerous guest survey forms in use today all share common faults. Exhibit 1 depicts four forms currently used by major hotel chains. Form A is based on an excellent-to-poor rating system for four different areas of hotel operations, with three or four subdivisions in each area. This form appears to use an ordinal scale, but actually employs a gross rating system that produces results that defy meaningful interpretation or appropriate management action. In fact, the form raises more questions than it answers.

Let us assume, for example, that most guests check "fair" under the category "front desk." This judgment might reflect a range of problems. One guest might have had a long wait before checking in. Another might have encountered a surly clerk. In other cases, the clerk might have been unable to find the guest's registration or might have been wearing a soiled uniform.

Or consider the category "cleanliness." How is management to interpret low ratings in this area? Do they indicate that the bathroom was untidy, or the bedroom, or both? Perhaps the guest gave a low rating because the room had not been vacuumed, or perhaps because paint was peeling

This article was originally published in the November 1981 issue of *The Cornell Hotel and Restaurant Administration Quarterly*, pp. 37-44, and is reprinted here with the permission of the Cornell University School of Hotel Administration. ©1981.

1. Thomas J. Beggs and Robert C. Lewis, "How the Industry Sees Inflation and Plans to Cope with It. 1981-1985—A Survey," (Paper delivered at the World Hospitality Congress, Boston, March 11, 1981), p. 12.

from the walls. Management cannot interpret what a low (or high) rating of "cleanliness" means from this type of survey. The same holds true for the category "swimming pool." Does "poor" mean that the pool was too small, or that it was too hot or cold? Were there no towels or were pool hours too limited? All mangement can do with the results of such a survey is gain a crude notion of various problem areas in the hotel's operations.

Given the exceedingly vague nature of the data thus obtained, management is also unable to interpret the responses in terms of the crucial consideration: the guest's general satisfaction. Does an "excellent" rating in some categories, accompanied by "good," "fair," or "poor" ratings in others, mean that the guest is satisfied and likely to return? The form provides little basis for making such a judgment or for comparing the management of one hotel to that of others.

Form B, a comment card used in the restaurants of a large hotel chain, provides a strictly nominal categorization that is even less meaning-ful than the previous form. Consider the first question, "Were you greeted as you entered?" What does a "yes" or "no" answer signify? (*Yes, I was greeted* . . . politely, abruptly, courteously? *No, I was not greeted* . . . did it matter?) This same difficulty in interpreting responses is found in all the remaining questions. Again, how does management interpret the responses and correct for any failings identified in this fashion?

Form C solicits guest responses on what could be construed as an interval-level scale. Although the scale may produce responses that are somewhat more meaningful than those in the preceding surveys, the questionnaire is still plagued by similar difficulties. What, for example, do three stars for "reservationist" mean in terms of management action and planning?

Form D is the most valid of the four formats pictured. By posing questions in terms of guests' expectations, the form gives some indication of guests' satisfaction with each area of hotel operations. Guests are also allowed to state specifically

---

EXHIBIT 1
Guest survey forms currently in use

FORM A

Please rate us ✔	Excellent	Good	Fair	Poor
CHECKING IN				
Reservation	☐	☐	☐	☐
Front Desk	☐	☐	☐	☐
Bellman	☐	☐	☐	☐
YOUR ROOM				
Cleanliness	☐	☐	☐	☐
TV/Radio	☐	☐	☐	☐
Bath	☐	☐	☐	☐
Bed/Furnishings	☐	☐	☐	☐
RESTAURANT/ LOUNGE				
Food	☐	☐	☐	☐
Beverages	☐	☐	☐	☐
Service	☐	☐	☐	☐
GENERAL				
Swimming Pool	☐	☐	☐	☐
Parking	☐	☐	☐	☐
Room Service	☐	☐	☐	☐

FORM B

TO OUR GUESTS: A moment of your time in completing and giving this card to your hostess will help us serve you better in the future. Thank you.

Date _____ Time _____ ☐ A.M. ☐ P.M. How Many In Your Party? ___

Server's Name _____ Are you: ☐ Local ☐ Out of Town

HOSPITALITY

Were you greeted as you entered? .... ☐ YES ☐ NO
Did the hostess/host seat you? .... ☐ YES ☐ NO
Did server introduce her/himself by name? .... ☐ YES ☐ NO
Were you thanked and invited to return? .... ☐ YES ☐ NO

FOOD AND SERVICE

Was food served promptly? .... ☐ YES ☐ NO
Was your order correct? .... ☐ YES ☐ NO
Was food properly prepared? .... ☐ YES ☐ NO
Did you receive smiling, courteous service? .... ☐ YES ☐ NO

ENVIRONMENT

Did our staff have a neat, clean appearance? .... ☐ YES ☐ NO
Were your dining area and dining utensils clean? .... ☐ YES ☐ NO
Was the restaurant clean overall? .... ☐ YES ☐ NO
Was the restroom clean and properly supplied? .... ☐ YES ☐ NO

why certain elements of the operation did or did not meet their expectations. Although this form should allow management to pinpoint the areas requiring corrective action, two problems remain. First, the form does not answer the single most important question: Overall, is the guest satisfied or dissatisfied (and will the guest return)? It is crucial to discover which categories of hotel operation are important to the guest in making this decision. The second problem is one of tabulation. Because the responses include written comments, coding them will be both troublesome and time-consuming, making it less likely that a busy managerial staff will attend to the survey's results.

Large-scale studies. Some companies have commissioned large-scale studies using random sampling techniques, as distinguished from the self-selection techniques of in-house surveys, to construct a profile of the hotel guest. Exhibits 2 and 3 show the results of one such survey, in which the response rate was approximately 35 percent from a sample group of 5,200. The study was designed to determine the importance of various facilities to hotel guests and their satisfaction with certain hotel services.

Exhibit 2 shows, for example, that beds were either very important or somewhat important to 98 percent of the respondents; that a friendly hotel staff was similarly important to 97 percent; that the bathroom was important to 96 percent; and that bars and lounges were important to only 68 percent of the guests. How does one interpret these data in a meaningful way? To be absurd, do the survey's results indicate that two percent of the respondents did not care about beds and that four percent did not care about bathrooms? Would the 32 percent who did not consider bars and lounges important be satisfied with the hotel as a whole if there were no bar or lounge?

Exhibit 3 indicates that 89.3 percent of the survey respondents were satisfied with the hotel's reservation service, but only 66.2 percent were satisfied with its bars and lounges. The correlation between importance (Exhibit 2) and satisfaction

---

FORM C

We'd like to know. Please help us make your future visits with us more pleasant by rating our service from one star (*) to five (*****)

	** ***	** **	***	**	*

Your arrival and reception

a. Reservationist

b. Doorman

c. Registration clerk

d. Bellman

e. Telephone operator

f. Cashier

g. Garage

h. Maid service

i. Concierge

Entertainment and dining facilities

a. Dining room—Breakfast/Lunch

b. Dining room—Dinner/Evening

c. Lobby lounge

d. Room service

e. Bar

f. Catering and banquets

FORM D

Your criticism is our most valuable source of information. If we did not meet your expectations in any area, your specific comments will help us to improve our services.

Exceeds Expecta-tions	Meets Expecta-tions	Below Expecta-tions	**Your Specific Comments are Appreciated**
			Doorman: _____
			Reception Desk: _____
			Did you have any questions the receptionists were unable to answer? Yes ☐ No ☐
			Bellman: _____
			Did you have to wait for service? Yes ☐ No ☐ Did the bellman explain the hotel facilities and the use of the bar? Yes ☐ No ☐
			Accommodations: _____
			Was your bed turned down in the evening? Yes ☐ No ☐ Were mints placed on your pillow? Yes ☐ No ☐ Was ice kept in your refrigerator? Yes ☐ No ☐
			Telephone Operator: _____
			Room Service: _____

EXHIBIT 2
Importance of various facilities to the hotel guest

	Very/ Somewhat Important	Very Important	Somewhat Important
Beds	98%	84%	14%
Friendly hotel staff	97	77	20
Bathroom	96	72	24
Professional hotel staff	95	77	18
Safety and security	95	69	26
Towels	94	65	29
Housekeeping services	93	64	29
Price—value	93	59	34
Restaurants	92	66	26
Reservation service	90	70	20
Check-in	86	51	35
Coffee shops	85	48	37
Size of room	85	33	52
Message service	83	55	28
Check-out	80	47	33
Decor and ambience	80	26	54
Wake-up call	79	57	22
Bars and lounges	68	34	34

Source: *Profile of the Profitable Guest* (New York: Time, 1979), pp. 12–14.

EXHIBIT 3
Percentage of guests satisfied with various hotel facilities

	Total
Reservation service	89.3%
Check-in	87.2
Check-out	86.2
Quality of Room Services	
Closet space	88.3
Safety and security	87.7
Size of room	87.4
Towels	87.2
Beds	86.9
Bathroom	86.7
Quality of General Services	
Housekeeping services	82.3
Wake-up call	81.5
Message service	73.8
Baggage handling	71.4
Room service	66.4
Laundry and valet	61.0
Recreational facilities	60.2
Courtesy airport service	53.4
Quality of Eating and Drinking Facilities	
Restaurants	68.7
Bars and lounges	66.2
Coffee shops	66.1

Source: *Profile of the Profitable Guest* (New York: Time, 1979), pp. 12–14.

(Exhibit 3) is close to 100 percent. Does this correlation mean that those who find services important also tend to be satisfied if they exist? What about those who find certain services unimportant? Are they satisfied or dissatisfied? If they are dissatisfied, is it because they think the existing services are unimportant, or because important services are not present? Finally, and most significant, if 89.3 percent of the guests are satisfied with a property's reservation service and only 66.4 percent are satisfied with its room service, which ones will return, and which ones will not?

The Problems

Such minute and exacting interpretation of survey responses is more than just an exercise. Rather, it vividly emphasizes the fact that hoteliers face serious problems when it comes time to interpret survey data and use them for planning or action. In summary, the guest-survey methods examined above suffer from the following deficiencies:

- It is difficult, if not impossible, to tabulate the data produced by these methods in a meaningful way. Eighty-six "yes" responses and 18 "no"s provide no revelations, nor do 28 "excellent"s, 16 "good"s, 20 "fair"s, and six "poor"s. Such data cannot be used to compare or rate management or to improve operations. Of course, if 86 percent of all guests rate a particular area "poor," it is clear that the area warrants immediate attention. But if 24 percent rate an area "poor," what should management do? This 24 percent might represent the most profitable segment of the hotel's market.

- These survey methods allow no measurement of the *relative* importance of different categories. For example, 98 percent of the guests might be dissatisfied with the swimming pool, but be quite ready to return to the hotel if they were completely satisfied with the cleanliness of the bathrooms.

- Existing survey types are entirely *product-oriented*. While this information is important to management (if it can be interpreted), equally important is a marketing orientation that deals directly with the *experience* of the guest. Is the guest satisfied? Will the guest return? Is the hotel satisfying the needs and wants of its target market?

In addition, there are statistical difficulties with current in-house surveys. These include the following:

• **Pragmatic validity:** Can the results be used to predict behavior?

• **Content validity:** Does the measurement instrument capture the most significant "domain of concern" (i.e., is the domain of concern—satisfaction—the same as the domain being measured—operations)?

• **Construct validity:** Is the instrument measuring what it is supposed to measure? Is it actually measuring satisfaction, or operations, or is it measuring something else (e.g., guests' expectations, guests' moods, operating expertise)?

• **Sample validity:** Is the sample truly representative of the hotel clientele? Or does it represent only those who are unusually satisfied or dissatisfied—based, possibly, on singular experiences or expectations?

All of these questions can easily be answered in the negative. Obviously, there is a need for a more meaningful survey instrument.

The Ideal Survey Format

A guest survey (satisfaction index) should measure dominant trends in consumer preferences, satisfaction, and behavior. These trends are sufficiently pervasive that they should be obvious in any carefully executed survey. Conventional market research focuses on the major consumer trends, problems, and opportunities that affect a company as a whole. Individual markets become the subject of investigation when the issues are important enough and the market is large enough to justify the effort.

In the hospitality industry, market research should provide reliable managerial and marketing information at the lowest level of market impact: the individual lodging property. Ensuring that the management of each property is aware of local market conditions and able to respond to them substantially enhances the market position of the company as a whole. To this end, the guest survey should provide straightforward information on the guests' needs and wants and their assessment of the hotel's facilities and services.

There is a tendency in consumer research to

want to ask *every* question that may be remotely relevant; after all, management needs to know about *every* facet of the operation and the consumer. Yet, as is evident in Exhibit 1, hotels pragmatically limit the questions they ask, to facilitate both response and interpretation. In this aspect of survey design, at least, hoteliers have been on the right track. A guest survey should deal with a limited number of issues at one time. However, although it should be parsimonious, a guest survey should also encompass all of the elements that may be significant.

Hotel units in a chain have a great deal in common with one another, from a researcher's perspective. Each unit is likely to have similar problems and opportunities, despite the unique characteristics of its market. Thus, a guest survey should be unique to the individual property, but, at the same time, should be sufficiently standardized for the purposes of research and comparison. The broad, comprehensive studies produced by conventional market research meet this latter requirement very well, but are often expensive and time-consuming to design, execute, and analyze. If the goal is to encourage more informed decision-making by the management of individual properties, it is better to conduct a few small studies rather than a single comprehensive one. Accordingly, a guest survey should be tailored to an individual property, keeping in mind the fundamental similarities of related hotel establishments. It should be executed quickly, and the results returned to management so that immediate and appropriate action may be taken.

Finally, a guest survey should address the pivotal issue of whether the guest will or will not return. This is the bottom line in assessing guest satisfaction and affects the interpretation of all other data gathered with the survey.

A New Approach

There are three essential steps in developing a guest survey that overcomes the shortcomings of existing surveys and fulfills the requisites described above. First, it is necessary to identify the prime determinants of hotel guest satisfaction. Second, the *relative* contribution of each of these determinants to the guest's overall satisfaction must be calculated and computed on a percentage basis. Finally, based on this information, it is necessary to develop a survey that:

• can be readily applied and analyzed by management,

- is easily adaptable to any individual chain, hotel, or target market, and
- is comprehensive and statistically valid.

Satisfaction determinants. To identify which variables of hotel satisfaction and dissatisfaction are important to hotel guests, the authors conducted a series of focus-group interviews. The findings provided the basis for a questionnaire consisting of 41 determinants of guest satisfaction to be rated on a 1-to-5 scale of importance for each determinant. An additional question, measuring the guest's overall satisfaction with a specific hotel stay, was added to serve as the dependent variable.

The questionnaires were placed with a cover letter on guests' pillows the night before check-out in three different hotels. At check-out time, each guest was reminded to submit the completed questionnaire. This method of administration differs significantly from the prevalent practice of leaving guest comment cards on a chest of drawers or nightstand. The method appeared to increase the response rate, and hence the representativeness of the sample, by reducing the probability that only highly dissatisfied or satisfied guests would respond.

Honing the survey. To develop a parsimonious instrument, it was necessary to reduce the number of determinants of satisfaction included in the final survey form through factor analysis, a procedure that allowed the authors to identify related determinants of guest satisfaction. These related determinants, or dimensions, were then used to develop the final survey instrument. When a particular dimension was identified, the components of that dimension were combined in a single question that addressed the range of determinants constituting the dimension. Thus, both parsimoniousness and breadth were achieved in the final survey form.

For example, factor analysis identified the following 11 dimensions (from the 41 original variables) for one hotel:

1. Room and bathroom quality;
2. Room and bathroom cleanliness;
3. Front-desk services;
4. Prices (relative and actual);
5. Restaurants—availability, quality, and services;
6. Professionalism of staff;
7. Convenience and availability of services;
8. Room service;
9. Prestige and aesthetic appeal of property;
10. Sports facilities; and
11. Bathroom condition and maintenance.

Weighting the dimensions. The guests' rating of the importance of each factor was computed as the first step in calculating the relative weights for each dimension. The factor ratings were then regressed against the overall measure of satisfaction with the hotel, producing coefficient weights indicating the relative importance or contribution of the guests' reaction to each dimension in determining their overall satisfaction with the hotel stay. For example, in the hotel mentioned above, the following three coefficient weights (significant at < .05) were derived:

1) Room and bathroom quality	.42
8) Room service	.33
7) Convenience and availability of services	.25

In other words, dimension 1 (room and bathroom quality) was 27 percent more important in determining guests' total satisfaction than dimension 8 (room service) and 68 percent more important in determining total satisfaction than dimension 7 (convenience and availability of services). Other weights, indicating the relative contribution of each dimension to the guest's overall satisfaction, are obtainable for the remaining eight dimensions. Similar weights may also be obtained for the variables within each dimension.

The final survey. The final survey instrument to be used by the hotel should employ the significant dimensions identified by factor analysis and revised in accordance with management's concerns. The guest's response to this instrument is interpreted in terms of the weight assigned to each dimension.

For example, assume that the five dimensions shown in the two tables of Exhibit 4 have been identified as the significant determinants of guest satisfaction. The numbers in the first column of the two tables represent the relative weight of each dimension in determining overall satisfaction. The numbers in the second column of the two tables are hypothetical mean responses, with 5 signifying a high degree of satisfaction and 1 indicating a high degree of dissatisfaction. In the first table, these hypothetical means run sequentially from 5 to 1. In the second table the order is reversed, although the sum, of course, is 15 in both cases. Using conventional methods of surveying, in which weights are not assigned to the various dimensions of guest experience, overall satisfaction is determined to be 60 percent in both examples. Using the weighted index, however, satisfac-

EXHIBIT 4
Weighted guest-survey responses

Table 1

Dimensions	Weights	Mean rating (1 to 5)	Maximum possible ratings	Actual weighted ratings*	Possible weighted ratings‡
Room and bath quality	.308	5	5	1.540	1.540
Room service	.262	4	5	1.048	1.310
Convenience and avail-ability of services	.172	3	5	.516	.860
Sports facilities	.150	2	5	.302	.750
Staff professionalism	.108	1	5	.108	.540
TOTAL	1.000	15	25	3.514	5.000
SATISFACTION LEVEL		15/25 = 60% (without weighting)		3.514/5.000 = 70.3% (with weighting)	

Table 2 (with reversed mean ratings)

Dimensions	Weights	Mean rating	Maximum possible	Actual weighted	Possible weighted
Room and bath quality	.308	1	5	.308	1.540
Room service	.262	2	5	.524	1.310
Convenience and avail-ability of services	.172	3	5	.516	.860
Sports facilities	.150	4	5	.604	.750
Staff professionalism	.108	5	5	.540	.540
TOTAL	1.000	15	25	2.492	5.000
SATISFACTION LEVEL		15/25 = 60% (without weighting)		2.492/5.000 = 49.8% (with weighting)	

*The weighted rating is obtained by multiplying the mean rating (column 2) × the weight coefficient (column 1).

‡The possible weighted rating is obtained by multiplying the highest possible mean rating (5) × the weight coefficient (column 1).

tion is determined to be 70.3 percent in the first example and 49.8 percent in the second, owing to the different importance of various dimensions in determining overall satisfaction. Obviously, there is a significant difference in the degree of guest satisfaction and the likelihood of repeat business. A conventional survey instrument, lacking a weighted index, would not detect this difference.

If management wishes to identify the specific problem areas in the dimension of room and bathroom quality, it may construct a survey instrument based on the determinants that gave rise to the broad dimension of room and bathroom quality through factor analysis. These determinants will again be accompanied by a weighted index, which will allow management to interpret the survey's results in terms of the crucial consideration of overall satisfaction.

Market segments. Still another important finding is available to management through the use of this survey instrument. The simple addition to the questionnaire of one or more demographic or purpose-of-stay questions would allow management to determine the satisfaction of a particular market segment. For example, the management of a hotel that has always had a largely male or business clientele might want to know how well the hotel is satisfying a small but growing female or pleasure-traveler clientele. With the addition of a demographic question, responses from one segment can be easily isolated and compared to those from another segment.

The Survey's Virtues

The use of this survey technique to gauge hotel guests' satisfaction provides a quick measure of overall guest satisfaction at various points in time. It identifies those dimensions in which satisfaction or dissatisfaction occurs and, further, identifies the individual determinants that constitute each dimension and that are the specific causes of satisfaction or dissatisfaction. The instrument is easily completed by the guest, and responses are easily tabulated and analyzed by management. The results will be valid and reliable for rating management, locating operational flaws, determining guests' needs and wants, determining marketing positions to target markets, tracking trends, making comparisons among properties, and measuring improvements over time.

The survey technique proposed here diverges from existing techniques in the following respects:

1. The final survey is based on an examination (through focus-group interviews) of the needs and wants of the specific market that the hotel serves. Consequently, it is directed to that market's concerns. For example, the dimensions of concern and the weighted satisfaction index used to interpret guests' evaluations of these dimensions will differ for mid-city hotels, resort hotels, convention hotels, and budget hotels.

2. Only those factors that have been found to be empirically related to overall guest satisfaction are included in the survey. Factors that by themselves might show high or low guest ratings, but that are not correlated with overall guest satisfaction with a hotel stay (and that are therefore of less significance), are eliminated.

3. Each satisfaction factor in the survey is assigned a differential weight reflecting the factors' contribution to overall guest satisfaction. In the guest surveys commonly in use today, equal weights are assumed for all factors—so that, for example, the availability of a sauna is judged to be just as important to overall satisfaction as the quality of the food in the restaurant or the efficiency of registration procedures.

4. The survey is easy to administer, code, and analyze because it is parsimonious—but not at the expense of important factors or variables. The number of variables and factors is reduced through fact analysis, which combines many variables into fewer common factors, and multiple regression, which correlates the factors with overall satisfaction and eliminates those that have little effect on satisfaction.

A representative sample. The problem of obtaining a truly representative sample and the related problem of a low response rate in the use of in-room guest questionnaires are inherent in the use of any survey. The alternative is research conducted in a different manner using standard sampling techniques. This method, however, has its own problems, not the least of which are the high cost of such techniques and the delay in obtaining useful data. To deal with the problem of obtaining a representative sample for the survey, the authors make two recommendations.

First, the survey should be used intermittently. There is little doubt that in-room comment cards have become so commonplace in hotels that they are usually ignored except by very irate or very pleased guests. If guests encounter surveys less frequently, they may be more inclined to use them, especially if the surveys are placed in conspicuous places (e.g., on the pillow), and if the cashier specifically asks for them at check-out time. Second, management should offer a reward for completion and return of the survey, such as a free drink in the bar or a free continental breakfast. Even if the incentive costs the hotel 50¢ per guest, the cost per 1,000 responses (a more than adequate sample size) would only be $500. If the survey were conducted ten times a year, the total cost would be $5,000. This is not an insignificant sum, but consider the alternatives; the current methods that produce invalid or unreliable results, or an expensive full-scale research study that yields a small sample and is often subject to sufficient delay to compromise the results.

Conclusion

A precise knowledge of the product and the market are essential in any business endeavor. In the hospitality industry, where a large part of the product is service, which can fluctuate widely, and where guests' full satisfaction is crucial to repeat business, such knowledge is particularly important. Developing a guest survey that yields the information hoteliers need is well worth the investment of time and dollars.

Marketing to Meeting Planners: What Works?

by Heidi Bloom

A recent study yields insight into the composition of the meetings market and suggests where hoteliers should spend their marketing dollars

Heidi Bloom is sales manager at Hyatt International's United Nations Plaza Hotel. A graduate of the M.P.S. program in hotel administration at Cornell, Bloom has also worked for the Dunfey Corporation. She holds a B.S. in economics from the Wharton School at the University of Pennsylvania.

As a volatile economy forces companies and associations to curtail their spending, hoteliers can expect a weakening in one of their major business segments: the meetings market. Some groups have already reduced the number, size, and duration of their gatherings; association meetings, in which participants pay their own expenses, appear to be most seriously affected.

In combination with a lower demand for rooms, the burgeoning supply of rooms in some areas—most notably, New York City—means that only those hotels with carefully developed and implemented marketing strategies will weather the troubled '80s successfully. Because the effectiveness of a marketing program depends on the marketer's knowledge of his customers, the hotelier who wishes to maintain a share of the potentially lucrative meetings market should obviously understand meeting planners' product requirements and the factors that affect planners' hotel selection. To investigate whether hotel operators actually understand the needs of the meetings market, the author undertook a study that compares hotel operators' current marketing programs and meeting planners' criteria for hotel selection.

The hotel sample consisted of 22 sales and marketing directors at New York City properties. [1] These participants were interviewed for information on their current business mix and marketing programs. The second sample consisted of 83 meeting planners, who received a mail questionnaire about their criteria for selecting a hotel and the importance of various marketing tools employed by hotels to their selection process. [2]

The Hoteliers' View

The meetings market represented an important source of business for the hotels in the sample. As shown in Exhibit 1, the commercial-group category accounted for 17.1 percent of the hotels' guests. As shown in Exhibit 2, 50.5 percent of the hotels' group business was derived from national corporations and associations; 62 percent originated from groups based in the northeast. Commercial and professional groups constituted 58.5 percent of the hotels' group business, with the remainder derived from special-interest, educational, and other groups. The hotel marketers estimated that roughly two-thirds of their group business was repeat business.

Marketing programs. The most pronounced

1. Individuals at 26 hotels belonging to the New York City Visitors and Convention Bureau were asked to participate in the study; 22 agreed to do so. Although the regional focus of the test sample may be considered a limitation of the study, the marketing strategies used by hotels in this important meetings center may at least be suggestive of strategies used in other cities.

2. Questionnaires were mailed to 200 individuals selected randomly from the membership of Meeting Planners International; 83 meeting planners (41.5%) responded.

EXHIBIT 1
Business mix at surveyed hotels

Type	%
Commercial	51.0%
Commercial-group	17.1
Social	18.7
Social-group	9.5
Other	3.7

EXHIBIT 2
Hotel group composition

Type of Group	% (Avg.)
Commercial (corporate)	36.7%
Professional (medical, legal)	21.8
Special interest (clubs)	20.2
Educational	9.5
Other	11.8

Group Profile	Avg.
Number of rooms	134
Number of delegates	201
Length of stay	3.23 days

Source of Group Business	% (Avg.)
Region	
Northeast	62%
Midwest	19
South	10
West	9
Scope	
National	50.5%
Regional	24
Local	25.5

EXHIBIT 3
Distribution of marketing dollars

Area	% (Avg.)
Advertising	40.6%
Sales	37.7
Public relations and special promotions	10.5
Support collateral	10.2
Direct mail	1.0

feature of the hotels' marketing programs was their great diversity. Marketing strategies ranged from the elementary to the complex: two hotels implemented strategies developed at the corporate level, while three had no formal marketing plans. (In fact, only 40 percent of the hotels had a designated marketing director.) Spending also varied widely from hotel to hotel, but averaged $730 per guest room annually. As shown in Exhibit 3, the largest portion of the marketing dollar— 40.6 percent—went to advertising, followed by sales, public relations and special promotions, collateral, and direct mail.

How the advertising pie was sliced is also worth noting. The hotels spent 90 percent of their advertising dollars on print advertising, with 56 percent of that allotment going to newspapers and 44 percent going to magazines. Most hotels concentrated their print advertisements in consumer periodicals, followed by meetings-trade publications and travel-trade publications. Of all advertising, 59 percent was regional or local, and 41 percent was national.

The hotel marketers said they were developing new marketing strategies in response to economic trends. Several hotels were enlarging their overseas marketing programs to attract international visitors. Others hoped to upgrade their image through property renovation, aiming at an upscale market they presumed would be less affected by recession than other socioeconomic groups. Other innovations included incentive packages for weekend travelers and special corporate programs for business travelers.

The Meeting Planners' Perspective

Of the 83 respondents to the meeting planners' questionnaire, 37 (45%) planned corporate meetings, 33 (40%) planned association meetings, and 13 (16%) planned both. Exhibit 4 summarizes the information furnished by the respondents.

Corporate versus association meetings. The data in Exhibit 4 reveal important distinctions between corporate and association meetings. On average, association groups met less often than corporate groups, but had a greater number of participants at each meeting. Associations also seemed more cost-conscious than corporations: Whereas corporations generally covered all expenses for their delegates, associations usually paid only the meeting costs, leaving their delegates to pay for lodging, food, and transportation. Furthermore, association meeting planners tended to select city and hotel sites further in advance than corporate meeting planners did. Both groups generally relied on an executive committee to select the city site, however, and over 50 percent of both groups used a rotating geographic site schedule.

EXHIBIT 4
Profile of planners' meetings

	TOTAL		ASSOCIATION		CORPORATE	
	Median	Mode	Median	Mode	Median	Mode
Number of overnight meetings	68.6	20	25	10	112	26
Percentage held on east coast	35.8	28	40.1	33	32.5	27
Percentage using rotating schedule	54	44	56	56	59	59
Number of meeting attendees	693	150	1,176	300	282	100
Number of nights	4.26	2.5	5.7	2.5	3.9	2.5
Number of hotel rooms	281	80	458	225	187	50
Square footage requirement	10,081	2,400	18,333	2,500	6,839	2,400
Dollars spent on meetings annually	$612,310	$200,000	$257,667	$120,000	$1,052,885	$250,000
Amt. time to select city site	2 yrs.	1 yr.	3.2 yrs.	2 yrs.	1.1 yrs.	.9 yrs.
Amt. time to select hotel	1.9 yrs.	.9 yrs.	3 yrs.	2 yrs.	1.0 yrs.	.9 yrs.

Sample Total—n = 83; Association—n = 33; Corporate—n = 37. The responses of planners responsible for both association and corporate meetings are not analyzed separately here, because of the small sample size (n = 13).

EXHIBIT 5
Factors influencing the choice of a hotel meeting site

Site-Selection Factor	TOTAL Avg. Rating*	(Rank†)	ASSOCIATION Avg. Rating	(Rank)	CORPORATE Avg. Rating	(Rank)
Recommendations by other meeting planners	4.57	(2)	4.61	(1)	4.44	(1)
Recommendations by others in organization	4.6	(1)	4.31	(3)	4.38	(3)
Hotel sales representatives	4.46	(3)	4.61	(1)	4.44	(1)
National and regional sales representatives	4.07	(4)	4.18	(4)	4.25	(4)
Post-convention reports	4.04	(5)	3.73	(5)	3.95	(6)
Hotel-supplier correspondence files	3.86	(6)	3.56	(7)	4.11	(5)
Recommendations by hotel associates	3.72	(7)	3.70	(6)	3.54	(8)
Articles in business publications	3.41	(8)	3.21	(9)	3.47	(9)
Convention-bureau sales representatives	3.37	(9)	3.52	(8)	3.08	(11)
Advertising by hotels in trade publications	3.21	(10)	2.94	(10)	3.61	(7)
Advertising by convention bureaus	2.88	(11)	2.47	(11)	3.29	(10)
Hotel associations	2.61	(12)	2.18	(12)	3.00	(12)
Airline sales representatives	2.19	(13)	1.91	(13)	2.56	(14)
Airline publications	2.11	(14)	1.78	(14)	2.58	(13)

Sample Total—n = 83; Association—n = 33; Corporate—n = 37. The responses of planners responsible for both association and corporate meetings are not analyzed separately here, because of the small sample size (n = 13).

*Respondents were asked to rate the importance of each factor on a scale of 1 (unimportant) to 7 (very important).

†Rank of the factor in relation to other factors; "1" indicates most important, while "14" indicates least important.

Meeting-site selection factors. Meeting planners were asked to rate the importance of 14 factors in the hotel-selection process. Their responses appear in Exhibit 5.

Whether the planners' client was a corporate group or an association, certain factors received consistently high ratings. The same two factors were ranked highest by both corporate planners and association planners: recommendations from other meeting planners, and the character of hotel sales representatives. [3]

Planners from all groups also agreed that some factors have little or no impact on site selection. These included hotel associations, airline sales representatives, and airline publications.

---

3. For recommendations on marketing to meeting planners, see: Raymond J. Hall, "Straight Talk to Hoteliers: A Meeting Planner's View," *The Cornell Hotel and Restaurant Administration Quarterly*, 20, No. 4 (February 1980), pp. 17-20.

Although corporate and association meeting planners gave similar rankings to the factors considered most and least important, there were some differences in their rankings of other factors. For example, hotel advertisements in trade publications and advertisements by visitors and convention bureaus were rated higher by the corporate meeting planners than by the association meeting planners. On the other hand, association meeting planners found the quality of sales representation from visitors and convention bureaus more important in their decision process than the corporate meeting planners did.

These differences suggest that hoteliers should view association and corporate groups as two distinct market segments, and that the hotelier's advertising dollar is better spent on the corporate meeting planner.

The need to distinguish. Responses to other questions underscore the need to distinguish between these segments. Planners were asked how they viewed New York City as a meeting site. Whereas 70 percent of corporate meeting planners found this city to be satisfactory, only 33 percent of association meeting planners felt similarly. We can speculate that the relatively high costs of New York City render it more suitable as a meeting site for corporate groups. Since, unlike corporate meetings, association meetings are rarely mandatory, attendance is likely to be low when the cost of the meeting destination is high. As a result, hotels located in costly cities and interested in attracting more association meetings might offer special packages to groups willing to schedule their meetings during slack periods.

The hotel marketers mentioned another difference between corporate meeting planners and association meeting planners: they maintained that persons responsible for association meetings were generally better informed than those planning corporate meetings. If this perception could be substantiated, it would argue for different emphases in marketing efforts directed at the two groups. Further research on the differences between these two segments would help hoteliers develop effective marketing strategies aimed at the needs of specific groups.

Conclusions

Given the small size of the sample and the diversity of the organizations represented, the findings described in the foregoing pages cannot be considered representative of the meetings market in general, but they do provide a starting point for further investigations. The most significant implication of the study is that association and corporate groups represent two distinct segments of the meetings market. They differ in planning horizons and hotel-selection criteria, and hotels' marketing efforts should reflect this fact.

One point came through loud and clear from members of both groups: meeting planners regard the hotel sales department as a vital factor in hotel site selection. It is crucial, therefore, that hotels provide informed, professional sales representation. Hoteliers should carefully segment and define their markets to ensure that hotel sales representatives can work efficiently, concentrating on various planners' marketing priorities.

The study also indicates that hotels must aim their marketing programs at the ultimate decision-maker. Whereas the hotel is generally selected by the meeting planner or convention coordinator, the site is most often selected by the group's executive committee. Depending upon the structure of the individual group, hotel sales and marketing directors may need to market only the hotel, or both the hotel and the destination.

The study suggests that no marketing plan can be applied universally. Each hotel is a unique product with a unique market. It is the responsibility of marketing and sales directors to know and understand the capabilities of their properties and to identify those market segments likely to yield the best prospects.

Examining the Eighties

A panel of experts predict substantial changes in the hospitality industry by the end of the decade

To plan successful strategies, hoteliers require an accurate picture of the future. Predicting the future, however, is a little like predicting the weather. As someone once observed, if you slip up, no one forgets; if you're right on target, no one remembers. In spite of the hazards of prophesying, a group of faculty members from the School of Hotel Administration at Cornell University met recently to identify the trends they felt would significantly affect the hospitality industry in the late 1980s.[1] If their predictions are accurate, here are some of the changes we can anticipate.

General Trends

Continuing inflation will aggravate a multitude of interrelated problems within the industry, from energy, material, and labor shortages to increased costs for labor, supplies, and capital. As capital grows scarcer and inflation maintains its hold, we are likely to see more renovation of existing facilities and less new construction.

The hospitality market will undergo slow but substantial changes through the 1980s. Such demographic changes as the shift in population (to the south and southwest), and the growing number of Hispanics, working women, dual-income and single-parent households, and older people living on fixed incomes will all influence the demand for services by the end of the decade.

Splintering market. The demographic bulge in the population still referred to as "the baby boom" will age. Members of this group, now in

their peak earning years, will boost the market for luxury accommodations. However, corporations, which have historically constituted a large share of the luxury market, will begin to restrict expense-account spending because of rising costs. The business traveler who must monitor his spending will probably seek less luxurious accommodations. We can also expect the expanded population living on fixed incomes to seek out those hotel accommodations that offer the greatest value. Many of these consumers will prefer more modest guest-room amenities, as well as less expensive food and beverage outlets.

On the other hand, in spite of the recent strengthening of the dollar, the increased standard of living in many foreign countries will continue to make the U.S. a vacation choice for the international traveler. Furthermore, this relatively new market is expected to offer little resistance to the rising cost of hotel accommodations. Consequently, the U.S. hospitality market will splinter into two relatively distinct segments, with one segment comprising financially secure, luxury-minded consumers, and the other consisting of value-conscious, budget-minded clientele. Luxury facilities within the hospitality industry will become more plush, and budget facilities will offer fewer frills than they now do. Hotels that attempt to straddle both markets may have difficulty maintaining one strongly recognizable image. Those that hedge their bets by catering to customers from the dwindling market in the middle may find themselves without a market by the late 1980s.

We will witness more shifts in food preferences (the renaissance of natural foods and the growing interest in nutrition are two examples of this trend). An older population with less disposable income will probably demand restaurant fare that provides the best value. We'll also see a rise in ethnic cuisine and U.S. regional themes, in response to the influx of international tourists.

Demographic shifts will hasten the demise of many established resort areas. Those parts of the

This article was originally published in the November 1981 issue of *The Cornell Hotel and Restaurant Administration Quarterly,* pp. 32-36, and is reprinted here with the permission of the Cornell University School of Hotel Administration. ©1981.

1. The panel met at the request of a large hotel corporation, and comprised faculty members representing a broad range of industry disciplines. Chaired by Michael H. Redlin, the panel included Paul Beals, John J. Clark, James J. Evster, Paul L. Gammer, A. Neal Geller, Richard G. Moore, and Richard H. Penner. The group's aim was to stimulate industry practitioners to think ahead and plan for the future.

country in economic decline may attempt to attract more tax revenues and business capital by promoting licensed gaming, following the Atlantic City example.

Travel

The growing number of elderly citizens with increased leisure time and the growing number of two-wage-earner households with increased disposable income will mean more vacation travelers. However, we are likely to see large changes in our modes and patterns of transportation because of rising energy costs and the deregulation of air fares. The cost of air travel on many routes will increase, but will still be a bargain for the long-distance traveler. Because air fares for shorter trips will rise at a steeper rate, however, more people will opt for short-drive vacations. Vacationers are also likely to depend more on cost-efficient, high-speed rail and bus transportation for short- and medium-range trips, as it becomes more costly to buy, maintain, and operate automobiles.

Managing and Operating Considerations

One of the significant problems the industry will face in the late 1980s will be the shortage of trained personnel; the number of hotel-school graduates will increase, but not sufficiently to meet rising industry demands. In addition, more graduates will pursue careers in other industries, or enter the field as consultants in response to the comparatively low pay and general lack of challenging entry-level positions within the hospitality industry. To offset this shortage, hotels will develop more sophisticated training programs and adopt compensation packages more competitive with those of other industries. We will see American firms recruiting more graduates from international hotel schools; there will also be more aggressive competition for those students who receive their training in American hotel schools.

A more difficult labor market is anticipated. Because of the lack of challenge inherent in most low-level positions within the hospitality industry, workers will continue to have little motivation to improve the quality of their work. Hoteliers will also be forced to cope with growing demands for higher wages. Some hotels will adopt profit-sharing or an improved work environment as incentives to attract and retain more and better workers.

Financing and Ownership Structure

Hospitality properties are, by nature, a risky investment. Lenders are likely to become even more cautious than they have been, if the rate of inflation continues as predicted. As a result, the industry will need to cope with higher fixed charges for initial financing. Operating loans, particularly short-term loans, will be more expensive and harder to secure. Investors will continue to view real estate as a hedge against inflation, but will attempt to share financial risk with others. For example, they may require that hotel operating firms invest in, as well as manage, their properties. Or they may be forced to attract outside capital by employing such innovative methods of financing as "hotel asset trust funds," an arrangement in which small investors are permitted to buy limited-partnership shares in hotel properties through national investment-brokerage firms. Operators who invest in the properties they run will have more of a say in investment and other financial decisions at those properties, as well as a share in profits. Hoteliers may also be able to borrow capital more readily and at lower rates if they seek out groups of small investors rather than a single large investor.

To counter continuing inflation and tight money, hoteliers aiming to increase profits will abandon antiquated capital-budgeting methods and adopt more sophisticated techniques. We will see more complex management and loan agreements, a greater use of tax-exempt bonds, more government incentives to encourage growth, and better planning for reinvestment of cash flow.

Timesharing will become more popular in the late 1980s, in part as a reaction to the anticipated shortage of investment capital for the construction of new hotels and in part as a response to the rising cost of hotel accommodations. The potential timeshare market will also expand because of more efficient exchange networks.

Placing experienced management in smaller properties will become prohibitively expensive, due to the rising cost of management expertise and the shortage of trained personnel. In response, we may see a growth in franchising and a related trend toward greater uniformity in products and properties.

Experts expect the hotel market to be saturated by the late 1980s, with fewer opportunities for continued growth. Hotel companies that are unable to increase profits through expansion will be forced to diversify. They may, for example, invest in such complementary enterprises as health care, real estate management, or travel packaging. Because of the new opportunities created by an increased number of elderly people in the population, owning and managing retirement communities are areas in which hoteliers may diversify. We will also see increased competition for prime locations among operators who choose to expand in spite of a saturated market, and more liquidation of equity through reverse mortgages among those who choose to diversify.

Planning and Design

Hoteliers who plan to construct new hotels will tackle formidable problems in the late 1980s. Because fuel is needed to construct and transport building materials and to operate construction equipment, the cost of new construction will increase dramatically as fuel costs rise. Delays in schedules caused by shortages of material and labor difficulties will produce delays in income and entail higher costs across the board. Room rates at new hotels may reach heights too steep to compete with rates at existing properties. To cope with spiraling costs, hoteliers will opt for more fast-track construction and build more prefabricated structures, or will choose to buy and renovate rather than build.

Newly constructed hotels will have less public space, larger central kitchens with fewer satellite pantries, and more versatile but less extravagant food-service equipment. Because the cost of owning and operating large, centrally located hotel buildings will continue to rise, hoteliers may attempt to economize by relocating such back-of-the-house functions as laundry, long-term storage, and accounting in facilities separate from the main hotel. We will also see more development of flexible interior space — rooms that can be enlarged or made smaller, and used for different functions.

Hotels of the future may share space with recreational facilities and offices. The Omni International in Atlanta—a building complex that combines offices, a professional hockey rink, and a hotel—is one multi-use facility now in operation. Investors who put their money into a multi-use property will incur less risk because even if one project fails to turn a profit, the loss can be absorbed by other money-making projects within the building complex. As this type of venture becomes more commonplace, more hoteliers will enter into joint agreements with such diverse investors as office developers, medical clinicians, proprietors of condominiums, and sports-team owners. Such facilities will have the disadvantage of requiring greater security and more elaborate housekeeping than single-use structures, however, and will offer less privacy. Furthermore, hoteliers who occupy a multi-use property will find it difficult to create a separate image for their own properties that consumers can readily identify.

As rising fuel costs make commuting to hotels in outlying areas more costly, more consumers will choose to stay in center-city hotels. Hoteliers who wish to pursue this growing market will seek out government- or community-sponsored financial incentives for center-city development.

Hotels that cater to the increasing luxury market will equip more guest rooms with complex entertainment centers, video games, computer terminals, and closed-circuit and cable television that can be operated at the flick of a switch from bedside.

Energy, Communications, and Computers

Cost-conscious hotel operators will attempt to offset rising energy costs by constructing buildings with more efficient heat-recovery equipment and energy systems. They may choose to install fewer large areas of glass, more multipane windows, and thermal shades or louvers for greater heat retention in their facilities.

Many managers will convert telephone systems into profit centers by using the telephone to transmit data in new ways. Advanced communications systems will link computers in various locations to provide hoteliers and guests with instant information. Telephone lines will also be adapted to control complex energy-management systems.

Advances in microcircuiting and large-scale integrated circuits will help bring down the cost of computers by the late 1980s, and more small hotels will be able to afford their own in-house computers. Internal control through computerization will hold many advantages for hoteliers. For example, reservations will be confirmed, customers billed directly, guest-room status monitored, and wakeup calls made automatically by computer. Hotel and airline computers will be linked to provide customers with information on flights and room reservations. Corporate and airline computers will also be connected with one another for more efficient direct billing.

There may be a greater demand for teleconferencing, brought about in part by the rising cost of travel. Hoteliers should be cautious about investing in computerized teleconferencing systems, however, until manufacturers have developed such systems more fully. Along with the positive aspects of electronic technology (e.g., better guest accounting, less risk of accounting fraud), we are already beginning to experience the negative side of internal control through computerization. Electronic records, we are learning, are vulnerable to vandalism, breakdown, and destruction from the environment; when breakdowns do occur, operators are often left without a paper audit with which to verify accounts. These problems will probably be magnified in the late 1980s.

Conclusion

In summary, the hotel market will undergo slow but substantial changes in the 1980s. The industry's biggest challenges will be to adapt to this new market while attempting to counter the pervasive effects of inflation, the dearth of qualified managers, and the shortage of energy, goods, and capital.

Hotels that are successful today may not be as successful five years from now, even if operators follow the strategies that have worked in the past. Those hospitality operators who wish to survive and flourish in the 1980s must adopt new policies for the future that take into account the demands of a changing market and that focus on the big picture as well as the details.

Part IV

Market Segmentation and Target Marketing

Markets consist of people. And as hospitality firms go about the business of servicing people, they quickly find that they cannot satisfy the diverse needs and wants of every individual. Therefore, each firm should identify the most attractive part of the market and attempt to provide goods and services that will satisfy the needs and wants of a homogeneous group of people. Each homogeneous group is a distinct segment and becomes a target market when a firm chooses to direct is marketing effort toward that segment.

Market segmentation doesn't just happen, nor does the selection and servicing of a target market. The process of developing sound marketing strategy to serve target markets is outlined below. The first three steps are concerned with segmenting the market and the last three with choosing and servicing target markets.

1. Select the characteristics or dimensions by which the total market will be segmented.
2. Discover everything possible about the resulting segment.
3. Develop ways to measure the business potential of segments.
4. Identify the most attractive segments and designate them as target markets.
5. Position the firm appropriately for each target market.
6. Construct a workable marketing mix for each target market.

There is no single or best way to segment a market. The simplest way to divide customers is on the basis of one variable or one characteristic. Dividing customers on the basis of age alone would be an example of single-variable segmentation. The market might be divided into two groups—those over 65 and those under 65. Another single variable segmentation might be according to sex or income. Generally, single-variable segmentation provides information of only limited use. However, several years ago the airlines did an outstanding marketing job by dividing the market between people who patronized airlines and those who did not. This segmentation and the accompanying research yielded a great deal of information about why people did not fly. The information provided the basis for a successful marketing program aimed at increasing airline usage.

A more productive approach is to use two or more variables to segment markets. The more variables used, the smaller the segment will be. The four most commonly used groups of segmenting variables are geographic, demographic, psychographic, and behavioristic.

Geographic variables are concerned with the location and numbers of customers and potential customers. Data on the distribution of population is readily available from published sources with information divided according to region, state, county, city (or standard metropolitan statistical areas), and so on.

Demographic variables are personal characteristics of the population such as age, sex, family size, income, education, nationality, race, and occupation.

Psychographics categorize personality, social class, and life style.

Behavioristic variables deal with benefits sought, purchase occasion, user status, loyalty status, and related factors.

One useful method of market segmentation is to divide variables into two groups. One is a group of qualifying variables; the other is a group of determining variables. Qualifying variables are those characteristics that qualify a person to buy a product or a service. Thus, income levels are qualifying variables. Generally speaking, certain income levels qualify customers to buy certain classes of products or services. Determining variables, on the other hand, address the question of why buyers choose one product over another. Qualifying variables are normally geographic or demographic in nature and relative information is fairly easy to obtain from secondary or published data. Determining variables usually are more elusive. They deal with psychographic and behavioristic characteristics and often require the gathering of primary data.

The purpose of market segmentation and targeting is not just to divide the total market into smaller groups, but to identify groups of customers who have similar needs and wants. By learning as much as possible about consumers' desires, marking strategies may be developed that will satisfy them better than the strategies of competitors.

The articles in this section have been chosen because they apply the art and science of market segmentation and targeting to the specific problems of the hospitality industry.

The Science of Target Marketing

by Robert C. Lewis, Ph.D.

Robert Lewis is Assistant Professor of Marketing and Management in the Department of Hotel, Restaurant and Travel Administration at the University of Massachusetts, Amherst. He is also president of Robert C. Lewis Associates, Inc., a restaurant consulting firm.

In just about every study conducted to determine what people seek most in a restaurant, the number one factor given is *quality of food.* In fact, any restaurateur can conduct his own "man-in-the-street" poll and obtain the same overwhelming response. Knowledge of this fact, intuitive even without research, has led to the predominant use in restaurant advertising of wording such as "finest food," "delicious," "fine dining," "gourmet dining," "continental cuisine" and other quality food implications.

There are two fallacies in this line of reasoning. The first is that food quality perception is relative to the type of restaurant. Thus, the customer actually thinks in terms of value for his dollar in making a restaurant choice, e.g., he is not necessarily impressed by gourmet claims when choosing a lower-priced restaurant. In fact, such claims may be a turn-off when used to describe certain types of restaurants.

The second fallacy is that customers actually see other factors as equally if not more important than food quality claims for two reasons. First, quality claims are so prevalent and often misused in restaurant advertising that they lack credibility. Second, the type of restaurant being sought has a major impact on the attributes or features that are important to the consumer and which interact with relative food quality. It is important, then, for restaurant advertising to reflect the particular attributes that are salient in particular restaurant choices.

From *Restaurant Business* (November 1, 1980) pp. 102-113. Reprinted by permission of *Restaurant Business.*

Segmentation and Positioning

No one restaurant can be all things to all people. Each owner/operator must decide what particular market he wishes to attract. In marketing terms this is called *segmentation* or target marketing. In the past the practice of selecting target audiences for advertising has been largely arbitrary or judgmental with little knowledge of how those audiences respond to advertising messages. Thus, to advertise "fine dining" is to try to appeal to the entire populace and not to specific market segments.

Once the operator has established his target market(s), his next strategic move is to *position* his restaurant for that segment(s). Positioning involves creating an image that differentiates your restaurant from the competition in such a way that it is seen as especially attractive to your specific target market(s).

Together, market segmentation and positioning are powerful tools for developing business. There are many who believe that those who survive in the 80s will be those who effectively use these tools. All of this makes for great theory, but how does the average restaurateur know how to use these tools in advertising? Recent research has shed light on a new segmentation strategy and cast doubts on old ones.

Segmentation Strategies

Probably one of the most common segmentation strategies used in the restaurant industry is socio-demographic. *Socio-demographic segmentation* involves establishing target markets by virtue of age groups, income levels, singles or marrieds, education, white and blue collar workers and so forth. But times have changed. Blue collar workers often have higher incomes than white collar workers. Older people eat in coffee shops and young people eat in gourmet restaurants. The "me" generation seeks instant gratification and has completely upset old socio-demographic traditions.

This is not to say that socio-demographic characteristics are useless in market planning. The baby boom, the gas crunch, the shifting population, and other socio-demographic trends are important to the restaurant industry. But how, for example, do you advertise both to the $40,000 a year, older, married steelworker and the $20,000 a year, younger, married, educated junior accountant when both are parts of your target market? Socio-demographics alone are of little help in this quandary.

One answer that has been suggested is *psychographic segmentation*. This strategy involves understanding consumers' personality characteristics and motives as well as their life styles. Psychographic analysis relates purchase inclination to peoples' activities, interests and opinions. These dimensions can be useful in defining target markets. Their use, however, is limited. Besides being difficult to measure, the relationships among psychographic variables and consumers' needs and wants are often obscure and vague. Further, the expense of acquiring the necessary data is prohibitive for most operators.

The most effective segmentation strategy for restaurants today is *benefit segmentation*. This procedure divides the market according to the benefits that customers seek. There are two very important distinctions between benefit and other forms of segmentation:

1. Benefits *are* the needs and wants of customers. Other segmentation strategies assume a relationship between the segment variables and consumer needs and wants.

2. Understanding benefits accruing to customers enables advertising to *influence* behavior. Other segmentation variables are only descriptive, which means we can only try to appeal to what exists and its assumed relationship.

Benefit segmentation is especially appropriate for restaurant advertising. Benefits sought by people must be identifiable so that people can be grouped into recognizable segments. Restaurant products and service readily pertain to this requirement. Advertising strategists have also learned that it is not the product per se that customers buy. It is the situation in which the product is used and the consumer attitude towards it that forms the basis of segmentation. These attitudes are what influence buyer behavior. Positioning the product in order to reflect positive attitudes is the basis of successful advertising strategy. This strategy reinforces positive needs and wants and modifies negative ones.

To implement benefits segmentation strategy it is, of course, necessary to understand: 1) consumers' needs and wants as they relate to your restaurant; and 2) how consumers perceive your restaurant in relation to the benefits they desire. Knowing these factors can identify a target market by benefit segmentation. Advertising is used to position the restaurant toward those segments where the greatest opportunities exist to create customers.

Benefit Segments

In using a benefit segmentation strategy in advertising, each segment is identified by the appeal strength of attributes to that benefit segment. The total configuration of attribute appeals differentiates one segment from another. It is the relative importance that people attach to benefit configurations that can differentiate one group from another and that can be used to segment markets. Once benefit segments are derived, they can be further contrasted with other segments in terms of demographics, volume, life styles, etc.

Let us now relate our earlier discussion on food quality—the benefit everybody wants—to other restaurant benefits to see how this strategy applies to restaurant advertising. Restaurant goers seek many benefits besides good food: romance, atmosphere, quick service, slow service, convenient parking, entertainment and so forth. Some would say that restaurant goers seek a "total experience." Regardless, research indicates that certain attributes are important to customers in combination for certain types of restaurants. These attributes should be reflected by the use of different advertising appeals.

Every restaurant will differ in the benefits it offers as they are perceived by the consumer. Each operator must do his own research to determine exactly what appeals should be featured, but we shall indicate here what research has shown in terms of broad categories of restaurant types.

First, and once again, let us accept as given that quality of food is on the top of everyone's priority list. But indications are when food quality is featured as an advertising appeal, that as many people would not choose a restaurant for that reason as would choose it. In other words, there is a disbelief among many that a high quality of food is really offered. Does this mean that restaurants shouldn't use this appeal? Not necessarily, but it does mean that it may have little or no effect. If you want to stress food quality you must make it believable. What exactly makes this appeal believable is still unknown as there are many variables that affect it. Apparently the well worn cliches that have been used for decades are largely ineffective. Most important, they are not generally effective in benefit segmentation, as was earlier pointed out, because "fine food" is a universal appeal.

There is an exception. This is the truly so-called gourmet restaurant. People who go to these restaurants indicate that quality of food is by far the most important benefit they seek. Atmosphere is nice, good service is desired but when these people decide to go to a gourmet restaurant and look at your ad there is one thing it has to convince them of—the food *is* great.

On the other hand, individuals who decide to go to atmosphere/specialty restaurants are looking for many benefits. They want conveniences, such as reservations, credit cards, parking facilities and easy to get to locations. Atmosphere, of course, is expected but so too are a cocktail lounge and entertainment. The advertising message must be appealing price-wise. These individuals seek many benefits and they are willing to let the strength of some compensate for the weakness of others as long as they know they exist. If this is your type of restaurant, advertise all the benefits you can offer. Make sure your food is good, of course, but don't worry about being gourmet and don't worry about stressing good food in your advertising. This customer expects a reasonable level but he's looking for other benefits that will compensate for the food not being of the highest quality.

Family restaurant goers represent a third type of benefit segment. They aren't as particular as the gourmet restaurant goers or as varied as the atmosphere restaurant goer. This segment is primarily concerned with menu variety, price and atmosphere.

The three types of restaurants discussed thus must be positioned to three different benefit segments for maximum advertising effectiveness. It is important to keep in mind that demographically or psychographically these segments may be the same or similar. It is the choice of restaurant type that distinguishes the benefits. Based on this, your own restaurant will have its own benefit segment.

Summary

Food quality is the predominant factor as a basis for restaurant choice. This attribute alone may be the only real benefit that consumers seek or it may be one of many, depending on the restaurant type. Most restaurant ads do claim to offer food that is of high quality. The restaurateur who can advertise to convince the reader that his restaurant serves quality food has a large head start in gaining patronage, at least on a first time basis.

Socio-demographic variables modify to some extent the relative importance of advertising appeals and add some insight to positioning and segmentation strategies. Socio-demographics alone, have little bearing on a consumer's decision to patronize a particular restaurant after reading an ad, nor are they very useful by themselves for segmentation purposes.

Socio-demographics have often been the sole or primary basis for marketing segmentation efforts. The inferences made here point very strongly to the conclusion that benefit segmentation could be a far more valuable tool.

In the 1980s the issue of market segmentation may be a critical one for restaurant marketers. Restaurateurs have been slow to adopt the positioning strategy in advertising used by their product-selling counterparts. The discussion here indicates that promoting certain restaurant attributes in a consistent way that images a distinctive personality and represents the specific benefits to the consumer could be the most effective form of advertising.

The astute restaurateur or his marketing colleague must know what attributes are important appeals for his particular restaurant, and how those appeals can be communicated via advertising to fit the benefit profiles of patrons and non-patrons. This information provides tools for positioning and benefit segmentation and for leading restaurant advertising out of cliches and demographics.

Marketing

First in a Series

Pinpoint Strategies for the 80s

by James M. Degen

Mr. Degen is Assistant Professor of marketing at Mundelem College in Chicago and president of James M. Degen Company, Inc., a marketing consultant firm.

There is a fundamental theory in marketing applicable to many products and particularly characteristic of the past decade. It's called segmentation—a "rifle" versus a "shotgun" approach that suggests that precise, pinpoint marketing can prove more beneficial and rewarding than a broadscale market strategy.

The primary reasons for, and benefits of, segmentation include:

• designing products that match consumer demands.

• channel marketing money and efforts to the most *profitable* markets.

• direct marketing programs and appeals to those submarkets where the response is greatest.

Soft drinks, cigarettes, automobiles and many others are good examples of products that once were marketed to everyone but today are targeted against specific and smaller segments of the total population.

There are four principal methods of segmentation. *Demographics* is perhaps the easiest to comprehend and most often used. Age, sex, income, ethnic background, occupation, etc., are all demographic variables.

Geographic segmentation is another obvious and common alternative. *Personality* is a less known segmentation approach that deals with the psychology of consumer demand—why consumers buy and demand various products. And *Buyer Behavior* which segments on the basis of current buyer activity, i.e., heavy users of a product represent greater potential than occasional users. Or, dissatisfied consumers of a competitive brand be-

come prime candidates to switch to another.

In the last five years the industry has witnessed a change. The primary product emphasis has moved away from food to liquor and entertainment. Part of this can be attributed to an apparent dearth of new menu ideas worth building an entire restaurant concept around. However, it has more to do with this same shifting of consumer segmentation variables. Personal freedom and affluence again surface but for different reasons: singles, two-person households, divorce and grown-up kids all minimize adult responsibilities. "I'm free, I'm me," is the cry.

The May 1, 1979 issue of *Restaurant Business* documented a number of demographic changes expected to impact on the foodservice industry of the 1980s. And in this census year, numerous reports come forth from government and the private sector predicting major demographic shifts in the next decade. So, having looked back on foodservice industry segmentation, let's make a closer examination of demographic variables and changes expected to occur in the 1980s.

Population

• 1980 population should be 222 million—that's 9% growth over 1970 but one of the smallest ten year percentage growths recorded. If the present trends continue another 21 million could be added by 1990.

• The West has grown by 15% since 1970, the South by 12%. However, the North Central region gained only 3%, the Northeast none. The growth of the sunbelt is expected to be substantial through 1990.

• From 1970 to 1978 metro area population grew by 4% while non-metro areas grew by 12%. This was the first time metro areas grew less rapidly than non-metro areas. Added to this is the return to downtown areas in several major markets like Chicago and New York.

From *Restaurant Business* (May 1, 1980) pp. 300-302. Reprinted by permission of *Restaurant Business*.

Households

• Household formation is up 26% in the past decade, however, average household size declined from 3.14 persons in 1970 to 2.78 persons in 1979.

• Contributing to smaller household size are "nonfamily households" or those maintained by a single man or woman which now represent 25% of all households and have increased 60% in the past eight years.

• Over 50% of all U.S. households consist of one or two people.

Age

• 1980 sees the baby boom generation—largest batch of babies ever born in a single year in the U.S.—reach the age of 18. From this point on the number of teenagers will begin to thin for some time.

• The next decade will see a dramatic decline of people between the ages of fifteen and twenty-four. This group increased its number four times faster than the total population in the 1960s.

• The single most populous segment of society in the 80s will be made up of people between twenty-five and forty-five.

Women

• Women *are* the new market.

• The number of single women has almost doubled since 1960.

• In 1978 there were 2.2 million marriages but over a million divorces. Most divorced women return to the work force and head up a household (25% of all U.S. households are maintained by women.)

• Seven out of eight young female college graduates are now in the labor force, often replacing older and less educated men who have been withdrawing because of more generous pensions and increased social security payments.

• Perhaps the most important statistic, however, is the increase in working women. From 1960 to 1978, 19 million women joined the work force, accounting for 60% of its growth. Fifty-one percent of all women sixteen and older work.

Income

• The influx of married women into the work force has contributed significantly to a steady increase in household income over the past decade with the trend continuing into the 80s.

• Family income is expected to increase by about 20% over the next decade or half the rate of the 1950s and 1960s.

• But virtually all of this growth is expected to come in the upper income bracket ($25,000 and above). One out of four families qualify for this bracket today but two out of five will qualify by 1990.

The restaurant industry has tried to capture shares of this very volatile population through numerous segmentation changes. These include the pursuit of teenagers, young families, young adults, higher incomes, higher education and, lately, working women. More affluent teenagers and ethnic food influences have shaped the emergence, alteration and often the demise of many menu and complete restaurant concepts in the past decade. But this may not necessarily be the demographic segmentation strategy of the 1980s. Rifle shooting product and marketing appeals may give way to a more undifferentiated approach.

An aggregate of many of the demographic forecasts of the 1980s lies in the *two-worker household:*

• greater affluence.

• more discretionary income particularly with no or few children.

• generally higher education, sophistication.

• a concentration of these in the 25-44 age group—the largest of the population.

• habitual "hard-core" eaters-out. These are the fifties and sixties drive-in users that have made eating away from home an integral part of life style.

• a tendency to concentrate with their peers—in condominiums, apartments, town houses, downtown areas.

• a need for self expression that the social environment of restaurants provides.

Making the single diner comfortable, increased seating for two, a re-examination of portion sizes all are suggested by these changes.

While this group has the income to frequent expensive restaurants on a regular basis, there are many other lifestyle demands for the same dollar. This group is not likely to regularly visit $2-$3 individual check average restaurants. But $5-$10 per person eating out costs are unacceptable. And in major urban markets or among certain sub-segments of this group, the price/demand ratio could equalize at substantially higher levels.

Price features will not be a major motivating factor. Product features with good price/value relationships will be. Already this group has demonstrated a willingness to pay higher prices for quality.

This emerging two-worker segment may do more to influence concept and positioning changes than any other demographic variable. In subsequent articles on the subject of segmentation, the personality and behavioral motives of this group will be more closely examined. But the recent cultural trends in dancing, exercise, designer clothes, etc., all reflect this new supersegment. Some restaurants have already begun to direct new efforts to capture this market. Others will have to reevaluate current restaurant concepts and either reposition or design a totally new and more impactive approach.

Promotion to this group will, by necessity, have to concentrate more on product rewards and social environment rather than on price and geographic location. To be sure there will be significant differences in apparently similar concepts as a result of local cultural and demographic influences. But the basic rewards will be identical.

The time to deal with this situation was yesterday. Closely watch the customer profile. Check with local sources such as newspapers or chambers of commerce for information on major demographic changes. Consider broadening geographic coverage to reach more of these consumer targets. Fit the product to this new restaurant consumer of the 1980s.

Segmentation Strategies for the 80s

by James M. Degen

The use of market segmentation—targeting in on a specific group of the population—is a strategy employed by marketers of most consumer products.

An analysis of existing demographic information and forecasted demographics for the 1980s (much of which will be derived from this year's census) suggests the emergence of a Super Segment.

- Single and 2 person households
- Age 25-44
- Household Income $25,000 +
- College Educated
- White Collar Workers

But demographics is only one way to segment the population. Other methods of segmentation include geographic, personality and buyer behavior segmentation alternatives. It is the application of these additional segmentation factors that begins to reduce the total Super Segment into more meaningful targets for the restaurant industry.

Much has already been written about the continued migration of all Americans from snowbelt to the sunbelt. This trend alone should have significant impact on chain restaurants seeking to exploit population concentrations.

But for restaurants of all types and concepts (chains and independents) there are more serious geographic concerns in almost every individual marketing area. The first concern has to do with energy—gasoline. The second cuts to the very fiber of suburban lifestyle versus urban alternatives.

The rising cost of gasoline, automobile prices and operating economics and the uncertainty of energy and transportation are in general causing a lot of rethinking among consumers. Gasoline consumption continues to decline, new car purchases are substantially off, all of which suggests that it is no longer an automatic reaction to jump in the car and make an extra trip. Advanced planning and

the elimination of unnecessary trips create a different set of decision-making steps that eliminate many impulse purchases affecting among other things restaurant usage and selection.

About sixty percent of metropolitan residents now live in the suburbs. Normally, continued movement to the suburbs would be expected. But many 25-44 year olds are finding that strong peer relationships concentrated in urban areas is more desirable than suburban isolation. With delays in the addition of children, these Super Segment members have little in common with suburbanites.

Finally, as the population matures, children grow up and leave home or go to college, there is a growing number of the older 35-44 year old couples that have suddenly discovered they have a new freedom, more time together and more discretionary income. Entirely new social alternatives are now available to this group that reaches far beyond their suburban community.

The addition of steak sandwiches and salads to previously hamburger oriented menus suggests more than a need to add menu items to attract new sales dollars. These types of foods significantly upgrade consumer perceptions at higher prices appealing directly to this new suburban and urban segment that is more affluent and more selective in eating out than just a decade ago. What is the viability of the concept of "Family Restaurants" given this set of circumstances?

Perhaps the most important characteristic of the Super Segment of the 1980's is income. It is estimated that in 1980 the 25-44 age group with annual household income in excess of $25,000 controls 20 percent of the aggregate consumer income. By 1990 this figure should climb to 30 percent.

The concentration of wealth among this group develops in three ways. The first is the increasing number of individuals with graduate degrees who tend to earn more than undergraduates to start with and progress up the economic scale at an accelerated rate.

From *Restaurant Business* (July 1, 1980) pp. 188-191. Reprinted by permission of *Restaurant Business*.

The second is the two income household that, regardless of educational levels (although at least some college is characteristic of one or both members), enters this upper income group just through coexistence. The working woman has and will continue to do more to reshape consumer marketing than any other segmentation variable.

Thirdly are the divorced whose salary is supplemented by alimony and child support. The split can help that person qualify as both a member of this upper income group as well as a one or two person household. Thus, divorce often creates two upper income households.

What is interesting about all of these groups is the similarities in social structure, lifestyle and peer group emulation. This phenomenon of self, affluence, education and youth is often used to explain the meteric rise in designer clothes, mineral water, exercise, health, and general sports activism.

It also explains the preference for exotic/imported automobiles, wine and imported vodka consumption, gourmet cooking, more frequent vacations, condominiums, etc. Originating in the 1970s, these trends caused sociologists and marketers to refer to this entire generation as the "Me Generation."

Socialists suggest that the 1980s may be the "We Decade" a decade when sharing, emotion, relationships and family become the driving social force. Expectations are that many of those two person households that delayed having children will do so during the 1980s possibly starting a minor baby boom.

The drive-in generation of the 1950s and 1960s through the "Me" generation of the 1970s to possibly the "We" generation of the 1980s carry with it 20-30 years of foodservice as an integral part of lifestyle. And the personality of the individual is often closely related to the image of an eating and/or drinking establishment. If early rock & roll and custom cars evolved through piano trios and station wagons to disco and economy compacts what does the 1980s hold in store? How will the individual seek to express his personality in his restaurant selection? And, how will the restaurant change its image to fit a changing consumer psychological outlet and need?

The last segmentation alternative to be explored is buyer behavior. There are two important factors that the Super Segment seems to demonstrate regarding eating out. The first is a high propensity to eat out—medium and heavy users of the restaurant product.

The implication is that this group does not have to be encouraged to eat out but merely given the choice of what to eat and where to go. Now, this is the typical eating out decision squeeze of virtually all consumers. The difference with this Super Segment however is the second important factor—quality or the perception of value.

This group is and will be less motivated to eat out because of low prices and promotional incentives. Quality and value are the prime motivators. The group already demonstrates this in its preference for branded products, premium selections, optional features, custom modifications, peer endorsements.

This group will go out of its way to receive a quality benefit and shows little price resistence. This benefit can come in the form of actual quality, perceived quality associated with restaurant reputation or aesthetic features or psychological qualities that enhance self esteem. But this group cannot be exploited. As soon as quality falls below expectations value is reduced and the consumer goes elsewhere to seek satisfaction.

So, this Super Segment of the 1980s is different from most others particularly when demographic characteristics are further modified by geographic, personality and buyer behavioral variables. For the restaurant operator—including chains, independents, urban/suburban/rural—the 1980s indicate the need to reassess existing marketing strategies and refocus efforts on this new group or groups.

In the final article in this series we'll explore the developmennt of alternative restaurant marketing strategies targeted against this Super Segment of the 1980s. We'll also take a look at some possible consumer expectations that might suggest new product and concept alternatives.

Marketing

Third in a Series

Segmentation Strategies for the 80s

by James M. Degen

In the previous two articles, we have attempted to demonstrate the need for a different approach to marketing a restaurant product. Now, segmenting markets for specific products is hardly new to restaurant marketing. But often it is done unconsciously or only by large chains with substantial staffs.

Marketing segmentation demands a consumer orientation. That is, the total consumer market for a product or service (a restaurant or multiple restaurants in a hotel for example) is systematically evaluated for particular characteristics, divided into submarkets or categories and specific products or other marketing elements focused upon them.

There are two major questions that arise from this discussion of segmentation. How is your current consumer base segmented? How is the consumer segmentation of your operation going to change in the 1980s, and what will you do in response to these changes?

Your Consumer Base

There are a series of steps required to determine the segmentation of your consumer base:

1. Identify as many segmentation variables that you feel best describe/characterize restaurant consumers in your marketing area and that you feel can accurately be measured or estimated. For example:

Age – even children, teenagers, young adults is definitive enough;
Income – high, medium or low or actual dollar ranges;
Families versus singles/couples;
Regulars versus infrequent/first timers;
Local residents (5 miles) versus non-locals (more than 5 miles);
Business versus social;

Meal occasion – even times within meal occasion: early dinner, late dinner, etc.
Check average – per person, per party; and
Menu item preference – as broad as beef, chicken, seafood or by specific menu item.

2. Eliminate common or less relevant characteristics.

3. Combine important characteristics and group into major segments representing the majority of the available restaurant business.

4. Give each segment an identifying name—it makes things easier.

5. Make a best "guestimate" of the relative importance of each group expressed as a percent of the total eating-out dollar in your marketing area.

6. Analyze the above in terms of how your customer base compares with the market. What share of each segment do you have? What share do you want to attain?, etc.

The more hard data that can be obtained from the sources such as chambers-of-commerce, local newspapers, parking lot surveys, comment cards, etc., the more accurate the information.

Here's two examples of what might emerge from this exercise. The first example might represent a suburban, full menu, table service restaurant with a lounge and per person check average of $15. The second might be a downtown hotel multi foodservice (lounge, dining room, coffee shop, banquet service and room service).

In both examples, the situation is clear. The suburban full-service restaurant probably is "the best show in town." That is, a hard core of local regulars and less frequent users who like to emulate the younger sociables at least once a year on their anniversary.

The problem for the suburban restaurant becomes finding more regulars. This can be done through word of mouth, promotion or by promoting the restaurant as the "in place" for social gathering.

This may never be a place for the Roving Reporters unless the house specialty is somehow made

From *Restaurant Business* (October 1, 1980) pp. 248-254. Reprinted by permission of *Restaurant Business*.

Example 1

Consumer segment	Young sociables	Annual eaters	Roving reporters	Family feud
Suburban Full-Service Restaurant				
Principle benefit sought	Social interaction	Memorable occasion	Food quality/ service	Lots of food for the least money
Demographic strengths	Young, couples, under 35, upper income	Middle age or older couples	Couples or foursomes, upper income	Young families of four, children under 16, middle-upper income
Geographic strengths	Local	Local/broad market	Broad market	Local
Special behavioral characteristics	Liquor intensive, heavy restaurant users, high brand loyalty	Conservative, unsophisticated, light restaurant users	Heavy restaurant users, low brand loyalty	Family oriented, light to medium restaurant users
Lifestyle characteristics	High sociability	Conservative, family oriented	Hedonistic	Value oriented
Menu concentration	Full menu	Steak or lobster	House specialty	Sandwiches, small steaks, desserts
Estimated share of market	30%	20%	30%	20%
Estimated share of restaurant's business	45%	35%	15%	5%

more unique. The 15 percent Roving Reporters currently dining are probably new at the restaurant review game and are attracted by the Young Sociables' influence more than the product. Once sampled, they will unlikely return.

This is not a place for families. Price may influence this. So too may the presence of the Sociables. The parents either feel the Sociables might be a bad influence on their children, or they are envious that they cannot be a member of the Sociables themselves.

The downtown hotel also has a clear situation. This is the place for a "good time, fun, action." The decor is probably modern, food and service quality need only be "acceptable" not outstanding.

The visibility of the unit is enhanced by the "good time" activity which is why it draws a higher local business for lunch and early dinner.

The Travelers probably see all the activity as a sign of poor value rather than a popular place to stay. If the unit, in fact, delivers a lower level of service their fears will be reinforced and they will not return. This can also influence travel agents when their clients report back.

The Professionals definitely desire and are willing to pay for a superior product. A quiet, more reserved atmosphere is more to their liking. Being recognized by name is a particularly important point-of-difference to keep them coming back.

The problem for the downtown hotel is that the market segments are very clear and rigid. The Professionals and Travelers will continue to decline in patronage at the hotel. Only a complete change in position will attract them.

The vulnerability of the "in place" position is its insecurity. Changes in entertainment by competition, new free-standing bars cut into the One Nighters' usage of the hotel's services. Price and package programs make every convention or sales meeting vulnerable. Predicting next year's sales to groups cannot be based on this year's performance.

But if both of these units have potential difficulties what about over the next decade?

Consumer Base of the 80s

In the last article we identified the Super Segment of the 1980s: single and two-person households, age 25-44, household income $25,000-plus, college educated, and white collar workers.

On the surface, the suburban restaurant example would appear to be in a good position to appeal to this group. However, one of the forecasted shifts

Example 2

Downtown Hotel					
Consumer segment	Professionals	One nighters	Conventioneers	Travelers	Locals
Principal benefit sought	Service	Action	Fun	Value	Price
Demographic strengths	Age 30+, higher income executive heavy traveler, male	25-40, medium-high income, heavy traveler, male	Varies with group	25-50, medium income couples, women, light travelers	20-40, secretaries or middle managers
Geographic strengths	U.S.	U.S.	Local/ U.S.	Local/U.S.	Local
Special behavioral characteristics	High self involvement based on achievement, heavy users	High self involvement based on expectation, heavy users	Critical, light users	Light users, insecure	Light-to-medium users
Lifestyle characteristics	Conservative	Active	"Middle class"	Social climbers	Value oriented
Food/beverage concentration	Dining room, coffee shop (breakfast)	Room service, Bar/ lounge, coffee shop (breakfast)	Banquet, bar/ lounge	Dining room, coffee shop (breakfast)	Coffee shop (lunch) dining room (early dinner)
Estimate market share	20%	25%	35%	10%	10%
Estimated share of hotel's business	5%	40%	30%	5%	20%

during the 1980s is back to the cities. Thus, this market will move to wherever their need for sociability can be fulfilled which may be out of the suburbs.

The forecast of smaller families makes this segment also unattractive as well.

Two strategic alternatives could be explored. The first would be to convince the remaining older couples to eat out more often. This would suggest a price/value approach aimed at the Annual Eaters. The second would be to develop and promote a reputation for a particular food or menu item and raise prices and thus appeal to the Roving Reporters.

The first strategy relies on higher traffic and attempts to make the Annual Eaters regulars—almost a new breed of Sociables. The second strategy is to build on lower traffic volume with increased pressure on food quality and service appealing to the Roving Reporter.

The downtown hotel example probably has had significant shifts in sales volume over the past several years and has changed the concepts of individual food/beverage facilities accordingly.

One of the first strategic moves to be made is to settle on a position and stick with it. Make changes only to improve the position.

The Super Segment of the 1980s will be looking for more leisure time activities and will have the money to participate. The Traveler segment offers potential particularly if the entire level of service can be upgraded.

By improving service, the Professionals now become a more stable target to pursue. By improving service, various elements of the Conventioners can also be attracted because of the "bidding" characteristics of this business.

All of this represents examples of how segmentation can improve a restaurant's marketing position. Every operator should be going through this type of exercise to identify his current consumer segment profile.

Changes cannot—or at least should not—be made in target segments or in redesigning or repositioning units until the current market position of the unit is clearly outlined and understood.

Keep in mind that the competition might be doing the same thing. Striving to be different should be a major objective. Thus, monitoring competitive performance and activity, and changes in concepts is more important now than ever before.

Confronting the 80s:

The Science of Market Segmentation and Positioning

by George Rice

Utilizing CREST data, George Rice identifies how restaurateurs can use market segmentation information to build additional sales and profits. And he explains how they can position themselves as unique in the marketplace by exploiting their competitive points of difference.

This article is rewritten from a prepared presentation by George D. Rice at COEX '80 (Chain Operator Exchange), an annual industry meeting sponsored by the International Foodservice Manufacturers Association, held in Atlanta March 3, 1980.

George Rice was one of the five original founders of CREST (Consumer Report on Eating Share Trends), an on-going market research tracking study of away-from-home consumer purchase behavior. Today Rice is president of GDR Enterprises, Inc., a management consulting firm specializing in foodservice marketing, and additionally serves as senior vice president of NPD Research, Inc. CREST Marketing Services is a service of NPD Research, Inc., and Rice is responsible for the sales, marketing, and general management of the CREST service.

Unfortunately, 1979 lived up to all of the advanced billing we gave it in 1978 as regards the looming "battle for market share." Increases in sales resulted from large increases in the average check size per eater rather than from increases in customer traffic.

For the period ending November 30, 1979, CREST showed that three successive quarters were characterized by declines in customer traffic.

As can be seen from *table 1*, the summer of 1979 reflected very poor performance in the commercial sector (restaurants), with traffic down nine

From *Restaurant Business* (May 1, 1980) pp. 226-232. Reprinted by permission of *Restaurant Business*.

percent from the prior summer quarter (Jun.-Aug.) of 1978. Summer 1978, incidentally, was one of the best quarters since CREST started tracking away-from-home purchase behavior in 1975, with sales up 16 percent from prior year comprised of 8½ percent increase in customer traffic and 7½ percent increase in average check size per eater.

The summer of 1979 is worthy of study for a variety of reasons, but primarily to identify and understand the loss in traffic.

As background: For every potential consumer, young and old, there are six eating opportunities per day: three meal (breakfast, lunch, dinner) and three snack opportunities (morning, afternoon and evening). Thus, there are 42 opportunities per week, or 2,184 eating opportunities per year per person. For each of these opportunities (which are referred to as the "source"), there are a variety of alternatives, as can be seen from *table 2*.

In the summer of 1979, 4.3 percent of all meal/snack opportunities occurred in the commercial sector (restaurants), down from the prior summer at 4.4 percent. On the other hand, the institutional sector increased its share of opportunities to 1.5 percent (up from 1.3 percent in summer 1978). The decline in restaurant traffic was, in fact, primarily a loss to the institutional sector, as opposed to meals prepared at home, or meals skipped!

So, the inflation-battered consumer, stifled by energy and economic problems, did not respond by eating at home or by skipping meals or snacks altogether, but rather opted for a lower cost alternative in the form of subsidized meals from school

TABLE 1

Source: CREST Series II . . . A Service of NPD Research

Analysis of 1979 Sales by Components

% Change to Prior Year)

	WINTER '79	SPRING '79	SUMMER '79	FALL '79
Sales	+16%	+12%	+ 2%	+ 4%
Customer Traffic	+ 4	− 2	− 9	− 6
Average Check per Eater	+12	+14	+11	+10

and employee cafeterias. This is only one of many situations where CREST has identified the cause and effect of price elasticity.

When viewed overall, CREST reveals that 38 percent of all meals and snacks are skipped, versus the remaining 62 percent, which involve the consumption of food and beverage. Viewed independently of meals and snacks that are skipped, restaurants satisfy the need on about 6 percent of food/beverage occasions, ranging from a winter and spring low of about 5 percent to a summer high of 7 percent (4.3 percent when meals skipped are included as discussed above).

Now, what does this all mean, and how do we in the foodservice industry use good marketing information to build sales and profits?

First, by understanding that the "battle for market share" is best defined by the statement "the consumer has a choice" . . . and the choice includes the opportunity to eat at home, skip the occasion altogether, or eat at an institutional alternative rather than at a restaurant.

Further, and of equal importance, the consumer now has a choice of products, services, price and convenience *at competitive restaurants.* In fact, supply has caught up with demand.

The impact of the unusual demographic and lifestyle characteristics of the 60s and 70s have been discounted, and the name of the game in the 80s will be *market segmentation* and *positioning.* The winners will be characterized by their ability to establish and communicate in a highly cluttered media environment, competitive points-of-difference that will motivate consumer trial and repeat purchase behavior.

Segmentation Management

Segmentation management simply involves breaking a given subject into a variety of its pieces (segments), and isolating and studying each segment independently in order to establish a priority order as regards the opportunity afforded by each.

For those segments that represent the maximum number that can be exploited (given your corporate resources), specific strategies and action plans

TABLE 2

Basic Source of Meal & Snack Behavior

Breakfast
Morning Snack
Lunch
Afternoon Snack
Supper
Evening Snack

Prepared At-Home → Eaten at Home / Eaten Away

Skipped → Skipped

Eaten Away-From-Home → Commercial-Restaurant (EATEN IN, TAKEN OUT, DELIVERED) / Institutional (SCHOOL, EMPLOYEE CAFETERIA, HOSPITAL, ETC.)

TABLE 3

Market Segmentation Matrix

	WEEKDAY	WEEKEND
BREAKFAST	1	2
	3	4
LUNCH	5	6
	7	8
SUPPER	9	10
	11	12
SNACK	13	14
	15	16

◻ EAT IN   ◻ TAKE OUT

are developed as part of an overall marketing or business plan.

The problem with most companies is that they get the cart before the horse. Before a marketing plan of attack is devised, the segmentation profile must be developed. For, it is the pieces that add up to the total, not the total that makes up the pieces.

Your ability to either build sales effectively, or to identify critical problem areas to be improved, depends on your understanding and use of segmentation management.

Put another way, segmentation is the link between the general and the specific, and provides the marketer with the disciplines necessary to identify and establish priorities, generate strategies, and subsequently develop and implement action plans. This isn't meant to represent a "motherhood" statement, but if you do not presently understand segmentation management as a basic systematic approach to managing your business, this article may provide you a new lease on building profits for your company.

Let's get to specifics.

The primary question is: "What business are you really in?" While such answers as "the restaurant business" or "the food business," or "the hamburger (or whatever) business," are not incorrect, it is important to be far more specific, as outlined by *table 3* "segmentation matrix."

The segmentation matrix suggests that any restaurant has at least 16 individual segments to define, isolate, and explore in terms of developing opportunities.

The first segmentation is by meal occasion: breakfast, lunch, supper and snacks. Snacks, in fact, can be broken further into three independent areas if snacks become a primary target, or be combined into one of the primary meal occasions, such as breakfast/mid-morning snack.

Next, we acknowledge that the peculiarities of the consumer during the week are considerably different than on weekends, and thus, potentially eight segments require attention.

And for any moment in time, your ability to sell products for eat-in consumption versus take-out consumption increases the opportunities to 16. Your actual number of segments can be more or less than this, depending upon your specific business.

Operational Variables

Next, in order to address each potential segment and to identify the opportunity that it represents

TABLE 4

Operational Variables
(Applied to Each Segment)

Consumer Mix
Product Mix
Pricing
Service Format
Staffing
Communication
Promotion/Merchandising

and thereby its priority, a study of seven "operational variables" is required, as outlined on *table 4*.

For each segment, determine: who are the consumers, their activities prior to restaurant purchases, their life styles, their demographics, their party composition? What products or product combinations, product presentation and portion sizes should be made available, and at what price? What service format is required, and how do we staff to service the customer? What do we have to offer, what points-of-difference do we have and how are they communicated? And, how do we promote and merchandise offerings?

Think through any one of the 16 segments listed in terms of these variables. There is considerable difference between "breakfast-on-weekdays-taken-out" versus "breakfast-on-weekends-eaten-in" or, "lunch-on-weekdays-taken-out," etc.

The isolation, analysis and development of each segment independently aids in a "free thought" process, unencumbered by the existing system and its "apparent" restrictions. When completed, the segments can then be ranked and, as part of the ultimate marketing plan, be developed in a priority order based on those segments which represent the maximum sales/profit opportunity with optimum utilization of corporate resources.

Strategies to Increase Sales

The next issue to be addressed has to do with strategies for each segment. For some reason, marketers get hung up on what constitutes a strategy when, in fact, there are only four that impact on our business, and they are very straightforward. Develop: reach, frequency, party size, or check size per eater (see *table 5* for detail).

For any given segment of your business, the ultimate strategies for building sales will involve some combination of these four: develop new customers, improve the frequency of existing customers, build larger party groups per dining occasion, or increase

TABLE 5

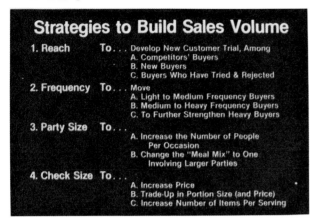

TABLE 6

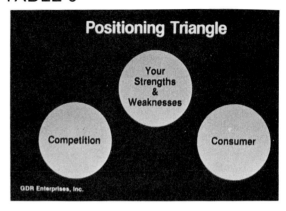

the amount of money spent per person. Each one of the operational variables, by any given segment under study, should be developed in these terms.

Positioning

Given all of the above, we are ready to pull the pieces together and establish your company's niche in the overall marketplace. The best way to view this entire activity is in terms of the positioning triangle (see *table 6*).

Your ultimate market plan involves the identification and understanding of three key elements, *both independently and collectively. They are:*

• First, your *true* corporate strengths and weaknesses, including an in-depth analysis of *every* asset that your company possesses; products, market penetration (store distribution), ability to change/adapt, company versus franchise-operated, vertical integration (food processing, distribution capabilities, etc.), consumer acceptance and awareness including mnemonic devices,* personnel and financial resources;

• Second, the consumer marketplace, its seg-

mentation (as discussed above), and trends of each segment;

• And lastly, the competition's strengths and weaknesses.

Your ultimate position must be condensed to a series of competitive points-of-difference that can be communicated in the highly competitive, media-cluttered environment that exists today.

The companies that will profit most in the next decade will be those which best understand the consumer and consumer segmentation . . . which can match the appropriate product mix with the appropriate value mix . . . which can match their corporate strengths with consumer needs through competitive points-of-difference, and can then effectively communicate these differences to that consumer.

The common denominator throughout the entire process of market development is information, and the management of information which results in the implementation of an effective marketing plan. The need for information grows incrementally with the size of your company . . . as does the cost of a bad decision!

---

*Mnemonic devices are trademarks, slogans, symbols, etc., which identify your products and services in the marketplace; McDonald's golden arches, KFC's red and white striped bucket, for examples.

Benefit Segmentation for Restaurant Advertising That Works

by Robert C. Lewis, Ph.D.

University of Massachusetts

Through the use of discriminant analysis, the traditional challenge to any advertising—"Will it sell?"—can now be answered in advance. A recent study identifies the attributes that should be stressed in advertising restaurants of three types

Robert C. Lewis is Assistant Professor of Marketing and Management in the Department of Hotel, Restaurant, and Travel Administration at the University of Massachusetts, Amherst. He received his doctorate from the University of Massachusetts, where his areas of concentration were communication theory and marketing.

As the concept of positioning[1] has gained currency in the hospitality industry, virtually all quarters of the industry have come to appreciate the importance of market segmentation to the success of their enterprises.[2] With some exceptions, less attention has been paid to the concept of *benefit* segmentation,[3] defined below. The purpose of the present article is to demonstrate how the identification of benefit segments can inform the development of a positioning strategy. Although the research reported below was intended to identify the benefits sought by *restaurant* patrons, the same techniques can be applied to the analysis of benefits required by prospective hotel guests.

This article was originally published in the November 1980 issue of *The Cornell Hotel and Restaurant Administration Quarterly*, pp.6-12, and is reprinted here with the permission of the Cornell University School of Hotel Administration. ©1980.

1. See "Advertising That Sells Hotels," *The Cornell Hotel and Restaurant Administration Quarterly*, 20, No. 4 (November 1979), pp 17-23, and Brian T. Sill, "Restaurant Merchandising for the Independent Operator," *The Cornell Hotel and Restaurant Administration Quarterly*, 21, No. 1 (May 1980), pp. 27-30.

2. William R. Swinyard, "A Research Approach to Restaurant Marketing," *The Cornell Hotel and Restaurant Administration Quarterly*, 17, No. 4 (February 1977), pp. 62-66.

3. For a summary of discussion of benefit segmentation, see: R.I. Haley, "Benefit Segmentation: A Decision-Oriented Research Tool," *Journal of Marketing*, 32, No. 3 (July 1968), pp. 27-30.

Understanding, Then Responding to, the Prospect's Needs

Demographic and volume segmentation strategies differentiate markets on the basis of distinct measures—for example, sex, age, income, and "heavy use" versus "light use"—that are easily compared. In contrast, benefit segmentation attempts to establish the strength of the appeal of various product or service attributes, and therefore requires the measurement and comparison of such elusive attitudinal qualities as consumers' perceptions and intentions. The problem of measurement and comparison is further compounded by the analyst's need to know not only whether an individual attribute represents a benefit but also how it interacts with other attributes to prompt the decision to use (or not to use) a product or service. Thus, it is the total configuration of benefits sought that defines a benefit segment, and a group of prospective users who weight the importance of the attributes of a product or service similarly constitute a benefit segment.

For the restaurateur able to identify his benefit segments, the next strategic move is evident: he must position his restaurant for the target segments identified. Positioning requires the consistent communication of a package of attributes through various channels, yielding for the restaurant a specific "niche" in the consumer's mind.

Together, benefit segmentation and market positioning are powerful tools for developing—or protecting—a firm's market share. Their effective use, however, depends on an understanding of consumers' choice processes.

How Consumers Choose Products and Services

For the prospective restaurant patron seeking specific benefits, the appeals communicated through advertising are especially important. Unlike products, the restaurant experience cannot be "tried on." If advertising fails to project *appeals* that involve the consumer by positioning the restaurant in the desired benefit image, the best orchestrated and most expensive ad campaign may be largely ineffective. The restaurant marketer's problem is that consumers employ different choice processes and seek different benefit "bundles," depending on the type of restaurant they want to patronize.

In general, the advertiser's objective should be to create a restaurant image that appeals to a particular segment of the population. Although the identification of the individual benefits sought by consumers has received considerable attention in various consumer surveys (e.g., Chain Restaurant Eating-Out Share Trends, the Gallup Monitor, and the National Restaurant Association's studies), little attention has been directed to (1) the joint effect of the benefits sought, (2) how the relative importance of those benefits varies by restaurant type, and (3) how consumers process advertising information in making a restaurant choice. The empirical analysis reported below contrasts the more common univariate approach—the identification of the individual benefits sought—with a multivariate approach that investigates the *joint effect of the several factors* underlying restaurant choice. Advertising strategies for three types of restaurants, based on the simultaneous processing of five perceived benefits, are also advanced.

Methodology

Data for the study were gathered from a systematic random sampling of 400 persons in a five-town area of New England. The usable sample numbered 110. The demographic characteristics of the sample (Exhibit 1) were diverse enough to permit the drawing of significant conclusions.

Three major and commonly defined types of restaurants were selected for analysis: family-popular, atmosphere, and gourmet restaurants (see Exhibit 2 for a full description of restaurant types). From a collection of over 1,000 restaurant advertisements in the print medium, six judges selected three advertisements, each deemed representative of one of the three categories of restaurants.

EXHIBIT 1
Demographic characteristics of respondents

Characteristic	Sample Size	Mini- mum	Maxi- mum	Mean	Standard Deviation
Age	109*	25	75	39.2	13.1
Annual income ($000)	91	0	75	18.7	11.9
Education (years)	109	6	22	14.8	3.0
# of children at home	109	0	5	.9	1.2
Average number of meals eaten out per month	109	0	14	4.8	3.3
Sex: Male	59				
Female	50				
Household status: Single	44				
Couple	65				

*Complete demographic data were not available for all 110 respondents classified using the discriminant-analysis function.

EXHIBIT 2
Definitions of restaurant types

Family-popular restaurant: A restaurant you would be inclined to frequent with your family, your spouse, or a friend for a casual meal. It is likely to be relaxed and unpretentious, featuring fast service; you probably would not make a reservation. The operation is popular in the sense that it is well-known and used by many, especially during meal hours.

Atmosphere restaurant: This is the type of restaurant that creates an atmosphere by virtue of its setting, decor, historic context, special artifacts, or view. Although you might take your family, you would probably have a special reason for patronizing this style of restaurant. You would be likely to dress better when going to this type of restaurant than you would when patronizing a family-popular restaurant.

Gourmet restaurant: You would patronize this type of restaurant because the food, service, and gracious atmosphere contribute to a relaxed dining experience. More formal than the family-popular or atmosphere restaurant, this type of operation is characterized by an unhurried pace. You might select this type of restaurant for a special occasion or because you seek especially good food and service on a particular dining-out occasion.

A content analysis of 270 restaurant advertisements identified, after refinement, five benefit appeals that served as independent variables: food quality, menu variety, price, atmosphere, and convenience factors. All subjects participating were interviewed in their homes and responded in two ways: by rating, on a scale from one to five, the strength of each of the five appeals perceived in each of the three advertisements; and by indicating whether they would choose to patronize the restaurant described if the only knowledge they had about it was that it was garnered from the advertisement.

EXHIBIT 3
Univariate significance-of-difference tests between goers and nongoers

Benefit Category	Goers' Means (Rank)	Nongoers' Means (Rank)	F(1,70) (Rank)	Significance
Family-Popular Restaurant				
Food quality	3.44 (4)	2.06 (4)	36 (1)	p .001
Menu variety	3.70 (2)	2.30 (3)	27 (2)	p .001
Price	3.61 (3)	2.72 (1)	14 (5)	p .001
Atmosphere	2.78 (5)	1.61 (5)	25 (3)	p .001
Convenience factors	3.80 (1)	2.70 (2)	16 (4)	p .001
Atmosphere Restaurant				
Food quality	4.10 (1)	3.10 (2)	20 (1)	p .001
Menu variety	3.58 (2)	3.25 (1)	2 (5)	p .22
Price	3.31 (3)	2.50 (3)	6 (4)	p .01
Atmosphere	4.10 (1)	3.10 (2)	12 (2)	p .001
Convenience factors	3.29 (4)	2.43 (4)	9 (3)	p .001
Gourmet Restaurant				
Food quality	4.30 (1)	2.70 (2)	38 (1)	p .001
Menu variety	3.36 (4)	2.14 (5)	23 (2)	p .001
Price	3.21 (5)	2.43 (3)	8 (5)	p .001
Atmosphere	3.57 (3)	2.36 (4)	19 (3)	p .001
Convenience factors	3.58 (2)	2.75 (1)	10 (4)	p .001

EXHIBIT 4
Significance and association tests for the discriminant function

	Chi-square	df	Sig.	R_c	EV	R_c^2
Family-Popular Restaurant	39	5	.00	.66	.78	.44
Atmosphere Restaurant	24	5	.00	.54	.42	.29
Gourmet Restaurant	36	5	.00	.64	.71	.41

Results

Univariate analysis. Significance-of-difference tests demonstrated that the five appeal categories distinguished those who would patronize a given restaurant (herein labeled **"goers"**) from those who would not patronize the restaurant (**"nongoers"**). As can be seen in Exhibit 3, the mean scores on the strength-of-appeal scale were higher for goers than for nongoers on each appeal across the three restaurant types. The difference between the means was found to be statistically significant in all cases, except for the appeal "menu variety" for atmosphere restaurants. A measure of the degree of difference between the goers' and nongoers' ratings of the individual appeals is provided by the F statistic, which expresses the ratio between the variances of the two samples. Here we see that food quality has the highest F value for each restaurant type.

The restaurateur presented with these findings might conclude that since all appeals, with the exception noted, differentiate significantly regardless of restaurant type, he should promote all the benefits in his advertising with special emphasis on food quality. Not surprisingly, the content analysis performed to identify the five appeals revealed that most restaurant advertisements are structured to achieve this end.

But note that food quality has been singled out as the predominant appeal by a comparison be-

tween the values assigned to the benefit by goers and nongoers. How important is food quality compared to other attributes in determining the "go" or "not go" decision? A comparison *within* restaurant types reveals that food quality is not necessarily the predominant appeal. For example, among goers in the family-popular restaurant type, convenience was given the highest appeal rating, while food quality was ranked fourth. In the atmosphere-restaurant classification, goers rated food quality first and atmosphere fourth. Similarly, the means of the appeals' ratings for nongoers differed across the three restaurant types.

Most restaurant surveys that seek to determine why patrons choose a certain restaurant—particularly in-house studies—produce similar results. Those variables that distinguish between goers and nongoers, when considered individually, are not necessarily those that form the basis of decision. Multivariate analysis is required to capture the total configuration of benefit appeals perceived by the consumer.

Multivariate analysis. The techniques of multivariate analysis permit the marketer to interrelate subjects' ratings so that categories of respondents with similar rating patterns may be distinguished. When the items rated are potential consumer benefits, the categories that emerge comprise persons who attach similar levels of importance to the various benefits. One statistical technique that is especially powerful in differentiating benefit segments is discriminant analysis.

Discriminant analysis statistically constructs linear combinations of independent variables that classify subjects into one of two or more mutually exclusive and exhaustive categories. In the present study, using the respondents' ratings of the five appeals (independent variables), a set of weights was derived to predict the respondents' classification into the two categories of the dependent variable: goers and nongoers. The process of discriminant analysis weights and linearly combines the benefit appeals so that the two dependent categories are forced to be as statistically distinct as possible.[4] The discriminant function thus developed specifies those appeals that differentiate goers from nongoers.

In analyzing the goer and nongoer categories determined by the discriminant function, we are concerned with the following.

• *How successful were the appeals in discriminating between goers and nongoers?* In other words, can we segment consumers by virtue of the total configuration of benefits perceived by them when selecting a particular restaurant? The degree of this success is indicated by the significance level of the chi-square statistic and by the size of the canonical correlation (R_c).

• If the discriminant classification is successful, *how much of the total variance is explained by the discriminant function* and what proportion of the variance is explained by the categories (i.e., is there still substantial unexplained variance)? The size of the total variance explained by the benefit variables is indicated by the eigenvalue (EV) of the derived function. The proportion explained by the categories is indicated by the size of the canonical correlation squared (R_c^2).

• *Which appeals contribute most to the differentiation between categories?* This information provides insight into the benefits that are important to the consumer, and permits the marketer to make inferences as to how the consumer processes the appeals when choosing a given type of restaurant.

In this case, as in multiple regression or factor analysis, the size of the weighting coefficients is used to identify the order in which variables contribute to the differentiation between categories. The accepted heuristic is to consider those variables having a standard coefficient with an absolute value at least as great as one-half the value of the largest coefficient as contributing most to the delineation of category profiles.

• *How successful is the discriminant procedure in classifying subjects as goers or nongoers?* Can we predict intention at a level greater than chance? A confusion matrix of predicted category membership is produced to indicate the percentage of cases

correctly classified. A t-test is used to determine the level of significance for the classification accuracy. The chance classification accuracy and the proportional error reduction (PER) are calculated.

As seen in Exhibit 4, the chi-square statistics indicate that all three discriminant functions were statistically significant at $p < .001$ in successfully separating goers from nongoers. Further, the appeals exhibited a high degree of association with the discriminant functions, as indicated by the canonical correlations. A large portion of the total variance was contained in the appeals variables (as measured by the eigenvalues), and a large percentage of the variance in the discriminant function (as measured by the canonical correlation squared) was explained by the two categories for the family-popular and the gourmet restaurants. The explained variances are somewhat less but still significant for the atmosphere restaurant. We can tentatively conclude that the intention to go to a restaurant is a function of perceived benefits, and that it is possible to discriminate between goers and nongoers—albeit with some reservations for the atmosphere restaurant—on the basis of the benefits they perceive.

Having established the discriminating power of the benefit variables, it is possible to predict a respondent's membership in a category, on the basis of the benefits he perceives, by analyzing the coefficients of the linear discriminant function. The weighting coefficients for all three restaurant types are reported in Exhibit 5. In addition to their use as a prediction tool, the weights provide valuable information about the restaurant appeals from the consumer's point of view. Here are some of the conclusions that may be drawn from Exhibit 5.

1. The most important factor in a consumer's intention to go to any of the restaurant types is quality of food.

---

4. The linear discriminant function is appropriate only when the categories' covariance matrices are equal or nearly equal. This assumption was tested and found satisfied in all cases.

EXHIBIT 5
Standardized discriminant coefficients of the discriminant function for GOERS

	Family-Popular	Atmosphere	Gourmet
Food quality	.51	.71	.69
Menu variety	.19	−.51	.41
Price	.28	.36	−.18
Atmosphere	.36	.32	.30
Convenience factors	.12	.28	.03

2. The second most important factor in intention to go to the family-popular restaurant is atmosphere. For the atmosphere restaurant, price is the second-ranking appeal; and for the gourmet restaurant, the second is menu variety.

3. The third most important factor in the intention to patronize the family-popular restaurant is price. For the atmosphere and gourmet restaurants, the third-ranking appeal is atmosphere, although the coefficient in each case is less than significant using the accepted heuristic.

4. Considerable menu variety has a *negative* effect on intention to go to an atmosphere restaurant.

The final step in the analysis is to examine the predictive power of the discriminant functions. Each function was used to predict respondents' intentions and to classify all respondents into the appropriate group by the "maximum likelihood" method. As shown in Exhibit 6, the discriminant function was highly successful in classifying respondents in all three cases.[5] Looking, for example, at the results for the family-popular restaurant, we see that the discriminant function predicted that 63 respondents would patronize this type of establishment on the basis of their ranking of the advertising appeals. Similarly, the discriminant function predicted that 34 respondents would not patronize the family-popular restaurant. Comparing the total classified by the discriminant function (97) to the total sample size (110) yields a classification accuracy of 88 percent. The lowest classification accuracy is a respectable 72 percent for the atmosphere restaurant, and all classifications are significant at the $p < .01$ level or better.

Further indication of predictive strength is provided by comparing the correct classifications produced by the discriminant function to the number of correct classifications that would be produced using a 125-percent-of-chance criterion.[6] In the case of the family-popular restaurant, a 125-percent-of-chance classification would have predicted category membership accurately for 75 of

the 110 respondents (68 percent)—a level considerably below the 88 percent of correct classifications produced by the discriminant function. In the case of each restaurant type, the discriminant function produced more accurate classifications than required by the 125-percent-of-chance criterion, as Exhibit 6 shows.

Finally, the proportional error reduction (PER) provides a measure of the discriminant function's predictive power by comparing the number of accurate classifications under optimal conditions to those produced by the discriminant function.[7] For the derived functions reported in Exhibit 6, the reduction in errors is substantial. The PERs also indicate that the total configuration of appeals selected as independent variables is more strongly associated with family-popular and gourmet restaurants than with atmosphere restaurants.

Three Models of Consumer Choice

The study's results also provide inferential guidelines regarding the prospective consumer's choice processes when selecting each of the three types of restaurants.

The choice process for the gourmet restaurant, for example, seems to fit the disjunctive model. In this model, the consumer establishes one or more attributes as dominant factors in his decision-making. If the requisite factor (or factors) is (are) present at a minimum level of expectation, all other attributes are of minor importance. For the gourmet restaurant, food quality stands out as a key factor; somewhat less important, but still significant to the decision, is menu variety. Thus, we can tentatively advance the conclusion that the way to appeal to prospective patrons seeking a gourmet restaurant is to emphasize food quality and menu variety. Support for this premise derives from the substantial amount of variance explained by the appeal variables.

The conjunctive model of consumer behavior specifies that each attribute must equal or exceed the minimum expectation of the consumer or the choice will be rejected. This pattern is apparent in

---

5. There is an upward bias in "canned" discriminant-analysis computer programs because they compute the confusion matrix by using all observations to calculate the discriminant function and then classify the same individuals using the same function. A method of cross-validation to attack this bias is one that splits the sample, using one part for analysis and the other part for validation. All classifications were successfully cross-validated in this study.

6. The proportion of correct classifications that would be predicted by chance is calculated using the proportional chance criterion formula
$$\text{chance portion} = p^2 + (1\text{-}p)^2$$
for unequal category sizes, here p = proportion of individuals in category 1 and 1-p = proportion of individuals in category 2. To warrant the interpretation of the discriminant functions for the development of category profiles, a rule of thumb is that the criterion of classification accuracy should be at least 25 percent greater than chance.

7. The PER measure is computed by the formula
$$\text{PER} = \frac{D\text{-}P}{N\text{-}P}$$

where D = the number of correct assignments produced by the discriminant function, P = the number of correct assignments under optimal prediction when the discriminant function is not used, and N = total number of respondents. The number of correct assignments under optimal prediction is equal to the number of respondents in the largest group.

EXHIBIT 6
Confusion matrices of predicted category member-ship

FAMILY-POPULAR RESTAURANT

	Predicted Membership		
Group	1	2	Total
1. Would go	63	8	71
2. Would not go	5	34	39

Accuracy: 97 (88%) correctly classified;
$t = 5.18$, p<.001.
125%-of-chance classification criterion would require
75 (68%) correctly classified.
PER: .67

ATMOSPHERE RESTAURANT

	Predicted Membership		
Group	1	2	Total
1. Would go	47	15	62
2. Would not go	16	32	48

Accuracy: 79 (72%) correctly classified;
$t = 3.08$, p <.01.
125%-of-chance classification criterion would require
70 (64%) correctly classified.
PER: .35

GOURMET RESTAURANT

	Predicted Membership		
Group	1	2	Total
1. Would go	41	13	54
2. Would not go	13	43	56

Accuracy: 84 (76%) correctly classified;
$t = 5.33$, p<.001.
125%-of-chance classification would require
69 (63%) correctly classified.
PER: .52

the weightings of the family-popular restaurant. Food quality is weighted most heavily again but at a much lower level than for the other two restaurant types. All other appeals are positive for this restaurant and higher in relation to the food-quality variable than was true for the gourmet restaurant. Thus, each benefit appears to have satisfied a minimum level of expectation. Again, the premise is supported by the large amount of variance explained by the appeals.

The atmosphere-restaurant weightings show a decidedly different pattern. Food quality is again rated highest. Menu variety is also weighted quite high, but as a *negative* influence; the other factors also have relatively high weightings. Further, only a low 42 percent of the variance was contained in the appeal variables. These two factors—a high

negative weighting and a low contained variance—lead to the premise that the consumer's choice process for this restaurant is a compensatory expectancy value model. Under this model, the sum across all weightings provides the basis for decision. The individual first determines that certain attributes exist and then attaches a negative or positive value to each one, with the highest net positive sum determining the restaurant choice. The variables used in the study tentatively explicate this model, but the low contained variance indicates that other variable interactions were not captured in the study.[8]

Summary

The limitations of the research reported above are apparent: the results derived from a limited sample and from data regarding consumers' stated *intentions* (rather than actual behaviors) cannot be freely generalized. More important than the specific results, however, are the implications of the study for future research in restaurant marketing.

The research demonstrates that a sophisticated methodology can yield results immediately and directly useful to the restaurant marketer. As confirmed by the empirical analysis, consumers process several appeals in selecting a restaurant, and it is possible to identify with reasonable reliability the relative importance of the appeals.

Perhaps most important, the empirical analysis shows a statistically verifiable relationship between perceived benefits and the intention to patronize a specific type of restaurant. In short, the traditional challenge to any advertising—"But will it sell?"—can be answered in advance by confirming the influence of the benefit variable on intended behavior.

Although the research techniques discussed above may not be available to the smaller operator, they can readily be purchased or developed in-house by multi-unit firms. Larger firms especially can derive significant competitive advantage from benefit segmentation because of their need to differentiate themselves from imitators in the market. With a thorough understanding of the benefits prospective patrons seek from their operations, multi-unit chains can position their firms to take advantage of consumers' needs.

---

8. For a detailed and substantive treatment of these and other processes of consumer choice, see: J.R. Bettman, *An Information Processing Theory of Consumer Choice* (Reading, MA: Addison-Wesley, 1979), chapter 7.

Part V

Positioning Strategy

From time to time new buzz-words appear in the lexicon of marketing. Positioning is such a word. It is now popular to talk about product positioning. But because product positioning is something that occurs in consumers' minds we don't know as much about it as we should and often we don't take advantage of what we do know. The position of a product or service depends upon consumers' perceptions or beliefs about the product or service in relation to similar products or services that are available. Positioning is concerned with image.

Positioning in a hospitality market begins with a hospitality product which can be a company, a restaurant, an individual hotel, or a chain. But the positioning of that product in the market has little to do with what is done to the product. Product design is important, of course. But name changes, refurbishing, redecorating and design changes are largely cosmetic in nature, although they are done to influence consumers' perceptions. More important than what is done to the product is what is done to the minds of consumers. In other words, products are not positioned in physical markets. Products are positioned in the minds of consumers.

What is the most desirable position in the minds of consumers and how does one get there? The most desirable position is to be number one, and the most effective way to get there is to be first.

People mentally sort products that they use into various product categories. There is a category for toothpaste, a category for automobiles, a category for suits, a category for restaurants and a category for hotels. There are as many categories as there are products used by the consumer. Hospitalty products are often sub-divided further according to purpose of purchase, geographic location, price range or some other criteria. Thus, restaurants may be subdivided into categories such as fast food, theme restaurants, or restaurants for special occasion dining. Hotels may be subdivided into categories such as resorts, convention hotels, or roadside motels. But, regardless of how categories are established or how they are defined, consumers to make these distinctions.

Within each category consumers mentally list brand names they know or have heard of. There may be few or many brands but seldom more than seven. Research suggests that the maximum number of items most people can compare is seven. Furthermore, people arrange brands in rank order of preference with number one being the most preferred. Therefore, the most favorable position would be to have a single product category with your product firmly established in the number one rank. In other words, the most favorable position is to be the only game in town.

But how is this number one rank achieved? The most effective way is to be first with a high-quality product that satisfies the needs and wants of a well-defined market segment. People tend to remember firsts and forget seconds, thirds, and fourths. For example, what was the name of the first company to introduce a chain of standardized, high-quality lodging accommodations located along major highways? Holiday Inns. What was the name of the second company? Few people know.

Being first implies innovation, doing new things, introducing new concepts. It implies in-depth knowledge of market segments, knowledge of needs and wants and the ability to recognize needs and wants that are not being satisfied. It further indicates the ability to provide products and services that will give satisfaction.

In summary, the position a hotel or restaurant holds depends upon what consumers think of it. The position depends upon customers' perceptions of how well the product satisfies their needs and wants. The articles in this section have been selected to show managers how to position their hotels or restaurants better in the minds of their potential customers—how to become number one.

Positioning: Crucial Marketing Tool

by Brian T. Sill

*Brian Sill, an associate with Cinci-Grissom
Associates, Inc., a planning and advisory
service to the foodservice industry, prepared
this article from a thesis he wrote entitled
"An Approach to Merchandising in a
Restaurant Operation."*

Traditionally, independent restaurant operators have marketed their restaurants based upon a "gut-feeling" approach to merchandising. Thus, marketing tools have not been utilized in the day-to-day activities of the operations. This, of course, is understandable since one can hardly expect all restaurant operators to have enough marketing background to realize the usefulness of these tools. Therefore, an active approach is in order; one that will allow you to make use of these tools. One of the most basic of these tools is called: *Positioning*.

The process of positioning is viewed as an ideal starting place because it lays the groundwork from which merchandising activities spring. The reasoning behind this process flows from the present day view that the product a restaurant offers is no longer just good food and service, but the dining *experience* as a whole. As you seek ways to differentiate your restaurant from your competition, it is important that all promotion and advertising tactics for building sales be consistent and flow naturally from the positioning objectives. It is the consistent and "natural" flow of these objectives that provides an enjoyable experience for the customer.

Inherent in establishing any restaurant concept are your attitudes as an owner. Your perceptions of your business establish the performance standards that shape the restaurant experience for the customer. Once the customer has tried this experience he develops an image of the restaurant. He then categorizes that image according to certain classifications he uses to define the experience.

These classifications tend to be similar for most customers. For example, some definitions that represent a different taste coupled with a specific atmosphere are ethnic or specialty restaurants such as Italian, Greek or Chinese. Some restaurants are categorized by the type of service offered such as drive-in, cafeteria, buffet or sit-down white table-cloth service. Additionally, many people classify their image of this restaurant experience by the level of expertise required in the preparation of the food. The tendency is to classify restaurants on a continuum scale ranging from fast food on the one hand to gourmet on the other. These are just some of the broader categories used to define the classifications of restaurants. It is apparent that many elements shape and influence the customer's image of the restaurant. These elements are the tools, activities and presentation methods that reinforce the placement, or positioning, of the restaurant as consumers perceive it.

A good way of determining this is to answer some questions. These questions require you to analyze the marketplace first: define the market, define your customers (target market); and then examine the relationship of these markets to the restaurant operation. Naturally one can assume this checklist would be marketing-oriented and that a marketing professional would be needed to administer the questions and help interpret the results. It is this writer's experience that a graduate student or professor of marketing at a local university can be retained for this exercise. Also, this person would have access to positioning checklists that can be found in the marketing literature.

The following is an example of exactly how positioning works.

The owner of The Rumble Seat Restaurant was distraught over the poor sales figures he was showing the past year. At the advice of a friend the owner decided to seek help from a marketing professional in the area. To begin, the restaurant operator gave a brief description of his operation, the

From *Restaurant Business* (July 1, 1980) pp. 98-102. Reprinted by permission of *Restaurant Business*.

Mini-market audit*

Social/Cultural

1. What attitude is the public taking toward business and toward products such as those produced by the company?

(O): Attitudes appear to range between total acceptance, on the high side, and confusion and lack of understanding of the product on the low end.

(M): Interest in restaurants is increasing. The public is becoming more discriminating in terms of taste, quality and originality.

2. What changes are occurring in consumer life styles and values that have a bearing on the company's target markets (customers) and marketing methods?

(O): There is a possibility that the consumer is becoming more conscious of good foods and good cooking, and tending to seek out foods that cannot be easily prepared at home.

(M): Consumers are coming to value fresh foods prepared to order. They are willing to pay a little more for "the real thing."

Markets

1. What is happening to market size, growth, geographical distribution, and profits?

(O): Market size definitely is increasing. However, because of an underlying economic weakness (i.e. wages not keeping pace with inflation and cost of living increases) for the area, there may be a temporary restriction in the amount of money spent in medium quality and above restaurants. Consistant growth is sure to continue after short side slow-down through mid-1979. (See the present location as a part of a regional area of high interest and service utility to the entire region (i.e. Pike Place Market and downtown retailing). Profits usually occur after the break-even point.

(M): no answer

2. What are the major market segments? Which are the heavy user and light user segments?

(O): Professional people living in the first and second ring of residential areas surrounding downtown Seattle tend to make up the major market segments. Shoppers and office workers in the downtown area and users of the Pike Place Market make up the heavy users. The light user segment would include the out-of-town business people and visitors, and those living in the suburban and outer residential areas of Seattle. (This would change with the introduction of a Class H license whereby more of a meeting place would develop for drinks after work and result in an increase in dining).

(M): Major market segments: (Beginning with heaviest users and decending to lighter users). Young successful businessmen/women, shoppers, people who "like Italian food", clerks and office workers.

---

location, and what he felt his strong and weak points were: "The atmosphere is a 1930's speakeasy motif. Limited menu, average entrees. The people that eat here are generally middle class, even though the immediate neighborhood is upper class. The present idea is that the atmosphere essentially sells the patron. In other words, the cuisine is superfluous to the concept."

After answering the questionnaire and discussing it with a marketing consultant (in this case, a local marketing professor) the owner was made aware of the surrounding environment in three major ways. First; he was catering to a casual middle-income, value-conscious clientele in an upper-income neighborhood. Since convenience plays a major role in consumer decision-making, the upscale group was the most logical target, especially since the convenience factor generally influences the decision-making of upper-income groups more so than middle to lower-income groups.

Second; although there were other restaurants in a two-mile radius, none of them had any type of lounge or cabaret entertainment.

Third; the atmosphere had always been appreciated by most of the patrons in the past, and had always been one of the major attractions. Thus, it was concluded that there needn't be any major concept changes—just an affirmation of the current concept with a re-targeting of clientele. Since the new target audience was chosen as the surrounding upper-income neighbors it was decided that the food would have to be upscaled to attract them. Hence, a new chef was brought in.

Except for the $75 charge by the marketing professor, the hiring of the more expensive chef ($400 more per month) was the only additional cost to the owner for changing his positioning approach to other restaurants.

In re-emphasizing The Rumble Seat concept, the menu nomenclature was tied in more closely. Examples of this menu merchandising:

Music programs for background dining music were changed to a nickelodeon-style music.

Employee training programs were instituted to place greater emphasis on the service function of the restaurant. Also, these meetings served a second purpose as a discussion period on customer reaction to the new concept. During these discussions the owner was better able to educate his employees to his approach with customer feedback fresh in mind. The result was a tighter bond between owner and employee in understanding the former's approach to merchandising based on his positioning objectives. Participation in these meetings was a key factor in the meetings being fruitful.

Employee feedback revealed customer acceptance based on the convenience factor. The neighborhood locals said "This is my type of food." Other feedback showed the customers to have an interest in entertainment. But they said they didn't want real active entertainment, rather, a passive, laid-back easy-going style of entertainment.

The owner started with a piano bar. Then he found the customers wanted more sophistication in the entertainment. So, he employed a 2-piece cabaret with guitar, piano and vocalist. Eventually the acceptance and desire for this entertainment grew and changed its nature completely.

It was concluded from word-of-mouth descriptions of The Rumble Seat that it was the "speakeasy" atmosphere that made the restaurant conducive to entertainment and drinking activities *on a par with eating activities*. It was further concluded that the primary desire of the upscaled clientele was in fact entertainment and drinks. But because of the social stigma associated with drinking activities unaccompanied with food, the upscaled, quality cuisine of the restaurant served as a cloak for shielding the customer from a "bar drinker" image. (The customer "imbibed liquor" vs "drank alcohol.")

Hence, the total package—a quality-merchandised image of cuisine coupled with a 1930's drinking emporium changed the restaurant emphasis from a dinner house to a supper house. In other words, *entertainment* with food, and not *food* with entertainment. The positioning change from beginning to end took eighteen months. Therefore, it should be noted that the process is an active, on-going approach that uses customer feedback and sales volume as a measure of successful positioning. In this example, sales tripled over the 18 months.

The foregoing is an example of an active approach taken by a restaurant owner to understand and improve his positioning in the marketplace. The first step was to seek help from a marketing professional. A checklist was used to determine the owner's present attitudes toward his business. The process of answering the questions is somewhat of an esoteric exercise. The purpose of the checklist was to internalize the situation with the owner. It focused the investigation on the person in control of the operation so external factors would not be used as alibis.

The approach is a therapeutic one: by answering the questions, the owner learned more about his motives and ambitions face to face with his restaurant operation. It forced him to write down in words exactly where he feels his business fits into the whole realm of things—not just the restaurant industry, but life as a whole.

The idea of this approach is to increase your self-awareness of the situation because self-awareness can enhance your position and increase your strength against the competition. By learning more about yourself in relation to your entrepreneurial attitudes, more insight is gained into your position in the marketplace; and you can gain some visibility, thus control, in the customers' dining decisions.

How to Develop a Positioning Strategy on a Small Restaurant's Budget

by Roy W. MacNaughton

The small-restaurant operator's market research and analysis lay the groundwork for a marketing plan that effectively sets the operation apart from other restaurants large and small

Roy W. MacNaughton is president of Hospitality Marketing, a consulting firm specializing in the international hospitality industry. A graduate in hotel, restaurant, and tourism administration from Ryerson Polytechnical Institute in Toronto, he received his M.B.A. from the University of Western Ontario.

Restaurateurs have begun to recognize the importance of positioning to success in the marketplace, but the independent operator—who generally lacks the time, expertise, and budget to develop a positioning strategy for his single outlet or small chain—is at a disadvantage when competing against large chain organizations with marketing departments capable of performing the analysis internally. The present article will help the independent food-service operator develop a positioning strategy for his firm.

The sequence of steps forming the marketing process is depicted in Exhibit 1. Although the discussion to follow centers on market segmentation (Step 3) and the development of a positioning strategy (Step 4), a brief discussion of marketing research is appropriate because the independent operator must systematically collect data to describe the essential attributes of his clientele: who they are, their food-away-from-home patterns, what they seek in a restaurant, and how they arrive at the operation.

Numerous sophisticated survey and analytical

This article was originally published in the February 1981 issue of *The Cornell Hotel and Restaurant Administration Quarterly*, pp. 10-14, and is reprinted here with the permission of the Cornell University School of Hotel Administration. ⓒ1981.

techniques are used by market researchers to answer these questions with a high degree of reliability, but the independent operator with limited financial resources must rely on less complex methods of market research. Nevertheless, he should not conclude that his data are necessarily less valuable for being obtained at a modest cost; if carefully gathered and objectively analyzed, the operator's in-house data can prove very useful in developing an accurate view of the firm's environment.

Basic market research might take the form of an in-house contest in which patrons are asked to complete entry forms with their names, addresses, and zip codes, thus permitting the operator to plot his customers' residences on an area map—and perhaps to use the information as a ready-made mail list when announcing special events. Informal after-meal interviews with randomly selected patrons can yield important information on such matters as their menu preferences, patronage habits, and basic demographics. Equipment currently available allows patrons to answer these and similar questions by punching their responses into a minicomputer placed near the cashier's stand or in the restaurant's lobby. These devices permit the operator to survey a large number of respondents cost-efficiently without compromising the objectivity of their responses—a potential problem when data are gathered through personal interviews.

Many data whose application has traditionally been limited to accounting and control functions—including sales by shifts, sales to labor-cost ratios, product mix, and average check—may also constitute valuable marketing information. Today's electronic cash registers make accurate and timely data of this type available to the operator at an extremely reasonable cost.

Finally, marketing research must include a survey of the operator's competition. It is especially important that this review be conducted and interpreted with objectivity; absent a realistic view of the marketplace, the operator cannot develop an effective segmentation strategy.

Market Segmentation

Market-segmentation strategies are based on the premise that all prospects are different, but not so different that they cannot be usefully classified into relatively homogeneous groups. Although it is possible to segment markets along psychographic dimensions (e.g., attitudes, opinions, preferences), it is more common to categorize prospects by such demographic variables as age, income, sex, education, ethnic background, marital status, and so forth. Segments of consumers residing or working in the overall trading area and described according to these variables can be isolated. Thus, instead of attempting to be all things to all people, the astute marketer can target his marketing efforts to distinct subsegments where consumer needs remain unfulfilled.

The operator can refine his definition of market segments by matching demographic variables to consumer preferences and behaviors. The matrix shown in Exhibit 2 suggests some of the numerous descriptions of patronage patterns that can be arrayed against demographic variables to help the operator develop a systematic description of market subsegments.

How it works. Based on research using mailed questionnaires (respondents' cooperation was enhanced by the use of a coupon offering them a free drink on their next visit) and personal interviews on the premises, an independent restaurateur found that 40 percent of his customers frequented his operation on pleasure occasions. In contrast to these patrons, who visited the restaurant primarily on weekends, more than 50 percent of the remaining traffic represented diners conducting business over lunch during the week. A review of the operation's accounting information revealed a well-known law at work: the smaller pleasure-oriented segment provided most of the restaurant's gross profits, while the larger business-lunch segment contributed only 20 percent of the gross profits.

Armed with this information, the restaurateur took action to increase the size of his more profitable segment—in this case, a drive-time radio cam-

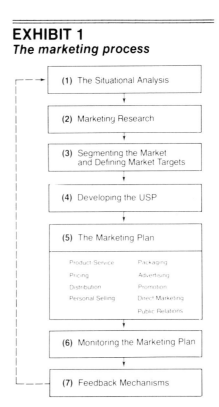

EXHIBIT 1
The marketing process

(1) The Situational Analysis

(2) Marketing Research

(3) Segmenting the Market and Defining Market Targets

(4) Developing the USP

(5) The Marketing Plan

Product/Service	Packaging
Pricing	Advertising
Distribution	Promotion
Personal Selling	Direct Marketing
	Public Relations

(6) Monitoring the Marketing Plan

(7) Feedback Mechanisms

paign emphasizing his operation's appeal as an elegant dinner house. Simultaneously, he restructured his luncheon menu to reduce the number of labor-intensive items, and—because he reasoned that his luncheon patrons were on expense accounts and therefore somewhat price-insensitive—raised his menu prices. As a result of this strategy, the restaurateur increased the contribution margin from his lunchtime segment and, more important, experienced 50-percent growth in his more profitable dinner market.

Segmentation Guidelines

There are three major criteria for choosing a potentially profitable market segment. First, the segment must be of sufficient size to warrant the expenditure required to exploit that segment. Second, the operation must have the physical capacity to service the demand the restaurateur expects to create for the outlet. Last, it must be economically feasible to reach the chosen segment using media currently available. If the costs to reach a specific segment are prohibitive, further analysis may uncover another segment that can be reached cost-efficiently.

The USP

Having identified his target markets, the operator can position his outlet to appeal to those patrons most likely to respond to the image he has chosen to project. Although advertising is a critical component of any positioning statement, it is not, as many practitioners seem to think, the sole means of communicating an operation's attributes to consumers. An operation's *unique selling proposition,* or USP, comprises all the elements—price, style of service, quality standards, cleanliness, and so forth—that differentiate the operation from its competitors.

"USP" is perhaps the most celebrated set of initials in the marketing and advertising business. The concept is also one of the most imitated and most misunderstood. A USP is *not* puffery, a blind advertising headline, a closing line that fails to sum up the benefits of the service, or a clever statement designed to attract attention without explaining the attributes of the service or the restaurant. Especially today, when the restaurant industry is awash with many comparable offerings, the astute food-service operator must distinguish what he has to sell from what all the others are selling. Therefore, each element of the marketing mix and each advertisement must answer this basic consumer question: "Why should I patronize this restaurant rather than others?"

The development of a unique and relevant positioning strategy demands a great deal of logical and creative thought. To prepare a preemptive and effective marketing plan, the operator must ask himself a single question each time he contemplates employing a specific tactic in his overall marketing strategy: "Is what I am about to do consistent with my positioning strategy?" Moreover, he must ensure that all elements of the plan are consistent and feasible. The road to ruin is amply populated with food-service companies whose managements attempted to establish a preemptive position but failed to execute all the components of their marketing plan. Many of these restaurateurs ignored the basic rule—deliver on the promises made. The food-service industry is unlike the manufacturing industries in that the delivery of the dining experience occurs at essentially the same time as the production of goods the consumer purchases. It is therefore critical that the operator scrutinize the operational aspects of his marketing plan to ensure that his outlets can consistently deliver the goods, service, and ambience commensurate with his positioning.

EXHIBIT 2
Market-segmentation matrix

Demographics	Food Product Types (e.g., chicken, burgers, pizza, Mexican food)	Group Composition (singles, couples, groups of people)	Eating Occasion (breakfast, lunch, dinner, special occasion)	Price Variations (average lunch or dinner check)	Convenience Variations (eat-in, take-out, drive-through)	Environment Variations (theme restaurant versus family restaurant)
Age						
Sex						
Marital status						
Income						
Occupation						
Education						
Ethnic background						
Address						
Number of children						

Harvey's: An Illustration

Although McDonald's maintains a huge lead in number of stores and total sales volume, Harvey's, a 110-unit Canadian chain that predated the American giant's arrival, continues to operate extremely profitably. Harvey's has positioned itself to appeal to the market segment seeking an alternative to standardized, prepackaged burgers. The firm's slogan, "Harvey's makes a hamburger a wonderful thing!," distinguishes the product from its mass-produced counterparts—as do the chain's operational procedures, which include charcoal broiling to order and allowing the customer to see his own burger garnished to his specifications. Finally, consistent with the firm's position as offering highly personalized service, the Harvey's unit is smaller than most other chain stores, and its lower cost yields a greater rate of return on the firm's assets.

In Conclusion

For the independent restaurateur, the proper development of a positioning strategy lays the groundwork for an effective marketing plan. Lacking an understanding of his competitive position and a rationale for dealing with it, however, the independent operator is likely to become an endangered species.

The Positioning Statement for Hotels

by Robert C. Lewis, Ph.D.

It is fairly simple to create an image for a hotel—but images may be good or bad, persuasive or not persuasive. Does your positioning statement include the three elements required for effective marketing?

Robert Lewis is Assistant Professor of Marketing and Management in the Department of Hotel, Restaurant, and Travel Administration at the University of Massachusetts, Amherst. He received his doctorate from the University of Massachusetts, where his areas of concentration were communication theory and marketing.

Although the concept of positioning has been widely accepted in a range of industries, by most appearances it has largely escaped the attention of hotel marketers. Whereas positioning relates to a property's *subjective* attributes (and how they differ from competitive properties' subjective attributes), hotel advertising has traditionally emphasized such objective product characteristics as number of rooms, prices, facilities, and amenities—characteristics in which competing facilities are generally quite similar.

The concept of positioning in a marketing strategy calls for the creation of an image—the consumer's perception of the subjective attributes of the property vis-à-vis those of the competition. This perception may be radically different from the property's physical characteristics. The distinction between the perception and the reality is especially important for hotel marketers.

The Purchase Decision for Services

A hotel's offerings comprise a bundle of goods and services ranging from tangible to intangible.[1] Because the lion's share of the hotel product—services—is at the intangible end of the continuum, it is often difficult to determine which attributes are most important in the consumer's purchase decision. Indeed, the intangibility of services makes the decision difficult for the consumer: he cannot taste, touch, feel, see, or try a service before making the decision; in fact, he "consumes" the service at the same time it is produced. Moreover, because every hotel property offers a heterogeneous range of services, the consumer's risk in the purchase decision is high. Finally, because service offerings are easily duplicated, the consumer cannot always draw clear distinctions among competitive offerings.[2] Thus, while a consumer can objectively measure, compare, and evaluate tangible products, and can actually consume them, he can measure and compare intangible services only subjectively; he finds it difficult to assign a monetary value to a service, and can consume it only passively. Services are critical to the consumer's perception of a hotel property, however, and generally have a long-term cognitive and affectual impact on that perception; the impact of tangible products is generally short-term.

This article was originally published in the May 1981 issue of *The Cornell Hotel and Restaurant Administration Quarterly*, pp. 51-61, and is reprinted here with the permission of the Cornell University School of Hotel Administration. ⓒ1981.

1. It can be useful to think of these goods and services as lying along a bipolar construct of tangible dominant and intangible dominant offerings. See: G. Lynn Shostack, "Breaking Free from Product Marketing," *Journal of Marketing,* 41 (April 1977), pp. 73-80.

2. For a more substantive treatment of these and other unique aspects of services, see: John M. Rathmell, *Marketing in the Service Sector* (Cambridge: Winthrop, 1974).

Hotel marketers who recognize the influence of intangible attributes on consumers' decision-making often react by advertising the abstract: the ineffable ("escape to the ultimate"); the euphoric ("surround yourself with luxury"); the euphuistic ("capture the spirit"); the ephemeral ("make any occasion special"); and the antithetical ("get away to it all"). The problem with such an approach is that the consumer will not buy a service, no matter what its intangible attributes are, until a certain minimum threshold of *tangible* attributes has been reached. In fact, a halo effect is possible: the existence of certain tangible characteristics is assumed to signify that a certain level of quality (an abstraction) also exists. Recognizing this, many goods-producing companies imbue their recognized tangible goods with abstract qualities in their advertising. For example, Charles Revson of Revlon Cosmetics reportedly said, "In the factory, we make cosmetics; in the store, we sell hope"—and this strategy is still apparent in Revlon advertising.

It is difficult to employ a similar strategy in hotel advertising because hotel products have a high degree of sameness and hotel services *are* abstract. To emphasize the concrete in advertising is to fail to differentiate oneself from one's competitors, while to compound the abstraction is to dilute the reality one wishes to represent. Thus, hotel marketers should focus on enhancing and differentiating a property's abstract realities through the manipulation of tangible clues: "The degree to which the marketer will focus on either tangible evidence or intangible abstractions for (positioning an entity to its target market) will be found to be 'inversely related to the entity dominance.'" [3] Compare, for example, the intangibility of Merrill Lynch services to the tangibility of its bull strolling through a china shop.

The Most Common Failing

Hotel marketers who have adopted positioning strategies sometimes fail to incorporate one basic marketing concept into otherwise good positions: they forget that any positioning statement must be directed to the needs and wants of the consumer. Many who have written about marketing strategies also make this mistake. Stating that positioning is the first of three steps in cultivating an image for a restaurant operation, Sill suggested establishing "an explicit statement of the type of restaurant (management) *wishes to present to patrons*" [4] (emphasis added). In the same vein, Tissian stated that after a hotel's management has "identified the property's competitive strengths and weaknesses, the results of this analysis are articulated in the form of a positioning statement. The positioning strategy reflects a conscious decision . . . to communicate to the market a definition of the property as a particular type of hotel . . . this definition must be consistent with the property it describes." [5] The *next* step, according to Tissian, is to select the target audiences. The concepts set forth by Sill and Tissian are essential to effective positioning and may lead one to develop a fine positioning statement. However, they may just as easily lead one to formulate a position corresponding to the image that management wishes to project or believes it projects, rather than one that differentiates the property from the competition in a manner reflecting the needs and wants of the target market.

The Three Elements

True positioning entails three elements. First— and least important—*it creates an image*. Why is this least important? Because images may be good or bad, persuasive or not persuasive, inspiring or uninspiring. It is relatively simple to create an image of some kind (although many hotel ads fail to do so), and images alone do not incline the consumer to buy.

The element that does influence buying behavior is the most important of the three: the perceived *benefits* of the product or service. Positioning a product or service along *benefit dimensions* in an attempt to reflect consumers' attitudes forms the basis of an effective strategy. Once the benefit dimensions have been defined, the marketer can isolate those target markets consisting of consumers who hold similar attitudes about a bundle of benefits as they relate to a particular hotel or hotel class.

The third essential element of the positioning statement is that *it differentiates the brand* from the product class—in other words, it distinguishes the hotel from other hotels, whether they are truly different or (as is quite likely) offer essentially the same products and services. To combine these elements, the positioning statement should be designed to create an image reflecting the perception

3. Shostack, p. 78.

4. Brian T. Sill, "Restaurant Merchandising for the Independent Operator," *The Cornell Hotel and Restaurant Administration Quarterly*, 21, No. 1 (May 1980), p. 28.

5. "Advertising that Sells Hotels," *The Cornell Hotel and Restaurant Administration Quarterly*, 20, No. 4 (November 1979), p. 19.

of the property that management wishes its target market to hold and reflecting promises on which the property can deliver and make good. The desired perception must be based on consumer benefits—first, on needs and wants, and second, on differences between the property and its competition. Consumers don't buy products or services; they buy expectations. Statements that both promise the consumer something and give him a reason to believe in the promise are most persuasive because they let the consumer know what he can expect and why he should stay at a particular hotel.

The three bases of persuasion set forth by Aristotle—ethos (credibility), pathos (emotional appeal), and logos (logic and reasoning)—are still the best tools we have; but first, said the philosopher, you must know your audience. The positioning statement cannot be developed until the strategy has been established, and the strategy must be based on the target market.

The Differentiation Element

One differentiates a property through the positioning statement by demonstrating the property's unique attributes to the consumer. The positioning decision is the most important factor in developing successful advertising, but "most brochures (and the properties they describe) look alike;"[6] few advertisements and brochures reflect any attempt at differentiation or positioning. When products or services are similar, the benefits unique to a property must provide the positioning differentiation.

Yesawich stressed this point in noting that lodging properties must become competitor-oriented to be successful in the '80s; knowing what one's guest wants is of little value if five of one's competitors are already serving his needs.[7] Identifying a property's unique attributes or benefits means not only knowing its strong points but also locating the weak points in the positions of competitors. Ideally, of course, the hotel marketer could discover an unoccupied position in which his offering could generate new business or lure customers away from competitors.

The task of the hotel marketer is to develop the desired consumer perception of the property's

Unique benefits differentiate

benefits as opposed to those of the competition—keeping in mind that the consumer seeks *tangible* clues to distinguish among the benefits of intangible services offered by competing properties. Research and self-examination should indicate how one property can be set apart from others, what its unique advantages are, and what positions remain to be filled.

A few hotels have developed positioning statements that differentiate them from the competition and that offer unique benefits. Some examples:

- **"A beautifully orchestrated idea in hotels"** (positioning a property in which every room is a suite)

- **"Soars 46 stories over Central Park"** (for a property featuring panoramic views not usually found in New York City)

- **"We think that vacation costs are outrageous"** (for a unique, inexpensive vacation experience)

- **"There *is* an alternative to high-priced hotels"** (directed toward the value-conscious business traveler; all the standard hotel amenities are mentioned, so the traveler can be sure that the low price does not signify low quality).

More often, however, hotel positioning statements fail to differentiate and to offer unique benefits. Consider the following:

- **"The flair and style of a Hyatt. The efficiency and courtesy of a Marriott:"** These

6. Jane Maas, "Better Brochures for the Money," *The Cornell Hotel and Restaurant Administration Quarterly,* 20, No. 4 (February 1980), p. 22.

7. Peter Yesawich, "Marketing in the 1980s," *The Cornell Hotel and Restaurant Administration Quarterly,* 20, No. 4 (February 1980), p. 38.

Low price doesn't mean low quality

phrases explicitly position the competition, but fail to define the position of the property they pertain to.

• **"The golden opportunity for the 80s:"** This approach is used by a chain that competes head-on with other "golden-opportunity" chains.

• **"We have room:"** This phrase simply announces an expansion that makes this hotel the largest in the state.

• **"We're the difference:"** This statement is weak because it is not accompanied by supporting evidence; the hotel looks like hundreds of others.

The Benefit Element

The benefits themselves are the real reason the consumer comes to a hotel. They *are* the image and they *are* the elements that differentiate a hotel from its competition. Benefits come in bundles, and it is the entire group of benefits offered that positions a hotel in relation to its particular target market. Benefits vary in the extent to which they are assigned importance by consumers, and their relative importance varies with different service

levels.[8] Positioning the benefits means marketing the correct expectation—because, in the final analysis, it is the expectation that hotels have to sell to the selected target market.

The first problem is to determine the key characteristic of the various benefit segments (groups of consumers who attach similar importance to a bundle of benefits). Such procedures as conjoint analysis, multi-dimensional scaling, and discriminant analysis can be applied for this purpose,[9] but it is also possible to adapt some older, simpler concepts with a consumer-behavior application to services and hotels. Let us begin by considering the utility model developed by Lovelock to explain purchase behavior as it relates to services. Lovelock suggested that a consumer evaluates a service on the basis of its *form* utility, *place* utility, *time* utility, *psychic* utility, and *monetary* utility.[10] This model allows the marketer to classify benefits from a consumer's viewpoint, identifying the positive utilities to be emphasized and the negative utilities to be minimized. By applying the tools of the behavioral sciences to create an image and using tangible clues to support that image, the marketer can translate the utilities (which are intangible) into realities that define the property to various target markets.

Lovelock's model is useful in understanding how consumers evaluate services, and can be made even more useful if combined with the following modified marketing mix for hospitality operations, proposed by Renaghan:

(1) *The Product-Service Mix:* The combination of products and services, whether free or for sale, employed to satisfy the needs of the target market.

(2) *The Presentation Mix:* All components directed by the firm and used to increase the tangibility of the product-service mix in the perception of the target market at the right place and the right time.

8. Robert C. Lewis, "Benefit Segmentation for Restaurant Advertising that Works," *The Cornell Hotel and Restaurant Administration Quarterly*, 21, No. 3 (November 1980), pp. 6-12.

9. For application of these techniques in segmentation and positioning, see: Paul Green, Yoram Wind, and Arun Jain, "Benefit Bundle Analysis," *Journal of Advertising Research*, 12 (April 1972), pp. 31-36 (conjoint measurement); Yoram Wind and Patrick J. Robinson, "Product Positioning: An Application of Multi-Dimensional Scaling," in *Attitude Research in Transition*, ed. Russell I. Haley (Chicago: American Marketing Association, 1972); Lewis, op. cit., pp. 6-12 (discriminant analysis); and Yoram Wind, "A New Procedure for Concept Evaluation," *Journal of Marketing*, 37 (October 1973), pp. 2-11.

10. Christopher H. Lovelock, "Theoretical Contribution from Service and Nonbusiness Marketing," in *Conceptual and Theoretical Developments in Marketing, Proceedings Series*, ed. O.C. Ferrell et al. (Chicago: American Marketing Association, 1979), pp. 147-165.

EXHIBIT 1
Hotel benefit matrix

Utility	(1) Product-Service	(2) Presentation	(3) Communications
FORM	Food, room, pool, beach, lounge, room service, bed; performance	Physical plant (interior and exterior), employees, tangible presentations	Product-service; tangible attachments, tangible aspects of use and performance
PLACE	Convenience, ease of use, ease of buying, facilities, reservations	Location; nearby attractions such as business, shopping, arts; availability	Where available, where can be used, use- and performance-related aspects
TIME	Convenient times; when needed, wanted, or desired	Pleasant use of time, time-saving, service level, seasonal aspects	When available, when can be used, use- and performance-related aspects
PSYCHIC	Good feeling, social approval, prestige, reassurance, personal service, satisfaction, rest and relaxation	"Atmospherics": light, sound, space, smell; accoutrements	Tangible attachments to intangibles, dissonance reduction, nature of guests, prestige address, satisfied guests
MONETARY	Cost, fair value, save money, how much	Price-value relation, easy payment, psychological effect, quality	Value perception, quality connotation, risk reduction

Based on Lovelock's utility model for services and Renaghan's marketing mix for hospitality operations

(3) **The Communications Mix:** All communications between the firm and the target market that increase the tangibility of the product-service mix, that influence consumer expectations, or that persuade consumers to purchase. [11]

Lovelock's utility model and Renaghan's hospitality mix can be combined in a benefit matrix that helps the marketer understand the key characteristics of various benefit segments. The hotel marketer can complete the matrix simply by noting the property's benefits, management's capabilities, and the market's perception of the property and its offerings. (Exhibit 1 shows abstracts of some listings such a matrix might contain.) If a similar matrix is prepared to describe the competition's offerings,

the marketer can perform an aggregated (non-segmented) positioning analysis. Even without a sophisticated knowledge of his target markets, the marketer is prepared from his own perceptions to develop that positioning statement, including the identification of the desired image, competitive differentiation, and consumer benefits. If target markets are identified, the marketer can also apply such techniques as conjoint analysis and discriminant analysis to evaluate the properties by benefit segment and determine the primary characteristics of the benefit segments. The benefit matrix can be used to identify the tangible clues that make the intangible benefits credible to the desired target markets.

The Positioning Statement

Communications used in the marketing effort should be both consistent and customized to fit the

11. Leo N. Renaghan, "A New Marketing Mix for the Hospitality Industry," paper presented at the National Conference of the Council of Hotel, Restaurant, and Institutional Education, August 13-16, 1980, Dearborn, MI.

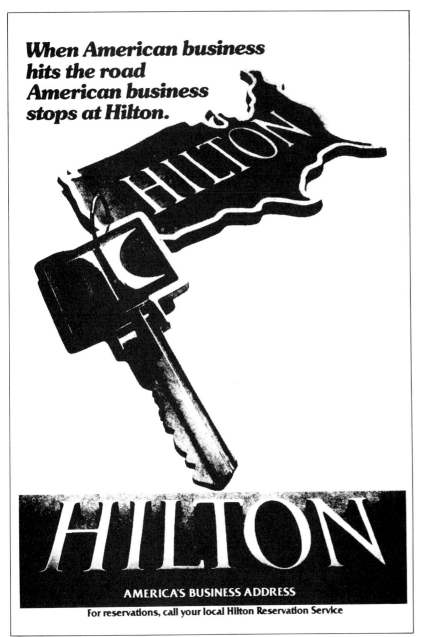

**When American business
hits the road
American business
stops at Hilton.**

HILTON

AMERICA'S BUSINESS ADDRESS

For reservations, call your local Hilton Reservation Service

The market is identified — but not the benefits

needs of individual target markets. Rather than attempt to crowd all information about every service into one campaign, the marketer should promote each service to its own target market, featuring the positioning statement in some form in every component of the campaign. This approach allows the hotel to implant its main services in the mind of the consumer, while giving each service its own image to, say, the businessman, the meeting planner, the travel agent, and the pleasure traveler.

The positioning statement is a unifying element: all subpositionings are promoted under one um-

brella. Applied with this flexibility and consistency, the positioning statement creates an *image* that personalizes the operation; the customer who is buying an abstract service is reassured. It *differentiates* from the competition; the customer knows why he is choosing one hotel over another. It promises *benefits;* the customer is promised that his needs and wants will be fulfilled. Finally, positioning supports these elements with clues of tangible offerings that the consumer can observe with his five senses, indicating to him there is substance behind the promises.

Attention-getting but tenuous

The advertisements that accompany this article all incorporate positioning statements—some good, some less good. The positioning statement in the advertisement that appears above is very specific: "America's Business Address." This statement clearly identifies the target market as business travelers, but it fails to provide an image, to indicate benefits, and to differentiate the properties advertised from the competition; there are no tangible clues to support the intangible contention.

The statement "Capture the Spirit Worldwide" (above) creates an image that is tenuous, nebulous, and intangible. It contains no reference to tangible benefits that differentiate these hotels from competing properties, relying instead on abstractions. According to Hyatt, the target market comprises pres-ent users who already *have* the "spirit," but this positioning is not clear in the advertisement, and the advertisement's approach ignores a vast potential market. In short, although the ad is one of an attractive series in an attention-getting campaign, it lacks a positioning statement that would commit it to the consumer's long-term memory.

In contrast, Marriott's advertisement incorporates all of the important elements of positioning: it is clearly directed to the businessman, creates an image, differentiates the benefits by place and time, provides tangible clues in its presentation and communication (see columns 2 and 3 in the benefit matrix), and supports these elements graphically so that the consumer can *believe* "The right hotel is never hard to find."

The 45-story Chicago Marriott stands just about where it <u>ought</u> to be—right in the middle of things.

The right hotel is never hard to find

The Marriott Hotel people have built their reputation on doing things <u>right</u>.

And one of the things they do most consistently right is to be, somehow, in just the right <u>location</u> for the business you want to conduct, in any given city.

In New York, for instance, Marriott's Essex House is right on Central Park. In Chicago? Right on Michigan Avenue (photo)—and also at O'Hare International Airport. In Kansas City, Cleveland, Miami, L.A. and Rochester, also conveniently right near the airport. In Philadelphia? Right at the edge of the Main Line.

Some cities already have <u>several</u> Marriotts.

Atlanta, four. Houston, three. <u>Five</u> in Washington, D.C. And new Marriotts are blooming worldwide. Marriott can now do it right for you in Saudi Arabia, Kuwait, Holland. Even right on the beach in <u>resorts</u> like Acapulco, Barbados, Santa Barbara, and Marco Island.

To reserve at a Marriott where you're headed, call a professional, your travel agent. Or dial toll-free 800-228-9290.

**WHEN MARRIOTT DOES IT,
THEY DO IT RIGHT.** **Marriott Hotels.**

Named after . . .

the great Armagnac District of France --

home of Armagnac, the world's finest brandy,

truffles, foie gras, roquefort cheese and

D'Artagnan, Captain of the Three Musketeers.

An extremely clear image

The Stanford Court's advertisement is another outstanding example of positioning. The image is extremely clear; the differentiation and the utilities (form, place, time, and psychic) are presented clearly and communicated with strong, tangible benefit clues; all elements are integrated; and the target market is identified in a single positioning statement: "For people who understand the subtle differences."

Smaller, lesser-known properties can be positioned just as well as large hotels and chain properties. The L'Armagnac ad at left identifies a target market, creates an image, and differentiates the property it advertises in terms of the benefit matrix. Note particularly the positioning statement "An uncommon inn," and the tangible clues that support it.

In the two La Quinta ads, we see one effective approach and one approach that falls short. Both ads appeared in *The Wall Street Journal.* The ad at right identifies the target market and differentiates the property; the other positions La Quinta only as one of many golf resorts, failing to share a differential advantage.

Conclusion

Any hotel marketer can devise a positioning statement, and, as the concept of positioning has gained currency in the industry, many marketers have done just that. However, most hotel positioning still fails to incorporate the elements crucial to effective marketing: communicating a unique benefit image, supported by tangible clues, to a defined target market. The marketer whose positioning statement encompasses all these elements will have a marked competitive advantage in the years ahead.

Golf in the Grand Manner
of La Quinta

A thoroughly championship course
designed by Pete Dye offers
the finest holes in golf.

La Quinta
HOTEL
GOLF & TENNIS RESORT

La Quinta, California
19 miles from Palm Springs
Call Toll Free: In California 800-472-4316
Outside California 800-854-1271

Dwight H. Hart, Jr., Director
Bob Silva, General Manager

Below right, differentiation; above left, no competitive advantage

Executive Conferences
accomplish more in our
pleasant seclusion

A new
Pete Dye Championship
Golf Course
is now in play

La Quinta
HOTEL
GOLF & TENNIS RESORT

La Quinta, California
19 Miles from Palm Springs
Call Toll Free: In California 800-472-4316
Outside California 800-854-1271

Dwight H. Hart, Jr., Director
Bob Silva, General Manager

Marketing for the Eighties
Creating the Right Identity for Your Hotel

Beginning a series edited by William Q. Dowling

AH&MA's first Advanced Advertising Workshop, sponsored with the Hotel Sales Management Association, was held in New York City, at the Sheraton Centre Hotel, in mid-1980. Major papers were presented on four topics:

1—How to Research the Market and Position the Hotel.

2—How to Develop a Marketing Strategy for a Hotel.

3—How to Evaluate and Select Advertising Media.

4—How to Plan an Advertising/Marketing Program and Prepare a Budget.

This intensive effort inspired development by LODGING and by Bill Dowling of 12 articles—eight of them hotel case studies—for a series in Lodging titled, "Marketing in the 80's," with Dowling as editor. This initial installment covers papers by: Martin Stern, executive vice president, Wells, Rich, Greene, on research and positioning, and Jay Schulberg, senior vice president and creative director, Ogilvy & Mather, on developing a creative strategy for advertising.

Introductory articles setting forth concepts on market research, positioning, strategy development, media selection, planning and budgeting, will be followed by eight hotel case studies. Each will tell how a hotel aiming at specified markets (business travelers, pleasure travelers, convention travelers, etc.) dealt with: (1) Positioning, (2) Strategy, (3) Media, (4) Planning, and (5) Budgeting.

Upon or before completion of this series, the reader may not agree with the leading advertising and hotel marketing experts of the country, but he will certainly know how they sell.

Every case study will follow the same path—positioning, developing strategy, and evaluating media, planning and budgeting.

The key to developing good advertising, according to Martin Stern, executive vice president of Wells, Rich, Greene, is to identify or "position" your hotel's benefits vs. other hotels. When you hear advertising executives discussing "positioning" of a property, they are talking about encouraging the proper consumer *perception* of one hotel's benefits vs. the competition.

There are a number of characteristics that make one hotel different from another. For example, is the property located downtown, near an airport, or in a suburban location? Does it depend primarily on commercial travelers, vacation travelers, groups, or a balanced mix of all three? Does this vary from weekday to weekend? Does it vary by season? How do the hotel's restaurants and lounges compare to the competition? How does its meeting space, if any, compare to that of other nearby hotels?

What size is the property? Is it a chain hotel or independent? Is it expensive, moderate or inexpensive? Are the facilities new or old?

Now that you know the *facts* about your hotel, it is necessary to consider a far more significant question: How do consumers *perceive* your hotel—regardless of facts?

The Key to Positioning is Research

Good positioning comes from good research. This is why most top advertising agencies insist that their clients allow them to conduct thorough research on their product before advertising strategies are developed. Martin Stern believes so strongly in the need for research that he often recommends clients reduce their advertising budgets in order to free up dollars for research.

A typical research study for a hotel should be divided into two parts: 1) a Market Study, and 2) an Attitude and Awareness Study. It is important for you to know the basic components of these two

From *Lodging* (September 1980) pp. 56-58. Reprinted by permission of *Lodging*.

types of studies. Your advertising agency can help you design the research or can recommend a qualified research firm, but you can evaluate their recommendations better if you understand the research.

A Market Study should contain statistics on the size and volume of the hotel industry in your local market, occupancy comparisons between your property and competition, seasonal and geographic factors which are unique to your area, mix of business (commercial vs. leisure, individual vs. group), sources of business (travel agents, tour operators, corporate travel departments, or direct bookings), form of transportation (percentage of arrivals by airline vs. train, bus or car) and any trends in these areas.

In many cities, this data is available from the local hotel association, Chamber of Commerce, Convention and Visitors Bureau or state tourism department. If it is not available, there are a few ways to obtain the market facts you need. First, see if the local hotel association will sponsor a market study in which all hotels submit their own guest statistics, on a confidential basis, to be used in tabulating market totals. Often, if a hotel manager is promised that his hotel will not be identified specifically, he will participate in such a study.

Another method, but a more costly one, is a tracking study. This requires hiring people to stand in airports, train stations, hotel lobbies, and other high traffic areas where they can get visitors to answer questions or fill in a questionnaire. This can become expensive and requires prior approval of airport managers, hotel managers and others, depending on where the research is conducted. A variation on this is to obtain names and addresses of visitors from many of these same sources and mail questionnaires.

A second part of the Market Study is to obtain as much information as possible from your own guests, using the same checklist used for the market in general. Many of these statistics can be obtained from your guest history files, daily occupancy reports and folios. A review of addresses (or zip codes) from the folios or registration cards will give you a *geographic* profile of your guests' origins, by month or season.

To determine a *demographic* (age, income, education, occupation) profile of your guests, by season, it will be necessary to use an in-room questionnaire or mail a questionnaire to guests after check out. You will have to offer them some incentive to fill in the form, such as a complimentary cocktail. You should be aware that the information you receive may be biased, because certain types of people never fill in forms and certain types do.

The other part of your research program, the Attitude and Awareness Study, will most likely give you the most valuable information. This is a basic study to determine the behavior, attitude toward and awareness of your property and competitive properties among 1) your guests and 2) guests of other hotels.

This kind of research is also most important in developing a precise definition of your prime target group of customers. It will make your future advertising more effective and tell you a host of things you can do to improve your positioning. And if the research is done well, it can last you for a number of years and you will be able to refer to it again and again.

There are three main questions an Attitude and Awareness Study should answer for you. They are:

1. How does my customer perceive my hotel vs. competition? (Is it thought of as expensive or moderate, full-service or not, better or worse than competition?)

2. What do customers of other hotels in my area think of my hotel and how aware are they of what we have to offer?

3. What are my customers' attitudes towards service, food quality, hotel facilities and amenities, and pricing?

When you sit with your ad agency or a research firm, you should give them as much information as you already know. Tell them who you think your customers are; who you would like your customers to be; what you think you offer vs. competition; and what you know about market statistics and trends. The more background you can provide, the easier it will be for the research company to design a study that pinpoints the questions you want answered. The easier it is for the researchers, the less costly it will be for you.

Pinehurst Resort in North Carolina conducted such a study in 1973 to see how the resort was perceived vs. The Greenbrier, The Homestead, Sea Pines Plantation and other competitors. They told the research company that their customers were mostly male golfers without their wives, the business was highly seasonal, and usage of resort amenities other than golf was minimal.

Research revealed that while the other resorts were perceived as all-around family resorts, Pinehurst was perceived as a "golf-only" resort, even though it had 16 tennis courts, a beautiful equestrian center and millions of dollars worth of other amenities.

What's "right" about this ad?

Answer: The ad is an example of good positioning by an advertising agency (Cavaliera Kleier Pearlman, Inc.) in terms of encouraging the proper consumer perception of one hotel's benefits vs. the competition.

Prepared by Cavaliera, Kleier, Pearlman, Inc.

The ad agency changed strategy based on the findings. They began advertising tennis packages instead of golf, and started promoting their tennis clinics. They changed the front of the rack brochure from a golf course shot to one of a couple horseback riding. And they began promoting family packages where the husband could play golf and the wife could play tennis or ride. In two years, Pinehurst's mix of business improved, seasonal skews leveled out, occupancy built to much higher levels and overall revenue per guest increased.

Complete a Situation Analysis

After you have conducted a Market Study and Attitude and Awareness research, and have determined the consumer and market profiles and perceptions, you must take one more step in order to complete a situation anlaysis. You and other members of your hotel's management team must analyze the hotel's services and benefits, corporate short and long range goals, and financial considerations. This leads to a definition of the problems, options and opportunities. Until this is completed, an advertising strategy cannot be completed.

Be careful not to get bogged down in too much detail. Look for main points. It is not important to rate the quality of your coffee, but it is important to rate the overall quality of each restaurant or lounge.

Martin Stern points out that Wells, Rich, Greene has developed its own system of strategic planning (see box) that they use as a checklist for any product or service they are advertising.

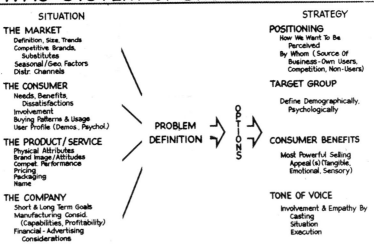

WRG SYSTEM OF STRATEGIC PLANNING

SITUATION	STRATEGY
THE MARKET Definition, Size, Trends Competitive Brands, Substitutes Seasonal/Geo. Factors Distr. Channels	**POSITIONING** How We Want To Be Perceived By Whom (Source Of Business-Own Users, Competition, Non-Users)
THE CONSUMER Needs, Benefits, Dissatisfactions Involvement Buying Patterns & Usage User Profile (Demos., Psychol.)	**TARGET GROUP** Define Demographically, Psychologically
THE PRODUCT/SERVICE Physical Attributes Brand Image/Attitudes Compet. Performance Pricing Packaging Name	**CONSUMER BENEFITS** Most Powerful Selling Appeal(s)(Tangible, Emotional, Sensory)
THE COMPANY Short & Long Term Goals Manufacturing Consid. (Capabilities, Profitability) Financial-Advertising Considerations	**TONE OF VOICE** Involvement & Empathy By Casting Situation Execution

PROBLEM DEFINITION → OPTIONS →

Wells Rich Greene's System of Strategic Planning is comparable to these procedures suggested in this article: (1) research the market; (2) determine customer awareness and attitudes; (3) get the management team to evaluate the hotel's products and services, and (4) state company goals and financial limitations—then proceed to strategy.

And Now Positioning— Keep Your Focus Simple

Once all of the complexities of the market place have been defined and analyzed, it is vital to the development of an advertising program that these facts be distilled to the one or two essential benefits that are most important to your potential customer. Typical hotel advertising has for years listed such detailed benefits as number of rooms, number of pools, number of tennis courts, number of restaurants and so on. These diverse statistics are the enemies of good positioning. "Kitchen sink" positionings don't work.

A review of any current magazine will expose examples of positioning that offers no unique benefit. Some recent examples are:
 "Elegance and Charm . . . "
 "The one hotel that stands above all others . . . "
 "The only number to call . . . "
Positioning normally requires a singleminded approach because the consumer does not easily assimilate complex messages. Advertising should have a simple focus. One chain promotes their unique room configurations as their one principal advantage over competition, with the headline: "Every room is a suite."

This does not mean that various substrategies do not need to be promoted, but if so, they should be done under *one umbrella positioning.*

Hints You Can Use in Any Situation

Whether you are positioning a hotel, motel, restaurant or lounge, there are eight questions Martin Stern suggests that you ask yourself about your product in determining your position:

1. Who are we? What do we stand for?
2. How are we different? How can we set ourselves apart?
3. What area can we pre-empt? Do we have an advantage we can capitalize on?
4. Do we need to overcome a liability and turn it into an asset?
5. Which target market segment is most important?
6. How can we expand or change usage patterns?
7. Do we use a tangible or intangible advantage?
8. What is the one thing the travelers look for most that we offer?

Positioning, according to Stern, is what makes potential customers choose your hotel rather than the competitive hotel. Properly targeted, single minded positioning affects everything a hotel does or stands for—not only advertising but also all of its promotions, brochures, facilities—even its decor. And once you have developed effective positioning, you should be willing to stay with it for a long period of time.

Marketing Services by Managing the Environment

by Bernard H. Booms and Mary J. Bitner

How hospitality managers can combine current service-marketing strategies with environmental-psychology theories to satisfy their customers

Bernard H. Booms, a faculty member at Washington State University's Seattle Center for Hotel and Restaurant Administration, received his Ph.D. in economics from the University of Pittsburgh. He has taught at Pennsylvania State University, and has served as a visiting fellow at Harvard Business School. Mary J. Bitner is currently a consultant for firms involved in marketing and tourism. She received an M.B.A. in marketing from the University of Washington, and has served as a research associate with Washington State University's Seattle Center for Hotel and Restaurant Administration.

At Morgan Guaranty and Trust, the desks are of mahogany, the chairs of leather, and the draperies of silk. At Skipper's, a chain of west-coast restaurants, dining areas are furnished with comfortable chairs and divided into small, intimate units by partitions. And at the Library of Congress, the long-closed great bronze front doors have been opened to the public.

These seemingly unrelated organizations have in common the following: their directors all recognize the power of the environment to influence customer perceptions. Elements of a firm's environment can be used to establish or reinforce an image, reposition the firm in customers' perceptions, or influence customer satisfaction or dissatisfaction

with the service they receive.[1] At Morgan Guaranty, for example, expensive furnishings project an image of stability, and give clients a sense of importance;[2] at the Library of Congress, open doors symbolize an open, approachable institution;[3] and at Skipper's, the recently modified decor suggests a relaxed dinner atmosphere rather than a fast-food environment (the firm's previous image).[4]

This article draws on the separate theories of services marketing and environmental psychology to suggest ways in which the physical environment may be used as a marketing tool. Examples of how such service marketers as restaurateurs and hoteliers are currently using the physical environment in their marketing strategies are presented to illustrate how these theories may be put into practice. The implications of the authors' observations—summarized in the final section—should be of interest to service-firm managers in general and restaurateurs and hoteliers in particular.

This article was originally published in the May 1982 issue of *The Cornell Hotel and Restaurant Administration Quarterly,* pp. 35-39, and is reprinted here with the permission of the Cornell University School of Hotel Administration. ©1982.

1. See: Theodore Levitt, "Marketing Intangible Products and Product Intangibles," *Harvard Business Review,* 58, No. 3 (May-June 1981), pp. 94-102; Carolyn U. Lambert, "Environmental Design: The Food-Service Manager's Role," *The Cornell Hotel and Restaurant Administration Quarterly,* 22, No. 1 (May 1981), pp. 62-68; Leo M. Renaghan, "A New Marketing Mix," *The Cornell Hotel and Restaurant Administration Quarterly,"* 22, No. 2 (August 1981), pp. 30-35.

2. Julie Salaman and Tim Metz, "Morgan Guaranty Acts to Improve the Image of its Investment Unit," *The Wall Street Journal,* September 19, 1980, p. 1.

3. Richard L. Williams, "The Library of Congress Can't Hold All Man's Knowledge—But It Tries," *Smithsonian,* April 1980, pp. 38-48.

4. Robin Ashton, "Skipper's Pipes a New Tune," *Institutions,* 86 No. 7 (April 1, 1980), pp. 47-49.

Using Tangible Clues to Sell Services

Morgan Guaranty, Skipper's, and the Library of Congress are all service firms.[5] The physical environment can be particularly effective as a marketing tool for these firms because the "products" they offer have many intangible characteristics, and are produced and consumed simultaneously.[6] Because customers must form their expectations about services through means other than actual physical contact with the product they are paying for, their perceptions are influenced by marketing messages (e.g., advertising, publicity, sales promotions) and by tangible clues (e.g., architecture, lighting, temperature, furnishings, layout, and color).[7] These elements communicate information to the customer about how the firm sees itself and about how it wishes its customers to behave. In service marketing, first impressions really count.

For goods manufacturers and distributors, the environment in which the product is produced has little impact on customers; they are often unaware of where the product comes from and how it is produced. Services differ from products, however, in that the customer is present when a service is produced and consumed, and the potential impact of the total surroundings can sharply influence the customer's behavior. As a result of this difference, service marketers must modify conventional marketing-mix theories to suit their own needs.[8] (In Exhibit 1, the authors propose modifications and additions that might be made to a traditional goods-oriented marketing-mix theory.)

Using the Environment to Reinforce or Establish an Image

A service firm that attempts to establish a new image can use the environment to do so. For example, at Speedi-Lube, an oil change and lubri-

---

EXHIBIT 1

Modifying the marketing mix for service firms

Services marketing and goods marketing share a concern with "product, price, place, and promotion"—Jerome McCarthy's four Ps. Each of these marketing-mix elements must be modified, however, to be fully useful to the service marketer. Additionally, they might be expanded to include the following three new Ps:

Participants: All persons (e.g., customers, employees) who play a part in service delivery and thus influence the buyer's perceptions.

Physical Evidence: The environment in which the service is assembled and in which seller and customer interact, combined with tangible commodities that facilitate performance or communication of the service.

Process of Service Assembly: The actual procedures, mechanisms, and flow of activities through which the service is delivered.

These new elements can be used by the firm to influence buyers' responses and, therefore, rightfully belong in the marketing mix.

Source: Bernard H. Booms and Mary J. Bitner, "Marketing Strategies and Organization Structures for Service Firms," in *Marketing of Services*, James H. Donnelly and William R. George, eds. (American Marketing Association Proceedings Series, 1981), pp. 47–51.

---

cating service recently introduced in the Seattle area, the environment enables the firm to project an image of speed, efficiency, and competence. Attendants are dressed in clean, starched uniforms, and the interior of each revamped Speedi-Lube service station is freshly painted and uncluttered—in contrast to most service stations. Customers are asked to drive their cars over open pits where each car is immediately attended to by several workers. While cars are serviced, customers are served fresh coffee in a clean waiting room whose walls are decorated with a graphic display illustrating the lubrication process. Work is completed within ten minutes, and each customer receives a friendly reminder three months later that "it's time for another oil change." Here, the environment is

---

5. For the purposes of this discussion, the term *service firm* is defined very broadly to include all firms that primarily perform *tasks* for their customers, rather than deliver or produce physical goods. This definition includes such service firms as banks, insurance companies, and educational institutions, as well as restaurants, hotels, and some retailers.

6. Renaghan, op. cit.

7. Bernard H. Booms and Mary J. Bitner, "A Services Marketing Framework," (working paper, Washington State University, School of Business and Economics, 1980).

8. Bernard H. Booms and Mary J. Bitner, "Marketing Strategies and Organization Structures for Service Firms," in *Marketing of Services*, James H. Donnelly and William R. George, eds. (American Marketing Association Proceedings Series, 1981), pp. 47-51; G. Lynn Shostack, "Breaking Free from Product Marketing," *Journal of Marketing*, 41 (April 1977), pp. 73-80.

USING THE PHYSICAL ENVIRONMENT AS A MARKETING TOOL
Implications for strategy and research

The environment is a critical marketing tool for service managers. *Implications:*

- Include environmental design and analysis in marketing mix for services; research the impact of the environment on customer attitudes, feelings, and behaviors.

The customer perceives the environment as a whole, and all environmental elements are integrated in this whole. *Implications:*

- Make all elements of the environment consistent with the service firm's image.

- Recognize the impact of small environmental changes on customer perceptions.

To be effective, the service-firm environment must elicit approach behavior from potential customers. *Implications:*

- Use the environment to reinforce feelings of pleasure in target markets.

- Use the environment to reduce potential negative responses.

To be effective, the service firm must recognize the emotional needs of its customers. *Implications:*

- Segment the market by emotional needs of clientele for high-load or low-load environments.

- Design the environment to stimulate approach behavior.

The environment influences customer expectations and satisfaction or dissatisfaction with a given service and therefore influences purchase and repurchase behavior.

This intuitive assumption could be tested in the following manner:

- Studying how customer expectations about services are formed and the role the physical environment plays in this process.

- Pinpointing which areas of service performance consumers have expectations about.

- Researching the standards customers employ to judge service quality and performance.

---

used to establish an image of efficiency and confidence, and the reminder card reinforces this image.

Using the Environment to Reposition a Service

Marriott Hotels is using the environment as part of a plan to attract a more upscale business traveler, introducing potential customers to two concepts dependent on new environments—the Marquis Club and the Concierge Level. Guests who have stayed five times at the Marriott hotel are eligible for Marquis Club membership; amenities include large, comfortable guest rooms and express check-out. Concierge Level guests have access to a private lounge area equipped with a color TV, current periodicals, and an "honor" bar. Guests who wish to use Concierge Level facilities merely pay a higher fee than do patrons occupying standard rooms.

Environmental modifications were an important element of the overall repositioning plan when Skipper's Seafood and Chowder Houses changed from a series of fast-food outlets to a group of casual, family-oriented seafood restaurants. Prior to the change, the environment at Skipper's—colors, signage, and dining-room decor—communicated fast food to the customer. When the shift to a dinner-house image was made, interior partitions, softer seating, natural wood textures, decorative photographs, and plants were introduced, and

signage was changed from stark (red, white, and blue) to subtle (yellow and brown).

In another successful example of repositioning, the Library of Congress recently opened up its massive bronze doors, set up picnic tables in its courtyard, and installed easy-to-use reader's guides and computer terminals for its patrons. The reason: the new chief librarian wanted to change the library's reputation from that of a "stuffy, closed-off, unapproachable" institution to that of an accessible information source. [9]

Using the Environment to Influence Customer Behavior

Many environmental psychologists contend that the use of particular colors may influence the actions of clients or customers. A California jail and a U.S. Naval Correctional Center both decided to paint holding cells pink after a study revealed that the color rapidly saps anger and aggression. [10]

The physical environment may also be designed to influence customer behavior by inhibiting or encouraging customer interaction with other customers. At Benihana, the chain of restaurants with Japanese cuisine, customer interaction is encouraged by capacious round-table seating arrange-

9. Williams, op. cit.

10. Judy Thorne, "We're Learning to Put Color's Power to Work," *The Seattle Times,* September 7, 1980, p. G1.

ments that permit large groups, whose members are often total strangers to one another, to be seated together. In other restaurants, physical barriers or dim lighting that limit customer interaction and enhance individual privacy help achieve the opposite effect.

Although there are many examples of the use of the environment to communicate the nature of the service experience, there are no established guidelines or marketing strategies that would tie these examples together. In addition to being able to catalog the elements that constitute the service environment and the ways in which they influence customers, service marketers need a framework to guide them in making decisions about the physical environment. The authors propose that a few theories drawn from environmental psychology provide such a framework.

Approach and Avoidance Responses

Environmental psychologists postulate that there are two basic reactions to any environment, *approach* and *avoidance*. Approach behavior involves such responses as physically moving toward something, exploring an unfamiliar environment, affiliating with others in the environment through verbal communication and eye contact, and performing a large number of tasks within the environment. Avoidance behavior includes an opposite set of responses. Because the decision to purchase is considered part of approach behavior, service firms should strive to create an environment that elicits approach behavior from their potential customers.

But to elicit approach behavior, the service marketer must first understand why people react to environments in the ways that they do. Mehrabian and other environmental psychologists assume that people's feelings and emotions ultimately determine what they do and how they do it. [11] They further assume that people respond with different sets of emotions to different environments, and that these reactions, in turn, prompt them to approach or avoid the environments. Service marketers who are able to predict accurately the likely emotional states of their customers, and to provide them with surroundings that set off positive reactions and encourage approach behavior, will profit. Holiday Inns' newly designed guest rooms for business travelers are a good example of this

strategy. The firm discovered that its business customers—after a stressful working day away from familiar surroundings—were most comfortable in rooms that had all the comforts of home. Accordingly, new rooms were appointed with large beds and colored sheets, telephones with long cords, clock radios (in lieu of a jarring wakeup call), large desks, comfortable, overstuffed chairs, and Home Box Office reception. If the environmental psychologists' theories are correct, these surroundings will inspire approach behavior because they satisfy business travelers' emotional needs for familiarity, security, and relaxation.

High-Load and Low-Load Environments

To design an environment that meets customers' emotional needs, service marketers must first understand the components of the environment as well as the components' impact on customers' behavior. One environmental psychologist uses the terms *high-load* and *low-load* to describe environments. [12] These terms are based on the concept of "information rate"—the extent of new stimuli in the environment to be processed by the observer. [13] A high-load signifies a high information rate; a low-load represents a low information rate.

Uncertainty, novelty, and complexity are associated with high-load environments; conversely, a low-load environment communicates assurance, homogeneity, and simplicity. Bright colors, bright lights, loud noises, crowds, and movement are typical elements of a high-load environment, while their opposites are characteristic of a low-load environment.

People's emotional needs and reactions at a given time determine whether they will be attracted to a high- or low-load environment. In the Holiday Inns example, the firm assumed its customers would be harried business travelers looking for a low-load environment in which to relax and unwind. Thus, they would seek out familiar surroundings that would not require them to process excessive new stimuli. Vacation travelers, on the other hand, might react more positively to a high-load environment, particularly if it symbolized excitement, new experiences, and change from the home routine.

To elicit approach behavior from customers, the marketer should endeavor to understand their

11. Albert Mehrabian, *Public Places and Private Spaces,* (New York: Basic Books, 1976).

12. Mehrabian, op. cit.
13. Mehrabian, op. cit.

needs and should present them with an environment that caters to these needs. For example, a restaurateur whose dinner customers are professional people, who come directly to his establishment after a long and stressful work day, should design a low-load environment to meet their needs. The same restaurateur could modify the environment through variations in lighting, music, noise level, or temperature to suit a different market segment during the lunch hour or on weekends, when a high-load environment might be more appropriate.

Similarly, a bank might modify its environmental design to suit the emotional reactions of that segment it caters to most often. A downtown bank might experiment with the Morgan Guaranty approach (mahogany desks and silk drapes) to elicit approach behavior from wealthy investors and corporate accounts. On the other hand, a suburban bank, whose customers might feel unpleasantly intimidated by such an environment, could adopt a more casual decor, serve coffee to patrons, or advertise with such slogans as "person-to-person banking."

Implications for Service Managers

Goods-manufacturing firms are very much aware of the power of packaging as a marketing tool. Market research and careful testing of package designs and increased professionalism among packaging specialists have made packaging "a science, not an art." [14]

For service firms, the physical environment plays much the same role as packaging does for manufactured goods. The total environment, including lighting, decor, temperature, and noise level, constitutes the "package" that cues the customer in to what the service is and what the firm can do. First impressions influence customers' ultimate purchase decisions, in the same way that the design of a package affects a potential customer's decision to purchase a product. Unlike goods packaging, however, the packaging of services is still very much an art. Hospitality firms and other service organizations that successfully meld services-marketing theories with environmental-psychology theories such as those mentioned in this article may be able to convert it into a science.

---

14. Bill Abrams and David P. Garino, "Package Design Gains Stature as Visual Competition Grows," *The Wall Street Journal,* August 6, 1981, p. 25.

Restaurant Merchandising for the Independent Operator

by Brian T. Sill

A three-step approach to cultivating an image, satisfying your patrons, and increasing sales

Brian Sill was assistant manager of Stuart's in Seattle when this article was written. He is now an associate with Cinci-Grissom Associates, Inc., in Potomac, Md. Sill designed a bachelor's degree program in restaurant management at the University of Washington, where his studies were concentrated in marketing and advertising.

The restaurant industry has grown at an astonishing rate in the last decade. Although much of the increase in revenues has gone to large food-service corporations grossing millions per year, thousands of enterprising individuals have also entered this often risky market.

Many challenges confront the restaurateur struggling to win or maintain his share of the market. Competition comes from new entrepreneurs entering the market, as well as from the growth of established restaurant chains. Inflation eats away at the bottom line as operating costs continue to rise. Vigorous merchandising to build volume frequently represents the only logical recourse for the restaurateur under competitive fire.

But in his pursuit of a differential advantage, the restaurant owner should never lose sight of the objectives behind his promotion and advertising. Successful merchandising flows naturally from a clear understanding of the restaurant's strategic objectives, but few operators expend the effort required to develop explicit statements of their goals. Restaurateurs who adopt a methodical approach and take a penetrating look at their business enterprises will enhance their prospects for survival and growth.

Merchandising in the restaurant business should

This article was originally published in the May 1980 issue of *The Cornell Hotel and Restaurant Administration Quarterly*, pp. 27-30, and is reprinted here with the permission of the Cornell University School of Hotel Administration. ©1980.

be based upon the widely held view that the product a restaurant offers is not merely food and service but the dining experience as a whole. The restaurateur's approach to merchandising his operation should comprise three basic steps:

- **Positioning.** The restaurant's management must first establish an explicit statement of the type of restaurant it wishes to present to patrons.
- **Personality.** Working from this view of the restaurant's positioning, management should endeavor to develop and project a consistent personality for the restaurant.
- **Merchandising.** Merchandising tactics should be creative extensions of the restaurant's personality.

Positioning

To develop an understanding of his competitive situation, the restaurateur should first analyze the marketplace—defining the makeup of the total market, his current patrons, and his target market—and put the results of his analysis in *writing*. After examining all the elements of the marketing mix as they relate to his restaurant, the owner should define his attitudes toward the operation. From his conceptualization of the restaurant flows not only the form of the physical plant but also the standards of performance that shape the dining experience and create, in the patron's mind, an image of the restaurant.

Most restaurateurs have never put this kind of information in written form, but the exercise will focus the investigation on the person in control of the operation, preventing him from citing external factors as an evasive defense. A searching analysis can illumine the owner's potential vis-à-vis his competitors. Without this analysis—and the explicit statement of its results in a structured form that permits the planning and implementation of marketing strategies—the owner will not know where to begin in developing an effective campaign designed to improve sales.

Case I: The owner and the manager of a failing restaurant in the downtown Seattle area asked for an analysis of their business situation. A general marketing audit questionnaire developed by Philip Kotler[1] was used as a format to elicit information. The overall tone of their responses might be characterized as frustrated optimism. Both the owner and the manager were convinced that a market existed for their product, but they could not seem to define it succinctly—or capture it. They agreed that consumers with more sophisticated tastes, a keener eye for value, and an interest in food preparation were willing to pay more for quality food and service. Thus, the needs and wants of a target segment had been outlined, but that audience was identified only as those who happened to eat at the restaurant most frequently, when instead it should have been defined in terms of the individuals the restaurant was trying to attract.

Beyond these obvious conclusions, owner and manager disagreed about most of the other aspects of the operation. Their answers also demonstrated that they were confused about their competition, blaming their downtown location for depressed sales while simultaneously defining Seattle's downtown restaurants as the operation's prime competition. The owner and the manager agreed on one point, however: the introduction of a bar was to be the operation's salvation. They proposed developing a new campaign to advertise the bar, but just how the message was to be presented and its desired effect were unclear.

In light of the magnitude of these discrepancies and the general confusion implicit in the responses of the owner and the manager, the restaurant's uneven performance was hardly surprising. Absent an understanding of the operation's positioning, the principals had no accurate idea of the restaurant they were attempting to create, and their merchandising efforts accordingly lacked direction and focus.

Restaurant Personality

Customers *personalize* a restaurant, forming an image of it based not only on the type and quality of the food but on many intangibles as well. The owner can guide the development of this image, imbuing his restaurant with a distinctive personality.

If the owner intends to convey a characteristic personality for his restaurant, his efforts must extend to the attitudes of his employees and all aspects of their service. George Wenzel, a well-known restaurant consultant, advises owners: "A smile on the face of the cashier when [the guest comes] in, and on the waitress when she approaches, and on the bus boy when he helps clear the table. These employees must be taught this. They won't do it if the owner doesn't set the example. . . . And, obviously, they must be rewarded to show that you appreciate their cooperation."[2] To the extent that the owner is able to accomplish this, the chances are better that his attitudes will live and grow beyond himself and be conveyed in the attitudes of the restaurant employees—attitudes that are the foundation of the restaurant's personality.

The personality should also be evident in every physical feature of the restaurant. The decor and furnishings should be more than just pleasant or comfortable; they should all make a consistent statement about the restaurant. Philip Kotler uses the term "atmospherics" to denote this total approach, maintaining that a well-designed atmosphere produces "specific emotional effects in the buyer that enhance his purchase probability."[3]

In developing a personality for the restaurant, the owner starts with a reassessment of his attitudes and objectives, then projects these into the operation of his business. His vision is effected in the attitudes and actions of the employees as well as in the style of presentation the owner wishes to employ. The presentation is made up of sensory stimulants (atmospherics) that play to the customer. The result is a restaurant personality to which the customer can respond. If the response is favorable, it can become a lasting friendship.

Merchandising Devices

By methodically going through each step—questioning motives, defining objectives, establishing standards, creating atmosphere—the owner has essentially developed the underlying merchandis-

1. Philip Kotler, William Gregor, and William Rodgers, "The Marketing Audit Comes of Age," *Sloan Management Review:* Winter 1977, pp. 25-43.

2. George L. Wenzel, Sr., *How to Build Volume* (Austin, Texas: George L. Wenzel, 1954), pp. 9 +.

3. Philip Kotler, "Atmospherics as a Marketing Tool," *Journal of Retailing,* 49, No. 4 (Winter 1973-74), pp. 48-64.

ing strategy for his restaurant. All that remains is the implementation of merchandising techniques and tactics.

A basic premise of merchandising techniques to induce purchase behavior is that people enjoy experiences that are novel and pleasantly surprising. The implication for the restaurant operator is that if he can keep the food, presentation, and service well-balanced, an element of novelty will enhance customers' dining experience and yield a competitive advantage. This requires a creative look at all elements of a restaurant's operation to determine which areas could benefit from the application of the concept. The owner should be aware of his competitors' innovations and be alert to ideas available from trade publications and organizations.

One of the best sources of ideas is the restaurateur's employees, who should be encouraged to brainstorm, along with management, to identify novel merchandising techniques. Brainstorming sessions with employees, as retailing experts point out,[4] can stimulate creativity by encouraging an open exchange of ideas in an environment free of criticism. Finally, the restaurateur should bear in mind that the restaurant's employees represent not only a pool of creativity but also the prime source of input from patrons, because they have the most firsthand contact with diners.

Case II: The owner of a family-run Italian restaurant just two blocks from Seattle's sports arena sought advice on means to increase patronage. In his discussions with a marketing consultant, it was revealed that sports fans seldom ate at the restaurant and that there was no advertising directed to this segment. After further analysis and market research, the owner decided to refocus his operation, positioning it to attract the middle-income sports fan frequenting the nearby dome. The restaurant

was to be given a more modern image and presented as a fresh but unpretentious operation whose most distinctive feature was its authentic Italian cuisine.

As he refurbished and redecorated his restaurant, the owner solicited his employees' suggestions for achieving the image of authenticity that was to be the key to the operation's personality. No small part of the restaurant's current success is attributable to the merchandising techniques suggested by the employees; homemade pasta dries in view of the prospective patron as he enters the restaurant; inside he can see the noodles being made, as well as observe the other operations taking place in the exposed kitchen. This openness and simplicity are complemented by robust food, presented in a fashion that emphasizes abundance and wholesomeness. In short, the restaurant now "works" because all the elements—from positioning through merchandising techniques—are coordinated to convey the underlying concept of authenticity.

Conclusion

The purpose of the three-step analysis outlined above is to help the independent restaurateur develop a perspective on his restaurant that will enable him to make a stronger appeal to his customers. The day-to-day operation of a restaurant can become very routine for the owner and his staff, but it is important that they remain attentive to patrons' needs. Periodic replication of the analytical process will help the restaurateur understand his operation's position in the market. That understanding will enable him both to satisfy his customers and to develop a merchandising strategy to increase his sales.

---

4. Roger Dickinson, "Creativity in Retailing," *Journal of Retailing,* 45, No. 4 (Winter 1969-70), pp. 3-18.

Marketing the Restaurant Personality

by Brian T. Sill

An understanding of how patrons psychologically identify your restaurant can be a useful tool not only in general marketing terms, but in specific positioning and merchandising strategies as well. A fundamental review of consumer behavior can be critical for success either in the *pre-opening* stage of concept development and design for a new restaurant or in the *repositioning/decline* stage of an existing operation.

Consumer research is an obvious and major component of any market feasibility study, be it for a major restaurant chain or the small independent operator. Traditionally, the consumer profile of a selected market area has been limited to demographic information such as age, income, sex, and religion. While this data is relatively inexpensive and easy to obtain (see list next page), many armchair marketers have misapplied its meaning—like the drunk who uses the lamp post for support instead of illumination.

Psychographic research, based on the consumer lifestyles of people in the restaurant trading area, comes closer to the mark in understanding how a customer will respond to your restaurant concept. Psychographic survey participants are asked to respond to such questions as:

• Food-innovativeness: When I am in a store, I am likely to pick up new foods (Yes or No).

• Nutrition-consciousness: I plan my meals so that my family gets proper nutrition (Yes or No).

• Price-consciousness: I go to stores where I usually do not shop in order to take advantage of food sales—every chance I get ( ) almost every chance ( ), seldom ( ), never ( ).

These questions are posed with the intention of spelling out the overt and latent psychological motives that cause acceptance/rejection of a given

restaurant concept. For example, do people patronize Lutece in New York City because they are strong followers of quality French cooking, or are they trying to achieve higher peer status by dining with the celebrity regulars?

Properly applied, psychographic research can help to segment trade area residents based on lifestyle characteristics that exhibit a homogeneous, or similar propensity to feel attracted to a particular restaurant experience. Simply put, it "humanizes" market data.

However, in the absence of sophisticated market research, a perspective that gets at the base of human interaction with the restaurant environment can be insightful to single and multi-unit operators. This perspective involves a consumer-oriented definition of the restaurant's *personality*.

Since the economics of a restaurant require the personal service function be spread over a number of customers at once, the actual time for personal contact is limited. However, human beings are creative and imaginative. Thus, they add their own subjective perceptions and images to the experience.

Stanley Marcus of Neiman-Marcus said in reference to the retail shopper: "The customer compensates for less personal contact by personalizing the store. He behaves in considerable measure toward this inanimate objective as if it were a person. It becomes a symbol to which he can form deep attachments or dislikes."

The legitimacy of this perspective is founded in the logic that human beings, before they can respond to something, however intangible, must first make it tangible. The metaphor devised by dining patrons is a personality for the restaurant. It allows the patrons to "put clothes on" an intangible experience so that they can visualize, and evaluate, the restaurant experience.

What is the significance of this perspective?

From *Restaurant Business* (June 1, 1982) pp. 108-114. Reprinted by permission of *Restaurant Business*.

While the restaurant produces physical products that can be readily experienced and evaluated—tasty food, efficient service, comfortable chairs and tables—there exist certain intangible qualities that add to or detract from the experience. Typical customer responses derived from intangible perceptions might be:

• A grateful patron: "The (restaurant) made me feel like a real VIP—comfortable, pampered, and recognized," or

• An insulted customer: "The (restaurant) is so boring and depressing. They'll never see me again!"

In each case, the restaurant is described in humanistic terms as a friend or foe.

Atmosphere is generally an all-encompassing term used to describe the experience "felt" but not always seen. Spatial aesthetics, more specifically termed "atmospherics," consist of elements such as brightness, size, shape, volume, pitch, scent, freshness, softness, smoothness, and temperature. Understandably, the effects of these elements on the customer are important in casting the image or personality of the restaurant.

Another major influence that shapes the personification of the restaurant experience is the study of "environmental psychology," which involves the interaction of customers and the environment (atmosphere) and the resultant effects on human behavior. For example, the amount of privacy afforded the customer directly relates to the freedom of behavior that individual feels. The standards of personal space are important dimensions of the experience perceived as follows:

1. **Intimate distance** occurs within 18 inches of the patron. Patrons not desiring such social intimacy may feel repulsed and hence, negative about the experience. In a cocktail lounge, however, this amount of space may be desirable where "forced" involvement is preferred.

2. **Personal distance** is from 18 inches to four feet. Adequate room is allowed for comfortable discussions and actions that may allow unfamiliar patrons to become more formally acquainted. Patrons may feel they temporarily "own" objects within this "zone."

3. **Social distance** ranges from 4 feet to 12 feet. Social actions become less personal and more casual in this area.

4. **Public distance** is space beyond 12 feet. People and objects become less familiar and less involved with each other.

Thus, the amount of square feet allowed each customer, and the objects allowed to interact with the customer within certain "zones" can positively or adversely affect the patron's experience.

Atmospherics and environmental psychology provide a means of defining physical relationships that the restaurateur can use to guide the restaurant personality. They help the operator bring to light certain phenomena previously unnoticed by the human eye and made visible through the metaphoric parallel.

The perspective, that seeks to "industrialize" an inanimate object, plays predominantly on the sensory perceptions of the patrons in terms of their sight, sound, touch, scent, and taste. The interplay between the senses and atmospheric stimuli is profound.

Yet, even more basic is the impact of social acceptability and the notion of customers' value systems in market segmentation strategies.

Any customer that walks into your restaurant is accompanied by a social structure influenced by fellow human beings. This structure defines that person's role in a group, thereby diminishing uncertainties about socially acceptable or unacceptable behavior. The bonds that hold this structure together in a cohesive manner are common *values* held by the "reference group" members (a group of people with similar behavioral attitudes and interests). Such values:

1. Are widely held beliefs;

2. Are thought to be desirable by members of a group; and

3. Serve as general guides or premises for activities within a group.

Values form the basis of a consumer's "self-concept" which is the prognosticator of purchase behavior researched in the psychographic surveys.

Identifying customers' values is important because interpersonal (word-of-mouth) influence is strongest between members of the same reference group. And, people with similar values tend to emulate each other with subtle/overt cues in their fashion and dress, etiquette, material ownership, associations, vacation spots, and other manifestations of their self-concept. Through their network of church, business, club or school, values are transmitted that decide acceptance or rejection. Target markets defined by value systems are surely the most "natural" form of market segmentation.

Sensitive restaurant marketers that pay close attention to these cues can use them in positioning their restaurant's personality to targeted market segments. Many independent operators do this without realizing it as they merchandise their restaurants as an extension of their own tastes.

Chain operators, on the other hand, must heed the differences in values over regions. An obvious example is the coastal diversity between the youth-oriented culture of Southern California where trendiness implies sensitivity, and the Northeastern states, such as New Hampshire and Maine, where conservatism and traditionalism are the norm.

In either case, the key is to understand, in general terms, the values of a trade area. This way, the operator can build in the "value cues" by applying atmospherics and environmental psychology in the interior design, ambience, style of service, and so forth that reinforce the desired personality. Once established, these values should be investigated to see if they are subject to long- or short-term trends for future planning.

The understanding of restaurant patrons' value systems may appear beyond the reach of most researchers. However, as foodservice trends become more fragmented and difficult to identify, and customers become more experienced and "individualized" in their tastes, this approach may well become the only path of certainty in the future.

Examples

The following are examples of restaurant personality positioning.

In some instances operators are providing more than one personality concept under the same roof. This allows the customer to "shop" for the personality that best suits his mood at the time. For example, a hotel in Cleveland, Ohio provides a "full entertainment" concept with five individually designed areas of the cocktail lounge for the hotel traveler and city locals.

1. A library room is surrounded by glass walls that minimize the noise from the adjacent disco. The glass walls help maintain good visibility so that patrons do not feel cloistered away. Shelves stuffed with books line one wall of the library. A television, a quiet electronic game, and pillowy chairs and sofas provide comfortable, passive entertainment. End tables with reading lamps are interspersed throughout the room for those desiring to peruse newspapers or magazines.

2. A raised conversational seating area, with tables larger than normal cocktail size, seat parties of three or more. This area separates the library room from the more intense and active disco area. While the tables are within the disco room itself, the area is farthest from the speakers, allowing the patrons to converse. The raised floor affords a good view of the disco activity. Groups of couples less in-

volved with the "singles" scene frequent this area. They are far enough away from the mingling dancers that they feel involved but not compelled to participate.

3. Two steps down from the conversation area are the stand-up bar counters. They are located on the bar level within the full volume area of the disco speakers. Patrons desiring to watch and be watched meander about, dancing here, stopping to chat there. The people themselves are the entertainment in this area.

4. In the middle of this area is the circular bar. Well dressed attendants mix drinks and joke with seated patrons. It offers a sense of security for those feeling uncomfortable out in the sea of bumping bodies.

5. Finally, on either wall of the large room are banquettes for two or three persons that face the "action." Couples enjoy the privacy of these canopied booths as they feel "cuddled" by the space, but still feel part of the overall activity.

Another example of a multi-personality approach is found in Clyde's of Tysons Corner, Virginia. The restaurant's heritage has been based on a "saloon" emphasis that serves as the "host" personality. However, surrounding the lavishly designed bar are four distinct areas, each with a distinct personality.

1. The Palm Terrace features a light menu consistent with the light and airy decor conveyed with the open room and large palm trees. A fireplace positioned at the edge of the Mexican ceramic tile floor underscores the casualness of the room.

2. The other side of the bar features a more secluded dining room, also with light foods. The Cafe offers the patron a European flavor with an attendant cooking assorted omelettes in full view of the diners.

3. The Oyster Bar presents a more serious fare of seafood entrees. Hard woods, brass, and a darker lighting scheme underscore the calm and sophisticated service style.

4. Finally, the Grill presents the most formal alternative of the different experiences. The art deco design and serious Maitre d' service augment a crisscross of continental menu items.

Another restaurant, in the Washington, D.C. area, was experiencing good success as a combination retail bakery and full service restaurant. Unfortunately, the restaurant's identity was more closely related to a breakfast and lunch restaurant than a dinner house. The baking equipment displayed in the center of the restaurant and baker's display shelves at the entryway were empty and not in use during the dinner hour. Coupled with numerous other factors, this presentation conveyed a closed, or unwelcome feeling.

The change, therefore, became one of re-positioning the personality of the restaurant from a French retail bakery with foodservice at the break-fast and lunch meal periods, to strictly a restaurant service at dinner—repositioning by meal period, so to speak. This approach appeared credible based on the assumption that people seldom frequent the same restaurant for dinner as they do for lunch.

Additional research has revealed that many downtown Washington, D.C. restaurants experi-ence poor business at night as residents refuse to drive back in from the suburbs. However, many operators are finding a bar or "saloon" emphasis will attract people from the suburbs. Thus a "French saloon" personality was defined for the restaurant at night and merchandised with a "peasant" food emphasis.

A movable partition, attractively designed, with "Follies Bergere" dancers was tastefully positioned to hide the retail baker's shelving at the front of the restaurant. The baking equipment in the center of the restaurant was surrounded by mobile book shelves stocked full with the restaurant's wine in-ventory. A counter was built in front of the wine shelves as a combination wine bar and food dis-play shelf; this became the new focus at night. After the lunch hour, five or six tables with chairs are removed from the dining room floor between the wine bar and restaurant entrance. More room is thus afforded for patrons standing at the bar and social interaction in the front half of the restaurant is encouraged. Free appetizers, such as cheese and pate, are provided on the wine bar counter throughout the evening.

In the back half of the restaurant, three or four tables are removed at night to allow more privacy than is necessary at breakfast and lunch. Table lin-ens on dining tables and dark lighting amplified the break in style from the wine bar area to the meal service areas.

The "peasant" menu consisted of small three ounce portions of seafood: scallops, crab, shrimp, mussels, and so forth, sauteed with ample portions of fresh vegetables and buried in various cream sauces. Bountiful baskets of crunchy French bread served at room temperature are supplied with each meal. The results are filling yet inexpensive quality entrees in keeping with the peasant cuisine and sa-loon price range of $5.00 to $8.00 per entree.

This example shows how the metamorphosis of a restaurant's personality can be achieved by alter-ing the atmospheric elements and applying en-vironmental psychology principles.

Part VI

Advertising

Promises, promises, promises. Hotels and restaurants sell promises of certain kinds of experiences. Buyers who are asked to purchase products and services from hospitality firms are, for the most part, asked to buy without the benefit of personal inspection. They can't feel in advance the products that they are asked to buy. They can't see them. They can't smell them. They can't hear them. Nor can they taste them. Yet they are asked to buy without being able to evaluate products in the same way that they can when they buy other products such as clothing, furniture, or automobiles. Buyers of hospitality products are asked to buy intangibles; to buy something that does not yet exist for them. And since they cannot inspect something that does not exist, they must base their buying decisions on someone else's word. In short, they must rely on promises that the experience will be a favorable one.

The problem for hospitality firms, then, is how to make an intangible product into a tangible one in the minds of buyers. To do this, modern companies develop and manage a complex marketing communications system made up of advertising, sales promotions, publicity, and personal selling. They use this system to reach consumers and middlemen such as tour operators and travel agents. While all the promotional tools are important and should have a prominent place in the total marketing communications mix of hotels and restaurants, this section of the book will be concerned with advertising.

Advertising comes in many forms and can be used for a variety of purposes. Generally speaking, advertising should be used to accomplish the following things.

Advertising is, first of all, used to attract buyers' attention and to make them aware of the hotel or restaurant.

Second, advertising is used to create an interest in the hotel or restaurant. It is one thing to make buyers aware that a product exists; it is another thing to get consumers interested enough to obtain information about the product.

The third general use of advertising is to turn interest into desire to experience the products and services that a hotel or restaurant has to offer.

Finally, advertising is used to create action on the part of buyers.

More specifically, advertising can be used for the image building and positioning of a company or an individual hotel or restaurant. It can be used to disseminate information about the advantages of a particular hotel or restaurant or about special events. It can be used to inform various publics about sales promotions such as special weekends or special packages. And advertising can be used to inform consumers on how to buy.

The articles that follow have been chosen because they discuss, in some depth, the ideas proposed above.

The Execution and Measurement of a Marketing Program

by Dr. Peter C. Yesawich

Peter Yesawich, Ph.D., is vice president of marketing for Robinsons, Inc., an advertising and marketing firm serving the hospitality industry. He received his doctorate from Cornell University, where his areas of concentration were psychology, marketing, and communication theory. He serves as a visiting instructor at the Cornell University School of Hotel Administration.

In the November issue of The Quarterly, *the author introduced a formula for the development of a marketing program comprising four distinct steps: (1) marketing research; (2) planning—objectives and strategy selection; (3) execution; and (4) measurement. Marketing research and planning were discussed in detail, providing the reader with the information required to build a program through the selection of a marketing strategy. The execution and measurement of marketing programs will be addressed in this article.*

Execution

Once the market planner has established the marketing strategy, the strategy can be translated into graphic reality. The execution must begin with the development of a "creative approach"—in other words, an expression of how the lodging property will be represented. Responsibility for synthesis of the creative approach typically lies with an advertising agency, although several large lodging establishments and chains have, in recent years, maintained in-house creative talent to assist with such assignments.

The development of the creative approach is one of the most important steps in the production of advertising and promotional material because it directly influences the image projected by, and as-sociated with, the establishment or group of establishments, as well as the extent to which the advertising and promotional materials attract and sustain the interests of prospective customers. Accordingly, the creative approach must be established carefully with a view toward achieving specific effects on the audience to be addressed.

The result of this exercise should be the crystalization of the marketing message to be projected through the various elements of the program. The message—be it one of newness, tradition, security, friendliness, or any of a number of other attributes—must be conceived with reference to the results of the research conducted at Step 1, as well as the known characteristics of the target markets. This process is known as "positioning:" the act of defining *precisely* what the audience's perception of the promoted product or service should be (particularly in relation to perceptions of competitive products or services, and to a conception of a hypothetical "ideal" product or service). [1]

Because the positioning permeates every aspect of the marketing program, it is advisable to test the concept prior to its wholesale adoption. Controlled evaluation of a positioning concept can be costly but it is often a judicious investment, particularly when planning substantial media coverage in the campaign to follow. Those who choose to test a concept can usefully conduct focus-group interviews, using a sample of individuals who are members of the defined target markets, to determine whether the approach is successful in communicating the concept it is intended to communicate, and to learn prospects' reactions to it.

With a creative approach accepted, management has the information needed to allocate the market-

---

This article was originally published in the May 1979 issue of *The Cornell Hotel and Restaurant Administration Quarterly*, pp. 41-52, and is reprinted here with the permission of the Cornell University School of Hotel Administration. ©1979.

1. Decisions about the positioning of a product or service are generally guided by the results of *multidimensional scaling.* In this type of research, subjects are asked to rate various brands on the basis of several *dimensions* (attributes) known to influence consumers' purchase of the product or service. Consumers are also asked to rate the dimensions of the "ideal" brand. The results of the scaling exercise are plotted on a map of "perceptual space" and a positioning judgment is made with reference to existing perceptions and anticipated market potential.

"Notch Brook is a New England portrait of rolling hillsides, ablaze with color.... guests find a multitude of outdoor adventures to fill each sunny day ... golf ... tennis ... horseback riding ... trout fishing ... Summer theatre is all around."

An establishment with dramatic seasonal changes in business composition should use a customized set of marketing tools for each segment of the market. The core design developed for collateral promoting Notch Brook, a resort in Stowe, Vermont, lends itself well to brochures for both summer and winter vacationers — with some features appearing in both pieces, and photographs and text geared to the specific interests of each market inserted in designated "windows." The result: Brochures that effectively address two specific and different markets, produced at a cost far lower than that of developing two discrete pieces.

"Notch Brook offers all the amenities of at-home living while you vacation and ski.... After an exciting day on the slopes ... enjoy cocktails and a good conversation by a crackling fire while you watch the deepening shadows on the ski trails through your picture window."

NOTCH BROOK . . .
is a wonderland of nature's elegance awaiting the New England-bound vacationer. This peaceful resort community created in the cool green forests touches the deep historic tradition of Stowe, Vermont . . . it is more than a "get-away-from-it-all" hideaway. Notch Brook is a New England portrait of rolling hillsides, ablaze with color and landscaped with a beauty most never see.

Our summers are cooled by the whispering breezes of Mount Mansfield, the renowned ski capital of the East.

Notch Brook guests find a multitude of outdoor adventures to fill each sunny day: golf on courses nestled in nature's own splendor . . . tennis on championship courts . . . swimming in our heated pool . . . sauna bathing, bicycling . . . hiking along nature trails, horseback riding into quiet forests and trout fishing in sparkling mountain streams . . . you can enjoy antiquing in the country of Smugglers Notch or the breathtaking view of three states and Canada from the summit of Mt. Mansfield.

Stowe's restauranteurs offer the elegance of gourmet cuisine and the grace of country dining in the Green Mountains' crystal moonlight. Summer theatre is all around.

You have a wide range of spacious accommodations at Notch Brook, from double rooms to one bedroom studios (complete with kitchens) to one, two and three bedroom townhouses. All are exquisitely decorated, and each has a terrace or balcony overlooking the surrounding mountains. Many have fireplaces and multi-level living areas. And our summer rates are most inviting.

Visit Notch Brook
for a leisurely vacation
or long weekend. For reservations
contact us
Notch Brook Resort
Notch Brook Road
Stowe, Vermont 05672
Telephone: 802 253-4882

Situated on a wooded mountainside overlooking Mt. Mansfield . . . Notch Brook is only minutes on our own shuttle bus from the best skiing in the East. For aprés-ski . . . picturesque Stowe is just 7 minutes away, with its enticing selection of shops, restaurants and colorful night life.

Visit Notch Brook
for a leisurely vacation
or long weekend. For reservations
write or call collect:

Notch Brook Resort
Notch Brook Road
Stowe, Vermont 05672
Telephone: 802/253-4882

NOTCH BROOK . . .
a superb resort complex that offers you all the amenities of at-home living while you vacation and ski. Our luxurious accommodations include everything from double rooms and one bedroom apartments to one, two and three bedroom townhouses . . . each with a panoramic mountain view from private terrace or balcony.

The quality of life at Notch Brook could only be surpassed by the skiing at nearby Mt. Mansfield, "the skiing capital of the East." There's cross country and downhill to challenge the most seasoned skier. For the "snow bunny", the novice slopes, fluffed with snow, make even falling down fun.

After an exciting day on the slopes . . . our shuttle bus brings you quickly and conveniently back to Notch Brook for the pleasant evening ahead. Relax in a sauna bath or take an invigorating dip in our outdoor heated pool. Enjoy our game rooms or the privacy of your own beautifully-decorated apartment. Spend a lingering evening enjoying cocktails and good conversation by a crackling fire while you watch the deepening shadows on the ski trails through your picture window. It's all part of your winter world at Notch Brook.

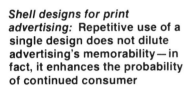

Shell designs for print advertising: **Repetitive use of a single design does not dilute advertising's memorability—in fact, it enhances the probability of continued consumer recognition. Shown above and at right are shell designs used in advertising various facilities at Holiday Inn's Executive Tower in Norfolk, Virginia. In addition to encouraging consumer recognition, the use of shell designs can greatly reduce the cost of producing promotional materials.**

ing budget over the different vehicles that will be used to deliver the message: print advertising, broadcast advertising, outdoor advertising, direct mail, audiovisual presentations, public relations, collateral (printed material), special promotions, and personal selling. Before deciding how the available funds should be spent, however, management must establish what percentage of its efforts will be devoted to securing repeat patronage and what percentage will be devoted to the development of new business, as this judgment will dictate the most appropriate mix of marketing vehicles.

Consistency and Flexibility

The establishment's or firm's logo should be adapted for use in every visible component of the program to produce thematic consistency among all materials to which the public will be exposed. Included on this list are advertisements, brochures, postcards, indoor and outdoor signs, guest checks, guest-service directories, matchbooks, and menus. The consistent use of the logo contributes to the projection of a unified property image. This design principle is supported by a well-established principle of the psychology of learning: it is easier to recognize a stimulus than to recall it. Thus, a marketing approach characterized by consistency is more likely to evoke repeated recognition on the part of the consumer than one that does not.

Using a *shell design*—a standard format that can be used in a variety of ways with only minor modifications—can greatly reduce the cost of producing printed promotional material. For example, consider an establishment with dramatic variations in business composition as a function of seasonal changes, where a customized set of marketing tools will be required to sell each of the seasonal segments of the market. The establishment can prepare a core design for its collateral material, with some features constant in brochures for all markets and "windows" left open for text and illustrations geared to specific markets; the different approaches requi   to   he various s   ents are then easily (and r   io y inexpensively) established through the insertion of appropriate photographs and copy in the windows. The flexibility of shell designs is apparent in the examples shown on pages 237-

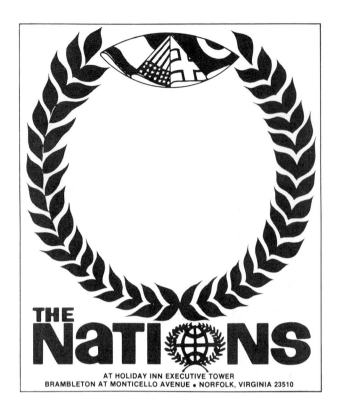

With only minor modifications in a shell design, a property can create a large number of different ads relatively inexpensively. Shell designs are particularly useful in developing advertising to promote food and beverage facilities, because advertising of this kind rarely requires major textual changes.

The Nations, located in Norfolk's Holiday Inn Executive Tower, downtown at Scope, invites you on the most elegant dining adventure in the Tidewater area. This fine restaurant, recommended by *Gourmet* magazine, specializes in international cuisine, carefully prepared and served in a gracious and intimate setting comparable to the finest on the Continent itself. Include The Nations in your Norfolk itinerary . . . no passport is necessary — just an appetite for an adventure in delicious dining! Open Tuesday-Sunday. Dinner 6 to 10 p.m. Reservations recommended: 627-5555.

238. The same cost-saving principle can be applied to the production of promotional material by multiple-location chains (as depicted on pages 245-246).

The concept of multiple use may also be applied to the design of advertising. For example, a single design format may be created for print advertisements in both consumer and trade publications, with copy and phtographs varied as a function of each publication's audience. An example of this adaptability is shown on page 242. Repetitive use of a single design does not dilute advertising's memorability. On the contrary, in accord with the principle cited earlier, such repetition enhances the probability of continued recognition.

Production economies may similarly be realized in developing advertising and signage to promote food and beverage facilities. Such advertising generally requires only occasional changes in copy to achieve its intended effect. Thus, shell formats provide an economical alternative to creating a number of different ads (see examples above).

Advertising

Most lodging establishments rely primarily on advertising through one or more media to convey the marketing message. Although they often make a significant investment in advertising, too many firms lack the basic understanding of advertising required to spend their advertising dollars wisely.

The question of how advertising contributes to purchase decisions is one that has challenged the patience of theorists for years. [2] Recent research on

2. It has been suggested that advertising influences consumers in the following sequence: it (1) makes consumers aware of the product; (2) teaches them relevant facts; (3) induces them to like the product through the use of reinforcements in the advertising; (4) intensifies the liking to the point of preference; (5) prompts a conviction on the part of the consumer that he will purchase the product the next time the purchase opportunity arises; and (6) leads to purchase (see R.J. Lavidge and G.A. Steiner, "A Model for Predictive Measurements of Advertising Effectiveness," *Journal of Marketing,* 25 [1961], pp. 59-62). Controlled studies of advertising influence have not always confirmed the accuracy of this contention (see, for example, K.S. Palda, "The Hypothesis of a Hierarchy of Effects: A Partial Evaluation," *Journal of Marketing Research,* 3 [1966], pp 13-24).

A marketing approach characterized by consistency projects a unified property image and is more likely to result in recognition on the part of the consumer.

A property's logo should be adapted for use in every visible component of the marketing program. The Rockley Resort and Beach Club in Barbados uses its logo and consistent design elements throughout its advertising and brochures, as well as on its letterhead, postcards, rate sheets, key chains, employee badges, promotional tokens, and all other materials to which the public is exposed.

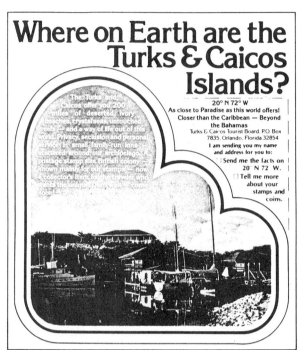

The shell design developed to promote the Turks and Caicos Islands is sufficiently flexible for advertising in both consumer and trade publications, in various sizes, in color or in black and white — and yet is used with sufficient consistency from one ad to the next to produce thematic coherence among the different ads (and to keep production costs down).

the cumulative effects of advertising suggests that advertising's influence on consumers varies as a function of the medium (print or broadcast) in which it is carried. Differences in influence stem from the fact that broadcast advertising (radio and television) obtrudes on its audience whether the audience likes it or not. Advertisements in print media, on the other hand, are unobtrusive in the sense that an individual may elect to spend as little or as much time examining the advertisement as he wishes, as determined by his interest. The difference between the two has been defined as the degree of "involvement" of the audience, and involvement is thought to be higher with print than with broadcast. Without delving into all of the theoretical considerations surrounding this issue, suffice it to say that advertising carried in print media stands a better chance of involving its audience than advertising carried in broadcast media. [3]

Other research indicates that long-term, repeated exposure to advertising is capable of achieving two ends: it can result in an "overlearning" of the brand name and its associated characteristics, and it can alter the "salience" of attributes affecting the brand image. [4] Through repeated exposure, it is possible to move the name of the product or service from consumers' short-term to long-term memories. Practically speaking, this means that consumers become more aware of the product or service and are therefore more likely to select it the next time around. Repetition may also be used to emphasize certain attributes of the product or service—to make the attributes more *salient*—to consumers, thereby affecting its brand image.

In summary, the following points should be considered by the individual responsible for advertising decisions:

1. Consumers' involvement with advertising appears to vary with the medium in which it is carried, and research results suggest that their involvement is higher with print than with

broadcast advertising. Therefore, if your message consists of more than one major selling point, or selling points that require some form of explanatory support, it is advisable to deliver it through some form of print advertising.

2. Repeated exposure to advertising leads the audience to "overlearn" the content and such repetition may be used in a planned alteration of consumers' perceptions of the product or service. Assuming awareness is a precursor of purchase behavior, the implication here is that tonnage, or the sheer volume of advertising exposure, will give one operation a competitive edge over the next.

Frequency. The frequency with which advertising is scheduled to run in selected print or broadcast media is another subject that warrants considerable thought. Intensive scheduling, with relatively brief periods of time between successive exposures, will build consumer awareness very rapidly, but this awareness will decline equally rapidly once the advertising has been terminated. On the other hand, less intensive scheduling with longer time periods between exposures will build consumer awareness gradually; this awareness will remain somewhat longer after the exposures stop than awareness that has been developed through intensive scheduling. [5] Scheduling should therefore be established in light of the desired level of consumer awareness, the amount of time the awareness must be sustained, and the purchase cycle for the product or service being promoted.

A second issue pertinent to the frequency decision is that of how many exposures it will take before the advertising begins to lose its ability to attract and sustain attention. In advertising circles, this problem is known as advertising "wear-out." Psychologists call it "satiation"— the point at which a stimulus no longer has the "psychological strength" to captivate its audience. Most practitioners agree that all advertising, regardless of its quality, will wear out at some point. The critical question for the practitioner is *when*.

Individuals researching wear-out have drawn a distinction between physical and psychological exposures to advertising, with the latter considered the true determinant of wear-out. The number of times a consumer is physically exposed to an advertisement is often quite different from the number of psychological exposures. In fact, several

3. Involvement has been defined as the number of "conscious bridging experiences" or "connections" between the contents of an advertised message and a consumer's salient needs (H.E. Krugman, "The Measurement of Advertising Involvement," *Public Opinion Quarterly*, 30 [1966], pp. 583-596). Involvement can range from low to high (depending on the number of "connections") as a function of the selling points made in an advertisement, the medium through which it is presented, and the economic, social, and psychological needs of the individuals composing the audience. Measures that have been used in experimentation on involvement include subjects' verbal reports and physiological indices such as brain waves (e.g., see H.E. Krugman, "Brain Wave Measures of Media Involvement," *Journal of Advertising Research*, 11 [1971], pp. 3-9).

4. H.E. Krugman, "The Impact of Television Advertising: Learning Without Involvement," *Public Opinion Quarterly*, 29 (1965), pp. 349-356.

5. For example, see: *The Repetition of Advertising*, (New York: DDY&O Research Department [undated and unpaged]); and H.A. Zielske, "The Remembering and Forgetting of Advertising," *Journal of Marketing*, 23 (1959), pp. 239-243.

physical exposures may occur before the first psychological exposure is experienced.

To understand wear-out, let us consider the forms psychological exposure can take. According to Krugman, all advertising is capable of engendering only three different psychological reactions, regardless of the number of physical exposures:

1. What is it?
2. What of it?
3. Decisional reaction. [6]

These reactions may be experienced at distinctly different points in time or simultaneously, depending on such factors as the interest of the audience, the complexity of the advertising, and so forth. In the first case, the prospect notes consciously that he has not "seen" the advertising before; his interest is aroused, and he evaluates its content. In the second reaction, the prospect evaluates the relevance of the advertising message to his own needs and desires. Finally, the third response—the decisional reaction—is that wherein the prospect determines whether he will act in response to the advertising message the next time the purchase opportunity arises. Krugman suggests that all subsequent psychological reactions are simply repetitions of this third reaction. If we accept this contention, we must assume that advertising begins to wear out once most members of the prospect audience have experienced this third psychological reaction.

Because the third reaction is dependent not only on frequency but also on the creative content of advertising, controlled lab testing would be required to investigate how many physical exposures to a specific advertisement could occur before the onset of wear-out. Establishments planning only a moderate volume of print or broadcast advertising would not find testing necessary, but establishments planning to run a substantial volume of advertising should seriously consider testing to ensure they will receive maximum market impact for the dollars expended.

Design Considerations in Print Advertising

To give the reader a notion of the number and nature of decisions to be made in developing advertising, we will now briefly consider three aspects of print advertising—the vehicle used most heavily to promote lodging facilities and travel services. Let us consider how size, layout, and the use of color affect advertising readership.

Contrary to popular belief, readership does not increase in direct proportion to the size of a print advertisement. Although readership does increase with size, it appears to level off as size approaches its maximum. [7] Perhaps the most notable research finding concerning this relationship is that the additional readership secured through increments in size normally comprises individuals who are not currently users of the product or service. Hence, size appears to be important if the advertising is intended to *expand* a market, but exposure to existing markets can be sustained through the proper design and placement of smaller ads. [8]

Studies of the relationship between advertising layouts and readership have generally indicated that placing an illustration at the top of the ad, with a single focal point, is most effective; in addition, photorealism appears to be more desirable than unstructured illustrations, like silhouettes. Copy headlines should be brief and complement the dominant focal point of the illustration. [9] These generalizations are by no means universally applicable, of course, and a test of readership recognition [10] can be helpful in determining which of several design formats to use.

Research studies regarding the effectiveness of color advertisements compared to that of black and white advertisements have had conflicting results. Rudolph, for example, found that two-color ads received only about one percent more readership than black and white ads, but that four-color ads averaged 54 percent higher readership: similar results were found by Starch. [11] Barkley, on the other

---

6. H.E. Krugman, "Why Three Exposures May Be Enough," *Journal of Advertising Research*, 12 (1972), pp. 11-14.

7. For example, one researcher found that, as the size of an advertising message increases, the permanency of the impression will increase approximately with the square root of the increase of the area (B.D. Copland, *The Study of Attention Value: A Review of Some Available Material* [London: Business Publications Limited, 1958]). Further refinement of this relationship has led to the following mathematical description: $x = N - .01N^2$, where N is the percentage of readers who noticed an ad of a given size, and x is the predicted percentage of readers who will notice an ad twice as large. (A. Anastasi, "Perceptual and Cognitive Factors in Advertising," in *Fields of Applied Psychology* [New York: McGraw-Hill, 1964]).

8. Anastasi, loc. cit.

9. Marplan, Inc., *The Measurement and Control of the Visual Efficiency of Advertisements* (New York: Advertising Research Foundation [undated and unpaged]).

10. A *recognition test* is a test of the impact achieved by a given advertisement; more specifically, it is a test of learning. In a recognition test, subjects are exposed to advertisements they may have seen at some point before (this is established through prescreening), and the researcher determines what percentage of the subjects: (1) have seen the ad; (2) have seen the ad and can identify the name of the sponsor; and (3) have read at least 50 percent of the copy. Starch tests, named for the individual who developed and refined the technique, are commonly used in advertising research.

11. H.J. Rudolph, *Attention and Interest Factors in Advertising: Survey, Analysis, Interpretation* (New York: Funk & Wagnall, 1947); and D. Starch, "How Do Size and Color of Advertisements Affect Readership?," *Tested Copy*, 74 (1956).

Still another application of the shell
design, in promotional material produced for a
multiple-location chain. Hotel Systems International operates
four widely different properties in equally disparate locations,
yet uses a single format for the four brochures used to promote
the properties. The format dictates the placement of photographs
and text, but the selection of photographs and the emphasis
of the text are dictated by the attributes of the individual property.

hand, found that page placement and the use of color *in combination* were related to readership, with black and white ads "out-performing" color ads under certain circumstances. [12] It can be argued that the value of color depends on the adaptability of the product or service to black and white portrayal as well as the skill with which the advertising is prepared. Because lodging facilities and destination attractions are portrayed most vividly in color, the use of color should be seriously considered for travel-oriented advertising.

Measurement

As is true of any allocation of a firm's resources, an investment in marketing should be evaluated through performance measures that will indicate the return received for the dollars invested.

It might seem that the most rigorous test of performance would be the application of a measure of sales over a specified period of time. Evaluating a marketing program's impact on sales is a troublesome task, however, because sales volume is affected by a variety of factors and it is difficult to isolate the influence of marketing from that of other factors. An aggressive marketing program can generate a substantial volume of new business, yet the quality of the product or service delivered will determine what percentage of this new business will be converted to repeat patronage. Furthermore, sales volume is affected by unusual climatic conditions, the rates competitive establishments charge for comparable accommodations, disruptions in transportation access caused by strikes or fuel shortages, the magnitude and effectiveness of competitors' marketing programs, and a host of other factors. As a result, increments in the volume of marketing often do not correspond directly to increments in sales volume.

Many operators have therefore elected to evaluate a marketing program's impact through *surrogate* measures of effectiveness, on the assumption that these are predictive of future sales activity. Commonly used surrogate measures include: (1) "couponing" to measure inquiries generated from newspaper and magazine advertising; (2) direct-response measures to evaluate inquiries generated through direct mail and selected forms of broadcast advertising; and (3) attitude and awareness studies to measure how well the program in general has communicated information to consumers. More controlled forms of lab testing may be conducted at the developmental stage of the campaign, yet these are rarely used in the hospitality industry because the industry's expenditures on media advertising are nominal compared to those by the marketers of consumer goods.

The use of both coupons and direct-response measures will provide the data necessary to compute the cost of generating inquiries, but the determination of actual conversions to business may be made only through periodic sample surveys of respondents. Unfortunately, these will provide only an approximation of the sales results of a campaign because many individuals who were exposed to the components of a campaign may have booked accommodations at the property but never responded to the advertising.

The most reliable way to evaluate the results of the program is to combine the surrogate measures with some form of sales analysis. The analysis should be structured in such a way that market segments (types of guests) may be isolated by origin market, [13] thus facilitating an examination of the relationship between marketing dollars invested in an area and room-nights booked. Some indices of market potential—such as population density, average household income, and transportation access—should also be incorporated into the analysis. An analysis comprising all of these considerations will provide a fairly precise measure of program performance.

The marketing process does not end at this step. Once the firm has researched, planned, executed, and measured the program in the manner set forth above, it is time to respond to the results of program measurement—and begin anew.

12. K.L. Barkley, "A New Method of Determining the Relative Efficiencies of Advertisements in Magazines," *Journal of Applied Psychology,* 15 (1931), pp. 390-410, and "The Demonstration of a New Method for Determining the Relative Efficiencies of Advertisements in Magainzes," *Journal of Applied Psychology,* 16 (1932), pp. 74-90.

13. For a discussion of origin markets and their definition, see the author's earlier article, "Post-Opening Marketing Analysis for Hotels," *The Cornell Hotel and Restaurant Administration Quarterly,* 19, No. 3 (November 1978), pp. 70-81.

Marketing for the Eighties

How to Develop an Advertising Strategy

Edited by William Q. Dowling

Bill Dowling is a marketing consultant to the hospitality and tourism industries and is president of Dowling Marketing, Inc.

An advertising strategy, known in advertising agencies as a creative strategy, is a blueprint, a map, a plan of attack, to make certain you're saying the right thing to the right people, simply and persuasively. That's how Jay Schulberg, Senior Vice President and Creative Director of Ogilvy & Mather, defines it.

Schulberg insists that a creative strategy be developed for every product his agency advertises. He believes it forces disciplined thinking by both the agency and the client. He points out that the most exciting advertising in the world, if executed to the wrong strategy, is practically worthless.

At Ogilvy & Mather, a creative strategy consists of six parts:
1. Positioning
2. Image
3. Objective
4. Target audience
5. Promise
6. Support

Good, effective advertising can be developed for your hotel or resort or restaurant or any tourist or guest accommodation by employing the following six steps:

From *Lodging* (September 1980) pp. 59 & 60. Reprinted by permission of *Lodging*.

1. Position Your Hotel Uniquely in the Customer's Mind

Ogilvy & Mather created these positioning statements for some of their well-known clients:
- TWA: The airline that's working hardest to make flying easier.
- American Express Travelers Checks: The safest way to carry travel funds.
- Marriott Hotels: The best all-around hotel for the business traveler.

There are a number of hotels or resorts that have positioned themselves uniquely in the highly competitive New York market:
- The Plaza: A famous hotel for top level executives. ("Nothing unimportant ever happens at The Plaza.")
- The Sheraton-Russell: A small deluxe hotel with personal service, appealing to European market. ("It's like a London Club in Mid-Manhattan.")
- The Tuscany: Sophisticated yet personalized service ("New York's biggest little hotel").
- The Park Lane: Luxury service and spectacular views of Central Park. ("The height of luxury in New York City soars 46 stories over Central Park.")

2. Create an Image That Reflects the Personality of Your Property

An image is the picture that comes to mind when your hotel is mentioned. For TWA, Ogilvy and Mather created a friendly image—"You're going to like us—TWA." For the American Express Card, they built the image of prestige by using successful people who most other people wouldn't recognize without their American Express Card—"Do you know me?" For the Pinehurst Hotel and Country Club, they are building an image of a special place that's an escape from the pressures of the '80s.

One of the images you'll encounter in the case studies of hotel advertising and marketing pro-

What's "right" about this ad?

Answer: The advertiser knows what distinguishes the Drake from other hotels: more employees per guest room. The message—better service—is communicated in creative terms.

grams in this series is for a small New York hotel with no meeting space. It features personalized attention to guest needs as "the hometown hotel in the heart of Manhattan."

3. Know What You Want Your Advertising to Communicate

The objective of your advertising should be written clearly and tersely in one sentence. It should state what you want your advertising to communicate. For example, the objective Ogilvy and Mather developed for KLM Royal Dutch Airlines—"is to create an awareness of Amsterdam as an exciting place to be."

We are all aware of the example of the rental car company that advertised "We try harder." The Drake in Chicago communicates a similar message of better service but in a different way. Their positioning is that they have more employees per guest room than any other hotel in Chicago, and used a headline which included ". . . A thousand years of personal service" (see illustration).

4. Decide Who Your Customer Will Be

The target audience is the best potential market for your hotel. It is determined by five things:
1. Age
2. Sex
3. Income
4. Education
5. Psychological Make-up

For example, the Turtle Creek Inn in San Antonio aims its message directly at business executives (they advertise "treats for Workaholics" such as sauna, tennis, et al following business meetings).

The Seven Seas Lodge in San Diego was positioned for the value-conscious customer by using the line "Hotel comfort . . . at motel prices." The Howard Johnson's Northside in Danvars, Massachusetts has been more straightforward in their travel trade advertising. Their headline to travel agents is "Send us your families . . ."

5. Understand Your Hotel's Most Important Benefit to Customers

The benefit is the promise to the consumer. What does your hotel or your hotel's services mean to your customers? What are the most important benefits to that customer? Ogilvy and Mather does a great deal of "promise testing" to determine the strongest, most meaningful promise.

In one of the case studies that will be reviewed in this series, a fictional chain of deluxe motor inns discovered they were the only chain of inns located exclusively on the North-South routes to Florida. Most of their guests were Florida-bound and were looking forward to leaving the fast, harsh pace of their Northern city. This chain was positioned as the only chain providing ". . . all the charm of the South" on the way to Florida.

6. Support Those Benefits With Facts

What supporting facts do you have for the promise you are making about your hotel? In the terminology of advertising agencies, *support* is sometimes called *reason-why*. For example, when American Express Travelers Cheques took the positioning of "Safest way to carry travel funds," the promise was quick, reliable replacement of funds around the world. The *support* or *reason-why* for this promise is that American Express has more offices around the world than any other competitor. A *reason-why* is not always necessary, but it gives credibility to your promise when that promise is similar to that of a competitor's.

If you watch television commercials for the packaged goods products of such giants as Procter & Gamble, General Foods and Lever Brothers, you will notice that they always support their promise. For example, the reason Dove is better for your skin (promise) is that it is one-quarter cleansing cream (reason-why).

Now put these six steps together in one complete strategy statement. Keep it all on one sheet of paper, stated simply. Include positioning, image, objective, target audience, promise and support. And remember, the purpose of a creative strategy is to make certain you're saying the right things to the right people, very simply, very persuasively.

Marketing for the Eighties

Why the Medium is the Message

Edited by William Q. Dowling

Parts I through IV summarize concepts on Positioning, Strategy, Media Planning and Budgeting. Articles V through XIII will follow the case study format.

Articles appearing on the following pages on media planning and budget development are parts of a series with subject matter as follows:
1. *Creating the Right Identity for Your Hotel*
2. *How to develop an Advertising Strategy*
3. *Why the Medium is the Message*
4. *A Guide to Planning the Marketing Budget*
5. *Marketing to the Individual Business Traveler*
6. *Marketing to the Travel Agent*
7. *Marketing to the Pleasure Traveler*
8. *Marketing to the Meeting Planner*

9. *Marketing Restaurants in Hotels and Motels*
10. *Marketing Lounges and Entertainment*
11. *Marketing to Build Chain Identity*
12. *Marketing a New or Renovated Hotel*
13. *Marketing a Tourist Destination (Location)*
14. *A Marketing Checklist for the Hotel Industry*

Contributors, in addition to editor William Q. Dowling, include top executives of 10 of the most successful advertising firms in America, and an equal number of the most effective hotel marketing executives. All participated in a 1980 Advanced Advertising Workshop presented by AH&MA's Marketing Committee and the Hotel Sales Management Association International.

Marshall McLuhan's over-quoted statement from the 60's, "The Medium IS the Message," is highly relevant today. The typical American is said to be exposed to as many as 1500 ads or commercials each day. He or she tunes out most of them but pays a great deal of attention to others. That's why the selection of proper media—like the projection of the proper image—is more essential today than ever before.

"You must provide a suitable environment for your message," Larry Stoddard told an AH&MA/HSMA Advanced Advertising Workshop this year, "because the proper medium will help insure that your ad or commercial will create the desired action or attitude from your customer." Stoddard is vice president and director of communications of Young & Rubicam, Inc. in New York. He said that "proper media selection can

add significantly to solving your marketing problems."

Packaged goods companies like Procter & Gamble, General Foods and Lever Brothers, pioneered professional media planning techniques. In the travel industry, airlines and credit card companies began making those techniques work for them only in the past 10 to 15 years. And the hotel companies have been even slower in adopting sophisticated media planning. Too often, hotel companies have selected media on a basis of personal preferences, special issues on specific destinations, or a promise of "editorial cooperation."

Before proceeding further, let me "position" this article in the series on "Marketing for the 80's," of which it is a part. The series will include 10 case studies of hotel marketing solutions. But before getting down to the case studies, we are basing four articles on four speeches made by distinguished advertising men at the AH&MA/HSMA Advanced Advertising Working mentioned above.

From *Lodging* (October 1980) pp. 62-65. Reprinted by permission of *Lodging*.

These reports will, I hope, help the lodging industry understand the basic principles of advertising that are applied by other industries and how they may be (and sometimes are) applied by this industry. The case studies will follow, showing actual application to marketing solutions.

Two introductory articles in the series discussed Positioning, or identifying your hotel in the market, and strategy Formulation.

Two additional introductory articles discuss Media Planning and Selection, and Budgeting.

So back to our series. Below, we consider how professional agencies such as Young & Rubicam use specific disciplines to insure that media planning is a vital part of the marketing process.

Five Essential Steps in Media Planning

Media selection is, at its most basic level, money management. You the hotel manager must select media, in which to spend your advertising dollars, with the same seriousness you would apply to the selection of vendors of food or beverages, supplies or equipment.

Here are five basic steps used by Young & Rubicam in media planning:

1. Assessment of the marketing environment (i.e., of your sales objectives, your prospects, and your competition).

2. Evaluation of important media considerations (among them, dollars available, target audience, how many people are to be reached and how often).

3. Media evaluation that is creative rather than limited to numbers (cost per thousand).

4. Review of available media research to understand how to reach potential and current customers most effectively.

5. Negotiation and purchase of the selected media.

I will try, on these pages—and with Larry Stoddard as the major resource—to provide you the hotel executive with information you need to work effectively with your advertising agency. I will not try to tell you everything you would need to know to write your own media plan. For that, you must rely on the media buyer and account team at your advertising agency. They have had years of experience from which you can benefit.

What this article will help you become is a better informed client.

1. Assess the Marketing Environment

The media planning process starts with an assessment of the marketing environment. This means defining the hotel's sales objectives, its best prospects, and its competition.

You will recall that previously we discussed how you and other members of the hotel's management team (a) make a written analysis of the hotel's services and benefits to the customers; (b) state corporate and long range goals as they relate to marketing strategy; and (c) define problems in meeting sales objectives; also, options and opportunities.

2. State Key Media Considerations

• *First, make a statement of the available budget.* This means dollars available, not how dollars will be spent (which is covered later).

• *Second, identify your target audience.* Your target audience—or best potential prospect—should be defined in numerical terms. For example, the target customer for a well-known Caribbean destination is stated as: "*. . . upscale adults with a family income in excess of $35,000 a year, college-educated, age 35-55, residing in the Northeast United States, with two children under age 16.*"

If you are marketing a city hotel, your target customer might be defined as "business executives earning over $25,000 annually, making more than 10 business trips a year, and residing in the following seven cities which are the major sources of visitors to our city . . . etc." You name the cities.

Remember, the more precisely you define your target audience, the easier it will be for your advertising agency's media buyer to develop your media plan.

• *Third, decide whether you want to reach many people a few times or fewer people many times.* You must decide whether to emphasize Reach (how many people see your ad) or Frequency (how often the same people see it).

Most marketing experts agree that Frequency is more important than Reach for hotel advertising because travelers tend to decide on hotel accommodations on the spur of the moment. If he can get by with it, the business man often makes his hotel reservation the day before he makes a trip. He is more likely to remember hotel advertising if he saw it this week than if he saw it a month or two ago.

By contrast, when a package goods company like General Foods introduces a new product, they may be willing to reduce frequency in order to reach more people with the news of the new product. Once a "user profile" for the product has been established, however, they may revise their media plan to emphasize Frequency over Reach.

• *Fourth, make yourself heard above the crowd.* Make an impact. If you cannot afford a television schedule that will be heavy enough to be noticed, forget television. Put your dollars into a medium where you can afford to make an impact.

For example, a half-page newspaper advertisement inserted every week will build frequency impact whereas a 60-second TV commercial scheduled once a week will not. The TV commercial will fail to dominate the medium or build any degree of frequency against anyone but the heaviest viewers—who are likely in the age/income category outside your target market.

Here's an example. The Bermuda Department of Tourism developed a high-impact, 4-color magazine campaign. Bermuda's competitor, the Bahamas, outspends them by a large margin with an effective TV spot. Since Bermuda lacked a large enough budget to be effective in TV, they chose to be a dominant advertiser in magazines.

3. Evaluate Media Creatively

The standard measure of media efficiency is called "cost-per-thousand" or CPM. That means the cost of your ad or commercial divided by the number of thousands of people reached by your message. In other words, a $5.50 CPM means it is costing you $5.50 for each thousand people you reach, or $5,500 per million.

With television and radio, CPM is a good measure of the effectiveness of a particular schedule once you have determined the type of programming in which your messages should appear. When considering magazines, however, Larry Stoddard of Y&R says, "We usually go beyond CPM and Reach."

At Y&R, a magazine is evaluated by questioning the quality of its circulation in addition to its CPM. Does it utilize significant amounts of cut-rate or discount circulation? Is the circulation growing or shrinking?

Stoddard says that a direct editorial analysis is done of each potential magazine. Is the editorial material likely to be of specific interest to the potential prospect of the advertiser? Does the editorial environment compliment the ad? Does the weight of the editorial matter enhance the believability of the ad?

Many times the cost per thousand makes sense but the editorial environment is wrong for the hotel ad. Don't be afraid to discuss your instinctive judgment with your agency.

4. Review Available Media Research

Stoddard says that media research is a critical element in day-to-day media evaluation and selection because it provides information in the following three critical areas:
a. Data about the target audience you are seeking.
b. Measurements about how each medium will deliver your message to its circulation or audience; how much duplication there will be from one medium to another (for example, how many readers of Business Week also read the Wall Street Journal); and how frequently you will expose your message to the same audience.
c. Feedback on how effective your advertising message is.

There are over 30 companies regularly involved in syndicated or special media research . Much of the expense of the various research studies is paid for by the individual publications or TV stations. The positive findings of these studies are used by the advertising representatives of the various media in their sales call.

You've probably heard a media representative say something like this: "Our magazine reaches more adults who earn $35,000 or more family income and who stay in first class hotels than any other magazine." Ask the rep if he will let you see a copy of the entire study the magazine commissioned—not just the excerpts. If he's allowed by the publisher, he will show not just the highlights but the entire study, from which you'll be able to judge the relative merits of all the magazines being compared.

Of all the major national research companies, there are two that are best known. The A.C. Nielsen Company, the largest, provides estimates of TV viewing (called "ratings") by use of a measuring device in 1200 sample homes. They supplement this with a diary sample to give data on people's behavior. Nielsen measures both network TV and local stations. Demographics are limited to age and sex. No product information is available.

The oldest of the existing magazine measurement services is the Simmons Company, now known as the Simmons Market Research Bureau (SMRB). SMRB measures about 140 magazines annually and also provides usage data on more than 500 product categories including hotels and motels.

There are many other research companies providing standard services and others offering custom services. If your advertising agency recommends use of a research firm you've never heard of, ask them to provide you with a list of the firm's clients and make your own judgments.

Whereas hotel companies often will commission market research studies themselves, most media studies are paid for by the media or subscribed to by the advertising agency for use by their clients. The larger the ad agency, the likelier it is to subscribe to at least Neilsen and Simmons.

Simmons Market Research Bureau reports that heavy travelers (adults who stayed 10 or more nights on business during the last year) skew to the 35-44 year old age group, have family incomes in excess of $35,000 annually, and hold professional or managerial types of jobs.

Not surprisingly, these heavy travelers are most frequently exposed to a combination of newspaper and outdoor advertising. Magazines also score heavily with frequent travelers.

Business travelers show up in high percentages among the audiences of upscale, special interest publications like *Fortune* or *Gourmet*. They do not show up as well in a publication like *Outdoor Life,* for example, where the blue-collar, male-oriented audience demographics do not parallel those of the frequent hotel user.

Stoddard is able to reveal general information from the SMRB reports subscribed to by Young & Rubicam, but he is not allowed to reveal specific details. He notes these general facts of interest to the lodging industry.

• There is a wide difference between media read by users of different types of hotels and hotel chains. One major chain found that customers of their hotels have a media usage (i.e., publications read, etc.) pattern that is diametrically opposed to that of customers of another major hotel chain.

• Frequency of travel is, obviously, not the only customer characteristic that varies; customers of different hotels will vary significantly in income level, education, life style, and business orientation.

5. Negotiate When Purchasing

Media costs are skyrocketing. Y&R's media department estimates that local radio costs will go up 46% over the next five years; magazine costs will rise 62%; newspaper advertising costs will increase 61%. Therefore not only proper media planning but also professional media buying is essential.

Don't be afraid to ask your agency to explain how they can get you the most for your money. Many times, radio stations will sell spots at a discount if you are willing to wait until the week before air time and buy what they haven't been able to sell. Princess Hotels did this successfully in the New York area. You have to weigh the risk of not getting the schedule you want against the price advantage in such a deal.

Some magazines will offer discounts if you give them the flexibility of scheduling your ad a month earlier or later, depending upon the availability of space. And during slow periods of the year, many media will offer special prices if you are willing to make a large commitment to them. Don't forget Stoddard's comment that "Media Planning is the management of money"

Always Monitor Results

The best media plan can sometimes be based on incorrect marketing assumptions. So it is important to monitor your results month by month. This is easy to do if you are in print, by coding your ads and by asking your guests where they read about your hotel.

If you have given a media plan time to work—say, six months or more—and you are not getting the response you wanted, analyze the results. If you think a particular magazine or newspaper is not working, ask your agency for an analysis of why and possibly an alternate recommendation.

If you have aimed your entire plan at upscale travelers and find that they are not interested in your hotel, try revising the plan to reach travelers with a slightly lower demographic profile. Even the best of plans can benefit from a little Monday morning quarterbacking.

Profiles of Heavy Users of Hotels

By age location employment household income

Index to total population

Adults who are:	Stayed 10+ nights on business
AGE	
18-24	72
25-34	129
35-44	153
45-54	117
LOCATION	
Living in North East	76
North Central	101
South	88
West	144
EMPLOYMENT	
Professional/ Managerial	300
Craftsman/Foreman	104
Clerical	95
LIVING IN HOUSEHOLDS WITH INCOMES OF:	
$35,000+	294
$25,000+	218
$20,000-$24,999	103
$15,000-$19,999	74

By frequency of exposure to media

Index to total population

Heavy users of:	Stayed 10+ nights on business
Newspapers/Outdoor	204
Magazines/Newspapers	187
Magazines	159
Newspaper	147
Outdoor	139
Television/Outdoor	97
Television-Prime	70

By frequency of exposure to six magazines

Index to total population

Read:	Stayed 10+ nights on business
Fortune	381
Gourmet	207
Elks	219
Time	199
Field & Stream	107
TV Guide	91

By chains: education, income and media usage

Adults who:	Chain A	Chain B	Chain C	Chain D
Graduated college	158	116	259	169
Have HH Income of $35,000+	171	105	320	192
Have HH Income of $15,000-$19,999	93	121	59	103
Who read:				
Fortune	111	70	296	192
Field & Stream	167	103	94	123
Listen to radio: (Type)				
Beautiful Music	110	128	99	138
Classical	83	74	184	94
Soft Rock	165	40	93	74

By courtesy of Young & Rubicam Source: SMRB '78/'79

How to Select Advertising Media More Effectively

by Howard A. Heinsius

Howard A. Heinsius, president, Needham & Grohmann, Inc., advertising agency, is a former boy soloist in New York City choirs, World War II navigator, USO entertainer, Cornell University Glee Club tenor soloist, hotel barkeeper, night housekeeper, sales manager, vice president, treasurer, director; president of the Cornell Class of 1950; president of the Cornell Society of Hotelmen. He is the husband of Marilyn Heinsius, the father of Diane, Lee and Lynn, a sometime convention speaker or tenor soloist, and an occasional sensation at whatever performance he happens to be giving at the time.

A competent advertising agency keeps abreast of marketing information and is certainly knowledgeable about the creative and media functions of advertising. It is important, however, for you as a hotel or motel marketer to also have a working knowledge of the various media at your agency's disposal so that there can be intelligent agreement with, or revisions of agency recommendations. This also helps in coordinating local and national efforts in advertising and promotion.

The most significant vehicles of the 20th Century are the electronic broadcast media: radio and television. In less than a half century, they have revolutionized communications, creating immediacy and shared experience on events, news and entertainments as they happen.

First radio and then television dazzled the world's population. Now they have become a daily habit (almost obsession). There is no question that these two electronic media dominate public interest. In fact, they have over 80% "share of mind" for major media (the exact amount depending on whose figures you believe).

Radio Advertising bureau currently puts "share of mind" of the major media at: television 45%,

From *Lodging* (May 1977) pp. 33-35. Reprinted by permission of *Lodging*.

radio 41%, newspapers 8% and magazines 4%. The Television Bureau of Advertising states that television's share of the time spent by adults is 53%, radio 32%, newspapers 9% and magazines 6%. Either way, radio and television enjoy at least 85% "share of mind."

Let's briefly examine each of the major media, first, in terms of their statistics, and then how each might fit into your media mix locally. (Magazines are excluded because they are seldom local.)

Television

Television has blossomed into the ultimate advertising medium: sight-sound and now color (in over 70% of U.S. homes) with an added boost from cable TV. Television now occupies about 25% of its listeners' 24-hour day—an average of 6 hours, 14 minutes.

The growing popularity of daytime TV adds another dimension to this medium. However, as a "success medium," television suffers from too many spot announcements.

Radio

Radio has found a new niche which complements rather than competes with television coverage. Where once radio was a mass medium reaching out for a total audience group, it now has become a "personal medium" that speaks to individuals in specific segmented groups. Thus, there are all-Black radio stations, Spanish radio stations, classical music, rock, top 40 and country music stations, all talk (including news) stations, etc. Each of these forms of programming can deliver a defined audience group with excellent cost efficiency.

Besides this, radio has become fully mobile— battery-powered sets, auto sets—to reach an almost exclusive audience on the move. This "drive-time", 7 a.m. to 9 a.m. and 5 p.m. to 7 p.m., is a prime listening period for radio. Significantly, radio has grown as a medium along with television (rather than declined) which demonstrates the compatibility of the two electronic media.

Newspaper

Newspapers are the original news and advertising medium. They are primarily a local advertising medium with over 1738 morning and evening newspapers reaching about 63 million circulation daily. As such, they dominate local advertising 72% (or $6,745 million) while having a 14.7% share of all national advertising ($1,165 million).

The local advertising dominance, however, is now under heavy attack from television stations who are aggressively seeking more local business. But newspapers provide an information medium that gives readers up-to-date news coverage in-depth and unmatched by any other media. Further, newspapers can cover local, state, regional, national and international news in a continuous manner.

Newspapers also offer excellent coverage of a wide range of special reader interests such as: business, finance, stock market, fashion, grooming, cooking, recipes, sports, hunting, fishing, science, society, television, other entertainments, travel and astrology and many others on a regular and continuing basis.

Newspapers enjoy a close identity with their community. They are, in effect, a "public utility"—a service medium for both readers and community. Besides this, newspapers, as a shopping medium, help create a market for products and services. Another important aspect of newspaper advertising is the structured format (and sections).

Newspaper advertising rates tend to favor local advertisers (particularly if on contract) with a rate differential of about 50% less for local advertisers. This has mitigated against the growth of national advertising.

Incidentally, our agency is one of the largest users of newspapers for travel advertising in the country. Over the years, we've sorted and sifted, analyzed and researched the newspaper as an advertising medium. We've developed 15 guidelines which are essentially error-proof.

I'm glad to share with you our 15 guidelines for publication advertising, and to add 12 essentials for media selection. The two checklists complement each other. I hope that, studied together, they will help make your advertising of your property and its facilities more professional and more profitable.

The 12 Essentials in Media Selection

• **Market focus.** Take a close look at your market by product category/brand, by areas/cities, etc., by identified product demand, by target market groups. In this context, how does your hotel fit in? How does it rank? And what do you want to advance?

• **Media focus.** Take a fresh look at the media in your market area. Get a current review/data on each newspaper, television and radio station, and outdoor plant. Keep an "open-door" policy for all media representatives, with "open eyes" and "open ears" for the facts. Be alert and watchful for changes, events, new programs, new editions for whatever opportunities they may offer you.

• **Periodic media update.** In terms of rates, costs per thousand, audience, circulation, etc., start with a new set of rate cards—and from there negotiate until you come to a firm market price. Constantly review new research data to see if it can deliver advertising more effectively for your hotel. Markets and media are in a constant state of change. Stay up with it.

• **Set basic media effectiveness yardsticks.** Set basic media yardsticks with which to measure the effectiveness of media advertising. Use such data as:

Reach. How many households/persons (unduplicated) does a specific medium buy deliver?

Frequency. Weekly/monthly, etc., per buy? How often does your message reach?

CPM. Cost per thousand readers/viewers/listeners.

Target Market Group. Since it's too expensive to reach the broad public at large, it is best to focus on the best target market group by sex, age, ethnicity, etc. *Continuity* and cumulative effort are necessary to achieve an effective impact on the market.

• **Advertising by objective.** Set definite objectives for your advertising, including a sales forecast, consumer awareness (before and after), and exactly what you are trying to achieve. Is your media effort the best way to do it? What other supporting elements will you utilize?

• **Coordinate your advertising with marketing campaigns.** Since advertising is but part of the marketing mix, it should be coordinated with the other elements, such as sales, distribution, promotion, etc., to work effectively. Don't just run ads. Make the ads part of a marketing program.

• **Use your ad budget properly.** Start with what you can afford and then allocate it by subject (entertainment, weekend package, C & I, etc.) and by market. Make sure that whatever you budget is sufficient to do what you set out to do. Don't overspend, or underspend, and don't fritter away your budget over too many small buys. When you make a buy, make sure that it is enough to create an effective impact on consumers. Achieve the reach and frequency needed to get the proper action.

• **Plan your way around "Media pollution."** No one talks much about the fact that there are now too many products, in too many ads/commercials aimed at a very finite and weary audience. Clutter comes in many forms: 100-page newspapers that are chock full of ads, back to back. The same with many magazines.

While radio and television have pushed back the "annoyance threshold" of listeners/viewers with the amount of commercial announcement that a person must be exposed to in a few minutes' timespan, clutter is still a problem. There is no simple cure for "media pollution," but a sensitive awareness can lead to stronger impact commercials/ads, and buys that sometimes are a little less cluttered. The smart advertisers are doing both and buying more spots to make sure that they get through.

• **Plan and coordinate local/national effort.** Make full use of national advertising as an "umbrella" of advertising on your market (this assumes your corporation runs a national campaign). Plan local advertising to work with it. Reap the harvest with well timed, follow-up effort. Also, coordinate sales and promotion efforts in such a way as to maximize the benefits of national advertising. It's a "tail wind" to drive home more sales.

• **Mix and match media.** Within the limits of budget and effective buy levels you should try various media combinations to see which works best and/or more economically for you. Using the proper mix of media is a fine art that pays big dividends in effectiveness.

• **Keep documented records of each advertising campaign.** This should fully document each advertising campaign, including: budget, media schedule, ad or commercial used; timetable, sales results (before, during and after). Thus, when you do something very successful, you have all the details to repeat it when desired.

• **Keep alert for special buys.** Radio and television time is a highly perishable commodity, somewhat like a block of ice on a warm, sunny day. It doesn't keep. There are times when radio stations (television less so) are anxious to sell time for a current, upcoming period. If you have the money, they have the time. Don't adopt the posture of a perennial "bargain hunter," but keep a sharp eye open and keep close contact with stations that you might want.

15 Guidelines for Publication Advertising

1. Color advertising has a 50 percent advantage over black and white.

2. Full-page ads have a 67 percent advantage over half-pages.

3. There is no distinct advantage for a lefthand page or a righthand page of advertising. Both get about the same readership.

4. Front, back or middle positions in a magazine or newspaper offer no significant advantage over each other.

5. The thickness of a magazine or newspaper has a moderate effect on readership—

   • For 80 to 160 pages, readership scores are 45 to 35.

   • For 40 or less pages, readership scores are about twice that high.

   • For more than 160 pages, scores drop to below 35.

6. Ads on the back cover pull much higher readership than those inside the publication. The back cover pulls 65 percent more readers than the middle section.

7. Readership does not increase proportionately with ad size. Message and position within the publication make for efficiency quite outside the space unit.

8. Tall-column ads attract more attention than square ads. Vertical ads pull better; horizontal ads don't stop readers as well as vertical ads.

9. The meaningful headline, and the dominant focal point, are the most important characteristics of an ad in stopping readers.

10. Continuity of advertising is important. Assuming a readership level of 20 per cent, it takes six insertions to reach 75 per cent of the publication audience, 12 insertions to reach 95 per cent.

A 40 per cent readership gets 78 per cent after three insertions, and 95 per cent after six.

A good ad should be run at least three times. This allows it enough exposure to begin paying its own way.

11. There are three levels of readership: first, when a reader notes your ad; second, when he sees it and associates with it; third, when he reads it actively.

The degree to which a reader will become a customer hinges on the readership he gives your ad.

12. The six points that generally attract high readership are: dominant attention-getter in headline or text; people in action around product; provocative claims; buyer benefits; specific and concrete offerings, and believeable copy.

13. Readership scores drop slightly with length of copy. A poster-type ad (75 words or less) usually pulls slightly better than a text ad (more than 75 words), but the difference is small, and the sales message dictates what will be read.

Though brevity is favored over wordiness, length of copy is a secondary consideration.

14. It is desirable to advertise in publications that have a built-in audience for your type of service or product, and in those publications, to advertise in sections appropriate to your offering.

15. Bizarre, attention-getting (but not thought-provoking) ads don't pull well. They may irritate instead of ingratiate.

Beware of the cute ad that doesn't really say anything.

Advertising That Sells Hotels

A veteran advertising practitioner discusses the principles of effective advertising for lodging properties

"Advertising for hotels is still unsophisticated—but it's improving," observes one of the advertising industry's most accomplished practitioners. As executive vice president of Spiro and Associates, Norman R. Tissian counts among his responsibilities the marketing and advertising functions for more than 40 individual hotels and hotel operating companies. To complement his 25 years of experience in advertising for the hospitality industry, Tissian calls on the wide-ranging expertise developed by his firm in serving diverse clients, from the manufacturers of packaged goods to accounting firms and universities.

Begin at the Beginning

Hoteliers embarking on an advertising campaign make their most crucial—and common—mistake, Tissian maintains, when "they fail to realize that designing the ad is the last thing to be done, not the first." Effective advertising is the result of a careful analysis of a property's strengths and weaknesses; only after completing this assessment can management proceed to develop a strategy, which is then translated into an advertising message. Tissian enumerates the requisite steps to be performed before advertising is created:

1. Establish management's perception of the subject property.
2. Ascertain the market's perception of the property.
3. Develop a positioning statement for the property.
4. Select advertising's target audiences.

This article was originally published in the November 1979 issue of *The Cornell Hotel and Restaurant Administration Quarterly*, pp. 17-23, and is reprinted here with the permission of the Cornell University School of Hotel Administration. '1979.

The rudiments of this approach are applied in various ways, depending on the property under analysis and the conclusions reached at the individual steps. To illustrate the process, Tissian cites examples drawn from his firm's numerous engagements.

1. Management's perception of the property. Deriving and expressing management's view of the subject property is not difficult, Tissian points out, but verifying its accuracy often is. Hotel managers hardly bear sole responsibility for their overestimations of a property's position in the market; in fact, the misconceptions typically commence with the developer, whose view of a property's potential is frequently colored by his personal commitment to the project. Developers' optimistic expectations are communicated to management and adopted without critical evaluation of their appropriateness to the type of property and the market it operates in. As a result, among the advertising executive's first responsibilities is to evaluate objectively management's perception of the property's position in the market, providing the impetus for management to reassess its strategy.

When analyzing the market segments they serve, many hotel managers fail to make full use of data available to them, relying instead on imprecise impressions regarding the origins of their business. Even managers who supplement firsthand observation with the review of registration requests, guest folios, and the pattern of commission payments to travel agents typically fail to define with accuracy the prime sources of their rooms business. Again, an orderly, objective review of the facts available will often yield a breakdown of the composition of the hotel's clientele that is divergent from management's view.

As an example of the difficulties management

The positioning statement can be explicit . . .   *. . . or more subtle.*

may face in correctly evaluating a hotel's status and appeal, Tissian describes the case of a downtown hotel located in a major U.S. city. A full analysis of the property's current position and its likely prospects in the future revealed that its primary market had become group business and that, based on the recent development of several luxury properties in the market area, the subject property could not hope to regain its former status as a rather exclusive transient hotel. Although management accepted some aspects of the plan developed to capitalize on the hotel's competitive strengths, Tissian observes, "the general manager believes deep down that the hotel can capture the top-rate, expense-account business traveler—and he's going to operate that way, all evidence to the contrary."

2. The market's perception of the property.
Testing the market's view of a property frequently requires field research, but this need not be intricate or expensive, Tissian points out. A methodology used by Spiro and Associates to assist

Chicago's Whitehall Hotel in discerning local residents' perception of the property offers a case in point.

To assure that the results of the research would reflect the views of members of the demographic group likely to frequent a hotel of the Whitehall's caliber, blind questionnaires were mailed to owners of late-model Jaguars and Mercedeses. Questionnaire recipients were asked to discuss their impressions of seven downtown Chicago hotels, including the Whitehall, five other exclusive properties, and—to test whether the respondent was able to distinguish a luxury hotel—a large convention property. The questionnaire results showed that many Chicagoans either thought the hotel was private (because the property also contains a private dining club) or that it served primarily "high-society dowagers." Since management and Spiro had determined that the hotel's location, amenities, and service positioned it to appeal strongly to top-level executives, evidence of the market's quite contrary perception was important information.

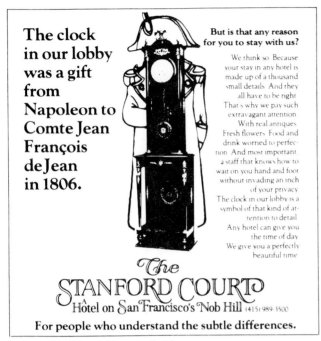

The clock
in our lobby
was a gift
from
Napoleon to
Comte Jean
François
de Jean
in 1806.

But is that any reason
for you to stay with us?

We think so. Because
your stay in any hotel is
made up of a thousand
small details. And they
all have to be right.
That's why we pay such
extravagant attention.
With real antiques.
Fresh flowers. Food and
drink worried to perfec-
tion. And most important,
a staff that knows how to
wait on you hand and foot
without invading an inch
of your privacy.
The clock in our lobby is a
symbol of that kind of attention to detail.
Any hotel can give you
the time of day.
We give you a perfectly
beautiful time.

The
STANFORD COURT
Hotel on San Francisco's Nob Hill (415) 989-3500

For people who understand the subtle differences.

A sense of tradition and a touch of whimsy

Similarly, a client operating a resort hotel was able to identify its ethnic clientele readily, but management needed to know the extent and nature of the property's appeal to a wider spectrum of persons in the same ethnic group. A telephone survey was conducted to poll both frequent guests and nonguests, asking for their impressions of the property. By comparing the responses from the two groups, the agency's personnel and the hotel's management were able to identify positive aspects of the guest's experience at the property that needed to be touted in the advertising subsequently developed. Conversely, both users and nonusers pointed to the negative images of the property that needed to be combated by advertising.

Finally, Tissian notes that there are two very simple forms of research that often yield important insights into the market's perception of a property. First, those responsible for developing a hotel's advertising should sample the guest experience, bringing to their evaluation of the property an objectivity management often cannot provide. Second, advertising executives can often provide helpful insights to management by discussing a property's position with other hoteliers. "After all," Tissian observes, "who's better qualified to help the GM analyze his property than another hotel manager?"

3. Developing the positioning statement. After management and its advertising agency have iden-

tified the property's competitive strengths and weaknesses, the results of this analysis are articulated in the form of a positioning statement. The positioning strategy reflects a conscious decision on management's part to communicate to the market a definition of the property as a particular type of hotel. Above all, Tissian emphasizes, this definition must be consistent with the property it describes, and it must be reinforced by advertising and management's delivery of the product promised.

A hotel's positioning statement is given full narrative treatment in its marketing plan, but a succinct version of it appears in the property's advertising. For example, advertising created by Spiro for Houston's Adam's Mark Hotel (preceding page), scheduled to open in 1980, is explicit in its description of the hotel's niche in the market: "... *the flair and style of a Hyatt. The efficiency and courtesy of a Marriott.*"

The advertisement designed for Chicago's Whitehall Hotel (preceding page) is more subdued in its tone but no less explicit in its positioning statement: the Whitehall is a businessman's hotel, but for the upper echelons. That the advertisement is aimed at the *local* business community is not a copywriter's whim but an important part of Tissian's strategy for getting across a hotel's positioning statement. In Tissian's view, the local business community is the conduit by which the business traveler to the area receives his impressions of a property and develops a perception of its position in the market. Moreover, Tissian notes that, in a very direct sense, the local resident controls much of the business channeled to an individual property by exercising veto power when meetings are planned in his home city and by making individual reservations for incoming business associates.

As another example of how a positioning statement is expressed in a hotel's advertisements, Tissian points to his firm's work for San Francisco's Stanford Court. The message (above) is a straightforward catalog of the old-world amenities and service awaiting the guest: "... *real antiques. Food and drink worried to perfection ... wait on you hand and foot ... attention to detail ...*" But lest the reader conclude that the hotel, in keeping with its turn-of-the-century traditions, is stuffy and pretentious, the playful device of sketching in a caricature of Napoleon lightens the tone and refines the positioning statement expressed by the copy.

4. Select your target audiences. Although management may be able to identify numerous market segments whose lodging needs, dem-

"Berkshire Place" opens to lavish praise from critical hotel audience.

"Superb. A personal hotel in the classic manner. The kind New York's needed for years." — *Floyd S. Glimert, corporate executive*

"What a splendid place! A welcome haven in an overcrowded, overhurried world, with service to match." — *Dyan Nelson, business traveler*

"The supporting cast is peerless. The *Rendez-Vous* is a wonderfully sophisticated restaurant/bistro. Their *Atrium Bar* is a perfect place to relax and have a drink, any time at all." — *J.P. Lowell, advertising executive*

"All New York's its stage. The Madison and 52nd location puts the city's business, shopping, shows, and museums right at my door." — *Isaac Segal, writer*

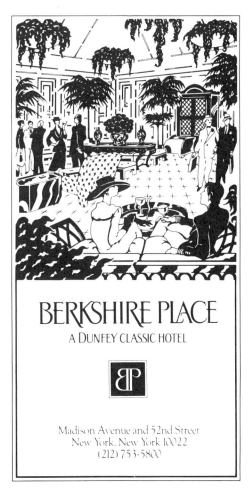

BERKSHIRE PLACE
A DUNFEY CLASSIC HOTEL

Madison Avenue and 52nd Street
New York, New York 10022
(212) 753-5800

"Couldn't imagine a better atmosphere for getting my business done. Efficiently. Productively. And pleasantly." — *Gerald D. Oakes, corporate treasurer*

"The Dunfey Hotel people have done it again. They've created another masterpiece of taste and style — just as they did with the Ambassador East in Chicago and the Parker House in Boston." — *H. Robert Lesnick, art consultant*

"BRAVO!"
— *Kathy Ivens, TV producer*

Other Dunfey Classic Hotels: Ambassador East, Chicago and Parker House, Boston. For all Classic Hotel reservations phone 800-225-2121.

Consumer advertising should be custom-designed for the medium used; the above appeared as a full-page ad in The New York Times.

ographics, and tastes match the product it is offering, advertising efforts must be directed to those segments likely to yield the largest number of room-nights. The target audiences selected for advertising describing American Hotels' new Puerto Vallarta property, for example, were carefully chosen to maximize the response. Puerto Vallarta's location, although a perfect illustration of the "splendid isolation" theme carried through all the property's advertising, removes the hotel from serious contention for the convention and association meetings market. For incentive travel, however, the remoteness and tranquility of the location enhance its appeal. Group-business advertising was directed therefore not to the meetings and conventions market but to some 200 incentive houses. In a decision motivated by similar considerations, consumer advertising was virtually omitted in favor of advertising to selected travel agents, including those engaged in tour wholesaling and west-coast

retail travel agents. It was reasoned that the latter would prove an efficient producer of business because of the modest air fares from west-cost origin cities and the greater likelihood of client familiarity with Puerto Vallarta. Travel-agent wholesalers were viewed as a means of generating business from the broad mass of consumers who, though unfamiliar with Puerto Vallarta, could be informed about the property by the travel agent.

Creating the Ad

Having defined the target audiences to which it will direct its advertisements, management and its advertising agency are prepared to develop the messages appropriate to each. Although there are subsegments within each target audience, Tissian identifies three broad groups and suggests considerations to bear in mind when addressing each.

- *Consumer advertising.* The cardinal rule gov-

The back and front covers of a brochure advertising Adam's Mark

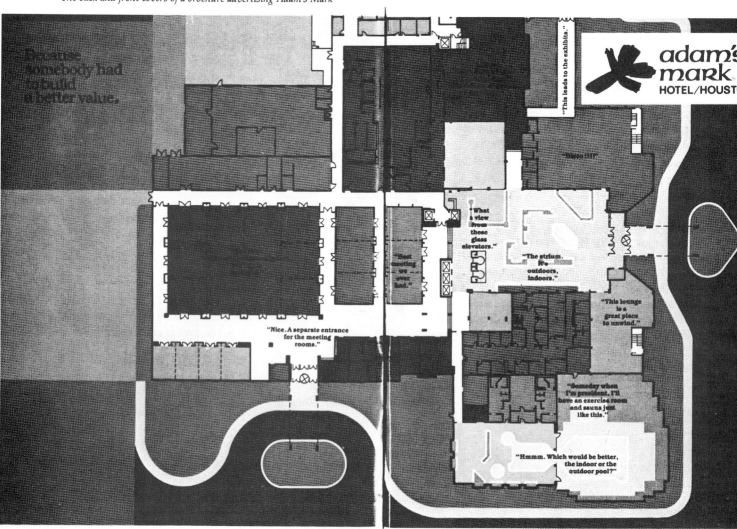

*In advertising directed to travel agents, communicating a distinctive image
is secondary. The primary intent is to impart
essential information about the hotel's positioning, facilities, and rates.*

erning this category of advertising is, according to Tissian, "Create with the prospect—not the general manager—in mind." The most prevalent violation of this precept is advertising that uses, as its primary illustrative feature, a photograph of the exterior of the subject hotel. "Very gratifying to the general manager," Tissian observes, "but what can the prospective guest learn about the hotel from an aerial view?"

Architecture's dictum, "less is more," applies to consumer advertising as well, Tissian notes. The aim of advertising directed to the consumer is to motivate him to try the property—but advertising has achieved its maximum impact if the prospect stays *once* at the subject hotel. Too many hoteliers, Tissian argues, ignore this primary intent of hotel advertising, succumbing to the temptation to overload advertisements with distracting detail describing minutiae of the services offered. The "one image, one ad" rule of thumb may *appear* to give the hotelier less than his money's worth, says Tissian, but it sells more rooms.

Finally, consumer advertising should be custom-designed for the medium selected to carry it. A recent example from Spiro that demonstrates the application of this precept is the advertisement for New York's Berkshire Place Hotel (page 263), which appeared as a full-page ad in *The New York Times.*

● *Advertising to travel agents.* Creating evocative advertisements that communicate a distinctive image for the hotel is a secondary concern in advertising directed to a travel agent. The primary,

more utilitarian objective of travel-trade advertising is to impart essential information regarding the hotel's positioning, facilities, and rates. The basic task of informing does not require the same subtlety as the effort to influence—as evidenced by the "Americana Man" cartoon appearing here.

Despite the simplicity of the approach, the Americana Man campaign displays careful thought and communicates much information. First, the Americana Man character, in addition to capitalizing on the Superman vogue, is an attempt to provide a unifying identity for the quite disparate properties Americana manages. While poking gentle fun at the travel agent unable to satisfy his persnickety—and price-conscious—clients, it provides full information on the property's amenities and recreational facilities, as well as a summary positioning statement ("the biggest Dutch treat in the Caribbean"). Finally, to facilitate the travel agent's day-to-day task, the advertisement provides a mnemonic rendering of the "800" number and an IT number.

Whenever possible, Tissian advocates the use of two measures of consumer and travel-trade advertising impact: coupons and packages. Although returned coupons are not necessarily converted to sales, they offer reliable feedback on advertising's ability to generate interest in the hospitality product. By offering packages in its advertisements, management can measure advertising's effectiveness directly by charting sales of the plans. Moreover, the pricing of packages constitutes an important positioning statement: travel agent and consumer alike are able to infer the price-value relationship of the subject hotel from the prices and features of the packages offered.

• ***Advertising for group business.*** The needs of this target audience are similar to the travel agent's: to derive an impression of the property's positioning and to learn the basic facts regarding its facilities. "Advertising for the group business market should be informational only," Tissian notes, "because personal selling consummates the sale."

The convention and meetings brochure designed by Spiro for Adam's Mark (page 264) illustrates Tissian's emphasis on communicating essential facts. Eschewing the typical architect's rendering as the cover illustration, the brochure features a complete floor plan of the hotel's public rooms and meeting facilities. The brochure's interior pages are similarly functional and direct, providing more details of the layout and design of the hotel, describing the food and beverage outlets and the expertise of the meetings-services staff, as well as depicting the hotel's location in relationship to Houston's attractions and transportation facilities.

In Conclusion

Colorful and creative advertising can be very impressive, Tissian concludes, "but it won't necessarily sell the property." First the hotelier must take a hard look at his hotel, and then apply logic and experience to create effective advertising.

Rediscovering Direct Mail:
A Primer for Hospitality Firms

by Robert T. Reilly

Robert T. Reilly is a professor of communications at the University of Nebraska at Omaha. He is the former vice president of Holland Dreves Reilly, Inc., one of Nebraska's largest advertising firms, has served as a consultant to the Ford Foundation, and is the author of several books on travel marketing. He received his M.A. from Boston University in 1948.

Direct mail is being touted in some quarters as a hot new marketing medium for American business. Far from being new, however, this advertising technique has been around in some form for over a century—helping to nourish organizations as diverse as Sears, Roebuck & Company and Amnesty International. Although it fell into disuse as a marketing tool when television lured away a large share of many firms' advertising dollars, it is now becoming both more prevalent and more reputable.

Is direct mail an appropriate advertising vehicle for hospitality firms? Managers considering adopting direct mail as a marketing tool should compare their firms' needs against the following list of direct mail's positive and negative attributes before making a decision.

Direct Mail: The Reasons For

On the plus side, direct mail offers these features.

• It is selective; it can deliver messages to very specific target audiences. (In comparision, television and print media deliver messages to a broad audience including large numbers of people with no interest in your product.)

This article was originally published in the May 1982 issue of *The Cornell Hotel and Restaurant Administration Quarterly*, pp. 46-51, and is reprinted here with the permission of the Cornell University School of Hotel Administration. ©1982.

• It permits a more personalized approach to advertising. Automatic typewriters and advanced printing techniques allow firms to produce mailings in which customers are addressed individually.

• Competition is limited. The number of competing direct-mail pieces your audience receives on a given day in no way approaches the clutter of radio, television, and newspaper ads they are exposed to. In fact, your message might be the *only* one some customers receive on a given day.

• Restrictions are far fewer than with other media. Without the constraints of 30- and 60-second time slots or limited column widths and color capabilities, you can make your message as long as you choose and select the color and paper most appropriate to your mailing. Additionally, your direct-mail offering can conform to one of hundreds of possible sizes and shapes and can include gimmicks, pop-up art, or other attention-getting devices.

• Scheduling is more convenient than with other media. Direct mail allows considerable control over when the material is produced and mailed. (In comparison, hospitality firms using magazine advertising and television spots are often boxed in by deadlines or forced to maneuver to secure prime-time spots.)

• Direct mail offers customers a convenient means of responding. Mailing packages may contain return postcards or envelopes, coupons, or other means of provoking and simplifying customer response.

• Direct mail offers hospitality marketers an easy method for monitoring results. Mailings can be specially coded to permit a count of replies by list, geographical area, alternate messages, or other variants.

Direct Mail: The Reasons Against

On the minus side, direct mail presents its users with the following problems and constraints:

- Compiling and maintaining accurate mailing lists have always been difficult tasks; an increasingly mobile population renders this job even more challenging today than in the past.

- As a medium, direct mail still has a somewhat tarnished image. Labeled "junk mail" by critics, it has historically lacked the prestige of other forms of advertising.

- Attractive and effective direct-mail packages are relatively difficult to create. While most firms develop imaginative advertising campaigns for other media, they often handle direct mail routinely. Even when the copy and layout are well conceived, too few firms do their "homework" in list selection and other aspects of direct-mail marketing.

- Although television is regarded as the most costly advertising choice, direct mail isn't exactly cheap. The price of paper, printing, and postage all have soared in recent years, as have the costs of compiling, buying, and maintaining lists.

- Direct-mail users must adhere to a multitude of postal regulations governing size, weight, compatibility, format, and zip coding.

Lists: Homemade

House lists are generally the most productive lists for hospitality firms. These are rosters of regular customers, clients, or guests, or a census of past consumers. Since the individuals on these lists are already familiar with your firm, having patronized it in the past, they make an excellent audience for direct mail.

Among hospitality firms, travel agencies use house lists most frequently as a marketing tool. In contrast, most hotel firms keep guest lists but rarely use them for promotional efforts. Instead, they should consider actively using such lists to direct follow-up letters to recent guests or periodic mailings to regular travelers. In doing so they may help position their properties in the minds of hundreds of potential return customers.

Restaurants have less access to house lists, but those that accept reservations could expand reservations information to include customer address. Some restaurants ask guests to deposit their business cards in a box—for prize drawings and so forth—thereby compiling their own lists. Such lists can be used to send good-will messages, newsletters, announcements, and special offers.

Assembled Lists. In addition to compiling house lists, some service organizations assemble rosters of names, using such sources as the Yellow Pages, city directories, club and organization lists, and collegiate files. Hospitality firms with a clear sense of their target markets could develop their own assembled lists.

Lists: Commercial

If your operation chooses to buy a commercial list, the list selected should be limited to include only the most likely prospects for your product or service. If you are selling something directly by mail, search for lists of persons who have previously made a purchase through the mails. The item or service purchased may have been totally different from what your firm is offering, but those on the list remain good sales prospects because they have previously demonstrated a trust in purchasing through the mails.

Available commercial lists are myriad. It is possible to buy lists of individuals in particular professions (e.g., doctors), persons who have donated money to particular charities, members of clubs and trade associations (including, for example, the American Hotel and Motel Association), owners of high-priced foreign cars, and persons subscribing to various magazines. One may also specify refinements of a given list—asking for names of doctors in the southwest, for example. Depending on the intended audience for a direct-mail piece, a commercial list broker should be able to offer the hospitality operator a range of potentially productive list choices.

Prices for such lists and regulations regarding their use may vary. The list supplier should point out these differences to the hospitality firms that purchase them. The cost of a list may range from $20 per thousand names to $50 or more per thousand names. The price differential is usually based on the quality of the list—which reflects how the list was compiled, the nature of the names, and the regularity with which the list is updated.

When you purchase a list, you are, in effect, renting access to a series of names and addresses. The firm marketing the list usually provides addressed envelopes or labels, allowing you to use the list only once for the specified charge.

Selecting the Best List

One obvious advantage of the purchased list is that the list broker "cleans" it at least once annually, dropping and adding names and addresses and correcting inaccurate information. A good list broker can also tell you what response a list has produced for other mailers and can point out some of its problems.

Lists compiled by a hospitality firm must also be maintained by that firm. If you choose this route, your company must develop some means of keeping the list (cards, Addressograph plates, computer cards, and so forth) and some routine for recording the numerous changes of address or title that will surely occur.

If you know what you want, selecting the best list is relatively simple. A travel agency desiring a list of middle-management personnel within a specific locale can probably locate one. A hotel seeking a statewide list of professional people should have little trouble finding one. In both of these cases, of course, the purchaser must be certain that the list he buys is the right one for his needs.

When you are not sure who your target customers are, research the field if you can afford it, and use common sense if you cannot. Pinpoint the most likely users of your service, and how they can be identified. Observe which age group dominates your clientele, and whether your typical customers are predominantly male or female. Find out whether their occupations or income levels affect their decisions about your product or service.

Once you have determined these things, read about available lists, investigating their demographic composition. In addition, be sure to ask the various list distributors for information on list "pull" (response) and available refinements. Finally, settle on several lists and try them out.

A word of caution: Perhaps you find a list of 150,000 professional men and women. Don't buy the entire list. Test 5,000 names first. If the test mailing pulls well, try 10,000. If the response holds up, pursue a larger number.

How can you tell whether the response is good? This will depend both on the nature of the list and the uniqueness of the offering. Most advertisers conducting an initial national mailing would consider two percent a more-than-adequate response. For a house list or a list that really zeroes in on the top prospects, a higher return might be expected. Some institutions, for example, have received a 30-percent return on a mailing to friends, but only a 1½-percent response on a "cold" mailing to persons never approached before.

The nature of the mailing also affects returns. Is the advertiser asking for donations, selling an expensive item, offering something for free, suggesting an office call, requesting a coupon response, or presenting news about a new program? All of these options have different degrees of appeal.

Writing the Direct-Mail Piece

Advertising copy should be terse, colorful, arresting, convincing, and complete. It needn't be grammatically perfect, but it must produce measurable results.

The writer who creates the copy for your firm's direct-mail piece should be familiar with your product or service. He must know what it does, how it stacks up against competitors' offerings, and which of its features are unique. Above all, he should be able to discern its specific benefits for prospective customers.

A good writer should emphasize the difference between your firm's product or service and the offerings of competing firms. As an example of this approach, one well-known hotel chain promises its customers a good night's sleep. Another builds a campaign around convenient locations. A third focuses on lower rates.

Good advertising consists of discovering something unique to say, and then saying it in a compelling manner. It should involve more than cleverly superimposing an image on a product. Accordingly, the copywriter you choose should know far more about your firm than will be captured in the few lines of prose.

Besides knowing about the product or service, the copywriter must also know something about the audience. A good copywriter arms himself with information about his readers and tailors his message to them, addressing them in their language and at a level they understand.

The Format and the Formula

How should your message be presented? A tried-and-true copy formula— "AIDA"— suggests stimulating *attention, interest, desire,* and *action* from readers, in the following manner.

Attention. In successful direct-mail pieces, reader attention is captured immediately. The prospective customer is enticed into opening the package by an intriguing message or design on the envelope that provokes curiosity. Inside, another arresting feature follows—a colorful illustration, perhaps, or a clever headline or the lead line or a well-written appeal letter.

Interest. Once the reader's attention is ensured, interest should be retained by the promise of a reward. Touting your restaurant as the oldest in the city or pointing out that your hotel was the first in the area with a computerized accounting system means little to the consumer asking the question,

SOME EXAMPLES: In a direct-mail effort targeted at top-producing travel agents, Princess Hotels issues "Travel Talk," an industry newsletter with information about new properties, renovations, expansions, and special packages. The source of a full 85 percent of Princess's individual bookings, travel agents are also among those on the rolls to receive "broadsides" like the one depicted above, created by Jessica Dee Communications.

Although most Americans who specify European delivery of a new Mercedes Benz spend four to six weeks touring Europe after the car is delivered, no hotels actively solicited the business of these prospects until Robinsons, Inc., created the package at right for Grand Metropolitan Hotels. The package included a description of the touring program and participating hotels, information on European auto delivery, and a price list.

The reply cards are still coming in from this recent mailing designed to inform meeting planners about the newly constructed conference center at the Palmer House in Chicago. The work of Gardner, Stein and Frank, this piece allowed the hotel's salespeople to identify qualified leads.

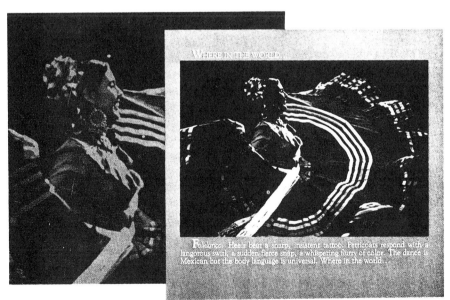
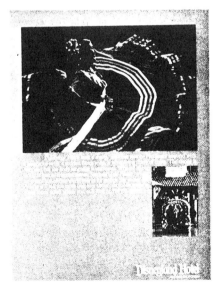

This second GSF effort targeted to meeting planners, with information about the Disneyland Hotel's new "Seaports of the Pacific," comprised several "teaser" mailings (in which the hotel's name was not divulged) and a final package encompassing four complete ads for the hotel.

"What will it do for me?" Specify the consumer benefit in the copy that follows.

Desire. Interest should lead to desire. The prospective customer now wants to sample this meal or this service. But doubts persist: *Nothing can be quite this good. Maybe there are hidden charges.* Good copy dispels such fears and makes the prospective customer know about, want, and believe in your offering.

Action. Finally, some form of action should be solicited. Your direct-mail piece should ask for a response: "Send for a free booklet today," "Phone us for a reservation, using our WATS line," or "Drop by our offices to pick up a brochure." Successful advertising copy emulates the sales approach in which the salesperson classifies a potential client, provides information, anticipates questions, narrows down objections, targets in on positive responses, and then closes the sale.

As with direct sales, direct mail involves presenting the hospitality firm's story to consumers in such a way that all their queries are answered. The tone should be conversational, with the writer eschewing long, latinized words and concentrating on ordinary language.

Make sure the copy leads off with your best selling point, and closes with a similarly potent statement calling for some form of action. Between these extremities, your story should be spelled out logically and punctuated, wherever possible, with your operation's name. Sentences should be short, but varied. Because everything counts, use no extraneous words. The emphasis should be on ways the reader will benefit, with secondary attention paid to qualities of the service and proof of claims.

Your brochure need not be extravagant to be effective. Sometimes exceptional copy can compensate for a modest printing job. Even if the brochure is simple and uses only a single color, the prospective customer will be inclined to read it from start to finish if it is written in a highly readable style.

Production Considerations

Graphic elements are just as important as text to the success of a direct-mail piece. While the copy sells the product to the reader by furnishing information, proof, and encouragement, the design induces him to open the package and further supports the offer—perhaps through strong illustrations, sharp color combinations, or a clever visual gimmick. Whatever the approach, the words and the pictures should be conceived simultaneously when your direct-mail package is designed.

Four Not-So-Easy Pieces

Direct-mail packages typically consist of four elements: the letter, the brochure, the return card, and the return envelope.

The letter. Modern style in mass-produced letters has moved away from cold salutations like "Dear Friend," and substituted such narrative hooks as "Do you feel awkward when the waiter presents the wine?", or "I don't trust any travel brochure . . ." These phrases, functioning as headlines, serve to get the reader into the body of the letter. Once the reader is hooked, the remainder of the message should be personal, conversational, and credible. The writer should not go into great detail here (he should save that approach for the brochure). Instead, he should focus on the strong selling points of your product or service, creating a receptive mood, and stimulating the reader toward further reading or a decision.

The brochure. This is the principal selling tool in every mailing. It spells out the case for your firm in greater detail, utilizing effective graphic elements, breaking up the copy with subheads, and focusing on claims and proof of claims. These pages show what your hotel or restaurant has to offer—with particular emphasis on those attributes that are unique.

Copy in the brochure should be terse and to the point, like the writing style of a magazine or newspaper ad. The story begins, unfolds, and ends, with a strong concluding statement. Whatever lends itself to illustration should be illustrated.

You can spend a lot of money on a brochure, or very little. For example, a three-week tour of Europe may require an elaborate four-color production, while a less expensive approach might suffice for a brochure advertising a weekend at a ski resort.

The response items. The card, return envelope, return postcard, coupon, or other device intended to elicit replies should be more functional than creative. It might contain some elements of a sales pitch or be decorated with typographical pleas to "Mail Now," but its main purpose should be to get all the information needed from the prospective customer and to make responding as simple as possible.

Virtually all direct-mail marketers supply postage-paid return envelopes. Prospective customers can mail back their replies without charge, and advertisers are billed only for the envelopes that are returned. Return cards and envelopes can easily be coded so that the mailer can identify the source of replies. Different box numbers, and inconspicuously placed letters and numbers, are typical coding devices.

Doing a Better Job With Direct Mail

How can you produce first-rate direct-mail packages that deliver results? A few suggestions:

• Collect and save direct mail that you find appealing, whether because of its graphics or copy. In particular, save samples that relate to your own industry.

• Consult the experts. Visit list houses and discuss lists with brokers. Inquire about varieties of paper available with paper-company sales representatives. Take a tour of a print shop and learn how publications are printed. Talk with copywriters, artists, and production specialists for their views on the production process.

• Attend professional seminars on direct mail. [1] Enroll in courses on direct mail at nearby colleges and universities.

• Read available materials. Journals like *Advertising Age* [2] and *Adweek* [3] often have features on direct mail. *ZIP*, a Philadelphia-based publication, is devoted entirely to direct mail, carrying articles on everything from collecting bills by mail to protecting house lists. [4]

• Consult available books on direct mail (there are a number of excellent ones); write to paper companies for free brochures on direct-mail techniques. [5]

• Experiment with lists and packages. Don't get in a rut with names or approaches. Look for new ways to appeal to consumers, and new ways to find them.

Conclusion

Hospitality firms that advertise should consider direct mail as a means of reaching existing and potential customers. To make the direct-mail route work for them, they should begin by selecting reliable lists and designing direct-mail packages that emphasize benefits to the consumer. Firms that follow these recommendations will rediscover an effective marketing tool and, through it, enlarge the market for their products and services.

1. For more information, contact: Direct Mail Marketing Association, 6 East 43rd Street, New York, NY 10017. The DMMA conducts regular seminars on direct mail in a range of locations.

2. For more information, contact: *Advertising Age,* Crain Communications, 708 Third Avenue, New York, NY 10017.

3. For more information, contact: *Adweek,* 820 Second Avenue, New York, NY 10017.

4. For more information, contact: *ZIP,* 41 North Broad Street, Philadelphia, PA 19108.

5. For more information, contact: S.D. Warren Company, 225 Franklin Street, Boston, MA 02101.

Newspapers: The Bread-and-Butter Medium for Hotel and Restaurant Advertising

by Harry A. Egbert

The immediacy, flexibility, and relative economy of newspaper advertising makes it a useful tool for filling hotel rooms and generating restaurant business

Harry A. Egbert is senior vice president of Spiro & Associates, a Philadelphia-based advertising agency with more than 80 hospitality clients. Formerly Spiro's media director, Egbert is now responsible for marketing and planning.

More advertising dollars are spent on newspapers than on any other medium, and for good reason. The advantages of newspaper advertising are many. While broadcast advertisements may seem a necessary evil to the radio listener or television viewer, whose primary interest is in being entertained, readers turn to newspapers in search of information—indeed, often specifically in search of advertisements. As a result, newspaper readers are in a frame of mind conducive to receiving advertising messages. Newspapers also offer advertisers the benefit of timeliness, in many cases allowing them to place an advertisement overnight. Furthermore, the cost of preparing and placing newspaper advertisements is far lower than the costs of radio and television advertising.

When a hotel or restaurant operator wishes to advertise in a local market or to reach residents of another area, newspapers are the logical medium. The immediacy of the newspaper renders it especially well suited for advertising designed to generate a direct response; the hotelier will find it useful for selling a weekend package, for example, while the restaurateur can use it to inform prospective patrons about a special holiday meal. Finally, because the medium is flexible, it can be used in a variety of ways. The operator undertaking a national campaign can design different advertisements for various papers, tailoring each advertisement to the local audience it will reach. Advertising can be designed to build image or to generate rooms, restaurant, and function business. The considerations applicable to newspaper advertising vary, depending on the objectives the advertiser wishes to meet.

Building an Image

The reputation a hotel or restaurant enjoys in its community is important to the facility's business, and newspaper advertising is one route by which a property's image can be enhanced. It should be noted that newspapers are generally not the first medium considered when a hotel or restaurant tackles the image problem, because the operator generally concentrates such advertising in media—especially radio [1]—that allow him to address specific demographic groups. Few newspapers are addressed to a specific, limited audience.

The broad base of the newspaper audience, however, can be useful in building awareness of an establishment among such individuals as taxicab drivers and the employees of competitive establishments—in other words, persons who are not generally themselves prospects but who are in a position to influence those who are. There are two basic approaches to take in advertising of this kind. The advertiser can run a regular leadership message (combined, of course, with a promotional

1. Harry A. Egbert, "Radio Advertising for Hotels," *The Cornell Hotel and Restaurant Administration Quarterly*, 21, No. 1 (May 1980), pp. 31-36.

message), or an occasional announcement regarding renovations, new services, and so forth. Many advertising practitioners believe that occasional large ads (such as a full newspaper page) are more effective for image-building than smaller, more frequent ads are.

Building Rooms Business

Newspapers are an effective medium for·advertising designed to attract the transient guest. As a first step, of course, the operator must define the desired effect of the advertising. Does he mean to stimulate weekend or weekday business? Whose business does he seek? To which end of the market does he wish to direct his efforts? The answers to these questions will determine such matters as the best position for the advertisements and their timing.

To reach the business traveler, for example, an advertisement should generally be placed in either the business pages or the early pages of the news section. Vacationers, however, are more likely to notice an advertisement that appears in the travel section. Although some hotel operators fear their advertisements will be lost in the clutter of competitive messages if placed in the travel section, most people considering a vacation already have a destination or two in mind and will turn to the pages in which they can "shop" for a hotel.

A different approach is required to advertise "escape weekends" and other special offers directed to guests in the property's area. Because most local readers are not actively looking for such offers, the amusement pages or radio-television section may be most appropriate; the sports pages can also be considered, depending on the nature of the offer.

Where in the newspaper an advertisement should run depends on its size as well as on its intended audience. The larger the advertisement, the less important its position. A small advertisement is likely to have the most impact if it is placed with competitive messages, because the reader looking for a specific type of offer will generally read all of the advertisements pertaining to such offers. Although the largest ad in a cluster will attract the most attention initially, such other factors as the advertisement's copy and design ultimately determine their relative effectiveness.[2]

An advertisement that makes a specific offer is usually more productive than one making only a general offer. As a result, the operator may wish to invite inquiries about a particular package rather than requests for a general-information brochure. When the advertisement is addressed to individuals other than local residents, the inclusion of an "800" number is generally helpful (along with the suggestion that readers contact their travel agents).

Building Restaurant and Function Business

Advertising designed to fill a restaurant necessarily differs from advertising designed to fill hotel rooms or to enhance an establishment's image. Many newspapers run "restaurant guides" in their pages, but the value of such guides is open to question. They are generally not an effective tool for reaching consumers at the upper end of the demographic spectrum unless the newspaper has developed an especially impressive and well-established format for the section in which the guide appears. Most restaurant guides are read only by locals contemplating a special-occasion visit to a restaurant they would not normally patronize, and by visitors from out of town (who have a range of other dining-out guides at their fingertips).

The most logical position for dinner advertising may well be in the entertainment section, because dinner out is so frequently associated with such other activities as going to the theater. Many newspapers publish a special weekend guide to entertainment, and such guides may be appropriate for restaurant advertising. In cities where major sporting events are held frequently, advertising on the sports pages should also be considered, while special holiday offers might best be placed in the early pages of the general news section, where they will be seen by most readers.

It is generally more difficult to promote luncheon business through advertising than it is to generate dinner sales. (Incidentally, that a restaurant serves lunch should be noted in its dinner advertising.) Although restaurant patrons are willing to travel a considerable distance for a dinner out, most people choose a lunchtime restaurant largely on the basis of its proximity to work or home; consequently, the results possible through luncheon advertising are somewhat limited. Patrons may consider a restaurant's prestige or decor when selecting a place to dine with business associates, however, so the operator might consider promoting luncheon facilities on the business pages of the local newspaper.

2. For a discussion of design considerations in print advertising, see: Peter C. Yesawich, "The Execution and Measurement of a Marketing Program," *The Cornell Hotel and Restaurant Administration Quarterly*, 20, No. 1 (May 1979), pp. 41-52.

In most restaurant advertising, the operator should note which credit cards are accepted (if no cards are accepted, this should be noted), and should provide a phone number for reservations. Depending on the type of restaurant and the purpose of the advertising, menu prices might also be noted. It is a good idea, for example, to mention price when advertising special holiday dinners.

Finally, although filling function rooms is the responsibility primarily of the sales staff, newspaper advertising can sometimes be of value in stimulating function business. For example, the operator may wish to alert office managers to the availability of function rooms for Christmas parties, or to announce expanded facilities for business meetings.

Placing the Advertisement

In most markets, the advertiser has a number of papers to choose from and can apply a number of criteria in evaluating their usefulness for his purposes. Total circulation is not the only important criterion in choosing among major metropolitan dailies. The demographic makeup of each paper's audience is unique, reflecting not only the paper's editorial tone and policies but also the time of day (morning, afternoon, or evening) at which the paper is published. Hence a precise definition of the advertisement's intended audience is essential to newspaper selection.

In addition to the major metropolitan dailies, the advertiser should consider suburban and regional dailies and weeklies, whose numbers continue to grow; because their rates are based on a limited circulation, advertising in such papers is often more cost-efficient than advertising in larger dailies serving a wider area. They offer a good value to the operator who wishes to reach the specific audience served by a limited-circulation paper.

Many metropolitan dailies have reacted to the proliferation of regional papers by publishing "sectional editions" devoted to the news of a specific community and included in only those copies of the newspaper distributed in that community. Rates for advertising in these editions are lower than those for advertising in the paper proper, and are usually comparable to the rates of the suburban or community newspapers with which these sections are designed to compete. Although sectional editions appear to offer a good advertising buy, many advertising practitioners believe their readership is limited and note that it is difficult to receive preferred placement (e.g., accompanying the business pages or the entertainment features)

for advertisements on these pages.

Further complicating the issue of newspaper selection is the plethora of special-interest and ethnic newspapers. In some communities, papers aimed at Spanish-speaking, Jewish, Catholic, black, or student audiences may be an appropriate choice, depending on the market the advertiser wishes to reach.

Especially in a major metropolitan market where daily and weekly newspapers abound, the advertiser is well advised to rely on professional help in the task of media selection. The advertiser wishing to compare newspapers himself, however, will find comprehensive information on newspapers' circulation, rates, and advertising requirements in the reports published regularly by the Audit Bureau of Circulation and Standard Rate and Data Service. (A sample entry from such reports appears in this article.) Most individual newspapers also conduct frequent readership studies, and—although a newspaper is likely to accentuate the positive in its presentation of findings—these studies can yield useful insight into the demographic composition of a newspaper's audience.

The Considerations

Although newspaper advertising offers many benefits to the hospitality advertiser, the unique requirements and problems of advertising in this medium must be considered when the advertising campaign is planned.

Rates

Most rate cards reflect an accumulation of practices designed to stimulate certain categories of advertising and to limit others. As a result, instead of giving a single rate predicated on an advertisment's size, a rate card will generally list separate rates for general advertising, retail advertising, classified advertising, and (often) hotel and restaurant advertising, as well as rates for advertising in special sections. A hotelier who runs several advertisements in a single edition of a single issue may pay a different line rate for each advertisement. Within each category, the rate is based on the number of agate lines (14 agates = 1 inch) in the advertisement. Many newspapers also offer discounts for prompt payment, as well as quantity discounts for several advertisements run at once or for a series of advertisements run on a regular schedule.

Many newspapers give a more favorable rate to local advertisers than to national firms. (In fact, most newspapers have separate rate cards for these two groups of advertisers.) Partially in response to this local-national rate differential, many national advertisers sponsor *cooperative advertising*—advertisements featuring the products or services offered by the national firm and available through a local business. Because the local firm places the advertisement, it receives the local rate. "Co-op" advertising is designed to generate business for both the local and the national adver-

tiser at a cost lower than each would pay if it advertised independently.

Sizes

All newspapers were once printed in one of two standard formats (eight columns per standard page and five columns per tabloid page), and an advertisement of a given width contained a certain number of lines, regardless of which newspaper it

---

Excerpts from a sample entry, Newspaper Rates and Data

The following items are representative extracts from *Newspaper Rates and Data,* a regular publication of Standard Rate and Data Service. They were compiled from entries for several newspapers listed in a recent edition.

MORNING AND SUNDAY

3. COMMISSION AND CASH DISCOUNT

15% to agencies; 2% cash discount. 15th following month, on general advertising only.

4. GENERAL RATE POLICY

60-day notice given of any rate revision.
Alcoholic-beverage advertising accepted.
All copy subject to publisher's approval.

ADVERTISING RATES

5. BLACK/WHITE RATES

	Daily	Sunday
Open, per agate line	6.00	7.10

General contract brackets in 1 yr:	Per agate line	
5,000 lines	5.88	6.98
10,000 lines	5.86	6.95
50,000 lines	5.79	6.89
100,000 lines	5.73	6.83

All full-page display ads (2,700 lines) will be charged 2,400 lines.

5a. ZONE EDITIONS

Sunday Metro	3.18
Sunday Non-metro	1.23
Saturday Metro	2.54

6. GROUP COMBINATION RATES — B/W & Color

General ads repeated in Saturday edition (within 3 weeks) 3.25 per line.

7. COLOR RATES AND DATA

Available: B/W 1c Monday thru Saturday.

Any special color inks other than standard colors not acceptable in main news nor all sections; Thursday: b/w 1c with special color inks acceptable. No color available Sunday main-news section; b/w 1c only in those Sunday sections printed early. No leeway required. All color booked firmly.

	Daily	
	b/w	b/w 1c
1 page	9,960.00	12,010.00
1,500 lines	7,125.00	9,175.00
1,000 lines	4,750.00	6,800.00

	Sunday	
1 page	11,640.00	14,100.00
1,500 lines	8,550.00	11,010.00
1,000 lines	5,700.00	8,160.00

Use b/w line rate plus the following applicable cost: 1,000 lines minimum to 1 page:

	b/w 1 c
Daily, extra	2,050.00
Sunday, extra	2,460.00

Closing dates: 2 days before publication date; 4 days for Thursday food section.

8. SPECIAL R.O.P. UNITS

POSITION CHARGE
Back page, 20% premium charge.

11. SPECIAL DAYS/PAGES/FEATURES

Best Food Day: Thursday. "Business Roundup," Tuesday. "Woman Alive," Wednesday. Automotive, Real Estate, Thursday. "Weekend," Friday. Television, Saturday. Travel, Sunday.

14. CLOSING TIME

Daily forms close: Midnight, 2 days before publication.

Sunday edition forms close: Main News Section, Friday 2:00 p.m.; Travel, Friday 5:00 p.m. (9 days before); Real Estate, Wednesday 8:00 p.m.

15. MECHANICAL MEASUREMENTS

PRINTING PROCESS: Photo Composition Direct Letterpress (Letterflex).

16. SPECIAL CLASSIFICATION/RATES

These rates are for ads ordered and accepted under designated classifications. Ads ordered elsewhere are charged general advertising rates, unless clas-

sification is higher. Position charges extra. Box charge 5.00; mailed 12.00.

Display ads of bonafide agencies promoting service of own agency, 20% from card rates, less contract discounts. No agency commission.

	Daily	Sunday
Amusements,[†] per agate line	6.00	7.10

[†]Ticket Agencies and ads with admission charge, min. 1 col. 14 lines; double column 28 lines deep. Amusement ads repeated Saturday (within 7 days) 3.25 per line. Ordered run of paper, amusement rates apply.

	Per agate line	
	Daily	Sunday
Restaurants	4.15	4.75
Within 1 year:		
13 days or 1,000 lines	4.00	4.60
26 days or 2,500 lines	3.95	4.55
52 days or 5,000 lines	3.85	4.50
Minimum 14 lines.		

*Political/Advocacy** (cash with order):

	Per line
Morn. & Eve.	3.22
Sunday	3.47
Saturday	2.55

*All Political/Advocacy advertising must enclose the name and address of the person authorizing publication.

POSITION CHARGES

Next to reading 15%; full position, publisher's option 33⅓%; special pages 15%. First and editorial pages not sold. Minimum depth for full position 56 lines.

18. CIRCULATION

Established 1881. Per copy, daily .10; Sunday .50.
Net Paid—A.B.C. 3-31-78 (Newspaper Form).

PRIMARY MARKET AREA CIRCULATION

	Total	Prim. Mkt.	Outside
MxSat	1,020,208	866,900	153,308
SatM	950,305	805,114	145,191
Sun	1,315,051	1,093,890	221,161

appeared in. About five years ago, newspapers made several format changes to conserve newsprint, which was then, and is still, in short supply. Because most newspapers acted independently, a lack of uniformity exists today among newspapers, with some using five columns, some six, some eight, and others nine. Many papers use different column widths for advertising columns and for news columns. As a result, a given amount of copy may be 100 lines long in one paper and 150 or more lines long in another. Many advertisers therefore prepare separate advertisements for each newspaper used. The alternative is to prepare one advertisement to the narrowest dimension among the newspapers used and to allow the ad to float in white space in the other newspapers used. In other words, the advertiser must choose between preserving the appearance of the advertisement and incurring the added cost of producing advertisements of the proper sizes for all of the newspapers used.

Position

Because newspaper pages are frequently made up under deadline pressure—when late-breaking news stories must be juggled into place alongside advertisements of many sizes and shapes—newspapers are not always able to give careful thought to the optimum position for each advertiser's message. A hotelier's small promotional message may be overwhelmed in a group of large advertisements or surrounded by advertisements for massage parlors. To avoid similar catastrophes, the advertiser should examine the makeup of several issues of a newspaper, and ask that his advertising be placed in sections where these problems are not likely to occur.

Reproduction

Because newspapers are printed by high-speed presses on a rough grade of paper, erratic ink coverage can compromise the reproduction of photographs. A photo that reproduces beautifully in a brochure or magazine may appear either dark and muddy or faint and lacking in detail when run in a newspaper. If a photograph *must* be used, it should be converted to a "screened" black-and-white print designed expressly for good newspaper reproduction. However, it is safer to use "line drawings"—art consisting only of solid black, with no tones of gray—for newspaper advertising.

Color

Most newspapers are able to offer the advertiser two kinds of color: *spot color*, one color (other than black) added to enhance an advertisement's ability to attract the reader's attention; and *R.O.P. ("run of paper") color,* full-color printing. The latter is rarely used by advertisers, primarily because the high speed at which newspaper presses roll can cause bad reproduction. However, research indicates that the use of spot color increases both readership and reader response significantly. [3]

Day of Week

The operator must consider his advertising objectives when deciding which day of the week an advertisement should run. An advertisement promoting a resort hotel's package clearly belongs on the Sunday travel pages, but hotel advertising directed to the business traveler probably belongs in a weekday paper.

Which weekdays are best? Monday is a light day for newspaper readership—except for the sports pages—because Monday's edition generally carries less hard news than other editions do. In most markets, either Wednesday's or Thursday's newspaper is cluttered with supermarket and food advertising. Since the advertising message should reach the business traveler early in the week, Tuesday may be the best day on which to use the business pages for advertising hotel accommodations.

In contrast to the selection of a hotel, the choice of a restaurant is often a last-minute decision. Consequently, the restaurant operator may find it most effective to run small advertisements every day rather than large advertisements on an infrequent schedule. However, in regard to advertising special-occasion meals—which generally require reservations—advertisements should probably be scheduled early in the week preceding the holiday. Finally, the weekend section published by many newspapers on Friday is the logical choice for promoting Sunday restaurant business.

Closing Dates

A newspaper generally accepts advertising up to a few days or even hours before an issue goes to

---

3. *Color in Newspaper Advertising: Is It Worth the Cost?* (New York: Newspaper Advertising Bureau, 1974).

Free newspaper "advertising"

In undertaking any campaign to generate local business or to enhance your establishment's reputation in the community, remember that many of your business activities are newsworthy.

• The opening of a new hotel wing, restaurant, bar, or discotheque should be announced in a newspaper's business pages or entertainment section. Distribute fact-filled news releases* and interesting, attractive photographs to the local media, and invite editors and reporters to your opening ceremonies (elaborate or unusual ceremonies may rate coverage in the paper's news pages).

• Any expansion, renovation, or relocation is worthy of ink. Even the acquisition of new equipment may warrant a news release — especially if it allows you to offer new products or improved service to customers.

• Publicizing the promotions of both employees and managers at your hotel or restaurant brings your establishment's name into the limelight, suggests to the public that you are a good employer, and has the added benefit of enhancing employee morale. Similarly productive is the announcement of employee awards, including service awards for long tenure and such other honors as you might devise ("Server of the Month," etc.).

• If a visiting VIP chooses to stay in your hotel or dine in your restaurant, take advantage of the opportunity for publicity by arranging for photographs or distributing an appropriate news release.

• Local readers should be informed of your community-service activities. If you've sponsored a local athletic team or youth group, raised funds for charity, established a scholarship program, initiated a program for needy citizens, or created a special rate for senior citizens, be sure the press knows about it.

• If you offer live entertainment, regularly distribute information (including a biographical sketch and a profile of musical style) on entertainers you feature.

• A good restaurant review can produce considerable business. If a newspaper that regularly runs reviews has not yet included you in its pages, try contacting an editor at the paper to extend an invitation to the reviewer.

• Many newspapers run occasional features about area hospitality establishments. Papers in areas with a sizable student population, for example, often publish a feature on area restaurants or taverns at the beginning of the school year. As a reader service, many papers also publish a guide to restaurants' offerings on special occasions — including Mother's Day — on which dining out is popular. To be sure your establishment is included in such editorial features, keep local newspapers informed about your activities — and keep yourself informed about the papers' editorial plans.

*The preparation of news releases and other aspects of publicity are covered in: Jacques C. Cossé, "Ink & Air Time: A Public-Relations Primer," *The Cornell Hotel and Restaurant Administration Quarterly*, 21, No. 1 (May 1980), pp. 37–40.

---

press. The advertiser should remember, however, that the closing dates for special sections—like the Sunday travel pages, which may be printed in advance—may precede the publication date by ten days or more.

"Pub-Set" Advertising

Many hotel and restaurant advertisers are tempted by the economies of "pub-set" advertisements—ads written, designed, and typeset by a newspaper representative, with the creative assistance of the advertiser. Although such advertising is far less expensive than that prepared by an advertising agency, most "pub-set" advertisements in a paper have a similar (often unattractive) appearance, limiting the advertising's effectiveness. Moreover, a newspaper representative is generally not the individual best qualified to develop advertising consistent with the operator's overall marketing strategy and objectives.

Conclusion

The newspaper may not offer the glamour of radio or television, but its timeliness, ability to generate immediate responses, and flexibility make it an important forum for hospitality advertising. Applied intelligently, newspaper advertising allows the hotelier or restaurateur to inform, persuade, and build image for both short-term and long-term results. The complexity of advertising placement and format, however, requires a professional, thoroughgoing approach to the definition of the advertiser's intended audience and the establishment of advertising objectives.

Radio Advertising for Hotels

by Harry A. Egbert

Like hotels, individual radio stations appeal to specific market segments. The ability to address an audience with the desired demographic and psychographic characteristics and the opportunity to strike trade agreements that allow you to promote your property without paying cash, make radio an ideal medium for advertising hotels.

In comparison to the manufacturers of toothpaste, automobiles, and other consumer products, hotel operators—particularly at independent properties—have relatively small advertising budgets. As a result, the dollars in those budgets must be carefully, yet skillfully, allocated for maximum effectiveness.

Radio is a medium often overlooked by the operator allocating his advertising dollars, but the nature of modern radio renders it a particularly appropriate tool for promoting hotels—both to attract rooms business from sometimes geographically dispersed target areas and to build the hotel's image in its own community. The importance of the local image to a hotel's success is well documented—many rooms reservations result from the recommendations of local residents or business contacts, and the volume of business in a hotel's restaurant and cocktail lounge depends to a great degree on local acceptance—and modern radio can be the most economical way to achieve local acceptance. It can be argued that radio is the only advertising medium whose audience is seg-mented along the same lines as the hotel industry's markets.

An Ideal Medium

Before the invention of television, radio was a mass medium, attempting to appeal to everyone through diversified programming. Today it is a highly specialized medium, with each station in a market tailoring its programming to attract members of a very specific demographic and psychographic group. It is this characteristic that allows hotels to advertise so cost-efficiently on radio in comparison to other media.

The rate paid for newspaper advertising, for example, is based on the total circulation of the newspaper. In effect, when a hotelier advertises in a newspaper, a good portion of his advertising investment is wasted on people in whom he has no interest—sometimes thousands of individuals who, because of their incomes, occupations, or other characteristics, are not members of his target market.

Although they are sometimes needed to provide directions to the property, outdoor signs are also priced to reflect the entire population of an area. Magazines, like radio stations, have become increasingly more specialized since the advent of

This article was originally published in the May 1980 issue of *The Cornell Hotel and Restaurant Administration Quarterly*, pp. 31-36, and is reprinted here with the permission of the Cornell University School of Hotel Administration. ©1980.

television; they offer many of the advantages of radio but do not allow the advertiser to achieve the frequency of impression or highly localized impact possible with radio.

In contrast to these other media, radio allows the hotelier to concentrate his advertising expenditures on persons with specific characteristics. One radio station can be used to reach executives and professionals, another to reach families, perhaps a third to reach young people or mature individuals. Even more important, different stations appeal to individuals with specific kinds of *tastes*.

Different radio formats and their audiences are discussed in the exhibit below. For effective, cost-efficient hotel advertising, the format of a station is more important than its power (geographic coverage), its ratings (the number of persons tuned in to the station), or the popularity of its personalities, because it is the format that determines the demographic and psychographic characteristics of a station's audience.

Because a hotel is also geared to attract members of specific demographic groups, radio advertising allows the operator to appeal to those groups only, avoiding the expense of advertising to the total population. An exclusive, prestigious hotel that caters to the executive traveler can direct its advertising specifically to upper-income, sophisticated individuals by using the appropriate radio station or stations. A commercial property can select the stations favored by salesmen, buyers, and other middle-management personnel. Similarly, a family hotel can confine its advertising to the proper demographic groups, a gourmet restaurant can be promoted to that segment of the population with gourmet tastes, and a swinging bar or disco can be advertised to young people only.

A Free Launch

Perhaps of equal importance to the hotel advertiser is the opportunity to use radio advertising without a major outlay of cash. Like unsold room-nights, unsold air time can never be recovered; like hotels, radio stations must dispose of their "inventory" every day. As a result, the hotelier will find radio stations receptive to "trade" or due-bill arrangements. Unfortunately, just as a hotel will honor a paid reservation ahead of a due-bill, radio stations tend to "bump" traded announcements if an advertiser willing to pay cash is interested in the same time period. To receive maximum cooperation, a hotelier contemplating a trade arrangement with a radio station should ideally work out a part-

trade, part-cash agreement, thereby ensuring that the advertising he depends on will actually be broadcast as scheduled.

There are a number of ways to work with a radio station for effective promotion. Conventional advertising, on a cash, trade, or combination basis, is one. In addition, most stations (particularly in larger markets) regularly need hotel facilities for promotional purposes. They will "trade out" radio time for cocktail-party facilities, or use hotel rooms or restaurant meals as contest prizes, often giving bonus announcements or extra commercials in exchange for such cooperation. Resort hotels can often achieve widespread coverage in target markets by developing mutually advantageous promotions with radio stations in those areas.

A cautionary note should be sounded in this discussion of trade or due-bill advertising: the rules pertaining to the *purchase* of advertising time should also be applied to the making of trade or due-bill arrangements. That no cash is involved is no reason to use a station whose audience is wrong for your hotel; indeed, it can hurt your image. If you cater to mature executives and you make a trade deal with a station whose rock-and-roll is beamed to teenagers, enough people will hear those commercials to create a suspicion that your image is changing; this perception could affect their recommendation or patronage of your property. As a good rule of thumb, if you wouldn't pay cash for it, don't trade for it.

Who, What, When . . . and How Much

You are well advised to obtain professional help in selecting a station and in creating commercials. Radio advertising calls for specialized skills, just as good newspaper and magazine advertising do. The following overview of the mechanics of radio advertising is offered on the premise that the more the hotelier knows about the medium, the better the job his advertising agency can do.

One consideration in selecting a radio station— AM stations versus FM stations—is no longer as important as it once was. In years gone by, AM was dominant and FM was thought to appeal only to those high-income sophisticates who could afford the static-free reception it provided. Most FM stations played only "good music," leaving news and other formats to the AM band.

All that has changed. Today, FM offers the same variety of sounds as AM—if not a *greater* variety—and in some areas, more people listen to FM than AM. Format and the skill of station management should now be given far more consideration than the broadcast band in selecting a station for advertising.

Similarly, the format of a station is more important than its ratings (reports on how many people are listening to a particular station at a particular time). Published by firms like Arbitron and Neilsen, ratings are constantly referred to by the sales representatives of the stations with the biggest numbers, but they are important only in a relative sense. It is not the size of the audience that counts for a hotel advertiser but rather the *composition* of the audience (by age, sex, etc.). This is the information to be evaluated in determining which station is most cost-efficient for your advertising. When rating data are submitted to you, make sure the statistics are organized in a way that provides the information you need, and always bear the format of the station in mind when evaluating these data. A classical station will usually have low ratings, for example, but the audience may contain the influential meeting planners or association members in whom your banquet manager is interested.

The Prime Times

When during the day or week should your commercials be scheduled to run? This is another

---

Knowing One's Station:
An Overview of Radio Formats

Most of today's radio-station formats may be categorized as *progressive, contemporary, MOR* (middle of the road), *news-information-sports, talk, good music, classical, country-and-western,* or *ethnic*. These terms can be refined further, but they cover the range of stations broadcasting today. Some of the terms are self-explanatory; others may be unfamiliar to the prospective radio advertiser. This overview will provide definitions of the less-familiar terms and sketch psychographic profiles of the audiences most likely to be tuned in to stations of each format type.

A **progressive** station — also called "AOR," for *album-oriented rock* — offers largely instrumental modern music, including rock-and-roll and jazz (not jazz of the type usually associated with New Orleans). The music of a progressive station generally does not appeal to those of conservative tastes; the audience comprises primarily young adults, with a few older individuals — among them, some executive types — who pride themselves on "thinking young."

Contemporary is a tricky term. Even an *"adult* contemporary" station plays primarily rock music but usually of a tamer variety than that found on the progressive stations. Its offerings generally include current hits and sometimes emphasize specific types of rock

(e.g., disco or "golden oldies"). This is another format appealing almost exclusively to the younger segments of the radio audience.

MOR or "middle of the road" is as close as today's stations come to offering a mass-appeal format. Preferred by middle-demographic, middlebrow audiences, the MOR station has traditionally enjoyed the largest audience in its market, but in recent years the format's popularity has begun to decline. Many MOR stations now inject contemporary or "light good-music" elements into their programming.

The radio industry coined the term **good music** to replace such pejorative earlier descriptions as "background music" and "wallpaper music." If you have ever spent time in a doctor's waiting room, or dined in a restaurant playing radio music, you have undoubtedly listened to a good-music station. The sound is designed to be relaxing and unobtrusive, and most good-music stations impose strict limits on the number of commercial interruptions. Almost all good-music stations are broadcast on the FM band. This format has experienced continual and often dramatic growth in popularity during recent years. Generally, it appeals to mature listeners with refined tastes, providing an audience with demographic decision that depends on your audience. The peak periods for radio listening are known as "drive-time" (periods when many persons are listening on car radios, in addition to those listening at home). Morning drive-time usually lasts from 6 to 10 AM; afternoon drive-time generally encompasses the hours from 4 to 7 PM. (These peak periods are longer in some areas, shorter in others.)

The period from 10 AM to 4 PM is known as daytime, and that after 7 PM as nighttime. On most stations, the most expensive period for commercials is morning drive-time, followed by afternoon drive-time, daytime, and nighttime. There are some exceptions to this rule: "good-music" sta-tions, for example, may charge more for commercials broadcast around the dinner period, or on weekends.

When you have decided which individuals you want to reach, the next step is to determine when those kinds of individuals are most likely to listen to radio. Business executives, for example, probably listen to the radio only during morning drive-time and, to a lesser degree, during afternoon drive-time. Housewives are listening throughout the day, but can be reached most cost-efficiently during the daytime period because commercials cost less then. Teens and (surprisingly) senior citizens are often most available during the evening hours.

characteristics attractive to certain types of hotels and restaurants.

One version of this format, sometimes called **light good music,** combines the basic characteristics of the good-music station with a more contemporary sound to attract younger audiences, and has achieved con-siderable success in reaching upwardly mobile indi-viduals not much taken with the progressive format.

The **news-information-sports** stations reach fairly mature audiences and are especially popular in the morning hours, when a substantial sprinkling of executives will be found in their audiences. **Talk** sta-tions, which broadcast telephone conversations be-tween program hosts, guests, and listeners, tend to attract older, predominantly female audiences; when they feature special topics, however, they often attract listeners in other demographic categories.

There is usually no more than one **classical** station in a single market. Classical stations have relatively small audiences but these listeners are at the top of the demographic spectrum in their areas. The appeal of the **country-and-western** format, and its "modern country" variation, depends to large extent on the geographic area in which it is broadcast. Less popular in the big cities of the northeast, C&W stations often have the largest audiences in other areas.

Although new radio formats appear with amazing regularity, they are almost always variations on the formats described above. The phenomenal success of disco music, for example, brought a rash of stations playing disco music exclusively. As the Hispanic popu-lation of certain areas expands, stations on which Spanish is spoken have proliferated.

Who's Listening

No discussion of the demographic groups tuned in to specific radio formats can be anything but sugges-tive, but the following *general* guidelines may be help-ful in station-selection for hotels.

To reach executives and professionals, advertise on the news-information-sports and good-music stations in the markets of interest to you. Younger members of the executive and professional groups may be found listening to the light good-music stations.

To reach families, vacation travelers, and to some degree, the traveling salesman, the MOR, adult contemporary, and talk stations may be the most effective.

If you operate a lively bar, the progressive stations may be the best suited for reaching your clientele. For group or social-function business, don't allow the rela-tively small size of the audience tuned in to the classi-cal stations to discourage you from advertising on them.

Most important, bear in mind that the summary def-initions provided above may not be applicable to the specific stations serving the markets you want to reach. Because statistics can be manipulated, a radio station's sales representative is not likely to be your most objective source of information on the station best suited for advertising your operation. Profes-sional guidance will help you evaluate the popularity and effectiveness of different radio formats in specific geographic areas among individuals with the demo-graphic characteristics you're after.

Radio advertising rates are determined by the time of day, the size of a station's audience, and a number of other factors. Commercials in morning drive-time can cost two or three times as much as a daytime commercial, and the leading station in a market (i.e., that with the largest audience) may have rates two to ten times higher than those of less popular stations. These dramatic differences are one reason professional advice is so useful in establishing a cost-effective schedule.

In creating the advertising, concentrate on 60-second (one-minute) commercials. The rate for a 30-second commercial is generally 75 to 85 percent that of a 60-second ad, so the one-minute length is the most economical buy. Ten-second announcements are generally wasted because they tend to get lost in the clutter of commercials on the average station.

Vertical and Horizontal, Reach and Frequency

Whatever the cost, it is important to see enough commercials to develop sufficient *reach* and *frequency.* * "Reach" is the number of people who hear your commercial at least one time during a week of broadcasting. "Frequency" is the number of times the average listener hears the commercial in that week. Reach and frequency goals vary so widely by type of advertiser that it is impossible to give general guidelines in this area.

Some help in developing appropriate schedules, however, can be found in the structure of radio stations' rate cards. Most are set up to reflect "package" rates for six, 12, 18, and 24 commercials per week. The suggestion that six commercials per week (per station) is almost an absolute minimum for any kind of impact is a valid one.

In regard to the number of commercials you use, there are two basic kinds of advertising coverage: vertical coverage and horizontal coverage. Vertical coverage—whereby commercials are "bunched," all run in one or two days of a given week—is an effective technique for promoting special events, such as a Thanksgiving dinner special or an escape weekend. The *horizontal* approach is to spread the commercials evenly over the week, and to repeat that exposure week after week. Horizontal coverage is especially useful in building local image, but requires greater dedication to continuing use of the radio medium than the vertical technique does.

One serious mistake made by radio advertisers is trying the medium without giving it enough time to develop genuine impact. If you are going to try radio, try it for at least six weeks, and preferably 13, before deciding it is not for you. Radio is not an "in and out" advertising medium: it requires consistent use to produce meaningful results.

Evaluating the Results

How will you know whether radio is producing results? The best source of information is the bottom line—particularly in regard to the facilities (rooms, restaurant, special offers) advertised—but the effects of other factors will make it difficult to discern which portion of a change can be attributed to radio advertising. The number of phone inquiries generated by commercials can be monitored; guests can be polled; or you can conduct a survey of local residents. Whatever evaluation method you use, give your radio advertising sufficient time to develop momentum before you attempt to judge its performance. You may find that, given an adequate chance, radio advertising is ideal for your purposes.

---

*For a discussion of these considerations, see: Peter C. Yesawich, "The Execution and Measurement of a Marketing Program," *The Cornell Hotel and Restaurant Administration Quarterly*, 20, No. 1 (May 1979), pp. 48-49.

Brochures That Sell

by Jane Maas

Jane Maas is president of Jane Maas, Inc., Advertising. She was recently selected to direct creative efforts for Helmsley and Harley Hotels. Maas directed the famous "I Love New York" campaign when she was a senior officer of Wells, Rich, Greene advertising agency.

Not every hotel has a large budget for advertising, but almost every hotel produces some type of promotional material, whether it is one simple flier or many elaborate brochures.

Some brochures are clearly more effective than others, in attracting attention, inviting readership, and most important of all, making the sale. The following rules and examples simply point out what usually works, and suggest some of the pitfalls to avoid.

The most important decision you will ever make for your hotel brochure is this: *what is our positioning?* Positioning is placing your product or service in a certain way in the consumer's mind. Do you want your hotel to stand for the utmost in modern efficiency, or for old-world charm?

Once you have decided on your positioning, you need a strategy to get you there. Put the strategy in writing, and get agreement in advance from everyone who will be involved in the creation or approval of the brochure. A good strategy always includes these five points:

1. Objective—what do you want your brochure to accomplish? For example, do you want to convince more customers to visit your hotel? Or do you want the same customers to stay longer?

2. Target audience—who is your customer? You cannot talk to everyone. If you do so, you are simply wasting money.

3. Consumer benefit—why should the consumer stay at your hotel? This is usually the hardest question to answer; it's also the key to your success. The answer should flow from what your property has to offer as well as what the consumer's perceptions and needs are.

4. Support—a reason to believe that benefit. Brochure readers these days are on the alert for over-promise and puffery. A reason to believe adds credibility to your story.

5. Tone and manner—the "personality" of your property. For many hotels, the personality is really the very thing you are selling; the element that distinguishes you from your competition. Yet few hotel brochures project a personality.

Stick With Your Strategy

It should not be changed lightly. If you have arrived at a strategy with thought, spend more thought—and work—before you discard it. You can change the appearance and copy of your brochure as often as you wish, but its basic nature should not change from year to year.

Before you review the copy and layout of your next brochure, review the strategy. Ask yourself if the brochure is on strategy and is consistent with your brand personality. If it is not, go back to the drawing board.

A good strategy, like a good map, gets you where you want to go—faster and easier. Follow the strategy, and your brochure will be successful in doing its only real job: making the consumer act.

Hotels and motels in the U.S. alone spend $30 million on brochures every year. Yet most lack positioning, a big idea, a strong selling strategy that sets them apart from the competition. Decide on the most important benefit your hotel has to offer; then communicate it in every piece of literature you give out.

From *Lodging* (October 1981) pp. 49-52. Reprinted by permission of *Lodging*.

15 Ways to Sell Harder

1. Put your name and location on the cover.

Most travelers choose a destination first, a hotel second. Flag your customer by proclaiming your name and location boldly on the cover. Many hotels rely on their names alone; yet few are famous enough to carry this off. Some hotels settle for just a photograph on the cover—a shameful waste of money.

2. Put your selling message on the cover.

The cover of your brochure should establish your positioning and your unique advantage.

The Whitehall Hotel in Houston sets itself apart with this positioning statement: "Welcome to the only four-star heart-of-Houston hotel." After the Whitehall began using this selling message, its occupancy rate increased 15 percent.

3. Promise the consumer a benefit on the cover.

Research says that brochures which promise the consumer something work harder than those which do not. Yet few hotel brochures bother to do this.

Consumers are selfish. Don't tell them how good you are; tell them how good the hotel will be for them.

One Omni Hotel promised: "At the Omni Hotel in Norfolk, you can sleep on the water."

Of course, the consumer benefit must be meaningful and important. The Omni Hotel knows that its waterfront location is a desirable one that gives it a march on the competition.

4. Identify your target audience on the cover.

If your brochure is talking to a particular audience, single them out on the brochure cover. Business travelers, Honeymooners, Golfers, Meeting planners.

"Six common convention complaints and how Indies Inn cures every one." In that cover headline, Indies Inn not only selects its target audience, the meeting planner, but states an important benefit.

5. Make the brochure reflect your personality.

A sleek, contemporary mailing piece is just right for a sleek, modern hotel. It would be all wrong for a quiet, hundred-year-old inn which promises tradition.

Does your hotel have a personality? If so, what is it? Are you the most convenient choice for business travelers; the utmost in luxury; or the best for economical family holidays? Decide. You cannot be all of them.

6. Avoid the smiling chef and other cliches.

Open almost any hotel brochure, and you will

arlington\ark towers
Chicago's new suburban hotel

The only hotel in the world with its own race track and golf course.

What distinguishes this brochure cover?

It goes straight to the point, in words and illustration, in stating the hotel's basic selling position: ". . . the only hotel in the world with . . . etc." Brochure covers are like advertising headlines: they either capture or lose the reader. Alas, four out of five lose the reader.

find a photograph of a smiling chef, complete with white toque, presiding over a buffet table. Most brochures also include the grinning bellman, the happy waiter and the couple posed in the bedroom.

Eliminate these photographs, and strive for freshness.

7. Use photographs that stretch the reader's imagination.

Allow readers to put themselves into the picture. Often, it pays to visualize what can be seen *near*

Houston, Texas

Welcome to
the only four-star
heart-of-Houston hotel.

The Whitehall

What is right about this brochure cover?

It does a cleancut job of setting the hotel apart with a positioning statement: ". . . only four-star heart-of-Houston hotel." This positioning boosted occupancy 15%. Further, the simplicity and elegance of the cover design convey the image of the hotel.

your hotel, not just within it.

The brochure for Sheraton's Nile Cruises shows far more than the comfort of the cruise ships. Photos of temples, Egyptian wall paintings and scenes of the river suggest what the traveler will experience.

8. Demonstrate your point of difference.

Television commercials make telling and believable points with demonstrations. This is a successful technique you can borrow.

The brochure for Del Webb's TowneHouse Hotel does not merely describe the huge convention hall. Enormous trailer trucks were driven into it, and a photograph was taken to make the point visually. It is a powerful demonstration of the dimensions of this convention facility.

9. Show activities, not just scenery.

Don't just show your swimming pool; show people swimming in it. Don't just show your discotheque; show people dancing in it. People are interested in people.

10. Photograph food in closeup.

The exception to the rule above is food. Research says food is more appealing when shown in closeup. And always show the finished dish, not the raw ingredients.

11. Make picture captions sell your product.

You have already read that, next to the cover of the brochure, picture captions are the best-read element. Yet most hotel brochures ignore this remarkable sales aid.

Kiawah Island Hotel captions every photo with informative, competitive material. "Historic Charleston, just 21 miles away," appears beneath a charming photograph of that city. "Plan a crabbing or fishing safari," suggests another caption, indicating some of the activities available.

12. Use maps for high readership.

Most travelers love maps. They are not only another way of giving important facts but can be used as a welcome graphic element. You might want to show exactly where your hotel is located in a city and indicate how close it is to other important sights, shopping or transportation.

The Bristol Hotel in London always includes a map showing it is just around the corner from Piccadilly. The Hay Adams Hotel of Washington, D.C., never forgets to tell consumers it has a view of the White House.

Resort hotels can give helpful information by using maps to show the layout of the resort itself.

Maps in a Ponte Vedra Club (Jacksonville) brochure depict both the club's layout (golf course, cottages, barber shop) and its location within the United States.

Maps are also helpful to the many hotel visitors who arrive by car, even in big cities. Several New York City hotels include maps that show their location in relation to various bridges and tunnels into the city.

13. Give the reader helpful information.

You are asking many readers to patronize your hotel sight unseen. The copy you include in your brochure may be the only information they have. Tell them what to bring, what to wear, what attractions are available in your area.

14. Use the brochure to be helpful to special audiences.

You do not usually have time or space in advertising to appeal to smaller "sub-segments" of potential customers. Do this important job in a brochure.

Women traveling on business represent over twelve million person-nights for hotels and motels. To appeal to this growing number, consider showing a photograph of a woman checking in, with attache case in hand. Or, to indicate that your dining room welcomes women alone, use a photograph of an unescorted woman having a pleasant dinner.

Westin Hotels hired a woman's travel consultant and conducted research which led them to add some simple features that appeal to women— skirt hangers, retractable clothesline, full-length mirrors and better bathroom lighting for makeup. They advertise these features in their brochures.

Other special segments you can address include families traveling with children. Spell out any special recreational areas or opportunities for youngsters. Potential visitors from overseas will be more likely to choose your hotel over your competition if you indicate in your brochure what languages are spoken.

15. Be alert to changing life-styles.

What is happening in the world must affect every aspect of your hotel business and be reflected in your brochure.

People are eating lighter meals, vegetarian meals and health foods. If such food is available in your dining room, why not replicate a menu in your brochure?

Exercise is in. If you have an exercise room, a swimming pool or a sauna, mention it in the literature. Photograph it.

Jogging is in. If your hotel is situated in an area where jogging is possible, indicate it. (You can even include a map.)

Sixty percent of all Americans go on picnics every year. Do you pack a picnic lunch? *Do you promote that fact?*

Don't worry if a good point about your hotel (such as a nice location) is shared by your competition across the street. You still reap the benefit if your brochure talks about it, and his does not. Preempting the truth is a technique that works very well in advertising. Use it in your brochures to the same good effect.

The Rules Work for Everyone

Let us dispel the myth that positioning is only for large properties or chains. It is just as important for the small unit operator, perhaps more important.

Why do most travelers love maps?

Because graphics often tell a story with great clarity. They tell—in this instance—where San Juan is located in Puerto Rico, where the hotel is located in San Juan, and where the air strip and local attractions are located in relation to the hotel.

When do trucks make good photo-copy?

When they pack a powerful message addressed to a target audience. Consider this picture of enormous trailer trucks driven into a convention hall at Del Webb's TowneHouse in Phoenix. This spread in a hotel brochure demonstrates the hotel's point of difference. No exhibition manager could fail to get the message.

The right positioning, executed with consistency, makes every dollar work harder.

The best positioning is a simple one, so the complexities of the hotel industry make the decision especially difficult. Promote substrategies if you must (weekday versus weekend business, for instance), but do so under one umbrella.

Your positioning is the motivation for a consumer to choose your property rather than another. Arriving at the right one is hard work, but it will pay off on the bottom line.

Follow these rules—especially the first two—and you will have a more effective brochure. Finally, once you understand what usually works and what usually does not, feel free to break the rules for good reason.

When are food photos most appetizing?

When they're close-up and show finished dish. This photo is from a brochure for the St. Moritz in New York.

Part VII

The "How To" Cases

The preceding sections of this book have been devoted to the structure of strategic marketing planning and the processes involved in developing a strategic marketing plan. This final section looks at some specific market segments.

In this section we gain insights into how some specific market segments behave in the market. The needs and wants of buyers in these segments are explored. The articles discuss what specific groups of people buy, how they go about making buying decisions, and what they consider to be value.

The conclusions reached in the articles are based on case studies that were conducted as part of the Advanced Advertising Workshop that was jointly sponsored and conducted by the American Hotel & Motel Association and the Hotel Sales Management Association. Each workshop was directed by high level marketing executives in the hospitality industry and followed essentially the same format. That is, each workshop followed, in a fairly consistent manner, the steps required in strategic marketing planning. The purpose of including these case studies in a book of this kind is to demonstrate how the principles of strategic marketing planning are applied to real life problems.

Marketing for the Eighties

Marketing to the Individual Business Traveler

Edited by William Q. Dowling

Bill Dowling is a marketing consultant to the hospitality and tourism industries and is president of Dowling Marketing, Inc.

"I've never met a client," quipped Julian Koenig, one of the best advertising copywriters in the last few decades, "who didn't fancy himself an advertising expert." Koenig used to complain that no one tells IBM how to make computers or Xerox how to make copiers, but everyone was always telling him how to write advertising.

Nowhere is this syndrome more prevalent than in the field of hotel marketing. Even the rank amateur has an opinion on the best way to fill a hotel with customers.

The series, "Marketing for the 80's," which began two issues ago in LODGING, has drawn on the techniques of professional marketing executives to provide a summary of the basic principles of preparing a hotel marketing plan. The first four

articles appeared in the September and October issues. They explained four major steps that are vital in the preparation of such a plan. They are (see box): (1) Research and Positioning; (2) Advertising Strategy; (3) Media Planning, and, (4) Budgeting. All other strategies for Sales, Public Relations and Special Promotions—even Pricing— will flow from the first four steps.

Once these general strategies have been completed, then specific sub-strategies must be developed for each segment of a hotel's business (e.g., individual business travelers, pleasure travelers, meetings and conventions, restaurant and lounge patrons, etc.). Beginning with this article, LODGING will examine the steps necessary to prepare for each of up to 10 sub-strategies. This article deals with the oldest and most lucrative market for lodging in history, the commercial traveler.

Individual business travelers are perhaps the most difficult segment of the traveling public to market to. Here are three primary reasons why:

1. The business executive buys location. Location is a more significant factor to business travelers than to any other segment of a hotel's clientele. The executive wants to be close to his appointments or business office. He will more often sacrifice amenities such as a restaurant or lounge in order to be in the right location than he will sacrifice location for amenities. This means you have to pinpoint the corporations closest to your hotel and target your marketing efforts against those who are most likely to be visiting those companies.

2. Business travelers are frequent travelers and have very specific needs. Some need a hotel with an outstanding restaurant to use for entertaining. Others may want a hotel with a 24-hour coffee shop. It is important to understand the most prevalent needs of most commercial guests of your hotel

and your competitors' hotels in order to satisfy those needs.

3. Commercial bookings have a shorter lead time than most other segments of a hotel's business (except perhaps weekend packages). Unless you are fortunate enough to be in a high-demand city like New York, where available rooms can be scarce during peak periods, you probably find that many reservations come in close to the arrival date. This creates a segment of business that is much more volatile and subject to wide fluctuations than group business.

Your marketing plan should contain enough of a contingency fund to enable you to respond quickly to changing market situations. Let's consider an example. When the Democratic convention was held in New York last summer, all of the major hotels were booked solid for the entire week. But when Senator Edward Kennedy withdrew from the race for the Presidential nomination, there was a mass exodus from the city, leaving many hotels with 15-20 point reductions in occupancy.

Many of these same hotels had turned down reservation requests from business executives for the convention period. Now, caught with empty rooms, the reservations departments of a few of the hotels—those set up to meet such contingencies—were able to contact their corporate clients and pick up instant business to replace the lost politicians.

A Case Study: Marketing a Commercial Hotel

Last summer, just before the Democrats were battling over the choice of a Presidential nominee, participants in an AH&MA/HSMA Advanced Advertising workshop were battling over a case history assignment involving a hypothetical New York hotel. Battle leaders were:

David A. Troy, vice president and director of marketing for Sheraton's North American Division; and

Michael Edgar, executive vice president of Needham and Grohmann, well known lodging industry advertising agency.

Troy and Edgar invented, out of their vast experience with hotels, a hypothetical hotel located in New York that was in trouble. They presented a case study of this hotel's problem to a workshop of the lodging industry's top flight marketing executives and some of the advertising world's best-known names.

The group worked, at length and in depth, on solutions to the Case Study Hotel's advertising and marketing problems. The hypothetical hotel will be discussed here as a real hotel—the Case Study Hotel—for purposes of showing the reader what would happen in an actual case of researching, positioning, formulating strategy, media planning and budgeting.

This case study is based on the development of the business traveler market as the hotel's predominant market. But the same principles would apply to development of business travel as a market segment.

Statement of the Problem

The problem: how to reverse declining occupancy trends in an 850-room hotel in mid-town Manhattan. Because the Case Study Hotel has very limited function space, it is forced to go after the individual business traveler for weekday business if the management hopes to raise occupancy from the current 68% level to the 82% it had attained in the previous year.

Research Methods

David Troy and Michael Edgar know that all future decisions must be based on research findings. They have heard the marketing director of one of the largest hotels to open in New York in 1980 say, "I was determined, before doing anything else, to gather more statistics than any of my competitors on travelers to New York."

So what about the Case Study Hotel? Its market is defined as "the Northeastern United States, Chicago, Dallas, Houston and the West Coast."

What about its competition? It is known that between 2,000 and 3,000 new hotel rooms (the number varies with what you count as new) will open in Manhattan in 1980, another 2,000 in 1981, and another 3,000 in the early to mid-1980's. While the annual growth of available hotel rooms in Manhattan is, therefore, projected at 2%-3% over the next few years, total demand for first-class hotel rooms is estimated, by industry executives, at the annual rate of 2%-4% for the same period.

Troy and Edgar decided that, in order to capture a larger share of this very competitive market, the Case Study Hotel would have to launch a research program that would accomplish the following four goals:

1. Define the Profile of the Case Study Hotel's Current Corporate Guests.

a) Where are current business travelers coming from and which corporations are they coming to visit?

b) What is the average age, income level, marital status and educational level of these guests?

c) What are their lodging needs when they visit New York City?

d) How do they perceive the Case Study Hotel's benefits? Is the hotel meeting their needs?

e) How does the Case Study compare to the competition in terms of: Location? Service? Security? Cleanliness? Amenities? Ease of making a reservation?

2. Define the Profile of Guests of Directly Competitive Hotels.

The same questions as above would need to be answered for each competitive hotel. Guests would need to be profiled to ascertain:

• Where business travelers are coming from and to visit whom.

• Their average age, income, marital status and educational level.

What's "special" about this hotel ad?

Answer: The Beverly is offering what most competitive hotels do not have: a quiet, serene atmosphere. The ad runs regularly in a business publication and is targeted against the business traveler.

• Their lodging needs.

• How they perceive each competitive hotel in terms of meeting their needs.

• How each competitive hotel compares to the Case Study Hotel by each of the six criteria listed above under (c).

3. Determine How These Executives Book Their Travel

a) Is it done by their New York office, from their own office in their hometown, or by a travel agent?

b) Who selects which hotel they will use: Secretary? Travel agent? Or do they decide themselves?

4. Analyze the New York City Hotel Market, Past, Current and Future.

a) What is the mix of business (commercial, pleasure travel, incentive travel, meetings and conventions)?

b) What are the seasonal occupancy trends, weekday and weekend, as reflected by occupancy over the past five years?

c) What is the Visitor and Convention Bureau projecting, in terms of conventions and trade shows, for the immediate future? Which periods will provide good overflow potential for the Case Study Hotel? Which periods will be soft?

d) What are the published rates of the hotels in the same general location as the Case Study Hotel that are going after the corporate market?

e) Which cities and countries provide the greatest volume of commercial traffic to New York?

The marketing team working with David Troy and Michael Edgar decided they would obtain the data on the Case Study Hotel's guests by a combination of two methods: in-room questionnaires and intercept interviews. To achieve the latter, guests would be interviewed in depth in the lobby of the hotel as they were checking in or out. The format for the two forms of research was therefore developed jointly by the Case Study Hotel's management team, its advertising agency and an outside research company that specializes in travel industry research.

The in-room questionnaire sought the answers to the basic quantitative data, such as questions "a," "b" and "c" under number one above, in the list of research goals; also, questions "a" and "b" under number three. In order to encourage the guest of the hotel to take the time to fill in the lengthy questionnaire, they offered a choice of free cocktails or free wine as an incentive.

The intercept interviews, where the guest was interviewed personally in the lobby of the Case Study Hotel, were designed to obtain quantitative data, such as points "d" and "e" under number

What's "right" about this ad?

Answer: This corporate ad for Hilton Hotels ran in The Wall Street Journal. *It is an excellent example of an advertising strategy and a media strategy targeting against the same customer: the business traveler.*

one. These interviews were designed to provide an understanding of the guest's *perception* of what the Case Study Hotel had to offer and how it ranked vs. the competition. This is perhaps the most valuable information that can be obtained when determining advertising strategy.

At this point in research, many hotels are surprised to find that customers have misconceptions about hotels. For example, a hotel with a fixed rate of $125 per day may be perceived as expensive whereas a nearby hotel with a rate range of $70 to $170 (and an average rate of $125) may be perceived as "a better value for the money."

The Case Study Hotel marketing group decided to compile New York City hotel market statistics from a number of sources. They would consult with the Visitors and Convention Bureau and the

New York State Department of Commerce. Further, they would send their sales people into the market place to have discussions with major corporate accounts to determine what they were paying for rooms and what services they expected for their executives. They would obtain additional market data from airlines, rail and bus operators serving the city.

Finally, the Case Study Hotel marketing group sought information on what services competitive hotels were offering to the corporate traveler. They correctly concluded that this information would be readily available from top corporate accounts.

Research Findings

The major conclusions from the research and

market analysis used in the case study were as follows:

- Primary corporate users of the Case Study Hotel in the past were frequent business travelers who were on limited expense accounts.

- These business travelers perceived the hotel as a medium-scale, mid-town commercial hotel that offered a fairly wide range of services. They perceived it as charging about the same as the competition but providing less service. They considered the attitude of those providing the service as poor.

- Guests perceived the Case Study Hotel as "tired," its cleanliness and housekeeping as "marginal," its performance in making reservations easy to make as "poor," but its location as "excellent."

- The guests of directly competitive hotels were found to be slightly more upscale. Their perception of the hotel they were patronizing was favorable but their perception of the Case Study Hotel was similar to that of the hotel's own guests. They complained of all New York hotels as "cold and unfriendly."

Methods of booking reservations were determined, but the conclusion was that the method of booking was less relevant than the experience in the hotel; in short—unless the business traveler liked the hotel, the recommendations of travel departments, travel agents and secretaries were not heeded.

The New York market was judged to be strong through 1981 and then slightly softer in the following years because of the infusion of new hotel rooms. Seasonal variations formed a fairly constant pattern from year to year.

Now that conclusions had been drawn from research and market analysis undertaken on behalf of the Case Study Hotel, the marketing team moved on to the next step: positioning the hotel.

Positioning New York's Case Study Hotel

Whenever a marketing executive begins to position a new product, or re-position an old product, the first question always asked is: "What does this product have, or do, that the competition doesn't?" Many of the most effective advertising campaigns in this century were based on unique positioning. Some advertising agencies call this unique positioning and strategy "a unique selling proposition" or "unique point-of-difference." How many times do you recall hearing, in television commercials, such phrases as ". . . cleans twice as

fast as . . .," or ". . . preferred two-to-one over . . .," or ". . . best on-time record in the airline industry." This type of unique positioning was what the Case Study Hotel group was looking for. They decided to capitalize on the market situation in New York by filling a need that research said was missing from competitive properties.

Research showed that most corporate travelers, especially those from smaller sized cities, felt that New York hotels were cold and unfriendly. Yet the new general manager of the Case Study Hotel had a reputation as being especially friendly and good on customer relations. Also, the owner of the hotel had just approved the general manager's request for capital expenditures that would improve the quality of guest amenities.

Therefore, the Case Study Hotel marketing team agreed that the most competitive and unique position for the Case Study Hotel was to be . . .

". . . the hometown hotel in the heart of Manhattan."

This positioning met the three criteria of being (1) unique—no other hotel was using it, (2) a benefit that would be perceived as important by customers—research showed that; and, (3) a promise that the general manager felt that the hotel staff could deliver on.

The next step was the development of a strategy.

Development of an Advertising Strategy

Hotel advertising should say the right things to the right people—persuasively.

In order to position your hotel uniquely in the traveler's mind, you must create an image that reflects the personality of the hotel, communicates the hotel's most unique and important benefits, and supports those benefits with facts.

The strategy developed by Dave Troy's and Michael Edgar's marketing team was as follows:

"The creative strategy of the Case Study Hotel's advertising will be to communicate the unique personal hotel experience for the business traveler that the hotel will provide. This will be supported with examples of uniquely personal services available at the hotel and by communicating a positive, friendly staff attitude."

Once this strategy statement was completed, the advertising agency developed the headline "We make you feel at home" and referred to the hotel in the copy and in the tag line as "your home away from home in New York City."

Marketing Planning Checklist

Research and Positioning

- Complete a market study
- Determine customer perceptions, attitudes and awareness
- Analyze hotel's services and benefits
- Position your hotel uniquely in the customer's mind

Advertising Strategy

- Create an image that reflects the personality of your hotel
- Know what you want your advertising to communicate
- Understand the hotel's most important benefits
- Support those benefits with facts

Media Planning

- Identify your target audience
- Use media research to find your customers
- Concentrate your dollars against customers of the highest potential

Budgeting

- Develop a formal planning process for budgets
- Get all relevant department heads together
- Segment the budget according to function and purpose

Selecting Media

Next came the challenge to concentrate advertising dollars against the highest potential customer. The decision was to target advertising against:

"... *the slightly more upscale market of the Case Study Hotel's competitors, rather than the customers the hotel is presently getting. The objective is to upgrade the Case Study Hotel's customer profile to someone making $30,000-$40,000 annually, college educated, married, and traveling with a reasonably generous expense account.*"

Advertising agencies usually have a great deal of media research that also shows which newspapers, magazines, and radio or TV shows reach the target customer profile you want to go after. So the marketing study group chose the *Wall Street Journal* for increased coverage of the upscale business traveler and supplemented this with newsweeklies like *Time* and *Newsweek*.

Then, to obtain frequency against the heavy traveler, they selected the in-flight magazines on the airlines that are the principal carriers into New York. But before laying out the media schedule, they referred to their overall departmental budget.

Budgeting for Results

A $20 million revenue for the Case Study Hotel for the next year was projected, assuming the marketing program was successful. After determining the amount necessary for the sales department and for other marketing-related expenses, it was agreed that an advertising budget of 3%—or $600,000—would be required. This was broken out as follows: $300,000 for media directed to the business traveler; $100,000 for broad-based media (newspaper and consumer magazine); $200,000 for printing, production and promotion.

As was pointed out in this series in LODGING, marketing budgets may vary from as low as 5.5% to as high as 8% for commercial city hotels. The split between advertising and sales may range from 60%-40% to 40%-60%, depending upon the amount of meeting space available in the hotel.

Accompanying this article are two examples of advertising directed at the corporate traveler. As you can see, in one the positioning is very specific in the headline ("America's most recognized business address."). In the other, more general copy is used (which nonetheless positions the hotel as distinguished from its competitors), but very specific media are selected to make sure that the ad is being read by frequent business travelers.

In the months ahead, this series will discuss the application of professional marketing principles to other markets.

Marketing for the Eighties

Marketing to the Travel Agent

Continuing a series by William Q. Dowling

"Travel agents are a necessary evil," a general manager once told me. "We don't like paying commissions but we can't get along without their business." A hotel reservations manager said recently, "It makes me angry to pay commissions to an agent just because they passed along a reservations request. They're just order takers."

Yet a travel agent told me during an ASTA congress a few years ago that "I cannot understand why hotel people feel they are doing us a favor to do business with us. If they only understood the right way to use us we could become an extension of their sales equipment."

These comments point out one of the paradoxes of the travel industry. In the past 20 years travel agency bookings into hotels have risen from $600 million to over $2 billion. Yet the relationship between agency people and hotel people is still characterized by lack of communication and misunderstanding.

Readers who have managed or directed the marketing for a resort hotel will have more of an appreciation for travel agents than those readers who have only been associated with commercial properties. Resorts could not survive without travel agents in the 1980's. The State of Florida's

tourism division just reported that in 1979, 53.7% of all visitors used a travel agent—an all-time high for the state. In destinations such as Mexico, the Caribbean, the Bahamas and Bermuda, as much as 80-90% of all individual visitors booked through an agent. General managers such as Cy Elkins of the Princess Hotel in Hamilton, Bermuda, attributes much of his success to his worldwide reputation among travel agents.

In the October, 1979, issue of LODGING, Melinda Bush, who is publisher of Hotel and Travel Index, wrote that "The travel agent should be viewed by the hotel operator as a sales opportunity." With hotel bookings over the $2 million mark and latest reports showing 17,000 ATC-appointed travel agents in the U.S., travel agents have become not just a sales opportunity, but a sales necessity.

Previous installments in this series have been on the subjects of (1) Research and Positioning; (2) Strategy Development; (3) Media Selection; (4) Budgeting, and (5) Marketing to the Individual Business Traveler. Future installments will include Marketing to the Pleasure Traveler, Marketing to the Restaurant Patron, Marketing to the Meeting Planner, and marketing to other market segments.

Travel agents are a difficult group to market to effectively unless you understand how they operate and what their needs are. There are four main points that you should remember when developing a marketing plan for the travel trade.

1. All travel agencies are not alike. They cannot all be marketed to in the same manner. In smaller agencies, the owner/manager reads most of the incoming mail and periodicals and has a great deal of contact with the client. But in larger agencies the owner may not be the manager, and may have little or no client contact. Even the manager of a large agency will most likely have his mail pre-

sorted by staff personnel, and only see certain periodicals and letters. This means your well-designed direct mail piece which was addressed to the manager may never make it to his or her desk. It may also never make it to the desk of the agent who is booking business.

2. Travel agents fish where the fish are biting. They are forced to concentrate on the types of business that make the best profits for them. The president of a major travel agency chain was quoted this November as saying, "For next year, we will be dropping the travel products that aren't producing high enough volume or enough profit." Therefore you must understand each agency's basic business thrust before you can market to it effectively.

If an agency is primarily concentrating on coast-

From *Lodging* (January 1981) pp. 38-40, 56. Reprinted by permission of *Lodging*.

to-coast packages or Hawaii or the Caribbean, you are wasting your time trying to interest it in sending business to a commercial hotel in Grand Rapids. You must conduct research to determine which agents, if any, are already sending commercial and group business to Grand Rapids.

Extra commissions will do little to entice an agency to change its pattern of business. If the agency has no customers for Grand Rapids, 20% commission (instead of the normal 10%) isn't going to make any difference. On the other hand, if the agent is already sending 500 room nights a week to your competitor and the competition is only paying 10%, you might capture a share of that business by offering a higher commission.

While agents will not do your marketing for you, they can be very effective in determining a client's selection of a hotel. The Lou Harris Survey in 1978 reported that 71% of travel agents' pleasure-travel customers asked for guidance on the selection of a hotel.

3. Travel agents want service, service, service. The same Harris survey reported that the three most important factors, other than general reputation of the hotel, affecting a travel agent's decision to recommend a hotel are the hotel's track record in honoring reservations, the availability of a toll-free reservations number, and the general attitude of the hotel management toward travel agents.

All of the hotel benefits a hotelier thinks of as being important—restaurants, size of rooms, chain affiliation, uniqueness of hotel's architecture—were at the bottom of the list.

Travel agents are looking for an easy and inexpensive method of booking a reservation and they don't want their client to arrive at the front desk of a hotel only to be told, "Sorry, but your travel agent must have made a mistake."

4. Travel agents suffer from "advertising clutter." They are bombarded with more advertising and direct mail literature than anyone in the travel industry. Therefore your message must be simple, clear and to the point. And, if possible, your message should be unique in order to make an impact and be heard above the crowd.

Case Study: Marketing a Resort Hotel to Travel Agents

A case study workshop on the opening of a new resort hotel in Puerto Vallarta, Mexico, was conducted at last summer's AH&MA/HSMA Ad-

vanced Advertising workshop. Michael Leven, one of the most accomplished and respected marketing professionals in the hotel industry, and senior vice president international operations and corporate marketing of Pick Americana Hotels, and Martin Kramer, vice president of Spiro and Associates, Philadelphia, one of the most successful ad agencies in the travel and hotel industries, ran the workshops. Not so coincidentally, Leven and Kramer were co-conspirators a year ago in the opening of the 280-room Fiesta Americana in Puerto Vallarta. So the hotel shown on the cover of LODGING in January 1981 can at least be credited for being the inspiration for the hypothetical case study.

Statement of the Problem

The hypothetical beach front hotel is located three miles from the international airport and about three miles from the town of Puerto Vallarta. The destination achieved world-wide recognition after the production of "Night of the Iguana" with Ava Gardner and Richard Burton. Yet Puerto Vallarta is still priced below other Mexican destinations such as Acapulco, and is 30-40% below other, better-known warm-weather destinations. The principal source of tourists is the United States, with the highest percentage coming from Los Angeles, San Diego, San Francisco, Dallas, Houston, San Antonio, New York and Chicago. Yet Canada is becoming an important secondary market.

Of the existing properties in Puerto Vallarta, only the highly successful Camino Real is direct competition to the case study hotel. Because 95% of all U.S. tourists visiting Mexico by air book through a travel agency, the key to the success of this new hotel will depend greatly on the effectiveness of the marketing effort to travel agents.

Research and Positioning

Leven and Kramer had 10 questions they needed to have answered by research. They were:
- what are the needs of travel agents' customers?
- what are the motivations for the trip?
- how do agents and their clients perceive prices?
- what is their awareness of and attitude toward Puerto Vallarta?
- what are the arrival and departure patterns? Length of stay?
- what is the mix of business? F.I.T. (individual foreign inclusive tour) or charter (group tour)?

- what seasonal differences exist in travel patterns? Which geographic regions produce the most business?
- how far in advance are bookings made? Does this vary from high season to low season?
- how do agents perceive the hotels in Puerto Vallarta? How do their customers perceive the hotels?
- is there a need for a deluxe hotel in this destination?

When preparing questions for a research study it is better to include every question you can think of rather than leave some out and wish, after the fact, that you had asked them. However, you will often notice after the research findings are in that some of your questions produced no relevant answers. With the workshop group, Messrs. Leven and Kramer sorted out the relevant questions and provided the group with the following hypothetical "findings:"

- agents said their clients are looking for good weather, lack of crowds and a foreign atmosphere in a Mexican vacation.
- agents and their clients were aware that rates and prices in Puerto Vallarta are slightly lower than Acapulco and much lower than in other warm-weather destinations.
- the destination was perceived as "exotic" and well-known because of the "Iguana" movie, but not much was known about the local hotels. (Note: this was perhaps the most important finding in the research, for reasons you will see later.)
- Nothing unusual was found in arrival patterns or seasonal variations; most business is from tours on scheduled carriers, rather than from charters (this is the opposite from Acapulco).
- unlike Acapulco, no one tour operator dominates the market; business comes from a number of different agencies.
- however, it was found that there was an unusually high interest in the destination by a couple of Canadian tour operators.
- agents reported their Mexico-bound tourists tend to be young, adventurous and interested in a deluxe vacation at a fair price.

Advertising Strategy

"There are two essential findings in the research," Leven said later when discussing the case study. "First was the fact that most travelers were not familiar with the names of any hotels in Puerto Vallarta."

"When people want to try an exotic destination but don't know the hotels well," he continued, "the travel agent makes the hotel selection for them." This meant that advertising efforts could be aimed primarily toward the travel trade rather than the consumer. "If we had the travel agent on our side," Leven said, "he would do the selling for us."

The second important finding was that travelers were looking for a deluxe product. "We decided to become to Puerto Vallarta what the Acapulco Princess is to Acapulco," Leven said. Marty Kramer summed up the conclusions of the workshop group when he reported that "We wanted to be perceived as the best in the market in terms of facilities, setting and product delivery." The group kept the advertising strategy simple and to the point, and supported it with factual details about the hotel and its amenities.

Developing Media Plan

When Leven and Kramer were opening the Americana in Puerto Vallarta, they first talked to the various airline sales people to determine who the top-producing tour operators were. "Canadian operators were identified as a major source of present business," Leven said recently, "so we identified the four or five who were the largest producers, went to see them, and developed good relationships."

When a situation like this exists, where the tour operators are marketing the destination to retail agents, it is often better to schedule "co-op" advertising with the operator rather than run separate advertising. All that is needed is to schedule advertising in the travel trade publications to create an image for the hotel and communicate the fact that packages are available through a certain tour operator. Many times it is better to have your advertising agency design the ad to look as though it is being run by the tour operator rather than the hotel company. In most cases, the hotel company and the tour operator will split the cost of the ad on a "co-operative" basis. (Note: when this is done, it is better to let your advertising agency control placement of the advertising so that you are sure the ads you paid for are actually running. Every now and then an unreliable operator will bill you for ads that never ran.)

When selecting travel trade media, Mike Leven and Marty Kramer suggested some guidelines to their workshop group for the case study. "If you are selling an expensive vacation," Mr. Leven said, "you will want to reach the owner/manager of a

Checklist for Marketing to Travel Agents

Research and positioning

- Analyze which agencies are high volume producers to destination and type of business they are sending.
- Determine what customers want and what their attitudes are toward destination and your hotel.
- Analyze hotel's reservation system, commission payment plan and agents' perception of "ease of doing business" with your hotel.
- Position your hotel as uniquely meeting needs of travel agent (including why clients will like it).

Advertising strategy

- Create one simple image of your hotel.
- Communicate only the hotel's most important benefits; do not include a multiplicity of selling points.
- Support your benefits with facts.
- Make it easy for the agent to know how to book your hotel.

Media planning

- Identify those agencies which can produce the most business and target media efforts towards them.
- Consider unique media vehicles for high impact, such as brochure, tip-ins, tip-in coupons, and magazine supplements.
- Obtain editorial schedules in advance and place ads in sections featuring your hotel's destination.

Budgeting

- Determine how important travel agents are in producing total business and allocate emphasis accordingly.

retail agency. If you are selling a low cost vacation package, you want to reach the agent on the desk." There are certain travel trade publications that reach more owners than desk agents and vice versa. Your ad agency can give you a breakdown of circulation for each publication and recommend which is best for reaching each segment of the travel trade.

The case study group decided to supplement their image advertising in the travel trade with a brochure insert which included a coupon to send in for more brochures. Many hoteliers are finding this technique to be a more economical method of brochure distribution than mailing to all 17,000 travel agents across the U.S. By doing this, you only send quantities of brochures to those agents who are interested in selling your property.

Budget Allocations

Because the research clearly showed the travel agent to be the decision maker in selecting a hotel for their client, the workshop group allocated $300,000 for travel trade advertising, only $100,000 for consumer advertising, and $100,000 for advertising production, printing and sales promotion material.

Considering the sales strategy—to work through tour operators and retail agencies—this lopsided budget was well justified. However, for most U.S.

resorts where travel agents play a less decisive role, the typical budget would be almost the opposite. The majority of the dollars would be allocated to consumer advertising and a much smaller amount would go to travel trade publications. Emphasis must be allocated according to the travel agents' role in producing customers for your destination. In a destination where all of the hotels are extremely well-known by the traveler, the agent plays a less important role and consumer advertising is vital.

One last essential point. Michael Leven makes one final, essential point in regard to marketing at hotels like the subject property in Puerto Vallarta: "When travel agents control your market, you must get top management of your hotel involved. Once a relationship is established between their management and yours, everything else will fall into place more easily." And this, quite naturally, includes the marketing plan.

Marketing for the Eighties

Marketing to the Pleasure Traveler

by William Q. Dowling

"The first thing to understand about pleasure travelers is that they buy mystique," said Mal Seymourian recently. He should know. In his former position as Director of Marketing for the Plaza Hotel in New York and his current job as Marketing Director of the new Helmsley Palace, he has marketed hotels that are surrounded by an aura of enchantment and mystique.

"Pleasure travelers want to share in, be part of, the hotel's mystique," says Seymourian. "They want to fulfill certain fantasies." The Plaza's now classic story is the result of a carefully planned five year marketing effort built around a combination of image-building ads and retail-type "price" advertising.

"We positioned The Plaza as a hotel with all of the mystique one would expect in a grand hotel in the world's most exciting city," said Seymourian. "Our promise was that if you stay at The Plaza you'll be a part of that exciting atmosphere."

The image building advertising showed celebrities using the hotel but did not identify those celebrities, implying that it was quite common to see Jack Lemmon having lunch at The Plaza. The headline used is "Nothing unimportant ever happens at The Plaza."

During soft periods such as July 1st through Labor Day and certain holiday periods, The Plaza's campaign was supplemented with a very competitive newspaper campaign offering a 20% reduction in rates.

During the five years this campaign has been running (it began in 1975), summer occupancy at The Plaza has built from 45% to 88% and overall occupancy from 63% to 89%. At the same time the hotel has achieved one of the highest average rates in New York City.

From *Lodging* (February 1981) pp. 23-25. Reprinted by permission of *Lodging*.

Marketing Musts for the Leisure Market

In an informal survey of general managers and marketing directors at AH&MA's 1980 convention in Washington in December, there were eight marketing musts that could be summarized from their comments regarding marketing to the pleasure traveler, and you will see how The Plaza's campaign is a perfect example of most of them. They are as follows:

1. Know your customers. Find out everything you can about the travelers who vacation in your area, and specifically those who use competitive hotels. You can't sell benefits until you understand customer needs. A good market survey and visitor profile should be the first step before you develop your advertising strategy.

2. Sell the vacation experience, not just the hotel. People travel to have new experiences or relive old ones. Their image of what that experience should be is part fantasy, part fact. This is the "mystique" The Plaza used so well.

3. Create an image for your hotel that convinces travelers that it can fulfill the vacation experience better than your competition. Cy Elkins, v.p. and general manager of the Princess Hotel in Bermuda, was quoted recently at the AH&MA convention in Washington, D.C. as saying that "our guests are buying a total vacation experience, and the Princess helps make that experience a special one. The hotel's image is very important in that for our guests it symbolizes everything that a Bermuda vacation hotel should be."

4. Never forget that leisure travelers are sensitive to price. One international advertising agency found that putting *price* in the headline of their client's ad increased response 30-40%. But make sure the way you present price should be consistent with the image you want to convey. In May Seymourian's soft period promotions for The Plaza, he always used the phrase "20% reduction" rather than "20% discount." It would be contrary to the Plaza's image to "discount."

"Most guests call about our resorts because of a special price they saw advertised," said Mark Kennedy, reservations director of Trust House Forte. "Of course once they are on the phone with us, our agents will attempt to upgrade them to higher rated rooms," he added. Trust House Forte owns the highly successful Nassau Beach Hotel in the Bahamas.

5. The ingredients of a vacation package must reinforce the hotel's positioning. Pinehurst Hotel and Country Club in North Carolina found from research that Pinehurst was perceived as a "golf-only" resort for male golfers back in 1973. By creative development of tennis packages, family packages and "choice of sports" packages, an image was created over the past seven years of a *complete* resort. Sea Pines Plantation, Hilton Head Island, South Carolina has achieved an image of a total resort for the entire family, using similar packaging strategies.

6. Ads featuring price work better when you run an image-building campaign simultaneously. The Plaza scheduled a campaign in magazines using celebrities such as Jack Lemmon and Gene Shalit having dinner at the hotel to build an image of The Plaza's mystique. At the same time, the hotel scheduled ads featuring "20% reduction in rates" in newspapers in order to obtain immediate response to the 20% offer. A special price has more impact when a customer knows the value of a product. (Would you respond to an offer of a 20% discount on Smith's Scotch? What about a 20% discount on Chivas Regal Scotch?)

7. As a general rule, magazines, radio and TV build image; newspapers and direct mail generate quick response. Advertising shows that people read magazines and watch TV for general information, but turn to the newspapers for most current details on "how-to-purchase." Newspapers and one other medium (print or broadcast) have historically been more effective than either medium alone. The Plaza's successful campaign used a combination of airline in-flight magazines and the Wall Street Journal.

8. Leisure travelers are booking with shorter lead time than ever before. Our society has become more flexible in its leisure activities in recent years; people buy vacations on last minute impulse, especially during summer months and off-season periods. Schedule your newspaper advertising to be in synchronization with the booking patterns in your area, and repeat your ads as often as you can afford. When selling packages or special prices, it is better to run a smaller ad many times than a large ad a few times. Frequency pays off when purchase decisions are impulse decisions.

Case Study: Repositioning a Resort Hotel

One of the most difficult assignments a marketing director or general manager will ever have is to reposition a hotel to the leisure travel market after it has failed with its original positioning.

At AH&MA's Advanced Advertising Workshop I had the opportunity to lead a workshop through this assignment along with Ian Kleier, Pearlman Advertising. Kleier and his agency have had extensive experience marketing a wide variety of hotels, from Loews Hotels and Princess Hotels International to the small Peter Island Hotel and Yacht Harbour. Prior to co-founding the agency six years ago, Kleier was Director of Advertising for Loews Hotels.

Statement of the Problem

We created a case study that combined some real problems experienced by a number of resort hotels. The hypothetical case can be summarized as follows:

- A 200-room resort in the Caribbean was purchased a year ago and refurbished for $5 million.
- A world famous general manager was brought in along with a top food & beverage manager and excellent chef, but an inexperienced marketing director.
- The resort was re-introduced with a new name, Island Beach Hotel, and an advertising campaign that used the line "The resort with guaranteed ocean view from every room."
- After one year, the hotel had failed to achieve any of its occupancy goals or any of its profit projections, it was too small to rely on convention business and had not been positioned effectively to attract leisure travelers.
- The owner of the hotel finally agreed that he should invest in a top-flight marketing director just as he had invested in other highly professional department heads, and try a new marketing approach.

The hypothetical destination was described as a combination of Bermuda and Bahamas, with up-scale visitors (average annual income exceeding $35,000). The island has, in addition to the 200-room Island Beach Hotel, a few small, medium-priced hotels, a wide variety of first-class hotels,

Nothing unimportant ever happens at The Plaza.

The Plaza

On the Park at Fifth and 59th. Call your travel agent or 800-228-3000.

Mal Seymourian: "We positioned the Plaza as a hotel with all of the mystique you would find in a grand hotel in the world's most exciting city." The promise was: Stay at the Plaza and be a part of that exciting atmosphere.

one large convention hotel, but only one *deluxe* hotel in addition to Island Beach.

Market Research Findings

The government of this hypothetical island has a large research budget and conducts attitude surveys of visitors annually. The hotel was able to analyze this existing research data and did not have to spend for a separate research program. Research revealed the following:

- most visitors agreed that the destination offered the best vacation experience they had ever had.

- over half said they were planning to come back again.

- some respondents said there was not enough nightlife; not enough places to go in the evening.

- others said that even though there were some excellent restaurants, there were not enough good ones.

- there were not enough deluxe hotel properties.

Obviously, "resort with guaranteed ocean view from every room" did not talk to the needs of the island's visitors.

Positioning in the Market

Under the circumstances, a new marketing director could have decided to mass market the Island Beach Hotel and develop low priced inexpensive packages to undercut competition. The objective of this positioning would be to take a share of the large market that the many first-class hotels on the island were going after.

However, because $5,000,000 had been invested in the Island Beach Hotel in refurbishing and upgrading it to the highest standards, and because the property had one of the best general managers in the world, the case study group decided to position the hotel as the most expensive hotel and the most luxurious hotel in the destination. They made that decision for four reasons:

1. There is only one other deluxe hotel on the island, therefore, competition is limited;

2. The general manager has a worldwide reputation for managing luxury properties;

3. The hotel's gourmet restaurant, nightclub and discotheque have become very popular and were catering to an up-scale crowd;

4. The hotel is not located on the part of the island where most of the other hotels are located. It is in a secluded area with its own private beach and has an atmosphere of exclusivity.

Developing Creative Strategy

The workshop group developed a creative strategy to communicate with high impact the promise that the Island Beach Hotel offers a more luxurious and complete vacation experience than any other resort or hotel facility on the island. The group decided that advertising would be created to appeal to the up-scale, well educated, adult traveler as well as honeymooners.

Since the hotel's name had been changed a year ago when it was purchased, it was felt that a further name change would be confusing to the public. But they did decide to modify the name from Island Beach Hotel to Island Beach Resort, in order to communicate the more complete nature of the facility and to be consistent with the positioning. Finally, everyone in the workshop group was in agreement that for the campaign to be successful it had to create a high impact immediately.

Developing an Aggressive Budget

Revenues during the past year were $7.5 million and based on the new marketing plan, the workshop group felt confident that with investment spending, the hotel could realize $10 million in total revenues for the coming year.

As a result the owners decided to spend higher than average amounts on a marketing budget for that year and established a budget that was 7.8% of projected revenues. However, a provision was made that as each quarter's results were reported, the advertising budget would be adjusted accordingly. For example, if sales were not coming in as high as were anticipated, the advertising budget would be reduced accordingly.

The $785,000 budget allocation broke out as follows:
- $400,000 media
- $60,000 production
- $185,000 sales staff
- $140,000 printing, promotion, public relations.

The sales staff allocation was small, because the hotel has no convention facilities and did not need a strong convention sales staff.

Formulating Media Plan

The strategy for the media plan was to get very broad reach and high impact against the target customers in those markets of highest potential. The government's research study revealed that 90% of visitors to the island came from four major metropolitan areas: New York, Washington, Philadelphia, and Miami. This provided a unique opportunity for a highly targeted media plan.

Magazines were selected for image building advertising and the Sunday travel sections of newspapers in these four major cities were selected for retail oriented advertising. The budget was split evenly between magazines and newspapers.

The workshop group decided to begin with two-thirds page four-color ads in the magazines for three months, followed by reduced size one-third page four-color ads that would run for a frequency of six times over the next six months. In newspapers, twenty ads were scheduled for insertion throughout the year, using a 400 line ad in the New York Times and a 300 line ad in the newspapers in the other three markets. The reason for the larger ad in the New York Times is that the travel section in the New York Times is more crowded, more cluttered with advertising than are the travel sections of other newspapers.

Additionally, a small portion of the newspaper and magazine budget was reserved for co-op advertising with the airlines and with certain wholesalers and tour operators. Finally, about 10% of the media budget was allocated to travel trade publications and travel directories.

The workshop group agreed that if the opening year extra spending levels were successful, then the budget for year two would be reduced to more acceptable levels consistent with island-wide averages, and years three and four would be reduced slightly below island-wide averages in order to recover the dollars that were allocated for extra spending on the first year.

Always Remember

In summary, when you market to the leisure traveler always remember:

- Know your customers.

- Sell the vacation experience, not just the hotel.

- Create an image for your hotel that convinces travelers that it can fulfill the vacation experience better than your competition.

- Never forget that leisure travelers are sensitive to price.

- The ingredients of a vacation package must reinforce the hotel's positioning.

- Ads featuring price work better when you run an image-building campaign simultaneously.

- As a general rule, magazines, radio and TV build image; newspapers and direct mail generate quick response.

- Leisure travelers are booking with shorter lead time than ever before.

Marketing for the Eighties

Marketing to the Meeting Planners

by William Q. Dowling

"The secret of success is to generate new leads, qualify those leads, and close the sales," according to Arthur Chernov. He could have been talking about selling insurance policies, encyclopedias or real estate. But because Chernov is vice president of sales and advertising for Loews Hotels, he was talking about selling hotel rooms and meeting space to groups.

There is no other segment of hotel customers who respond to basic Dale Carnegie-type selling methods as well as meeting planners. This is because a group booking is a specific piece of business which has a specific value and can be finalized by contract or letter of agreement.

Marketing Musts for the Meetings Market

1. To find out who your best prospects are, use a shotgun instead of a rifle approach.

Market research is often not as productive for pin-pointing group prospects as it is for targeting types of individual travelers. Many times it is impossible to limit your marketing efforts to a small list of companies or associations. When you don't know who your prospects are, develop a broad marketing effort and see who responds.

Says Arthur Chernov: "Our hotel in Monte Carlo had been depending on a handful of corporations and incentive houses until 1979. Then, because of a shortage of aircraft available for charter, most of our clients' volume dropped sharply.

"We had to start all over again, generating new leads for our Loews Monte Carlo. We increased advertising, direct mail and trade show attendance to generate new leads and find new prospects. As a result, a majority of the groups on the books for '81 and '82 come from companies that are new customers of the hotel."

From *Lodging* (March 1981) pp. 17-20. Reprinted by permission of *Lodging*.

2. Decide on your positioning and do everything you can to maintain it.

Evaluate your hotel's facilities and those of your competition. What can you offer that they can't?

The new Harley Hotel of New York opened in February, 1981 with 800 bedrooms and only 8,000 square feet of meeting space. It is one block away from the new Grand Hyatt, with 1400 rooms and a 20,000 sq. ft. ballroom. The Harley was positioned as a hotel for small, personalized meetings with the headline "We want to be your favorite hotel for meetings, not conventions."

For a hotel to pay off a promise like that, it must prove to its customers that it can, in fact, offer more personalized service because the groups are smaller. Be careful not to promise something you cannot deliver.

3. Fill your advertising with benefits and factual information.

"Hotel ads directed at meeting planners never have enough facts," according to Robert Rosenbaum, publisher of Successful Meetings magazine. "I look through Successful Meetings each month and am amazed that hotel companies will spend the money for a full page, four color ad, and include no factual information on the hotel or its amenities.

"Most corporate executives are amateurs at planning meetings," Rosenbaum continues, "and they need to be told why they should consider one hotel instead of another." Does your hotel have any unique room configurations? Any unique services? Is it closer to the airport or convention center or shopping center than your competition? Does the hotel have any special theme parties (one hotel tripled its volume from one incentive house when it developed a Roman toga party for groups).

4. Schedule your advertising to coincide with editorial coverage of magazines.

The meetings magazines publish schedules at the beginning of the year that outline the editorial subjects to be featured in upcoming issues. Find out which issues will have a feature on your destination and schedule your advertising accordingly. Also notify whoever handles the hotel's publicity so that timely press releases may be sent to the magazines.

Most of the meetings publications also have an annual issue that lists hotels with meeting space. Even though the advertising environment is cluttered with too many ads, the issues are important to be in. Meeting planners keep them around all year as reference books.

5. Always include a device in your advertising or direct mail to generate response.

Two techniques have worked for Loews Hotels in their advertising: a) package prices for groups and b) guaranteed rates for future years. (See illustration). Also, a coupon in the ad, or a postage paid tip-in coupon (like the magazine subscription cards you find in Time magazine every week), or a listing in the magazine's reader service card will increase response.

6. Don't expect advertising to book business for you.

All it will do is generate leads. You then have to qualify those leads and make sales calls. The only purpose of advertising for group business is to communicate information about your hotel and produce leads.

7. When making sales calls, never make a "cold call."

"That doesn't mean that you should never call on new prospects. But before you make the sales call, qualify the customer. Find out as much as you can by telephone about the customers' needs, any rate limitations they may have, the types of meetings they hold, hotels they have used in the past.

There's the story about the salesman who called on a meeting planner in another state, took him through all the benefits of meeting in the salesman's hotel, and then tried to close the sale. "I'm sorry to have wasted your time," the meeting planner said, "but our association is never allowed to meet out of state." One qualifying phone call in advance would have saved a lot of time and expense.

8. If you're not using a "trace" system, begin today.

A trace system, or tickler file, is a systematic way of following up with prospects on certain dates in the future. For example, if you talk to a meeting planner and he or she tells you that they won't begin analyzing sites for their 1983 convention until the first week of October 1981, you should "trace" the file for the first week of October. The

standard method of doing this is to make an index card for every account in your files. Every time you pull the file, indicate on the trace card when the file should be traced again. Your secretary should put the file back in its original location but put the trace card in a file box that is arranged chronologically by date. When that date next appears, the card is a reminder to pull the file.

9. Know the four secrets to working a trade show.

1. Obtain the pre-registration list and call or write important prospects to let them know you want to get together with them at the show. If you can't get the list until the day before the show, leave notes at the front desk of their hotel.

2. Find out which of your current customers will be there and arrange to see them. There are always details you need to discuss with them face to face.

3. Arrange to have someone who is well known, such as an officer of the association, take you around the floor of the trade show and introduce you to the top contacts he has.

4. Keep thorough notes and follow up with each new prospect the first day you are back in the office.

10. Don't be afraid to spend money on familiarization trips.

One of the quickest ways to convince a meeting planner that your hotel is all you say it is, is to bring him to your hotel. Familiarization ("fam") trips can be very effective if you carefully qualify your prospects before inviting them for a visit. You will see in one of the case studies presented below how one hotel overcame a negative image of its destination by paying meeting planners to visit it.

So much for the 10 marketing musts in reaching the meetings market. Some readers will improve on these guidelines. Some might want to abstract them—with or without improvement—for use as a checklist of marketing musts.

Before getting into case studies of marketing to the meetings market, here is an additional checklist: the basic sources of group business.

Basic Sources of Group Bookings

1. Corporations: especially companies with large sales forces, such as insurance companies and pharmaceutical companies, which hold a large number of meetings annually.

These meetings can involve local, regional or national offices of corporations. In almost all cases with corporate business, there is one person who books the business and pays the bills. Sometimes this person is not a full time meeting planner, and may be somewhat inexperienced, so it is important that you make it as easy as possible to book.

2. Associations: Most statewide associations are located in your state capital; most national associations are in Washington, ·D.C. Successful Meetings magazine's research division, SM/Databank, reports there are 9,000 national and international association meetings annually, 37,000 state and regional meetings, and over 200,000 conferences, workshops and clinics averaging in size from 25 to 200 people.

Meeting News magazine (1515 Broadway, New York 10036) listed 27 industry associations in their January, 1981, Directory of Sites, Suppliers and Services.

3. Training/Educational: Hardly a week goes by that an executive fails to receive in the mail an announcement of a management seminar or three-day educational course. These are being conducted by a wide range of individuals and companies, from free lance trainers to moonlighting college professors to universities and professional training companies.

4. Incentive Travel: According to Incentive Marketing magazine, $875 million was spent on incentive travel in 1980. While this is "corporate" business in the true sense, it is booked differently and therefore is being singled out for special attention. If your hotel is in a resort destination, it is a prime property for incentive travel trips awarded to corporate executives or dealers/distributors for reaching certain goals (usually sales). Much of this type of travel has traditionally been booked by the major incentive companies, such as E. F. Mac-Donald, Maritz, S&H, to name a few.

You can obtain a complete list of incentive companies from the January, 1981 issue of Incentive Marketing magazine (633 Third Avenue, New York 10017). But an increasing number of travel agents are beginning to book incentive business as another service they provide to their corporate accounts.

This business is commissionable and highly competitive. Many times two or three different agencies or incentive houses are bidding on the same piece of corporate business. They will all come to you asking for a special rate. Always give everyone the same rate. Don't play favorites, because it will not take long for the others to find out and decide to quit using your hotel.

Every two years Meetings and Conventions magazine (1 Park Avenue, New York, New York 10016) publishes a comprehensive study of the entire meetings and conventions and incentive travel fields titled "The Meetings Market." This is an excellent source for additional information.

5. Social/Fraternal. This category of business is primarily local and will generate little rooms volume. Social and fraternal groups do, however, constitute a major source of banquet volume.

Case Studies in Marketing to Groups

Two case studies follow that exemplify marketing to groups in off-line destinations. One is hypothetical (the first) and the other is actual. But both illustrate the components in a marketing program that have been discussed in every article in this series: Research, Positioning, Strategy Development, Media Selection and Budget Formation.

The first case study is from the AH&MA/HSMA Advanced Advertising Workshop in 1980. The problem of a hotel with many meeting rooms but few meetings was studied by a workshop group led by John Drake and Bruce Lucker. Lucker is president of Lucker & Inkamp, Inc., Atlanta, and Drake is principal of Cole Henderson Drake, Inc., Atlanta.

Here is the case study:

A 400-room independent hotel, with a 1,200 sq. ft. ballroom and eight meeting rooms, plus three conference suites, is located in a secondary, or off-time, market, which is not recognized by most meeting planners as being a group destination. The hotel has had to exist primarily on transient business and a limited amount of state, regional and national association business. The state and regional associations were booked at very low rates which pulled down the hotel's average rate significantly. This is a situation that many hoteliers in the United States find, because state association groups traditionally travel on tight budgets and request low rates.

The case study hotel had as its objectives, to increase its occupancy from 50% to 84% over the next five years, and to increase its average rate from $40 to $58 during the same period.

Research: Low Awareness, Negative Image

Market research indicated that the hotel was not known among corporate meeting planners, nationally or regionally. The city in which the hotel is located has a negative image, not because it has undesirable characteristics, but because it is generally unknown and not used by corporate groups at the present time.

Loews advertising to meeting planners

*Excerpt from Loews Hotels ad offering to guarantee rates three years in advance
with gold-colored tip-in reply card.*

Invest in Loews'
<u>NEW</u> guaranteed three year group rate program.
It's as good as gold.

Once again this year you can look to Loews Hotels to make your
meeting dollar go even farther than ever before. With an even better golden
opportunity for the 80s.
Here's how it works: Choose one or more of the dazzling destinations
listed below. Confirm it for a minimum of 75 rooms (150 people). And Loews
will guarantee the rate quoted for a full three years and beyond. Guaranteed
meeting rates. What better way to help your group fight inflation.
To find out more about this unique program, just send in the attached
reply card.

*Above is the top quarter of a full-page Loews ad in a meetings magazine. The full ad displays a gold
bar with this large caption: "Loews Hotels: The Golden Opportunity for the 80's." The ad lists Loews
Hotels in Monte Carlo, Quebec City, Washington, Dallas, etc. It is accompanied by a tie-in self-
addressed reply card.*

Yes, Arthur . . . I would like to take advantage of Loews Hotels
Three Year Guaranteed Rate Plan . . .

_____

_____ Have someone contact me concerning the following:
_____ Send me information on the following:
_____ **Loews Monte-Carlo Hotel**
_____ **Loews Paradise Island Hotel**
_____ **Loews Churchill Hotel**
_____ **Loews Westbury Hotel**
_____ **Loews Le Concorde Hotel**
_____ **Loews Anatole Dallas Hotel**

Company Name _____

Address _____ _____

City _____ State _____ Zip _____ Tel (___) _____

Attn _____ Title _____

*This is the copy on the tip-in reply card addressed to Arthur L. Chernov of Loews Hotels, 666 Fifth
Avenue, New York. It is of course postage-free to the meeting planner.*

However, the hotel is an attractive property, is easily accessible by air, and although it is not a tourist destination in itself, is in close proximity to two major tourist centers. The hotel is a superb facility with a highly professional staff and has all of the amenities of a luxury hotel. Its principal competition for national corporate group business were other luxury hotel properties in primary markets, such as Atlanta, Miami, and New Orleans. One clear advantage that the hotel had over luxury hotels in the other destinations was that its room rates were about 25% lower than competition.

Therefore, the positioning statement which was developed by the case study group for the hotel was as follows: "The Case Study Hotel, a new luxury hotel in a new meeting destination, is easily accessible by air and represents excellent value."

Creative Strategy and Media Selection

In order to reinforce the professionalism of the hotel, the quality of the facility, and the good value offered by the case study hotel, the creative strategy was to use testimonial statements from meeting planners who had had successful meetings at the hotel. Because the hotel had not had many national corporate groups, they selected quotes from well known state or regional association executives who had professional images.

Rather than scheduling small space advertising at heavy frequency levels, the group decided to schedule their ads less frequently but to use large full page ads in the meetings publications in order to create high impact for the destination. This is a case where media strategy and creative strategy work together because the large space advertising created the image of "major destination" and "major resort facility."

The case study group allocated an aggressive 8.5% of total revenues to the marketing budget for the first year, and allocated 60% of that to advertising, 40% to sales. Because the hotel did not know specifically who its customers would be, they chose to allocate a higher percentage to advertising and a lower percentage to sales during the first few years. Once they determined who their specific prospects were, they would reduce their advertising budget and increase the size of their sales force.

The case study workshop group felt that the aggressive-spending, high-impact creative and media strategies would produce the results needed to introduce a new hotel in a new destination and effectively compete against more established hotels in primary destinations.

Swiss Hotel Seeks U.S. Meetings

The second case study involves the Victoria Jungfrau Haus in Interlocken, Switzerland. This deluxe hotel long relied on wealthy European families and a total transient occupancy. But the operators decided to seek out a share of the U.S. group market. They made this decision at a time when travel to Europe by Americans was declining and the use of Europe as a group destination by corporations and associations was shrinking rapidly. Further, Interlocken had never been accepted as a group destination and is not accessible by air.

The board of directors of the hotel hired Emanuel Berger, a Swiss hotelier who had experience in the United States at the Pinehurst Hotel and Country Club in North Carolina and at the Waldorf Astoria in New York. They also retained Jaro Fisher Associates as their marketing representatives for North America.

Using the Airlines to Find Customers

Jaro Fisher went to Swissair to request their help in finding group customers for the destination. Together with Swissair and the Interlocken Tourist Board and Convention Bureau, Fisher planned a series of audio-visual presentations in the major markets from which airline traffic to Switzerland was originating.

At the same time, a personalized mailing was done by the general manager of the hotel to all regional managers of Swissair who were involved in the group and incentive markets in North America. Further, Fisher sent a personalized letter to each of the major incentive houses, top corporate meeting planners and top association executives in the United States who had used Europe in the past years.

In new sales promotion material, the hotel was positioned as: a) easily accessible by train or motor coach from Zurich or Geneva, b) a totally deluxe property with $10 million worth of refurbishing and renovation, c) served by a general manager who is Swiss but who understands the needs of the American market, and d) offering new low rates which allow American groups to put together their own tailor-made packages at prices which are an exceptionally good value.

Selling the Destination

The best way to convince corporate meeting planners and association executives that a destination is easy to get to is to bring them to the destination. The Victoria Jungfrau Hotel developed an aggressive program of familiarization trips. They agreed to provide a first class round trip ticket to any meeting planner or incentive house executive who was willing to come over and inspect the hotel for future meetings. This aggressive offer was announced at every audio-visual presentation during the sales blitz of major cities, and was announced by the regional Swissair managers to all the top prospects in their regions.

This initially sounds like an expensive undertaking, but the first four people who were flown over at the hotel's expense booked 26 back to back groups resulting in $1,200,000 worth of business.

In order to emphasize the ease and accessibility of the destination, the hotel made it possible for guests returning to the United States to check their luggage in at the hotel, then take a motor coach or train to Geneva or Zurich, fly back to the United States on Swissair, and, when they arrived at the airport in the United States, find their luggage waiting for them. This unique offer was featured in sales promotion. It was a major selling point in every sales call.

The important point to learn from this case history is that a hotel can make very effective use of the airlines serving its destination. In the case of the Victoria Jungfrau Hotel, they were able to use Swissair to: a) find meeting planner prospects in the major gateway cities in the United States, b) organize sales calls and luncheons, dinners and receptions for top prospects in these cities, c) develop a familiarization trip program for serious prospects, d) work out a unique baggage handling plan to overcome Americans' fear of lost baggage on European trips and e) utilize Swissair sales managers' help at trade shows.

Marketing for the Eighties

Marketing a Hotel Restaurant

by William Q. Dowling

*"A hotel restaurant has a life of its own." So
says Robert M. Campbell. He explains, "A hotel
with a declining rooms volume may have an
increasing restaurant volume. Obviously, the
opposite may be true."*

*Campbell is vice president marketing of Stouffer
Hotels, Cleveland. He continues: "Hotel
management may find it necessary to create a
marketing plan for the restaurant department as a
key profit center that is separate and distinct from
the marketing position of the hotel itself."*

*The restaurant department is second only to the
rooms department as responsible for a hotel's
profitability. In many spectacular successes in hotel
operation, the restaurant department exceeds the
food and beverage department in volume.*

*So, much care and planning must go into the
development of a marketing plan for the
restaurant department or for a particular
restaurant, within the department, that is in
trouble. The plan should include the same
elements that have been discussed in every
previous article in this series: (1) research of the
market; (2) development of creative strategy; (3)
budgeting; and, (4) media selection and follow-up.*

*This article is based on a case study of an
unprofitable hotel restaurant and how it was
repositioned in the market to make it more
profitable. The case study was presented to the
1980 Advanced Advertising Workshop presented
by AH&MA and the Hotel Sales Management
Association. Robert M. Campbell, in presenting
the study, was assisted by Jim Hunt of Wyse
Advertising, Cleveland.*

The Problem

A 600-room combination commercial and convention hotel located in the downtown business
district of a large mid-western city has three food
outlets: a roof-top fine dining restaurant; a 24-hour
coffee shop; and a medium-priced lunch and
dinner restaurant.

From *Lodging* (May 1981) pp. 15-18. Reprinted by permission of
Lodging.

• Both the roof-top restaurant and coffee shop
are successful operations catering to clearly defined
audiences.

• The medium-priced restaurant is experiencing
steadily declining guest counts and lower average
checks principally because the physical plant is old,
and the decor and menu have remained the same
for approximately ten years.

Sales in the medium-priced restaurant closely
parallel hotel occupancy, since the facility is unable
to attract any business from the local market.

• Hotel management found it was losing many
second-night guests to other restaurants in the
downtown area.

Research

Before making any decisions as to positioning,
advertising strategy or media placement, additional
information was needed about the market place,
the competition and the target customers. Some of
the questions that needed answering were:

• Who is the competition, what are its strengths
and weaknesses?

• What are the demographics of the market
place?

• Who is our target audience?

• What does our potential customer want in
terms of atmosphere, menu selection and type of
service?

• What type of entertainment do they desire in
a restaurant in our price category?

• What is their perception of price vs value?

Management needed to know if there was a void
in the market place that this restaurant could be
positioned to fill.

There are various ways this research can be
conducted: staff surveys, surveys of past and current hotel guests or by a research firm. Management wanted to give this project the highest priority; it was going to be the hotel's biggest financial
endeavor for the year. Therefore, a decision was
made to use a professional research firm to obtain
the most reliable information possible.

Checklist for Marketing Restaurants

Research and positioning

1. Analyze demand for luncheon business, early evening dinner business and late evening dinner business in your immediate neighborhood.
2. Determine what those customers want and what their attitudes are towards existing restaurants in the area.
3. Analyze where the business is coming from (luncheon business may be from the immediate area, but dinner business may include people who drive to the area from other parts of town).
4. Analyze the needs of your hotel guests and determine whether or not other restaurants in the area are meeting their needs better than you are.
5. Position your restaurant to fill a need not being met presently by other restaurants.

Advertising strategy

1. Create one simple image for the restaurant.
2. Communicate the restaurant's single most unique benefit in a way which will make a high impact.
3. Determine whether you want to communicate price, atmosphere or convenience of location, but do not feature all three; concentrate on the one that is most important to your market.
4. Make it easy for people to make a reservation at your restaurant.

Media planning

1. Identify your target market carefully, and determine whether or not they can be reached effectively by print or broadcast media, or whether they need to be pinpointed with direct mail.
2. Consider unique ways of reaching your target market.
3. Tie-in advertising to editorial coverage in your local newspapers and magazines.
4. Don't be afraid to trade advertising for meals or rooms in the hotel, if volume is low; they may allow you to afford television or magazines which you could not otherwise afford.

Budgeting

1. Determine the mix of business you want between hotel guests and outside customers, and allocate the budget accordingly.

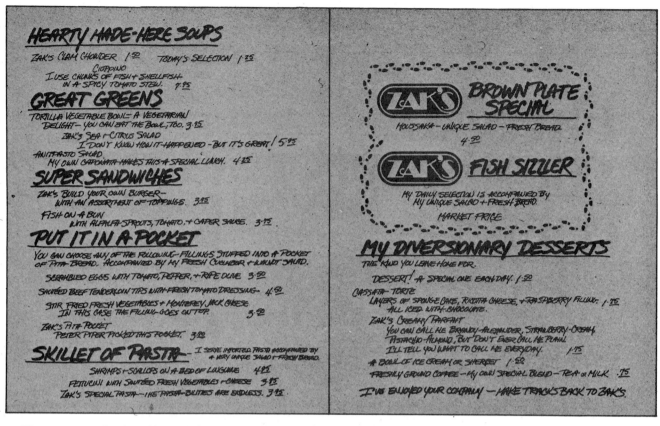

The case study in this article closely resembles Stouffer's introduction of Zak's Restaurant in Cincinnati Towers. A "Make Tracks to Zak's" self-mailer went to a large neighborhood mailing list to establish the location and lively atmosphere. Then came "Make Tracks to Zak's" newspaper advertising (illustration) to position the restaurant in the market and clearly define the type of business they were after. Note the limited but highly stylized menu. You can be sure it has a "Make Tracks" cover theme. "Doggie bags" (Zak's Snacks) are highly styled; so are little brown bags (Zak's Sacks) for wine bottles.

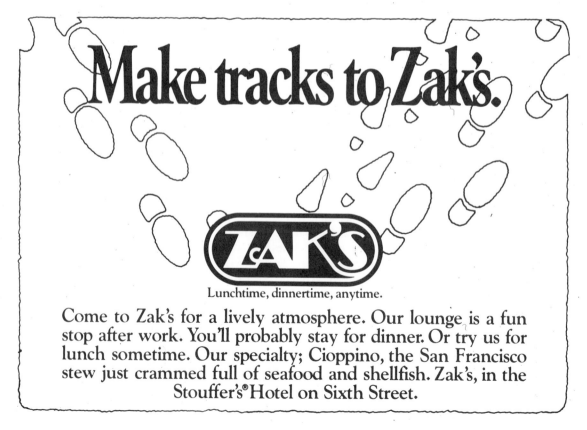

A year later, in celebrating its first birthday, Zak's sustains its lively image with join-the-party promotion.

Party to your heart's content.

A Valentine, Birthday, 3-day hearty party. To celebrate Zak's first birthday, we've got exZakly what you need. It's a three-day party this Tuesday, Wednesday and Thursday — February 10, 11, 12 — that's guaranteed to get you through the winter blahs. The drinks are big, the food delicious and the people ready for a good time. There's a lot going on this week at Zak's. Join the party.

Prizes, prizes, prizes. You get the prizes at this party. Just stop into Zak's and enjoy our special birthday dinner sometime during our 3-day party and register to be eligible. And here's what you could win: First Prize, a weekend for two at PineIsle. PineIsle is a Stouffer Resort Hotel on beautiful Lake Lanier Islands in Georgia. There's golf, swimming, tennis, and a lot of peaceful countryside to enjoy. And it's all expenses paid. Second Prize, a baseball weekend for two at Stouffer's Cincinnati Towers. Third Prize, dinner for four at Zak's. Three terrific prizes.

Now that we're one, we've got a special on dinner for two. It's a terrific meal and a terrific deal on our special birthday dinner package. It includes seafood cocktail, prime rib of beef, dessert and beverage, plus a ½ bottle of champagne. The complete dinner for two is just $29.95.

Research Findings

The research firm's surveys revealed the following facts about the area and potential customers:

- There is a substantial luncheon demand in the downtown area that is not currently being satisfied by any existing facilities, especially in the medium price range;
- Most of the luncheon facilities are frequented by secretaries and businessmen.
- Currently there are no successful cocktail lounges in the downtown area.
- Businessmen and secretaries in the area would be willing to go to a cocktail lounge after working hours, particularly if they could walk to it.
- There is a market segment that comes downtown in the evening for dinner and late-night activities.
- Ease of parking for dinner is important, as few people live in the downtown area.
- The hotel guest is a businessman looking for a place to go after dinner.
- Potential late-night customers tend to go from place to place, with no preference for any particular nightspot.
- Potential customers do not want to dress in blue jeans but don't want to be required to wear a tie.
- Their entertainment preference is Top 40 rather than disco or rock.
- Young, friendly, casually attired waiters and waitresses are preferred.

Positioning

Based on research results, management decided to create an informal but colorful restaurant, with a limited menu selection presented in a highly stylized way. Prices would be moderate.

The menu for lunch would feature hearty soups, "great greens" (salads), super sandwiches, pita bread with savory fillings, and a couple of more conventional items such as Moussaka and a daily seafood special.

The menu for dinner would be geared almost exclusively towards Italian seafood and continental dishes offering mainly traditional selections but with less traditional dishes offered as specials.

The lively but informal atmosphere would be incorporated into the decor of the facility as well as in table settings and graphics.

Physically the lounge would be located separate from but near the main entrance to the facility with easy access to and from the restaurant. Live entertainment would be offered early in the evening, either a violinist or guitarist during the cocktail hour. No entertainment was planned for the dinner hours and Top 40 music would be played later in the evening. Half of the restaurant area would be designed to be integrated with the lounge later in the evening to increase the lounge area.

Creative Strategy

Objective. The advertising objective was to successfully introduce the new restaurant to the market place. The target audience was adults 24-49 years of age, earning $18,000 plus, primarily white collar professionals who dine out on an average of three or more times per month. Therefore, luncheon advertising was not necessary, but it was important to promote the cocktail lounge and dining room aspect of the restaurant.

Advertising was developed to *position* the restaurant as the only informal restaurant with live entertainment in the market area, create a contemporary image as the place to be, while at the same time positioning it as being casually sophisticated and affordable.

Budget

Management agreed to a renovation program of approximately $650,000. Based on a projection of $867,000 in first year sales, the grand opening marketing budget was set at approximately $50,000 of which $35,000 was set aside for advertising.

Media Strategy

Initial strategy called for a quiet opening without major advertising support. This would give the refurbished restaurant and new personnel time to work out the various rough edges found in all new establishments. This initial quiet period would be followed by an intensive four-week advertising campaign. $10,000 of the total advertising budget was held in reserve for use after the results of the initial advertising campaign could be analyzed.

Media Selection centered on newspapers and radio. Although these are low reach vehicles, they are affordable, allowing for additional frequency. Television was eliminated due to its high cost. City magazines were included in the media plan to reach suburbanites coming into the downtown area for sporting events, plays, etc.

After researching initial results, the additional $10,000 of the advertising budget was used for outdoor and transit advertising.

Marketing for the Eighties

Marketing Entertainment

by William Q. Dowling

For many years hotels relied on big name entertainment as a basic marketing tool. Whether in New York, Chicago, San Francisco or cities like Jacksonville, Memphis or San Antonio, travelers could always find one of their favorite performers in the lounge or nightclub of the most successful hotels in town.

Then two things happened that changed the pattern of hotel entertainment in the U.S.: television and Las Vegas. Performers found they could earn higher fees on television. And casino operators in Las Vegas, in an effort to revitalize their destination, began featuring these TV stars on their marquees. The result was that hotels could no longer afford well-known stars. By the mid-1970's, most of the hotels in even the largest cities closed their nightclubs.

Day of the Disco

The hotel industry began shifting from live entertainment to discotheques with recorded music in the 70's. Rooms where Frank Sinatra and Peggy Lee had once captivated audiences were converted to flashing lights, elaborate speaker systems and the latest recorded disco sounds. It was not unusual for hotels to invest anywhere from $40,000 to $200,000 in disco conversions. Entrepreneurs in New York opened clubs like Studio 54 and Xenon, spending $3-500,000 on elaborate sound and light systems.

Today, most professional entertainment company executives are predicting that new, more creative uses of live entertainment may slowly replace disco as the disco era begins to fade.

In this article we'll review the experience and advice of two entertainment company executives and see how one hotel in New York, the St. Regis-Sheraton, used new entertainment concepts

From *Lodging* (June 1981) pp. 9-12. Reprinted by permission of *Lodging*.

as a basic marketing tool to revitalize dining room and lounge business and create a new image for a landmark hotel.

The New Concepts

"Anyone can fill a room with Tony Bennett," says Jerry Kravat. "But the challenge today is to put together an entertainment package that is economically viable yet still draws." Kravat, who is president of his own entertainment company and acts as entertainment director to a dozen or so of the best known hotels in America, speaks from experience.

"The trick is to create unique entertainment concepts," Kravat continued, "that will appeal to the type of customer the hotel wants in its public rooms." Many hoteliers have seen the problems that occur when the wrong type of customers mix with hotel guests in the lounge or dining room. Discos, while generating high revenues for many hotels, had the disadvantage of sometimes attracting local customers who were not of the same demographic or social profile as the hotel's guests. Yet a piano player or trio which did appeal to the right clientele often resulted in half-empty rooms.

The general manager knows that a balance must be maintained between protecting the hotel's image and making money. The following case history shows how one hotel in New York met that challenge.

Case Study: St. Regis-Sheraton

"The well-known entertainers who used to perform in our Maisonette lounge priced themselves out of our reach over the last few years," said Guenter H. Richter, vice president and managing director of the St. Regis-Sheraton. "The unknown entertainers or middle-of-the-road performers didn't draw customers," he continued, "so we were forced to close the room."

"Furthermore, the King Cole dining room, as it was designed originally, was meant to be strictly a restaurant serving breakfast, lunch and dinner," Richter said. While breakfast and lunch business was satisfactory, from in-house as well as outside guests, the King Cole room—like many city hotel dining rooms—died at night.

During the last two years the Maisonette room was converted to an elaborately designed lounge, called Astor's, and the King Cole Room was completely redesigned and redecorated. Clearly a new entertainment concept was needed in both rooms to attract guests in the evening.

Richter, with the approval of Sheraton's New York Area Vice President Klaus Ottman, developed a budget and a marketing strategy for pumping new life into these two rooms.

"The first thing we did was engage an entertainment director," said Richter. "We wanted a professional who had talent, know-how and contacts with writers, producers and performers." Jerry Kravat Entertainment Services, Inc., was hired and the first concept created was for the King Cole dining room.

Research and Positioning

Kravat looked over the room, considered the seating capacity and the size of the stage. He then had to determine the type of clientele to go after. He says, "We analyzed the market profile, the activity of competitive hotels, and what we thought would be appropriate for this well-respected, landmark hotel."

Perhaps the most important decision made by Richter and his management team was to develop an image for the room, not just for the entertainers. The second decision was to make a commitment to stay with the new concept for the long haul—to give it at least a year to prove itself. Fortunately, the managing director received the support of his corporate management.

Concept and Strategy

The concept developed for the King Cole Room almost a year and a half ago was to produce a cabaret show that was "A Salute to Famous Composers and Producers."

Examples included:
"Rhapsody in Gershwin"
"From Rodgers and Hart with Love"
"The Sounds of Rodgers and Hammerstein"
"It's Delightful, It's De-Lovely, It's Cole Porter"
"Thank Heaven for Lerner and Lowe"

Many of the performers booked had appeared in the original Broadway shows but many of them were not top stars.

The entertainment director put together the producers and writers necessary to create the shows and negotiated the contracts with most of the cast. Richter then took the following four steps:

1. Retained a public relations firm that had excellent contacts in theatrical and musical circles, especially with critics and columnists.

2. Developed advertising and promotional pieces and guest reply cards that were directed at the hotel's target audience—in-house guests and upscale local residents and visitors in Manhattan.

3. Reworked the dinner menu to offer an a la carte menu to dinner guests and a supper menu to late show customers. A cover charge of $7.50 in midweek and $10 on weekends was added to dinner guests' checks ($10 midweek and $12.50 weekend for guests who did not have dinner).

4. Established a reservations system, using the hotel's own reservations system as well as Ticketron and Chargit (outside, independent reservation systems).

The results have been outstanding, both for the room and the hotel's overall business. Room covers have increased dramatically in midweek and on weekends it is not unusual to see lines all the way into the lobby, waiting to get in for the first or second shows. Favorable quotes have appeared in all of the major media, including the following comments:

". . . the food and service are as impeccable as the 22 Rodgers & Hart selections . . ."
"This room is one of the best buys in New York."
"The Sheraton St. Regis' tribute to composers is one of the successful nitery policies around town."

And the National Academy of Concert and Cabaret Arts nominated the shows for Best Revue, Best Producer and Best Writer.

At the same time that the entertainment strategy for the King Cole room was being planned, a completely different but compatible strategy was being planned for the lounge downstairs, Astor's. Richter decided to position Astor's toward the local business community for early evening business, with piano entertainment from 5:30 to 8:30 and complimentary hors d'oeuvres and a two-for-one cocktail hour.

From 8:30 to 9:30 p.m. Astor's picks up some of the pre-show crowd before they go into the King Cole, and from 9 pm to 1 am (2 am on weekends) the room offers live entertainment and dancing.

In order to draw a good local crowd into Astor's,

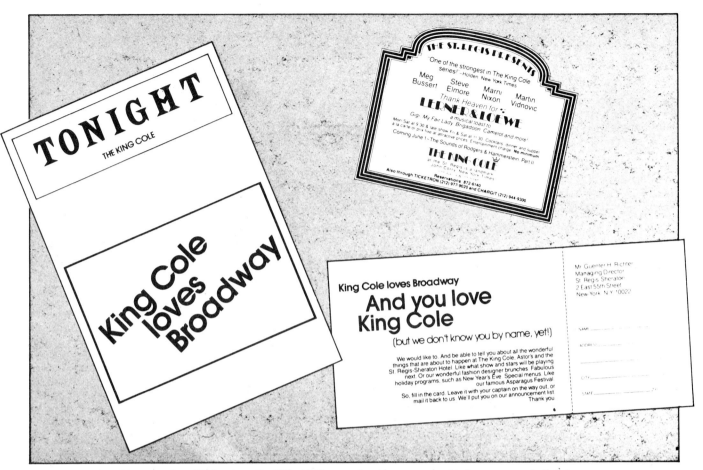

Small space advertising was placed in local media; "Playbill"—type booklets were provided to guests and all dining room guests were given a reply card to build a mailing list for promoting the dining room and lounge.

some of the stars who had appeared in previous King Cole shows were encouraged to visit Astor's as guests of the hotel. This resulted in such a strong following from the Broadway theatrical community that when Joey Bishop took over Mickey Rooney's role in Sugar Babies temporarily, the cast party was held at Astor's.

It was decided not to charge a cover charge or a minimum in the lounge, in order to get more pre- and post-show guests. Promotional material used the lines "Rendezvous at Manhattan's hottest new bar. Right out of New York's golden slipper days."

Various entertainment concepts have been used at Astor's, including an all-female band.

Both entertainment concepts and the marketing of those programs have helped to build a new image for the St. Regis-Sheraton. It has strengthened the hotel's rooms clientele at the same time that it has significantly increased evening activity in its two public rooms.

"No hotel has done what the St. Regis has done," commented Jerry Kravat. "They looked at the marketing of entertainment as a long term commitment that would eventually benefit all departments in the hotel."

Part II: Four Steps for Marketing Entertainment

"Entertainment can be one of a hotel's most valuable marketing tools," according to James Fauvell of Park West 58 Theatrical Productions. Fauvell, whose company also assists hoteliers with production and planning, suggests the following four steps general managers should consider before marketing a lounge or nightclub.

1. *Research your market, then position your facility.*

a) Find out what your present image is. Do guests expect a family atmosphere or a singles scene? Is the hotel informal, elegant, quiet or active?

b) Would you like to change or broaden this image? Do you want to attract young singles to supplement your regular guests? Do you want local residents mixing with your hotel clientele? Do you want your commercial travelers thinking of your hotel as quiet or full of activity?

c) If you want local guests, what are the demographic and geographic profiles? Are they close by or do they have to drive across town?

d) Who is your competition? Which hotels, lounges and clubs in your area are being visited by the target customers you are attempting to attract? What is the appeal of these establishments? Is there room for another?

e) How can your facility be unique? What kind of entertainment will attract these audiences, yet be different from competition? Will it be consistent with the image you want your hotel to project? Will your hotel guests like it?

2. Prepare a budget and an R-O-I analysis.

Analyze the costs of construction as well as the cost of operating and marketing, compared to the projected revenue generation, to determine whether or not the effort is justified. If you utilize a large-scale entertainment program, you may want to build in the cost of an independent producer who would be responsible for production, staging, lighting, sound projection and booking the entertainment. Some will conduct market research and will help with budget planning as part of their services. The budget should also include the comp rooms and food and beverage checks provided to the talent and local columnists.

Most entertainment service companies work in one of three ways:

1. A flat monthly fee; or

2. Strictly commissions they can make as agents for the performers they book; or,

3. A package price for the show they produce, the price to include all costs.

However, these companies will often agree to pay a fee to the hotel in return for having exclusive rights to sell their services to banquets and meetings booked into the hotel.

The marketing budget would include: local advertising, printing (tent cards, flyers, posters, direct mail), postage for direct mail, public relations, and any special sales promotion expenses.

3. Create advertising that enhances your hotel's image.

Once you have agreed on positioning, and have selected the type of entertainment that is consistent with the hotel's positioning, make sure the advertising reinforces that image. Too often a hotel's rooms advertising will be very professionally prepared, but advertising for entertainment will project a totally different image.

4. Consider these four other ways of marketing your facilities.

a) Obtain free media coverage through public relations. All local media and some nationally distributed magazines cover entertainment on a regular basis. Either use a good public relations firm or have someone in the sales department make sure that entertainment editors and reviewers are invited to your lounge. Suggest that your entertainers would make interesting subjects for radio, TV and newspaper interviews. Make sure your lounge or nightclub receives regular coverage in the local media.

b) Market your entertainment to meeting planners. If you are using live entertainment in your hotel, groups may also want to use them for banquets, sales meetings or special parties. As mentioned earlier, if you have an entertainment company on staff they will often do this marketing for you.

c) Let travel agents and tour operators know about your facilities, especially if your lounge features live entertainment. This is an added benefit that they will promote to their clients.

d) Use special seasonal promotions to attract new target audiences and generate publicity. Seasonal, ethnic and holiday festivals can be created in your hotel's restaurants, lounges and other facilities, especially with the use of live entertainment.

Then all you have to do is serve good food, large drinks and have outstanding entertainment and you are sure to succeed.